The Archaeology of Traditions

The Ripley P. Bullen Series

Florida Museum of Natural History

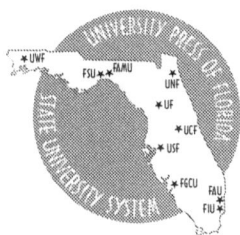

Florida A&M University, Tallahassee
Florida Atlantic University, Boca Raton
Florida Gulf Coast University, Ft. Myers
Florida International University, Miami
Florida State University, Tallahassee
University of Central Florida, Orlando
University of Florida, Gainesville
University of North Florida, Jacksonville
University of South Florida, Tampa
University of West Florida, Pensacola

The Archaeology of Traditions

Agency and History Before and After Columbus

Edited by Timothy R. Pauketat

Foreword by Jerald T. Milanich, Series Editor

University Press of Florida

Gainesville · Tallahassee · Tampa · Boca Raton

Pensacola · Orlando · Miami · Jacksonville · Ft. Myers

First cloth printing, 2001
First paperback printing, 2003

Library of Congress Cataloging-in-Publication Data
The archaeology of traditions: agency and history before and after Columbus / edited by Timothy R. Pauketat; foreword by Jerald T. Milanich.
p. cm. — (The Ripley P. Bullen series)
Includes bibliographical references and index.
ISBN 0-8130-2112-X (alk. paper); ISBN 0-8130-2745-4 (pbk.)
1. Indians of North America—Southern States—Antiquities. 2. Social archaeology—Southern States. 3. Southern States—Antiquities. I. Pauketat,
Timothy R. II. Series
E78.S65 A79 2001
975'.01—dc21   00-066785

The University Press of Florida is the scholarly publishing agency for the
State University System of Florida, comprising Florida A&M University,
Florida Atlantic University, Florida Gulf Coast University, Florida Interna-
tional University, Florida State University, University of Central Florida,
University of Florida, University of North Florida, University of South Flor-
ida, and University of West Florida.

University Press of Florida
15 Northwest 15th Street
Gainesville, FL 32611–2079
http://www.upf.com

Dedicated to an earlier generation of hard-working archaeologists who dug up history, tradition, and ethnicity, and who enjoyed the hell out of it.

Contents

Figures

Tables

Foreword

Archaeologists long have divided themselves into two camps, historical archaeologists and nonhistorical archaeologists, those who studied pre-Columbian cultures. As Timothy R. Pauketat of the University of Illinois notes, historical archaeologists, blessed with written records as a source of data, had the luxury of examining documents to help them document historical processes and determine "what regularities owe their origins to common historical linkages." On the other hand, archaeologists studying the pre-Columbian past searched for those common processes that explain "all people in all places."

In recent years the theoretical schism between historical and "pre-historical" archaeologists has begun to blur as a new paradigm dubbed "historical processualism" has emerged, one which recognizes that we can better understand the past in terms of history, defined here as "cultural construction through practice." What people and groups did in the past is best understood within the context of their histories and cultures, within their traditions. History defined in this fashion is not the purview solely of historians or of historical archaeologists, and the archaeology of historical process becomes an important guide to explaining the past.

In his introductory chapter, Pauketat offers a cogent discussion of this theoretical approach, which is then amplified and demonstrated in twelve case studies, each penned by an archaeological scholar working in the southeastern United States.

Kent Lightfoot supplies a commentary that assesses how well the volume's individual authors accomplished their task, focusing in part on their multiple uses and multiscalar approaches to cultural/historical traditions. He also examines the concepts of traditions and historical processes beyond the Southeast.

Archaeology continues to evolve as a discipline, refining new theoretical approaches that help us to model the past in novel ways. These are exciting times that are providing fresh tools for understanding all of human history and the dynamics that have made the world what it is today. *The Archaeology of Traditions: Agency and History Before and After*

Columbus is at the forefront of applying this paradigm shift to archaeo-logical data sets. I am pleased that the University Press of Florida and the Ripley P. Bullen Series can share in what is certainly an important challenge for the discipline of archaeology.

Jerald T. Milanich
Series Editor

Preface

This book spotlights a part of the world, southeastern North America, as a means to an end. That end can be summed up as the search for how history happened, a search with considerable relevance beyond the Southeast. Figuring out *how* change in human identities and relations happened, more than *why* change may have happened, is the guts of American archaeology at the beginning of the twenty-first century. In point of fact, I am not altogether certain that *why* questions can be resolved without bringing a truckload of metaphysical baggage to the table.

In archaeology, answers to such *why* questions have tended to do little more than reify their initial assumptions about how human beings "behave." *How,* in that case, is an unchanging quality of humanity that *why*-researchers believe to be true. It is not the subject of investigation, and that is a mistake. Permit me a brief digression to explain what I mean. Someone at a Southeastern Archaeological Conference recently asked me *why* people built pyramids of earth, stone, or mud brick around the world throughout history. My response went something like this: perhaps there is some innate human tendency to build toward the sky, but that's a question of human nature, not human culture. It is a question for a psychologist, a biologist, perhaps a theologian, but not an archaeologist. What do we learn from this answer that we didn't already accept or reject in the beginning? Not much.

It is more satisfying to compare *how* cultural phenomena happened at various points in time and across space. That is what this book is all about. The Southeast is well suited to the investigation of what we label "historical processes" and exemplifies a direction in which archaeology in general must move. Perhaps, if we try to figure out how history happened, we may one day be able to answer the ultimate metaphysical questions of our day (emphasis on "our day"). However, this will come only after dealing with the proximate *how* questions that archaeology has asked too infrequently and too timidly. Moreover, the relevance of those *why* questions may have faded before we get a chance to answer them.

This volume is an outgrowth of a symposium titled "Resistant Traditions and Historical Processes in Southeastern North America" at the 64th Annual Meeting of the Society for American Archaeology in Chicago, March 1999. I would like to thank the original participants of that session, all of whom are represented in the present volume except for Kathleen Deagan, who served as a discussant alongside Kent Lightfoot. The original idea for the session was the study of resistance before and after Columbus. However, that theme began to drift almost immediately toward a broader focus on tradition and tradition making. In this regard, the Southeast and all things traditional go together remarkably well. Archaeologists in the Southeast are fortunate to have a wealth of data that speaks directly to issues of an archaeology of traditions, and for this many individuals, private foundations, and public organizations are owed debts of gratitude. Of those directly supportive of my own research (spilt into this volume just a little), I would like to thank the National Science Foundation, the National Geographic Society, the Wenner-Gren Foundation for Anthropological Research, the University of Illinois, the Illinois Department of Transportation, the Illinois Transportation Archaeological Research Program, and Cahokia Mounds Museum Society.

|

A New Tradition in Archaeology

Timothy R. Pauketat

People have always had traditions, practiced traditions, resisted traditions, or created traditions. Archaeologists cannot avoid dealing with the concept. Broken potsherds, stone tools, and the remains of houses, farms, and fields virtually scream "tradition!" But this seemingly simple concept is not as straightforward as one might assume. Power, plurality, and human agency are all a part of how traditions come about. Traditions do not simply exist without people and their struggles involved every step of the way. This book reexamines that human involvement by analyzing a series of historically divergent and yet interrelated traditions from one macroregional "tradition": the American Southeast (see fig. 1.1).

In everyday parlance, "tradition" means something learned from the past, something persistent or unchanging, or something old-fashioned. As commonly understood, traditions impede change by constraining what can be done by the people living with them. Believing this, an earlier generation of archaeologists isolated different traditions and attempted to explain why they were where they were (see Caldwell 1958; Haury 1956; Willey and Phillips 1958). A later generation of "processual" archaeologists adopted a more utilitarian view; traditions, as learned ways of doing or making things, allowed a group to survive (see Binford 1965).

The earlier generation's theories of cultural change and those of the processual archaeologists, not to mention time-honored methods of sequencing cultural remains, rest on taken-for-granted notions of tradition (cf. Marquardt 1978). Sometimes stated, but often unstated, they adhere to a deeply engrained view that ideas, cultures, or styles change gradually and slowly while political and economic spheres change rapidly. For them, traditions are conservative and cultures are seen to lag behind the times, retaining vestiges of earlier periods. This adherence, which cannot be assigned to a specific school of thought, is increasingly called into question

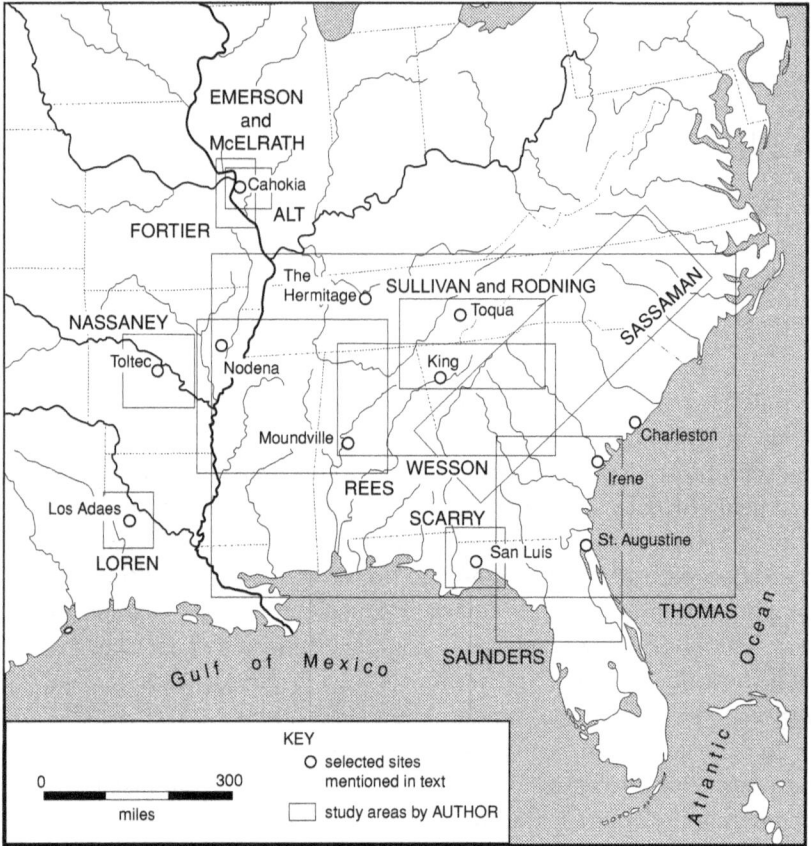

Fig. 1.1. Locator map.

by more recent studies that place people back into anthropological models of how change comes about (see Rees, this volume).

Today, tradition and related concepts are reappearing in discussions that purport to redirect how we explain the past (Dobres 2000; Hendon 1996; Joyce and Hendon 2000; Lightfoot et al. 1998; Pauketat 2001). From a contemporary perspective, a tradition is some practice brought from the past into the present. It may be a personal practice, a group practice, or an entire population's practice. By opening up the definition thus, I do not intend to make it so general as to lack explanatory utility. Technically, certain traditions at the personal or population ends of the spectrum may not be useful abstractions. However, opening up the definition allows one to argue that traditions are not passive and benign ways of doing things but are malleable, subject to politicization, and always "negotiated" between persons and among peoples at multiple scales. Tradition in this sense is part of the dynamic and contingent "cultural construction" process, a fluid "reactualization" of the past (see Borofsky 1987; Hobsbawn and Ranger 1983; Sahlins 1985; Toren 1999; see also Comaroff and Comaroff 1991). Given this broadened sense of tradition, archaeologists should be able to address a central question of the human experience. How do people throughout history become separate *peoples* with seemingly distinct identities, ways of doing and thinking, and specific technologies to cope with the outside world?

David Kertzer (1988) offers a series of examples that reveal traditions (or traditional symbols) to be potent media for negotiations that generate cultural change. For instance, fundamentalist religious leaders and politicians use traditions to attract followers. Traditions used in such ways are the basis of social movements, coalitions, or revolutions. These are cases of tradition in the service of high-order political interests. In the course of world history, such coopted traditions have built cathedrals and pyramids, overthrown governments, and revitalized religions.

Other, lower-order traditions are also open to negotiation and change. Stephen Shennan (1993) argues that representations or practices that are beyond conscious reflection or without well-established cultural meanings do, in fact, embody traditions. That is, the meanings of practices (if any are even identifiable) may not be entirely clear to people who nonetheless actively reproduce them. People may not know why they dance or sing or cook the way that they do, but they may do so because of habits that seem consistent with the past (see Hendon 1996). "We do not believe our religion," says one Plains Indian informant, "we dance it!" (J. E. Brown 1977:123). The question remains: How susceptible might such embodied traditions be to change?

Traditions, that is, present us with a conundrum. Do they thwart or promote change? If the latter, then when does a tradition cease to be traditional? Can cultural change even occur outside of traditional practices? This puzzle indicates the need for better concepts to deal with the process of tradition making. A series of such concepts are used throughout this volume, including practice, doxa, ethnogenesis, community, resistance, and official and unofficial traditions. With the aid of these, the resolution to the conundrum will be found in the revised understanding of southeastern history and the fundamental "materiality" of southeastern traditions. I begin in this introduction by focusing on two facets of the process of tradition making: constraints and practice.

History as Tradition Making

History and tradition are closely intertwined. In fact, I define history as the process of tradition building or as "cultural construction through practice" (Pauketat 2001). Before I elaborate, let me note what history is not. First, history is not merely the background noise, window-dressing, or irrelevant details of social or cultural evolution (cf. Bamforth and Spaulding 1982). Second, history is not "narrative," and archaeological remains are not "texts" to be read in different ways depending on one's contemporary biases (see Hodder 1989).

A dismissal of history as mere detail was common to the processual archaeology of the 1970s and derives from an often unstated commitment to the insidious notion of behavior (see Pauketat 2001). As used in archaeology, behavior has implied a uniformity of action that allows a population to cope with some condition. This is insidious because it means that actual people and their traditions have little explanatory value.

The history-as-narrative argument is a "postmodern" position, taken most often by nonarchaeologists, that locates history in the present-day interpretive narratives of some person or group instead of in the past (e.g., Errington 1998). The argument goes: there are many narratives about the past, and who are we to claim that archaeology can deduce the truth from among them (see Shanks and Tilley 1987)?[1] Fortunately, we may dispense with this history-as-narrative position. Narratives do exist, but only as part of any process of tradition building. They are acts of interpretation with reference to the past, not the entirety of actions—not the diachronic series of actions—that gave shape to the present or to any moment in time. One might think of history as a whole series of interconnected narratives, the point being that how those narratives were constructed relative to each other is something concrete and very different from a single narrative. Archaeologists can measure such concrete, diachronic series using the residues of what people actually did. Narratives can lie; people's garbage seldom does (see Rathje 1974).

My definition of history as the process of tradition building or cultural construction through practice is considerably broader than history as either noise or narrative. History is the practicing and embodying of traditions on a daily basis. "Practice" in the sense that I use it refers to any enactment, embodiment, or representation of one's dispositions (see Archer 1996; Bell 1997; Bourdieu 1977, 1990; de Certeau 1984; Giddens 1979, 1984; Ortner 1984; Sahlins 1985). One is disposed to do and to be in certain ways because of one's experiences in social settings. The doing and being is practice, not behavior, because doing and being are contingent on historical context.

Constraints

At various times and places, what people did, how they identified themselves, and who they became was constrained in different ways by those times and those places. Individuals were not free to act as completely rational decision makers although, within preexisting parameters, they would have thought and acted in ways that continuously altered those parameters. Meanings, environments, identities, regional cultures, or other traditions all could be called constraints.[2] Southeastern North America, for instance, has been characterized as a cultural and an environmental constraint; it involved distinctive biomes, panregional cultural patterns, and creolized "southern" traditions. Such constraints, so very large in scale, may seem beyond the realm of direct change through daily practices. Environmental change, for instance, might seem to stand apart from social change, if not to be a cause of it (see Anderson et al. 1995). Likewise, the myths and cosmological themes of the pre-Columbian Southeast—the quartered circle, the bi-lobed arrow, or the earth mother— may appear as unchanging structures that constrained cultural practices (see R. L. Hall 1997).

This view of constraints, while not altogether wrong, is deceptive. The principal problem with the concept of constraint is the extent to which it allows us to think of the process of cultural construction as a series of transformations between constraints, as if the latter were static states that stood apart from the process of tradition building itself (for a parallel argument, see Plog 1973). With specific regard to the use of tradition as constraint, archaeologists mistakenly assume the existence of widely shared, unchanging, and homogeneous cultures. Hence, they do not view traditions as requiring explanations. However, from the dynamic-tradition position advocated here, cultural heterogeneity is the rule rather than the exception. Consequently, continuity demands an explanation.

By taking a dynamic-tradition position, one need not disavow descriptive units of cultural-historical or sociological reconstruction that connote homogeneity and continuity. We can still isolate and name traditions, meanings, environments, identities, regional cultures, and the like. Indeed, recognizing and naming macroscale patterns are first steps toward processual explanations. These patterns are real and, depending on how they are recognized, may have considerable interpretative utility. For instance, an archaeological ceramic tradition or a chronological phase may correlate with some past social upheaval, demographic shift, popular movement, residential unit, or labor coordination (see Alt, Emerson and McElrath, Fortier, Sassaman, Saunders, this volume). In my own research, phases established thirty years ago based on pottery styles seem to correlate relatively well with new information on major developments in the formation and disintegration of a pre-Columbian polity (Pauketat 1998b). This is perhaps not surprising to many archaeologists who retain an implicit faith in their ability to account for the past. Given the present views of practice and materiality, it is even less surprising.

Nonetheless, we must remain cognizant of the fact that the recognized cultural patterns—traditions, meanings, identities, environments, phases, and so on—are only imperfect abstractions of past cultural processes. Even seemingly ancient myths, icons, or cosmological themes are not truly static (see Nöth 1990 and Turner 1967 for common uses of these concepts). The "deep" thematic qualities that lend an appearance of cultural persistence also made the myths, icons, or cosmological themes especially effective political symbols to be displayed, manipulated, and co-opted by social movements or astute politicians (see Cohen 1974; Kertzer 1988). Consider the varied uses and emotional evocations of the Christian cross, the Confederate flag, the color red, or the southeastern cross-in-circle motif (Emerson 1999:271). The basic and seemingly uniform meanings of these symbols continue to be manipulated; referents are reconfigured; values and associations are altered (see Barth 1987). For instance, a pre-Columbian pot featuring cross-in-circle symbolism would not have meant quite the same thing as the same symbol in another medium or another context, owing to the novel referents and associations of the pot's contents, the time or place of the pot's use, or the people who made, used, or possessed the pot (Pauketat and Emerson 1991; and see fig. 1.2).

Note that I am not saying that *things,* such as the pot or the pot's symbolism, are *subject* to negotiation. Rather, I am saying that the very idea of "thingness" is problematic. The pot and its symbolism are themselves negotiations. As put into practice, they are the process of cultural construction. This realization, in fact, constitutes the first step in the abandonment of materialist explanations in archaeology. Once these are abandoned, archaeology will have to seriously modify an array of commonly accepted processual generalizations in which antecedent conditions—strategies, population levels, ideologies, political systems, or various sorts of traditions—are treated as if they possessed causal power to produce

Fig. 1.2. Pre-Columbian pottery bottle from Arkansas with quartered motifs and cross-in-circle design field.

some effect apart from people. It is true that materialist arguments in archaeology have produced significant advances in our general knowledge about the relationships between constraints. For example, insightful correlations have been made between group size and hierarchy, political institutions and ideologies, domestication and sedentism, and artifact distributions, ethnicities, and centralization, among many other things. Such studies have enabled archaeologists to obtain understandings of the broad parameters of cultural processes.

Given this, we could conclude that broad correlations of constraints, econometric indices, or demographic measures, and so on, are not only necessary steps in explanation; they are the primary goal of much archaeological study. However, correlation is not causation. Such correlations, indices, or measures do not themselves explain the processes of cultural construction, because they rely on macroscale concepts already one or more steps removed from the historically constituted practices of people.

Practice and Materiality

Practices are not the links between structures or constraints in a causal chain. Instead, they are the continuous construction wherein constraints are always "becoming" constraints (Sztompka 1991). That process is a complex one, since all people enact, embody, and represent, and they do this in all social contexts. It involves practices of all sorts ongoing everywhere and everyday. Thus, tradition making is not only continuous; it is a human universal. In theory, how hunter-gatherers made projectile points at, say, 8000 B.C. can be explained with reference to a process that also helps explain the dramatic cultural clashes or the plantation society of the colonial and antebellum South, respectively. There are a growing number of archaeological explications of practice that promote a similar sense (Clark 2000; Dietler and Herbich 1998; Dobres 2000; Dobres and Hoffman 1994; Hendon 1996; Pauketat 2000b, 2001).

Practices can be habitual, ritual, or strategic. They may be second nature and beyond the realm of thoughtful reflection or planned and politicized. Practices may be keyed to specific meanings, abstract referents, and emotional associations that were inculcated in children or inscribed in social settings (see Toren 1999:83ff.). Whether understood or unknown to practitioners, "practices are always novel and creative, in some ways unlike those in other times or places" (Pauketat 2001).

People always relate to other people or to other socially defined and meaningful things or precepts. As they do so, however, practices—and associated meaningful referents—change owing to the unanticipated associations or circumstances of any particular act, performance, ritual, or event (Sahlins 1985). Thus, practice always alters that which seems merely perpetuated. For instance, eating might seem like a monotonous behavior, but it changes daily. The people who share a meal change from day to day. Guests come and go, the experiences of the day are brought to bear on the meal, and relations between genders, ages, or interests are all infused in the experience. Even if changes in practice are in some ways intentional or planned, there are always unintended consequences of that particular practice (see Giddens 1979).

The consequences of practices exist at multiple scales of social life simultaneously. A hunter makes a projectile point in a familiar shape that is identifiable to outsiders as an ethnic marker (see Sassaman, this volume); a family builds a house in a "traditional" manner, intentionally or unintentionally countering the architectural style and meanings of the "dominant" group (see Alt, Scarry, this volume). Hunters making points or

Fig. 1.3. Wall-trench building floor, ca. A.D. 1100, southwestern Illinois.

homebuilders constructing houses are engaged in a kind of dialogue with the others around them and with their own sense of tradition. The acts of small groups, even if not designed to achieve some large political goal, can resonate at regional and panregional scales.

For instance, a meal at one's home with one's immediate family may seem rather inconsequential to most other people in the world. And it may be. However, the same meal eaten while entertaining visiting dignitaries carries much more historical import, as it would presumably impart an impression about oneself and one's household to the visitors, who might communicate that impression to others. The scale of an ordinary household practice, in that case, simultaneously exceeds the household. In a similar vein, a speech made to one person will have a smaller-scale effect, regardless of content, than the same speech carried by the mass media. The practice is the same, the circumstances and the scale of the historical effects quite different. A good example of this is the spread of wall-trench architecture within certain regions (e.g., Alt, this volume) and across regions of the Southeast after A.D. 1050 (see fig. 1.3).

Besides being multiscaled, the process of tradition making always occupies space or matter. It is cultural construction figuratively, as the building of collective sentiments, values, and meanings, and it may be construction literally, as the physical act of building, production, and manufacture. In this way, the process of tradition making or cultural construction through practice differs little from Giddens's (1979) sense of "structuration," except in the insistence on materiality and in the artificiality of "structures" or constraints. Even speech, music, or bodily movements have a spatial and material dimension that is archaeologically visible (see fig. 1.4). This may be obvious in dance halls or grounds, less obvious in terms of the acoustics of space, and seldom even considered in terms of the proxemics of talk, body language, or gesture (see Farnell 1999).

Shennan's (1993) useful characterization of practices as "surface phenomena" allows us to carry this observation of the manifest qualities of all practice a step further. Arguing against treating institutions, organizations, or cultural meanings as real things, Shennan (1993) and others propose that, in a way, practices embody institutions, organizations, or meanings. The institutions, organizations, and meanings do not exist outside of the doing of them, and people are not necessarily conscious of their supposed deeper meanings. Likewise, traditions exist only in the practicing of them or in the "moments" of construction, even though meaningful referents are rooted in the "genealogies" of traditions (see Clark 1998; Robb 1998; B. W. Thomas 1998).

The crux of the matter is that material culture "as a dimension of practice, is itself causal. Its production—while contingent on histories of actions and representations—is an enactment or an embodiment of people's dispositions—a social negotiation—that brings about changes in meanings, dispositions, identities, and traditions" (Pauketat 2001). Unlike materialist scenarios where material culture merely reflects, expresses, or correlates with some unseen transformation between constraints, *the spaces and artifacts analyzed by archaeologists are themselves the processes of tradition making.*

This is the essence of the idea of materiality (Conkey 1999; Joyce and Hendon 2000; Pauketat 2002; J. Thomas 2000). Once adopted, the idea of materiality (not materialism) forces anyone seeking to explain the past to shift attention away from interpreting things and toward understanding them as continuously unfolding phenomena. The idea of the *chaîne opératoire,* or technical-operational chain, has been offered as a useful heuristic device for understanding this process in a technological sense (Dobres 1999, 2000; Stark, ed., 1998). That heuristic involves focusing on how tools were made and used by various people through time as a way to

Fig. 1.4. Plains Indian pow-wow dance ground.

explain the process of tradition making, rather than focusing on the functionality of the tools or tool styles to explain "why" the tools took the forms they did (for additional background, see Dobres 2000; Lemonnier 1993; Pfaffenberger 1992). The latter explanations rely on unseen processes to explain change between static tool types.

The *chaîne opératoire* is a specific example of tradition making. However, it engenders a near microscopic view of cultural process that may not resonate with researchers grappling with larger-scale problems of history and tradition (little reference to it, for instance, is made in this volume). Similar variants of the dynamic tradition concept are necessary for understanding the construction of person, ethnicity, hierarchy, or community (Toren 1999; for archaeological examples, see Clark 1998; Dobres 2000; S. Jones 1997; Pauketat 1997a; Sassaman 1998a). For instance, Thomas Emerson and I have claimed that political centralization in the pre-Columbian Mississippi valley was effected through a "traditional" community-building process (Pauketat 2000a; Pauketat and Emerson 1999). Feasting, craft production, and pyramid building (among other practices) under a set of novel circumstances were the material processes that caused profound cultural-historical change.

Practice, Power, and Plurality in the Southeast

In this volume, community identities, ethnicities, political cultures, regions, polities, and various other traditions are cast as cultural constructions. In instances ranging from native hunter-gatherers (discussed by Sassaman, and Emerson and McElrath) to African slaves (analyzed by Thomas), cultural construction always involved "power." This is not power as a coordinated force, but it is power as an ability to effect some cultural construction (Bourdieu 1990; Foucault 1978; see also Wolf 1990, 1999). Archaic flintknappers chipping projectile points negotiated power and technique between generations and across space with their projectile point–making neighbors (consider Sassaman, this volume). An aged potter extolling the virtues of using a particular surface treatment or temper in pottery manufacture exercised power over technological know-how in her negotiations with younger potters (consider the chapters by Alt, Saunders, and Scarry, this volume). The members of a village who reprimanded another villager for some "nontraditional" act were defining tradition via collective power (consider the chapters by Nassaney, and Sullivan and Rodning, this volume).

In other words, politics and tradition are quite inseparable. Pierre Bourdieu (1977) discussed this same inseparability using the notion "doxa." Doxa, the taken-for-granted, nondiscursive knowledge of people, becomes "heterodoxy" and "orthodoxy" via the historically situated negotiations of doxa and power. For instance, native political-cultural orders in the Southeast were not simply imposed on tradition-minded people; these orders "appropriated" doxa to create orthodoxy or heterodoxy (e.g., Pauketat 2000b; Pauketat and Emerson 1999). These included Cahokian attempts to homogenize a cultural landscape or to counter homogenization (Alt, this volume). In the case of Toltec, the anti-homogenizing forces may have carried the day (see Nassaney, this volume). They did among the Creeks (see Wesson, this volume), and they may have among the Cherokee (see Sullivan and Rodning, this volume). These cases point to the dynamic quality of tradition as a negotiated balance—Gramsci's (1971) "compromise equilibrium"—of conflicting or alternative cultural practices (see Lears 1985). The compromise equilibria may take the appearance of political cultures (Rees, this volume), village-level diversity (Alt, this volume), embedded countercultures (Nassaney, this volume), distinct ethnic histories (see Emerson and McElrath, Sullivan and Rodning, and Sassaman, this volume), and communalization (Wesson, this volume).

Another way of putting this is that orthodoxies, political cultures, or power-tradition negotiations always appear to involve some degree of resistance (see Lears 1985; Paynter and McGuire 1991). Here, I am not limiting the idea of resistance to those conscious, objective, and intentional acts of defiance documented, for instance, among peasant communities (Halperin 1994; J. C. Scott 1990). In its broadest sense, "cultural resistance" could be located within any contrary practice where knowledge exists of the alternatives. Following Scarry (this volume), we might also label such contrary practices as an alternative "discourse" or "counter-hegemony." This would be dissidence of the latent everyday sort, done less to oppose some dominant persons and more to reproduce one's sense of tradition in the face of alternatives. Such is the point of studies that stress the persistent culinary practices, community arrangements, and artifact forms among southern slaves in spite of their knowledge of and access to Euro-American utensils, recipes, and worldviews (see L. G. Ferguson 1992; Orser 1998; Thomas 1998, and this volume). It is also suggested in the studies of the routines and practices of hunter-gatherers and village agriculturists (see Alt, Sassaman, Saunders, and Scarry, this volume). That contrary practice as tradition making was a real force with which people reckoned seems verified whenever politicos, especially of the imperial and colonial sort, took pains to break up and relocate "traditional communities" (see Hassig 1988:208; Patterson 1986, 1987:122–123; Redmond 1983; Saunders 1998). The purpose of resettlement, as in the ethnic cleansing of recent history, was the elimination of cultural resistance and "persistent traditions" (Nassaney, Sassaman, this volume).

Of course, resistance is not an explanation (M. F. Brown 1996; Lightfoot, this volume). Neither is practice, tradition, doxa, ethnicity, habitus, or any other single concept in this volume an explanation. Explanations come from analyzing concrete historical cases using (and improving) conceptual tools. The conceptual tools deployed in this volume allow us to begin to study tradition making as a multilevel, syncretizing, and hybridizing process shot through with contestation, defiance, and contrary practice. Given that concepts are tools and not explanations, it may be preferable to think of them—especially resistance—as part of a continuum.

The papers in this volume fall at various points along this continuum (see fig. 1.5). At one end are overt, conscious actions of resistance projecting identities or defying the powers that be (e.g., Loren, this volume). At the other end of this continuum is the lack of interaction with and knowledge of other people (e.g., Fortier, this volume).[3] In between the two extremes, power and tradition were accepted, accommodated, co-opted,

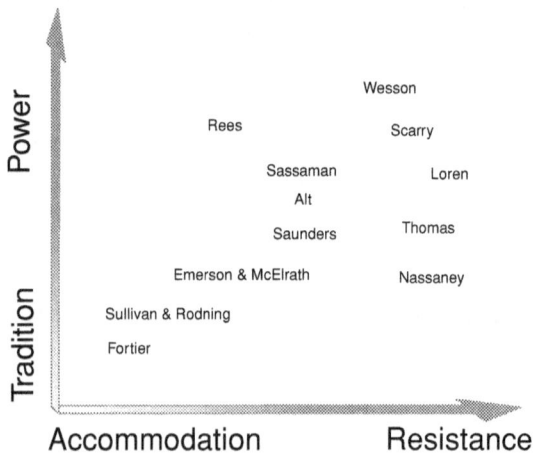

Fig. 1.5. Positions taken by volume authors along the tradition-building con-tinuum.

rejected, and resisted. Traditions were politicized and power was tradi-tionalized. The historical consequences ranged from syncretism to ethno-genesis and whole-group migration.

Add to this, cultural pluralism. Kathleen Deagan, Kent Lightfoot, and others consider the pluralistic side of culture contact (see Deagan 1995; Graham 1998; Lightfoot et al. 1998). The ideas of pluralism, "syncre-tism," and "hybridity," encourage us to understand the negotiation pro-cess as multiscalar and multidimensional (Stewart and Shaw 1994). Syn-cretism, or the notion that parts of traditions might be perpetuated and articulated with other historically distinct practices, should help us con-ceptualize how one group might accommodate practices foreign to their own experiences at one level while preserving those at another level. This might especially be pertinent under circumstances of rapid or large-scale contact, conversion, social disruption, or re-integration (consider the cases made by Alt, Loren, Saunders, Scarry, and Thomas, this volume).[4]

In the Southeast, part of the problem is first identifying regional discon-tinuity. Emerson and McElrath (this volume) and Fortier (this volume) make this a central point, as it implies a very different historical process compared to the standard evolutionary explanations of the eastern Wood-lands. The Mississippian problem analyzed by Alt (this volume) rests in part on evidence of intraregional settlement displacement, as do the Mis-sion period cases presented by Saunders (this volume) and Scarry (this volume). Given that evidence, displacement can be examined as a moment of cultural construction wherein traditional practices were exposed to a suite of novel contexts. Abandonment, culture contact, migration, depopulation, enslavement, and warfare are other instances of the tradition-making process under exceptional circumstances (see also Nelson 2000). In this volume, the chapters by Loren and Thomas most clearly reveal how creative and proactive human agents can be in such radically altered contexts.

To be sure, southeastern North America before and after Columbus is constructed of locally and regionally diverse histories (e.g., Rees, this volume). This book is ample testimony to that fact. So how could this diversity give birth to a southeastern culture area or to distinctive southern traditions? On the one hand, the answer may reside in the compounding of regional-scale patterns created as part of daily practices going all the way back to Archaic foragers. On the other hand, the Southeast is also being produced today, as people select traditional practices and bring them forward into the present. To sort through this particular instance of the conundrum of tradition, the case material in this book is presented in reverse chronological order. The reverse order engenders an appreciation for the universal process of tradition making regardless of time or place. The reverse order also recapitulates how we in the present and our predecessors at various points in the past create and created tradition by reaching selectively back further and further into the past. The result, I hope, is an archaeology of tradition that better explains and, at the same time, transcends the Southeast.

Notes

1. Of course, denying that we can know the past, oddly, denies the people of the past their voices at the same time that it enables today's politicians—academic, governmental, and tribal—to co-opt those voices. Archaeological interpretation is not simply the creation of a narrative. Rather, it is itself a historical and self-correcting process. This is the scientific method, which need not be distinguished from historical understanding. The goals of science and humanism are not antithetical (e.g., Harré 1986). True, there may be a number of ways to interpret the past, especially at the outset of some interpretive venture (à la Hodder 1985, 1986). However, as more and more independent lines of evidence are brought to bear, the array of interpretations narrows, constrained by accrued evidence (Trigger 1991).

2. Neo-Darwinists have correctly attacked the "essentialism" inherent in these macroscale concepts (e.g., Lyman and O'Brien 1998; Shennan 1993).

3. This continuum was approximated by the 1980s debates on style. At one end were the information-exchange and political-ideology models; at the other end are the old interaction models and more recent emphases on "technological style" (Conkey 1990; Dietler and Herbich 1989; Graves 1994; Lechtman 1977; Stark 1999; Stark et al. 1998).

4. It is also relevant in understanding the apparent persistence of some of the thematic symbols, icons, and linguistically encoded precepts, including those considered by Hall (1997) and, possibly, observed by Emerson and McElrath, Fortier, Sassaman, and Saunders (this volume).

2

African-American Tradition and Community in the Antebellum South

Brian W. Thomas

Enslaved African Americans negotiated a social landscape during the antebellum period that was filled with struggle. Some struggles centered on the many well-documented physical hardships entailed in slavery. However, many of the struggles in which African-American slaves participated were ideological. At the core of these conflicts, the participants wrestled over who would define what it meant to be a person of African descent living in the American South—not simply in legal terms, but in human terms. Such struggles were ideological because they were intimately bound up in the power relations inherent to the institution of slavery. The specific arenas in which African-American slaves engaged these tensions ranged widely, from the contradiction of defining people as property to more subtle conflicts over social categories and work roles, or the form and practice of religion. While these various conflicts took place at an ideological level, they often carried with them indirect—if not direct—physical and material consequences.

As African Americans negotiated the terms of their existence in the antebellum South, there always was at least one source of strength they had to draw upon: the cultural practices and traditions that they retained, adopted, created, and modified. The process of putting traditions into practice—that is, living them day-to-day—provided coherence to African-American identity and acted as a means to deal with the social and material demands imposed by slavery.

Despite the implied meaning of its common usage, I do not define traditions simply as longstanding, time-honored practices or values that reflect an unchanged past. Although they recall the past, traditions are constantly defined and redefined in the present. Such certainly was true for enslaved African Americans in the U.S. Southeast. They forged in North

America a new set of cultural practices out of various African and European cultures, tempered by a new physical environment and a new set of social circumstances. In particular, the African-American traditions practiced during the antebellum period developed and changed in a social milieu where asymmetrical power relations dominated life. Consequently, these traditions were important as African Americans mediated antebellum power relations throughout the plantation South.

In this chapter, I focus on two realms that illustrate the tensions between tradition and power relations in the antebellum South, drawing on evidence from the historical and archaeological records. The first case explores the ideological and material struggle over slave ownership of property. The second case examines how new traditions defining kinship helped enslaved African Americans better cope with the disruptions that slavery caused to families. These new constructions of kinship operated at several levels, from providing ties to strengthen the slave community to offering a means to engage the ideological struggle over how social roles were defined within that community (see Loren, this volume). Taken together, these examples demonstrate the fluid nature of tradition and its importance in negotiating plantation power relations during the antebellum period.

Central to this study is the idea that tradition is established, maintained, and revised only within the context of practicing communities. As I discuss more extensively elsewhere (B. W. Thomas 1998:532–534), communities are formed by individuals who recognize common interests, and are defined and contested through power relations. Tradition may participate in this negotiation in a number of ways, but always as a constituent part of the struggle to define and maintain community.

A second and equally critical point is the importance of history in understanding both the institution of slavery and the developments that took place within it. The ideological construction of African and African-American slavery in North America has a history, one that is tied to unique historical contexts and the racial constructs that developed within them (e.g., Berlin 1998; Davis 1999; Fields 1990; Kolchin 1993; Smedley 1993). Furthermore, the institution of slavery was not uniform through time and space, a point Berlin (1998:14) makes when he cautions:

> Projecting the regimen of seventeenth-century tobacco production, the aesthetics of African pottery, or the eschatology of animistic religion into the nineteenth century is no more useful than reading the demands of blackbelt cotton production, the theology of African-

American Christianity, and the ethos of antebellum paternalism back into the seventeenth century. It is important to remember that at the beginning of the nineteenth century . . . the vast majority of black people, slave and free, did not reside in the blackbelt, grow cotton, or subscribe to Christianity. That the character of slave life in North America was reversed a half century later is a striking commentary on a period that historians have represented as stable maturity.

Accordingly, I have attempted to limit my focus in this chapter to conditions as they existed during the half century leading up to the Civil War and emancipation, roughly the 1820s to the mid-1860s. Although I draw upon examples from different regions in the South, I endeavor to be explicit about the similarities and differences that likely existed among them.

Ownership of Property Through Public Display

A convergence of factors during the colonial period—including the shortage and temporary nature of indentured laborers, at the same time that cash crops found expanding markets—made the use of African, and particularly Afro-Caribbean, slaves profitable in North America. Although economic viability may have been the primary reason to acquire and maintain slaves as a labor force, it did not provide the ideological underpinnings to sustain the institution. Ideology developed over time, helping to describe and affirm as natural the new sets of social relations that slavery entailed. The most powerful ideological construct surrounding slavery was, of course, race. Racial constructions were always a backdrop to other social definitions contested during slavery, as they were in other colonial contexts (Loren, this volume). One aspect of Euro-American racial constructions—and one that defined the institution of slavery—was the legal acceptance of some people (mainly those of African descent) as chattel property.

By the beginning of the nineteenth century, the legal restrictions on African-American slaves, as well as free blacks, were well established across the South. There existed, however, some fluidity across time and space, and slave codes indicate the waxing and waning concern that the planter/ruling class had over perceived liberties practiced by slaves. One of the areas of negotiation through time involved the extent to which slaves, themselves defined as property, might possess property of their own.

Although there existed no legal basis for slaves to own property in the antebellum South, archaeological and historical information demonstrates that they sought out and obtained a wide range of possessions (e.g., Deetz 1993; L. G. Ferguson 1992; Heath 1997; Morgan 1982, 1983; Otto 1984; Penningroth 1997; Singleton 1998; Young 1997). Slaves acquired personal possessions by various means and for various purposes. Precisely how slaves obtained the objects we find on archaeological sites is not clear from study of the material record alone. Masters likely provided some items that slaves possessed, while others were acquired as gifts or through purchase, barter, or theft, or were made by slaves themselves. Although it would be valuable to know how specific objects entered slave households (Orser 1992), it is unlikely that this could be determined with any amount of certainty. However, it is clear that slaves did participate in a thriving economy that involved cash as well as exchange, and a growing body of research indicates that slaves were very active in seeking out items they desired (e.g., Berlin and Morgan 1993; Foster 1997; Olwell 1996; Wood 1995).

In the Low Country of Georgia and South Carolina, where labor was organized according to the task system, it was not uncommon for slaves to acquire property, sometimes substantial amounts of property. The task system, along with the gang system, was one of two principal labor systems used on plantations (Gray 1933, 1:550–551). Under the task system, slaves were given specific tasks that had to be completed by the end of the day. Upon completion of assigned tasks, slaves had the remainder of the day to pursue their own goals. The gang system, on the other hand, involved groups of slaves working the entire day under the supervision of a driver or foreman. The task system allowed some slaves to earn money by hiring themselves out or selling produce, fowl, or livestock that they raised during their spare time. Although slaves working under the gang system often had access to small gardens, the scale of self-employment and of the potential to earn income was significantly less than for those working under the task system.

Historical records make clear that slaves in the Low Country did, in fact, accumulate property—ranging from livestock to farm equipment. Morgan's (1983) research on former slaves who submitted claims for property losses during the Civil War illustrates this fact. The Southern Claims Commission was established in 1871 to allow individuals "who could prove both their loyalty and their loss of property to Federal troops" an opportunity to seek reimbursement for their losses (Morgan 1983:405). Drawing on depositions and supporting testimony from Liberty County, Georgia, Morgan discusses some of the types of property that slaves had owned. The claims, mostly by former field slaves, were limited to items that Federal troops were able to take legitimately, such as food and supplies. Therefore, the claims do not list all the property the individuals had possessed. According to Morgan (1983:409): "Virtually all the Liberty County ex-slave claimants had apparently been deprived of a number of hogs and a substantial majority listed corn, rice and fowls among their losses. In addition, a surprising number apparently possessed horses and cows, while buggies or wagons, beehives, peanuts, fodder, syrup, butter, sugar, and tea were, if these claims are to be believed, in the hands of at least some slaves. The average cash value (in 1864 dollars) claimed by Liberty County former slaves was $357.43, with the highest claim totaling $2,290 and the lowest $49."

But even beyond the special situation of the Low Country, where slave ownership of property is amply documented, it is clear that a limited form of slave property ownership was in place throughout the South. While the gang system of labor did not provide the opportunity to accumulate wealth to the extent possible under the task system, upland slaves still had opportunities to earn money in other ways. In up-country Georgia, for example, many slaves working on cotton farms and plantations used Sundays to hire themselves out; their earnings allowed them to purchase necessities or desired goods (Reidy 1993:143–145). Slaves also accumulated goods by exchanging items they raised, caught, or made, as well as by providing various services to other slaves, such as midwifery, medicinal treatments, and so on. Thus, despite the differences inherent in the distinct labor systems, opportunities did exist for slaves to obtain provisions and other goods beyond what planters provided them.

Archaeologists have encountered numerous examples of personal possessions once belonging to enslaved African Americans. The evidence comes from archaeological sites spanning the Colonial to the antebellum periods, and ranging geographically across the entire slaveholding South. The objects recovered from archaeological sites represent a different realm of possessions than those discussed in the Southern Claims Commission documents. Rather than wagons, livestock, and perishable foodstuffs, the material culture from former slave sites ranges from ceramic dishes and glass containers to marbles and sewing kits. Many of these items likely were considered to be the possessions of individuals (a piece of jewelry) rather than something used communally (a ceramic serving bowl). It is within the realm of personal items that property ownership likely was acknowledged most explicitly (see fig. 2.1). Precisely how ownership of such items was established and maintained is unclear, but historical evidence suggests that display played an important role.

Fig. 2.1. Copper alloy purse clasp found at slave cabin site at the Hermitage. Photograph courtesy of the Ladies' Hermitage Association.

While there is little doubt that slaves *possessed* various items, from ornaments to livestock, did they truly *own* them? And if so, how was ownership established? Penningroth's (1997) recent research on Southern Claims Commission documents from Liberty County, Georgia, is one of the first attempts to explore precisely how slaves established ownership over property in the Low Country. Building on Morgan's work, Penningroth (1997:411–412) explains: "Since no law protected a slave's property from other slaves or from his or her master, slaves depended on an informal system of display and acknowledgment to mark the boundaries of ownership. Their ability to transform mere possession into ownership depended on their ability to substitute informal public recognition for public law as the anchor of their title." Such recognition, he convincingly argues, was established by displaying possessions at public occasions and in public spaces, a process that was repeatedly acknowledged in documents from the Liberty County claims cases.

Penningroth's research focuses specifically on the last years of slavery in Low Country, Georgia. How applicable were these observations to up-country Georgia farms or Upper South plantations in general during the decades preceding emancipation? Clearly, the situation for Upper South slaves differed in many ways from that witnessed at coastal plantations in

Georgia, with distinctive labor systems being the most notable contrast. Nonetheless, the practice of public display and acknowledgment that validated property ownership in the Low Country may have operated similarly in other regions.

There certainly is ample evidence that slaves possessed a wide range of material items, many of which likely were acquired by individuals making choices based on personal tastes and/or needs. Archaeological research on former slave sites at the Hermitage, the plantation home of Andrew Jackson, helps to illustrate this point. Located near Nashville, Tennessee, the Hermitage has been the locus of archaeological research on slavery for nearly fifteen field seasons. Fieldwork first took place in the mid-1970s and has been on-going since 1988 (e.g., Galle 1997, 2001; McKee 1991, 1993, 1997; McKee et al. 1992; McKee et al. 1994; Russell 1997; S. D. Smith 1976; S. D. Smith et al. 1977; B. W. Thomas 1995, 1998; B. W. Thomas et al. 1995). Archaeologists have uncovered hundreds, if not thousands, of objects of adornment and personal use from former slave cabin sites dating from the 1820s into the 1860s. These objects range from buttons (with over ninety distinct styles represented),[1] beads, and buckles, to combs, pipes, musical instruments, and parts of firearms. The presence of coins at the sites suggests that money was circulating among the slaves (see fig. 2.2). It is likely, therefore, that at least some of these items were purchased rather than obtained as hand-me-downs from the Jacksons or overseers.

Entries in the Hermitage Farm Journal and Account Book (Ladies Hermitage Association, 1817–1832) indicate that money was sometimes paid

Fig. 2.2. Gold 1853 U.S. dollar recovered at slave cabin site at the Hermitage. Photograph courtesy of the Ladies' Hermitage Association.

out to slaves at the Hermitage. The amounts were small, ranging from $1.00 to $1.50 per entry, but they nonetheless indicate that slaves were earning money for specific tasks or products. The presence of coins indicates that slaves were active players in the local economy—despite laws generally forbidding such activity (e.g., Public Acts of Tennessee 1799:§28; 1803:§13; 1813:§135; 1839:§47). Evidence of this economic activity in the Nashville area also comes to us through the memoirs of John McCline, a former slave from the nearby Clover Bottom plantation. Recalling his time at Clover Bottom, he wrote: "The cabins, or quarters, of the people on the place, were seldom visited by either master or mistress unless some one was sick. Neither, therefore knew of the elegance and prosperity displayed in some. None of the people were supposed to have money, or to know its use and power. The fact is many of them had some, and spent it in the usual way, just like people who had always enjoyed freedom, liberty, and happiness" (Furman 1998:24).

On Upper South plantations such as Clover Bottom and the Hermitage, enslaved African Americans also had the opportunity and means to purchase selected items they sought, if at a smaller scale than that witnessed in the Low Country. Likewise, the tradition of display that helped establish ownership in the Low Country seemed to be a practice shared in other areas of the South as well.

There is considerable evidence indicating that the practice of display was an important tradition among African Americans. One important form it took was the display of dress. As early as the eighteenth century, paintings and drawings depict slaves in special dress for occasions such as weddings, and such practices extended into the antebellum period when attendance at churches became more commonplace (e.g., Kelso 1984:27).

A tradition of display of dress among enslaved African Americans, at minimum as a means of personal expression, is evidenced in written sources and in archaeological remains (H. B. Foster 1997; Heath 2000; B. W. Thomas and Thomas 2001). Written accounts of this practice come to us in the form of advertisements for runaways, planter diaries, traveler accounts, slave narratives, and interviews with former slaves conducted early in the twentieth century. Slaves sought to display personal possessions for a number of reasons, many of them tied to communicating social identity (B. W. Thomas and Thomas 2001). But public display of items such as beads, buttons, and garments also may have acted to establish ownership of such items. Showing other members of the community that objects were in an individual's possession created a public record of ownership. Thus, similar traditions for establishing property ownership appear to have applied to substantial property like livestock, as well as to small personal items, in various parts of the antebellum South.

Understanding the importance of display also casts a different light on the development of Christianity among African-American slaves. From the early days of slavery in North America, slaves were provided time off from their labors on Sundays, and this custom was well entrenched by the antebellum period (Berlin 1998:57, 61; Blassingame 1979:106; Genovese 1976:315–316; Kolchin 1993:107, 130; Stampp 1956:79, 167, 172, 218). Christianity spread rapidly among African Americans in the nineteenth century, and as many African-American slaves restructured their spiritual life, Sundays assumed new meanings for them. One important aspect of Sunday worship was the opportunity to dress up for the social gathering. For some, it also provided a public venue to display other property such as horses and wagons (Penningroth 1997:420–421). But public display was not restricted to clothing or other possessions African Americans might have acquired. A tradition of spiritual display also developed among the growing numbers of black Christians as they worshipped. Ecstatic conversions, shouts, and ring dances characterized many black Christian religious services and provided a vehicle to publicly demonstrate faith (Frey and Wood 1998; Raboteau 1980; Sobel 1988; Stuckey 1987:3–97). These practices were another manifestation of display—in this case, of a spiritual experience rather than of property. The effect, however, was the same from a community perspective. Through this ritual practice, the community witnessed and acknowledged an individual's participation in faith.

It was within the context of a tradition of public display that enslaved African Americans established ownership of property in the antebellum South. Display functioned at many levels. At different times and places it provided a creative outlet, reflected competitiveness among individuals, and expressed and reinforced shared beliefs, aesthetics, and identity. Perhaps most importantly, display was a shared event that was practiced, witnessed, and understood by a collection of people who shared common interests—that is, a community. This widespread practice of display, documented as early as the colonial period, took on a new form and meaning with respect to property in some areas of the South during the antebellum period, most notably in the Low Country. In doing so, it joined with broader social and economic trends within which the restrictive institution of slavery existed and provided enslaved African Americans a tool for negotiating important aspects of their day-to-day existence.

Negotiating Community Through Kinship

Establishing ownership of property among slaves took place within the context of a practicing community, where a broader tradition of display helped slaves establish socially recognized claims of ownership to possessions. Display, as a means of establishing ownership, resulted from a unique set of historical events and social conditions—namely, oppression by whites and laws banning legal ownership of property by slaves—that created greater cohesion with the African-American community. Display of property was connected to struggles of a larger scale over the material and social existence that slaves experienced on antebellum plantations. Its impact on material conditions was tied, in part, to the items over which slaves were able to assert ownership. But the issue of slaves—themselves defined as property—having ownership of property also needs to be viewed as part of a broader negotiation over social identity that was taking place at this time.

The process by which slaves established ownership of property relied upon social networks that validated their identity as a member of a larger community. By relying on community acknowledgment to assert ownership, individual slaves were forced to subject themselves to public scrutiny of their personal acquisitions. Thus, the practice of slave community reproduced traditions (display, in this case) that strengthened the community itself. The meaning of this community, however, also was under a constant process of negotiation.

Communities exist only through practice. That is, they exist only when a group of people who recognize common interests act upon those interests (Roseberry 1989:225–232). Community is not a static concept; how it is defined and put into practice is in a constant state of negotiation among individuals and groups pursuing different interests. As Roseberry (1989:226) notes, communities are formed "around particular social and cultural oppositions that create a group or community feeling among heterogeneous folks." The images—that is, the constructions—of community "are products of and responses to particular forces, structures, and events ... and they derive their community forming power from their apparent relationship to those forces and events" (Roseberry 1989:227). For African Americans living in the antebellum South, the image—and practice—of community was formed in a historical context dominated by institutionalized slavery.

Because the interests of African-American slaves and planters were, for the most part, inimical, obvious tensions existed between slave and planter communities. One area in which these tensions were apparent was in how social relations within African-American slave communities were defined and played out (B. W. Thomas 1995, 1998:533–534). Planters viewed slave communities as social hierarchies that mirrored white southern society. Enslaved African Americans, however, viewed internal social relations much differently than whites. One of the means by which they opposed the planters' image of slave community was with a tradition of kinship that had formed in the New World, a tradition that grew out of the social insecurities of slavery itself.

One of the most common views of slavery articulated by whites during the antebellum period was that slave society contained a strict social hierarchy defined by work role. Simply put, whites viewed house slaves as more cultured and more intelligent than field slaves, who were considered lower class. A few examples from contemporary observers help to illustrate this point.

Joseph Ingraham, a northern native who spent some time as an Episcopal minister in the South, noted that "the domestic slaves and field slaves are two distinct classes" (Ingraham 1860:35, cited in Harper 1978:42). The domestic slave, Ingraham observed, "is more sprightly, better clad, more intelligent and animated, apes polite manners, and imitates the polished airs of the well-bred 'white folk'" (Ingraham 1968, 2:254). James Sterling, an Englishman who traveled throughout the South in 1856 and 1857, noted that house servants were better off than field slaves. While a fervent opponent to the institution of slavery, Sterling clearly believed that domestic slaves, who were exposed to "the civilizing influence of Anglo-Saxon industry," were far more intelligent than field hands owing to their "association with the superior race" (Sterling 1969:59, 296).

Similar observations were made by Fanny Kemble, whose letters described conditions on her husband's rice plantation on Butler Island, Georgia, in 1838 and 1839: "The slaves on this plantation are divided into field-hands and mechanics or artisans. The former, the great majority, are the more stupid and brutish of the tribe; the others, who are regularly taught their trades, are not only exceedingly expert at them, but exhibit a greater general activity of intellect, which must necessarily result from even a partial degree of cultivation" (Kemble 1984:63).

In contrast to the putative civilizing effect of white contact on domestic slaves, whites explained "the 'loutishness' and 'coarseness' of the field hand . . . by the lack of close contact with masters and mistresses" (Doyle 1937:74). Such a view was shared by many southerners and slavery sympathizers; but it also reflected the view of antislavery visitors to the South such as Sterling. James Redpath, another abolitionist who traveled through the South in the 1850s, described field slaves in a similar way: "The field negroes, as a class, are coarse, filthy, brutal, and lascivious; liars, parasites, hypocrites, and thieves; without self-respect, religious aspirations, or the nobler traits which characterize humanity" (Redpath 1968:256–257).

Planters and their families did much to reinforce their image of slave society, one that projected social divisions among slaves. For example, they segregated domestic, and to some extent skilled, slaves from field slaves by constructing separate housing areas. They provided house slaves with nicer clothing, referred to them as their "black family," and limited their contacts, in some cases, with slaves who worked outside the mansion. Through these acts, planters presented an image of the enslaved African-American community that was divisive and antagonistic. Mediating this process, however, was a tradition of kinship that did not square with that image.

Kinship connections structure many aspects of social life, and they helped African slaves adjust to a new social existence in the Americas. Gutman (1976:218–224) observes that slaves adjusted African patterns of kinship transplanted to the New World by placing a growing emphasis on fictive kin relations, a common practice in many African societies. Gutman suggests that the fictive kin relations among slaves developed through several interrelated stages (Gutman 1976:223). Prior to enslavement, Africans had well-established sets of family and kinship beliefs and practices. Gutman believes that after enslavement, first in Africa and then in the New World, slaves began to invest non-kin relations with symbolic kin functions owing to disruption of traditional kinship and family patterns through the sale of family members. New patterns of symbolic or fictive kin relations were strengthened because there was a need to enlarge social relationships among slaves, who were often cut off from blood kin. Over time, the linkages within and between generations of different slave families helped to transform conceptions of family and kin obligation rooted in blood and marriage into conceptions of quasi-kin and non-kin social obligation.

Thus, slavery led African Americans to modify traditions of kinship to meet needs experienced during enslavement. There was nothing inevitable about these changes; rather, they developed based on social needs within a specific historical context. As they developed, they also participated in broader negotiations over how slave community was defined and practiced.

Historical and archaeological research at the Hermitage illustrates the tensions between planter and African-American slave images of community, as well as the importance that kinship had in negotiating them. Precisely how fictive kinship relations played out at the Hermitage is unknown. However, information does exist on ties of blood and marriage on the plantation. Because African-American families at the Hermitage were relatively stable—at least before the 1850s—these ties played a crucial part in structuring social relations there. Marriage ties, for example, were extensive and crosscut all segments of the Hermitage slave community. There exists enough documentary evidence to piece together much of the family structure and marriage ties of Jackson's slaves, as well as work roles assigned to individuals. Farm journal entries from 1829 (Ladies Hermitage Association, 1817–1832) and 1846–1849 (A. Jackson, Jr., 1845–1877) present glimpses of the family structures at two points in time. In addition, the occupations of many slaves at the Hermitage have been gleaned from correspondence between Andrew Jackson and family members or colleagues, visitors' accounts, and an 1841 Hermitage farm journal entry (Parker, 1840–1841). This information, together with the family structures, sheds light on the threads of kinship woven through the African-American community of the Hermitage.

Documents indicate that the highest proportion of all slave marriages at the Hermitage was between field slaves. Such a situation is to be expected, given that most African-American slaves worked in the fields. The marriage patterns do show, however, a large percentage of marriages crosscutting occupational roles, suggesting close connections between all segments of the slave community, regardless of occupation (see table 2.1). Over time, for example, skilled slaves married both domestic and field slaves in roughly similar proportions.

A similar pattern existed for domestic slaves, who more often married nondomestic slaves. In fact, there is only one marriage recorded between two domestic slaves. Between 1829 and 1855, well over half of the marriages involving domestic slaves were to skilled slaves, while a quarter to a third were to field slaves.

Written sources from elsewhere in the South do indicate that some domestic slaves embraced the planters' hierarchical image of slave community and segregated themselves physically and socially from others within the slave community (e.g., Frazier 1930:209, 211; Rawick 1972: 183, 221). However, the historical information from the Hermitage suggests that kinship ties mediated such tensions, and that planter-defined work roles and conceptions of slave community were not central to social

Table 2.1. Summary of marriages by occupation at the Hermitage, 1829–1855

Domestic and domestic = 1
Domestic and skilled = 4
Domestic and field = 6
Skilled and skilled = 2
Skilled and field = 4
Field and field = 14

Domestic slaves: total of 11 marriages
 54.5% to field slaves
 36.4% to skilled slaves
 9.1% to other domestic slaves

Field slaves: total of 24 marriages
 58.3% to other field slaves
 16.7% to skilled slaves
 25.0% to domestic slaves

Skilled slaves: total of 10 marriages
 40.0% to field slaves
 20.0% to other skilled slaves
 40.0% to domestic slaves

relations within the slave community itself. We can assume that fictive kinship ties contributed to this process as well.

Such a view is further supported by the material culture recovered from former slave house sites in three areas of the Hermitage plantation. Despite Jackson's efforts to segregate slaves by housing area, with house slaves living directly behind the Hermitage mansion (see fig. 2.3), the archaeological remains indicate that material items circulated extensively among slaves living in other parts of the plantation. These items included those more likely to have been differentially distributed by Jackson, such as meat and serving vessels (B. W. Thomas 1995:61–151, 1998:537–547). Fancy ceramic table settings, for example, have been found at cabin sites located near the mansion as well as in a field quarter about a third of a mile away. Faunal remains, to the extent that they accurately reflect access to food items, indicate that quality cuts of meat were distributed similarly across the plantation.[2] Additionally, items such as glass containers and a wide array of small personal items indicate that material items circulated within the community regardless of location of housing or work role. Although the precise process by which these goods made their way into specific households is unclear, it is likely that the kinship connections just documented played an important role in redistributing material culture and food items among members of the Hermitage slave community.

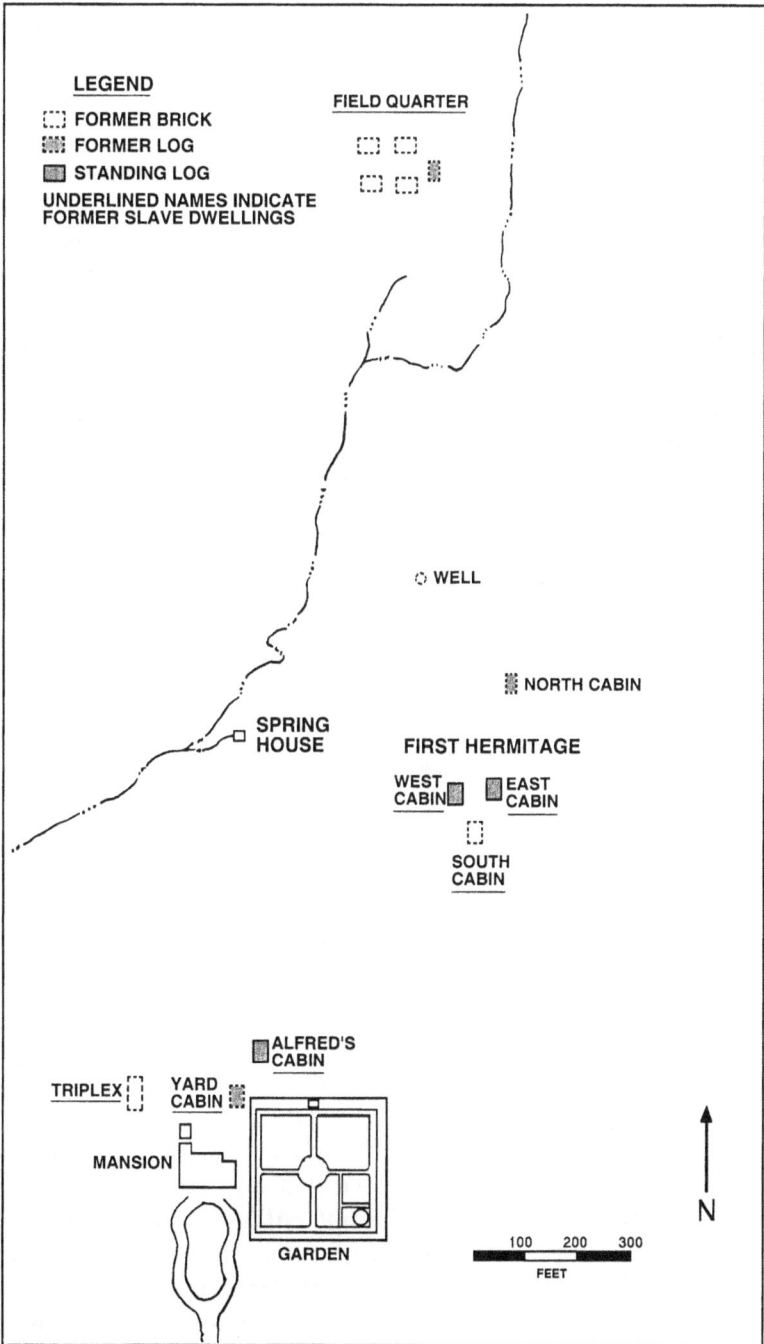

Fig. 2.3. Map of the Hermitage Plantation showing slave housing areas.

One material consequence of the kinship patterns among Hermitage slaves was that the spatial order imposed by Jackson, as by other planters, which reflected a hierarchical image of community, was undermined by intermarriage across occupational roles. Such intermarriage resulted in slaves of different occupational roles living together in housing ostensibly segregated by those roles.

Individuals' identities and the social networks that helped to define them were fluid, but both were closely tied to concepts of kinship that developed among African-American slaves. These concepts of kinship helped slaves to define community for themselves. They also helped to define social relationships in a supportive manner, strengthening bonds within the slave community in the face of external pressures from owners that held the threat of destroying African-American family and community. Kinship, as a dynamic tradition, played a crucial role as slaves negotiated the definition of community.

Conclusion

Enslaved African Americans in the antebellum South negotiated the meaning and content of their lives, in part, through the traditions they adopted, created, maintained, and modified. Slavery entailed a constant process of negotiation between owners and those they enslaved, and tradition entered into this process because it was fluid enough to fit the new social conditions that African-American slaves experienced. A tradition of display, for example, articulated with a historically contingent legal system and provided a means for African-American slaves to establish ownership of property. Originating from the same broader tradition, display also became important in African-American religious practices during the antebellum period. Similarly, by modifying traditional kinship ties, African-American slaves were better able to cope with the family dislocations that slavery brought. This tradition of kinship also helped enslaved African Americans to define community for themselves, countering a divisive, hierarchical image of community espoused by planters.

As the examples discussed here illustrate, African-American slaves involved traditions in the give-and-take of slavery in many ways. For example, traditions helped to provide a sense of identity that assisted African Americans in negotiating the material and ideological struggles of day-to-day life under enslavement. However, traditions were made meaningful only by virtue of the communities within which they were practiced and experienced. This connection to community is paramount, for without a community that sanctions certain practices, traditions could not exist.

People do not, of course, practice and modify tradition or community in a vacuum. They do so in a social arena influenced by past events and contemporary power relations, and with a view toward the future. The traditions that African Americans practiced on antebellum plantations were central to defining African-American identity and community and provided the means to navigate the experience of slavery. Furthermore, the forms that these traditions took in the nineteenth century could not be predicted when enslaved Africans first arrived in North America. They resulted from a host of factors, including the myriad African cultures of the enslaved, the cultural practices belonging to slaveholders in the Southeast, the material conditions of slavery, and the asymmetries of plantation social relations. These traditions were tied to a given place and a given time, just as the communities that practiced them were. Neither can be divorced from history.

Tradition is a process that is neither static nor timeless. On the contrary, it is a dynamic process that is historically contingent, shaped by people as they create and modify communities. Like communities, traditions exist only through practice, and practice exists only through human agency. However, traditions cannot be fabricated out of thin air, for the choices that people have before them are constrained by what took place in the past and power relations that exist in the present. It is in that tension between past and present that both tradition and community exist. Indeed, it is through this very process, whereby people negotiate past and present, that humans create history.

Acknowledgments

Funding and support for field research at the Hermitage was provided by Earthwatch and the Ladies' Hermitage Association. Additional funding for analysis of the historical and archaeological remains was provided by the National Endowment for the Humanities and the National Science Foundation.

Notes

1. C. Lynn Rodgers, University of Nevada-Las Vegas, performed analysis on the button assemblage from the Hermitage.

2. Emanuel Breitburg, Tennessee Division of Archaeology, conducted the analysis of faunal remains recovered from the Hermitage slave sites.

3

Resistance and Accommodation in Apalachee Province

John F. Scarry

In the early sixteenth century, the native Apalachee people of northwestern Florida came into increasingly intense and frequent contact with Europeans. This contact began in the early sixteenth century, when the armies of Panfilo de Narváez and Hernando de Soto invaded Apalachee territory. It continued in the seventeenth century when Spanish missionaries established a number of missions in the province. Ultimately, the Apalachee lost their independence, were incorporated into the Spanish colonial empire, and were destroyed as a distinct ethnic and cultural group.

While all this was happening, the world and culture of the Apalachee changed dramatically. Some of the changes were the result of the actions of Europeans; others were the result of the actions of Apalachee. Some changes the Apalachee accepted, others they opposed. The patterns of acceptance of and opposition to specific changes varied among the Apalachee. That variation depended on the social position of the individuals and the nature of the changes.

How did the Spaniards achieve their ascendancy and ultimate domination? How did the Apalachee act during the process? Further, how did historically and environmentally contingent constraints on practice shape the actions of the Apalachee?

Practice and the Construction of Culture

One of the long-term benefits of the postprocessual movement in archaeology has been an increase in the attention paid to individuals and the impact of their actions on the course of history. More and more, we seek to examine how individuals create, re-create, and modify cultural patterns through their actions, through practice. This focus on individuals has led some of us to draw on the theoretical works of scholars like Pierre Bourdieu (1977, 1990) and Anthony Giddens (1979, 1984) to build individual actors into models of both historic change and daily living.

We can think of practice as, in part, the routinized patterns of action that embody cultural traditions and meanings (see Pauketat, this volume). It follows that much of what we see in the archaeological record is the product of (and reflects) practice (Lightfoot et al. 1998; following Ortner 1984). Patterning in the archaeological record is the result of repetitive practice. Thus the archaeological record allows us a glimpse of past practice. As practice embodied tradition and meaning, so the archaeological record allows us a glimpse of the structure and meaning of the lives of people.

Practice is much more than the simple, mindless following of tradition or the *reproduction* of culture. It is through practice that people (actors) *produce* culture and its structures. The constant, ongoing creation of cultural patterns (such as social structures or identities) through practice allows (if not mandates) innovation and change. Individuals innovate when faced with choices among possible alternative actions. They innovate when faced with conflicting demands or expectations. They innovate in novel circumstances and in situations that lie outside past practice. Individuals differ and have differing agendas. There is a constant tension among individuals with different viewpoints and goals. The resolution of these tensions can also lead to innovation and change.

However, there are constraints on actors and on practice. Particularly important are the constraints resulting from past practice: from structures, traditions, and meanings created in the past (what Giddens [1984] would call the unacknowledged constraints on action). Important facets of structure, perhaps the most important, are the identities that individuals and groups of individuals create for themselves and for others. One's social identities give meaning and help shape the understanding of oneself, others, and the broader social and material world. Social identities and the traditional patterns of practice attached to them shape interactions among individuals and groups. Social identities constrain and enable action on the part of individuals and groups. Social identities, and the meanings and sentiments attached to those identities by their holders and by others, shape societies and the actions of individuals. Individual and group practice, however, creates social identities. They do not exist outside the social world, nor are they separate from daily practice. They are not immutable. People change their identities and the meanings attached to their identities. Individuals do so unconsciously as they act in response to immediate circumstances, and by acting they provide precedents for future actors (Holland et al. 1998). They also do so consciously, as they deliberately manipulate and change identities (see de la Cadena 1995; J. F. Scarry 1999).

One important way that people produce and reproduce cultural patterns and social identities is through social discourse (through things like systems of classification, myth, and ritual). Classificatory systems shape and constrain identities and embody understandings of the world. Myth and ritual lend meaning and evoke sentiment.

The power of discourse to reproduce or produce cultural patterns involves both ideological persuasion and sentiment evocation (Lincoln 1989:9). While ideological persuasion based on rational logic or supernatural rationales is significant, Bruce Lincoln (1989:11) has argued that "ultimately, that which either holds society together or takes it apart is sentiment, and the chief instrument with which such sentiment may be aroused, manipulated, and rendered dormant is discourse."

One area where the impact of discourse (and practice in general) on the construction of society and the changing of society is especially telling is in the production of social identities. Rituals and myths can be manipulated and used to reinforce particular identities, to modify identities, or to create new identities. Daily practice can reinforce or subvert the meanings and sentiments attached to particular identities. In both cases, the evocation of sentiments of affinity and estrangement among individuals and groups is crucial to the ongoing creation.

Hegemony, Resistance, and Accommodation

Hegemony is social ascendancy, but we can distinguish it from dominance (social ascendancy based on power). I find Connell's description of hegemony to be especially useful. For Connell, hegemony is "social ascendancy achieved in a play of social forces that extends beyond contests of brute power into the organization of private life and cultural processes" (Connell 1987:183, cited in Holland et al. 1998:290). That is, hegemony is ascendancy embedded in practice and achieved through discourse. The "power" of hegemony rests on the understandings and feelings of the individuals and groups involved. It may not always result from conscious or otherwise deliberate acts, but it does emerge from practice that persuades and evokes acceptance and belief in the reality or appropriateness of the ascendancy.

Hegemony is, obviously, important in all societies, particularly those where there are asymmetries that involve individual and group status. However, while hegemony is important in state societies where there is also domination based on asymmetries in the distribution of coercive and economic power, it takes on even greater importance in those situations where ascendancy is coupled with relative symmetries in the distribution of power.

One such situation involves the institutionalization of social inequality. Another can be found in chiefdoms, like those of the late pre-Columbian and early historic Southeast. Still another can be found in early colonial times in many areas of the world when the power of colonial societies was limited by distance, by the numbers of colonists, and by the technology available to the colonists. The Apalachee of the sixteenth and seventeenth centuries fall into both of the latter two cases.

James Scott's *Weapons of the Weak* (1985) and his later writings on resistance (see J. C. Scott 1990) have had a powerful impact on anthropology—so much so that "resistance" has become something of a fad in our field. This has been a good thing for us. It has helped focus our attention on historically contingent worlds peopled by live actors. It has also focused our attention on people outside the dominant social group (women, peasants, commoners, the oppressed, and other people who are too often overlooked).

While attention paid to resistance has been good, we can carry it too far. It is possible to see resistance everywhere (M. F. Brown 1996). This is a trap that we must be wary of, for it will dilute and trivialize the concept. As Holland and Eisenhart note, "resistance can be a seductive but ultimately infertile concept when promiscuously applied" (1990:57). However, colonial situations and other circumstances involving the imposition of asymmetrical relationships of power or social ascendancy do appear to be particular areas where we might expect to observe resistance. They are also situations where the concept of resistance may be an appropriate and useful tool for examining stability and change in daily practice. For Scott, the "everyday forms of peasant resistance include practices like . . . foot dragging, dissimulation, false compliance, pilfering, feigned ignorance, slander, arson, sabotage, and so forth. . . . They require little or no coordination or planning; they often represent a form of individual self-help; and they typically avoid any direct symbolic confrontation with authority or with elite norms" (1985:29).

While not inevitably successful, peasant-style resistance is not a trivial exercise doomed to failure. The resistance that Scott describes clearly has an element of intentionality at its base. Scott's resistance is also a counter to oppression (dominance) backed by coercive force. While he notes its existence, he tends to downplay the role of hegemonic ascendancy in the contexts he addresses. Instead, he sees the reality of asymmetric relations of coercive force as having greater impact on modern peasants (on whom much of his thinking about resistance is, of course, based).

Tim Pauketat has argued for an expansion of the concept of resistance. He suggests that "'cultural resistance' could be located within any contrary practice where knowledge exists of the alternatives. . . . This would be dissidence of the latent everyday sort, done less to oppose some dominant persons and more to reproduce one's sense of tradition" (see Pauketat, this volume, chapter 1). Pauketat has an important point here. As Terry Weik (1997:88) notes, viewing resistance as part of a simple dialectic with domination (opposition to domination) can be a real barrier to understanding historical processes because it masks multiple interests and levels of interaction. Much of the practice we see in contested arenas can be seen as this second kind of resistance. It is every bit as important as the conscious opposition to the oppression backed by coercive force that Scott addresses. But it is different.

Thus, we might think of two forms of resistance. Both consist of actions taken that oppose attempts of one group to gain or maintain social ascendancy over another group. The first form of resistance consists of deliberate actions taken to counter ascendancy based on force (dominance). The second form consists of acts that counter ascendancy based on ideological persuasion and sentiment (hegemonic ascendancy). This second form includes both deliberate, conscious acts and the unintentional following of prior practices (consequences of the unacknowledged constraints of prior practice).

I think this second resistance is especially important in those worlds where ascendancy is not backed by coercive force to the extent that it is in modern colonial situations. Where social ascendancy is hegemonic rather than domination backed by coercive or economic force, we can see this second form of resistance. We should remember that "what is hegemonic is contested and variable according to situation" (Holland et al. 1998:290). What I seek to describe here for the Apalachee clearly includes this second kind of resistance.

I think it important to distinguish between the two forms of resistance. The distinction between conscious actions to resist oppression and latent resistance to hegemonic ascendancy (or failure to move beyond the constraints of prior practice) is an important one. The distinction may also (as I will suggest) reflect other factors, such as social position.

The Apalachee

The Apalachee were a Mississippian people who occupied a small territory surrounding present-day Tallahassee, Florida (Hann 1988; J. F.
Scarry 1994). Most of the Apalachee were farmers who could (and did in
later Mission times) produce substantial agricultural surpluses. They lived
in farmsteads—small residential sites occupied by one or two families—
scattered across the landscape (J. F. Scarry and Smith 1988; M. F. Smith
and Scarry 1988). But some Apalachee lived at larger sites with prominent
public constructions (mounds) (Payne 1994; Payne and Scarry 1998).

Some of the residents of those larger sites had access to raw materials or
finished goods from foreign sources that the residents of the scattered
farmsteads did not have (B. C. Jones 1982, 1994). Some of them occupied
social positions that entitled them to the possession of those things while
they were alive and after they died, as well. Access to those positions was
restricted, apparently to a small group of related individuals (Storey
1991).

Apalachee society was hierarchically organized, with institutionalized
political offices. There were pronounced differences among individual
Apalachee in terms of sociopolitical status and access to those political
offices. The Apalachee polity was a complex chiefdom (*sensu* Steponaitis
1978; H. T. Wright 1984). The social ascendancy of the Apalachee elites
was real, but it was a hegemonic ascendancy. The elite had no monopoly
on coercive power, and they lacked the ability to exercise effective economic control over other Apalachee. Households or corporate kin groups
were most likely economically independent of elites for their basic needs
(food, shelter, and reproduction). Individuals and families were capable of
making most of the things they needed to survive (tools and shelter). Individual farmsteads had their own granaries and presumably controlled the
stores they contained (J. F. Scarry 1995; J. F. Scarry and Scarry 1995).
Agricultural fields were cleared communally, and there were large communal hunts associated with field clearing (but both of these took place at
the level of the local community) (Wenhold 1936).

The economic riches of the Apalachee made them an attractive target
for Spanish explorers, missionaries, and colonists. It is not surprising that
they came into contact with Spaniards early and that their contact continued and intensified. In the first half of the sixteenth century, Spanish
armies led by Panfilo de Narváez and Hernando de Soto entered Apalachee territory. In the early seventeenth century Franciscan missionaries
traveled to Apalachee province (in response to requests from some Apala-

chee chiefs). In 1633, the first of the Apalachee missions was established. Except for a brief period following the 1647 revolt, there was a continuous Spanish presence in Apalachee until the destruction of the province in 1704 (Hann 1988, 1994).

Over the course of the seventeenth century, the Apalachee experienced profound changes. They lost political independence. They converted to Christianity. Some Apalachee men engaged in wage labor as carpenters and other craftsmen. Other Apalachee, both men and women, labored for Spanish colonists. And many Apalachee were compelled to work outside the province as bearers, taking goods to St. Augustine and in St. Augustine itself. Dozens of Spaniards (friars, soldiers, and civilian ranchers) took up residence in Apalachee province. The Spaniards brought European foods to the province and by the end of the seventeenth century the Apalachee were exporting substantial quantities of beef, corn, and wheat to St. Augustine and Havana.

Apalachee-Spanish Interaction During the Mission Period

In the sixteenth century, Spain attempted to establish ascendancy over the native peoples of the Southeast. The initial attempts relied almost exclusively on coercive force. The Spanish Crown chartered seven major expeditions to the Southeast (Lyon 1981). Six of these (those led by Juan Ponce de León, Pánfilo de Narváez, Lucas Vásquez de Allyón, Hernando de Soto, and Tristán de Luna) failed. The seventh, led by Pedro Menéndez de Avilés, was successful and led to the establishment of St. Augustine and the colony of La Florida.

Two of the failed expeditions, those led by Panfilo de Narváez and Hernando de Soto, entered Apalachee territory. Panfilo de Narváez stayed for about two months in 1528 before the remnants of his army sailed for Mexico. Hernando de Soto stayed for five months over the winter of 1539–1540. In both cases, the relationship between the Spaniards and the Apalachee was one of unremitting hostility. There was little contact between the Apalachee and Spaniards in the decades following these two expeditions.

Contact between the Apalachee and Europeans was renewed in the early 1600s. In 1608, some Apalachee nobles journeyed to St. Augustine. There, they swore allegiance to the king (and became legitimate vassals in the eyes of Spaniards). They also requested that missionaries be sent to the province. In response to this request, several Franciscan missionaries traveled to Apalachee province. When they returned to St. Augustine, they advised against sending missionaries to the province because "the chiefs could not control their people." I have suggested that there was factional competition among Apalachee elites, and the elites who sought an alliance with the Spanish Crown and missionaries represented one faction. The people they could not control (and who were presumably opposed to missionaries) were the other faction (J. F. Scarry 1992; 1999).

The Apalachee and Spaniards maintained a low level of contact during the first quarter of the seventeenth century. Eventually, the faction seeking links to the Spaniards was successful. The first of the Apalachee missions was established in 1633. Within a decade, there were eight missions and a small secular force (a deputy, his family, and five soldiers) in the province.

In 1647, the Apalachee rebelled against the Spaniards. The rebellion failed, largely due to factional conflict among the Apalachee, and the missionaries and secular authorities returned. The leaders of the rebellion were punished. The Spaniards instituted a system of *repartimiento* labor (conscription), and they increased the size of the garrison. They constructed a fort at San Luis (Hann 1994:339).

In the second half of the seventeenth century, the Spanish presence in Apalachee province increased. Ranchers took up residence and began to grow wheat and raise cattle. The governor's deputies brought their families to settle at San Luis. The Florencia family became rich and powerful at San Luis.

During this period, the Apalachee labored for the Spaniards, constructing the fort, churches, and houses for Spanish civilians. At San Luis, some Apalachee women worked as household servants for Spanish families. Some Apalachee men worked for wages as tradesmen or as bearers, taking agricultural products to St. Augustine under the *repartimiento* system. Apalachee commoners raised corn and other products for the church and the secular authorities. They paid portions of their produce to the Crown as tax. During the period of interaction between the Apalachee and the Spanish, we can see evidence for both opposition to Spanish attempts to achieve ascendancy and cooperation with (or acquiescence to) those attempts.

If the social ascendancy of the Apalachee elite was hegemonic, and their coercive power limited, the situation of the Spanish authorities was different. The coercive power of the Spaniards was real, although it too was limited. The Spanish garrison in Apalachee was quite small. There were five or six soldiers in 1638, and they served mainly as fiscal agents for the governor (Hann 1994:336). The Spaniards did suppress the 1647 Apalachee revolt with the aid of several hundred Timucuan warriors and factions within Apalachee society that opposed the rebels. Even following the failure of the 1647 revolt, the garrison never exceeded fifty men.

Apalachee Opposition to Spanish Domination and Hegemony

Apalachee actions to counter attempts by Spaniards to achieve ascendancy took three forms. There were reactions that involved force. There were attempts to utilize Spanish practices (such as legal avenues). Finally, there was resistance.

Military Force and Opposition to Spanish Dominance

In the sixteenth century, the Apalachee effectively countered the attempts of Narváez and Soto to establish domination with military force. While horses, dogs, and weaponry gave the Spanish armies advantages in pitched battles, the Apalachee quickly turned the struggle into one of guerilla warfare. Here, the Apalachee had clear advantages. Neither of the sixteenth-century Spanish expeditions succeeded in establishing dominance over the Apalachee, not even for a limited time. The Apalachee had a regional reputation for military prowess, and the experiences of Narváez and Soto suggest the reputation was justified.

In 1647, the Apalachee rebelled against the Spaniards. John Hann has suggested that one or more specific acts by the Spanish may have triggered the rebellion. In particular he points to the placement of a deputy governor in the province (who may have curbed the independence of the caciques) and the establishment of a large hacienda on the Apalachee border near Ivitachuco (a major Apalachee political center and mission) (Hann 1994: 337). An alternative possibility is that the rebellion was a consequence of continued factional competition among the Apalachee elite (as was the initial solicitation of missionaries in 1608 [J. F. Scarry 1996b, 1999]). During the rebellion, the Apalachee killed three friars, the governor's deputy, and his family. They burned seven of the eight mission churches (Hann 1994:338). In a single stroke, the Apalachee had essentially eliminated the Spanish presence in the province.

Governor Benito Ruiz de Salazar y Vallecilla quickly dispatched 31 soldiers to the province. This Spanish force (with 500 Timucuan warriors) then engaged a large rebel force of Apalachee. After a day's (apparently inconclusive) fighting, the rebel force withdrew into the province and the Spaniards withdrew to St. Augustine. The governor subsequently entered the province with 21 soldiers and about 60 Timucuan warriors. A pro-Spanish faction of Apalachee joined him. Within a month the rebellion had collapsed. The rebel leaders were handed over to the Spanish authorities for trial (Hann 1994:338).

The Spaniards executed 12 rebel leaders and sentenced 26 others to forced labor. Following the rebellion, the Spaniards also instituted *repartimiento* labor requirements for the entire province. Missionaries returned almost immediately. The seven burned churches were rebuilt within a year. Until the English and Creek drove them out in 1704, the Spaniards never left Apalachee province again (Hann 1994:339).

Following the revolt, the friars persuaded the interim governor, Pedro Benedict Orruitiner, to remove the garrison and dismantle Governor Ruiz's hacienda. In 1654, Governor Diego de Rebolledo reestablished the Apalachee garrison. He also developed plans for a fort, an expanded garrison, and the introduction of Spanish settlers into the province (Hann 1993a:6).

Spanish Legal Avenues and Opposition to Spanish Dominance

The Apalachee opposed Spanish domination in other ways as well. In many respects, those other methods proved more successful than armed struggle. During the Mission period, the Apalachee made use of several avenues within Spanish culture to oppose actions that tended to subordinate them or that they perceived as injurious or bad. Literate members of the elite appealed in writing to higher Spanish authorities—the bishop, the governor, and even the king—to redress wrongs (see Bushnell 1979). Apalachee leaders made use of Spanish institutions like the visitations conducted by governors and bishops to voice their opposition to specific actions (Hann 1986b, 1993b, 1993c). Finally, the Apalachee leaders also negotiated with local authorities—friars and the governor's lieutenant—concerning other perceived wrongs.

One area in which the Apalachee made use of Spanish channels was to lodge complaints against Spanish ranchers for damage done to fields and to forest areas where Apalachee harvested acorns and palm fruit (Hann 1986b:131, 143). The Apalachee were successful to a degree in their attempts to use the visitations. For example, in 1694, the visitor Joachín de Florencia ordered several Spanish ranchers (Francisco de Florencia, Marcos Delgado, Diego Ximénes, Pedro de Torres) to move their haciendas to insure that their herds did no damage to the fields of the Apalachee (Hann 1993c:182–186). He specifically ordered Pedro de Torres to move his corral three leagues from any Apalachee village, with a penalty of fifty ducats for failure to comply (Hann 1993c:186).

The Apalachee used Spanish institutions to oppose actions of individual Spaniards and general demands placed on them by Spanish authorities. However, the use of Spanish institutions was a means of opposition that the Apalachee elite (or those who held recognized political positions) were able to use. It was not an avenue that commoners could use. The role of the Apalachee elite in making these appeals to Spanish authorities was consistent with the elite identities as mediators between the Apalachee and the "other" (J. F. Scarry 1999).

Resistance and Opposition to Spanish Dominance and Hegemony

The resistance to Spanish ascendancy that we can see in the archaeological record appears to be largely reaction to Spanish hegemony rather than to Spanish domination. That is, the resistance largely consisted of the failure (or refusal) to adopt Spanish practice. This retention of Apalachee practice is especially evident in the area of domestic life (not surprisingly since this is the area from which most of our archaeological data are derived).

I want to consider the evidence for resistance in three areas of Apalachee practice: domestic life, ethnic and community identities, and elite identities. The Apalachee created, through daily practice, multiple identities. All of these practices served to create identity at the individual, kin group, community, and ethnic levels. The identities they created by these practices were more like pre-Mission aboriginal identities than identities of members of a Spanish colony. It is evident that the patterns of resistance and accommodation varied among these areas. I would argue that two of the dimensions that structure this variation are the gender of the participants and the public-private nature of the practice (see Sullivan and Rodning, this volume).

Evidence of Resistance in Domestic Life

We can observe this resistance to hegemonic ascendancy in four areas of domestic life. First, the Apalachee maintained earlier patterns of settlement distribution (and views of landscape). Second, they continued to employ aboriginal styles of domestic architecture (and division of space and labor). Third, they continued to make and use aboriginal ceramic forms (and patterns of cooking and dining). Finally, they retained the aboriginal diet.

Settlement Patterning

One important area in which we see resistance to Spanish practice is in the social landscape constructed by the patterning of settlements. Throughout the Mission period, the majority of the Apalachee continued to live in scattered farmsteads. This was despite the development, in the late seventeenth century, of more or less nucleated Spanish-style settlements at San Luis (and perhaps other mission communities). There was no *reducción* (forced nucleation of settlement) like that seen in California missions.

The scattered Apalachee farmsteads were grouped into dispersed communities (Payne 1981; M. F. Smith and Scarry 1988). In the Mission period these communities were recognized, named entities. Members of these communities cleared and prepared agricultural fields cooperatively. The members also collaborated in large hunts associated with the field clearing (Wenhold 1936). Finally, the members of the community worked communal fields that were used to support widows and orphans and to provide produce for the caciques and for the church.

Beyond these communal economic activities, the scattered farming families appear to have been largely self-sufficient. Storage (and presumably control) of agricultural produce was maintained at the household level. We have archaeological evidence of large granaries at a number of Apalachee farmsteads dating to the protohistoric and Mission periods (J. F. Scarry 1995; J. F. Scarry and Scarry 1995). I argue that maintenance of household independence was an important component of Apalachee resistance to Spanish ascendancy.

Domestic Architecture

We can also see resistance to Spanish ascendancy in the continuation of aboriginal patterns of domestic architecture (J. F. Scarry and McEwan 1995). Throughout the Mission period, the Apalachee living outside the major mission communities continued to construct their traditional round, unpartitioned houses. Rectangular common-plan Spanish-style houses with interior partitions were constructed at San Luis (McEwan 1993; J. F. Scarry and McEwan 1995; Vernon and McEwan 1990), but they appear to have been occupied by Spaniards. The distinction between the common-plan house and the Apalachee house is significant. The common-plan house divided interior space into two areas, one of which was probably a work area. The Spanish pattern (at least at St. Augustine) also involved outdoor space placed behind the house, removing it from public view. The Apalachee house enclosed a single, undivided space. Major activity areas appear to have been located outside the house. The major focus of exterior space was to the front of the house (J. F. Scarry 1995; J. F. Scarry and McEwan 1995).

The differences between the patterning of daily activities suggested by the two house forms affected the division of public and private spaces. It also involved the classification of labor as public or private. This would have affected the visibility of domestic labor and (consequently) the visibility of women. I would argue that the Spanish pattern made women less visible and increased the likelihood of their subordination. Resistance to Spanish architectural forms resisted that subordination. As McEwan (1992a:35) notes: "The retention of traditional Apalachee architecture at San Luis (also see Shapiro and McEwan 1992) underscores how the Apalachees' sense of domestic and community organization failed to change despite sustained contact and direct involvement . . . with Europeans and their architectural traditions."

Ceramics

We can also see resistance in domestic life in the retention of aboriginal ceramic assemblages and vessel forms. There were clear differences between Apalachee and Spanish ceramic vessels used for food storage, cooking, and serving. During the Mission period, the Apalachee manufactured ceramic vessels in Spanish forms. These Apalachee copies of European vessels are collectively referred to as Colono-wares. Richard Vernon describes three basic forms for Apalachee Colono-wares: "pitchers or vertical-sided storage vessels with flat bases and handles, brimmed plates with foot ring bases, and cups with footed or foot ring bases" (1988:77). As Vernon notes, each of these forms has unmistakable European features.

The differences among the traditional Apalachee vessels, Spanish vessels, and Colono-wares are particularly evident in serving vessels. Spanish-style serving vessels were designed for individuals (Vernon 1988:78), while Apalachee serving vessels, which took the form of simple and *cazuela* bowls, were designed for communal (probably family) servings. The distinction between Spanish plates and Apalachee bowls reflects a very real difference in the kinds of foods being served.

Colono-wares have been recovered from several Apalachee sites dating to the Mission period. A large sample has been recovered from San Luis de Talimali, the late seventeenth-century capital of the province (Griffin 1951; McEwan 1992a; Shapiro 1987; Shapiro and McEwan 1992; Vernon and Cordell 1991, 1993; Vernon and McEwan 1990). We also have samples from several secondary mission sites, among them San Pedro y San Pablo de Patale (Allison et al. 1991; B. C. Jones et al. 1991a, b; Marrinan 1993; O'Connell and Jones 1991), San Juan de Aspalaga (Morrell and Jones 1970), La Concepción de Ayubale (H. G. Smith 1951). Finally, we have samples from two outlying rural sites (Apalachee Hill [Bierce-Gedris 1981] and Spanish Hoe [Bryne 1989]).

Vernon argues that Spaniards manufactured the Apalachee Colono-wares for use. He points to two contrasting patterns. First, Colono-wares and Spanish pottery are found in association with each other at San Luis and other Mission period sites (1988:79–80). Second, Colono-wares are relatively rare at Apalachee sites where there were no resident Spaniards, as in the Apalachee Hill farmstead (Bierce-Gedris 1981).

Vernon and Cordell (1993) note that the frequency of Colono-wares varies significantly by context at San Luis. They found that the frequency of Colono-ware sherds varies from over 10 percent in the Spanish fort to only 2 percent in the Apalachee council house. The frequency in the Spanish residential area was approximately 10 percent, while that in the church complex was about 2.5 percent (Vernon and Cordell 1993:fig. 16.2). Except for the church complex, the relative frequency of Colono-wares appears to be higher where frequencies of Spanish pottery are higher.

McEwan has also conducted excavations within what has been interpreted as an aboriginal residential area at San Luis. There she recovered surprisingly high frequencies of Colono-wares. She states: "Of particular interest was the regularity with which colono-wares were recovered from the Apalachee village which may have been occupied by the native ruling class. It has always been presumed that these native reproductions of European vessel forms were manufactured by local women for use by Spaniards (Vernon 1988; Vernon and Cordell 1991). The presence of these wares suggests that individualized vessel forms may have appealed to high status Apalachee. However, it is unknown if the native elite had a functional preference for these vessels or if they were viewed as symbolic and/or status items" (McEwan 1992a:38).

Based on their analyses of ceramics recovered during Marrinan's excavations at Patale, O'Connell and Jones (1991, cited by Marrinan 1993:275) argue that Colono-ware ceramics were rare at Patale. Presumably, they were also rare at other mission sites. Patale was an early mission, however, and the difference between Patale and San Luis may reflect the several-generation time gap.

At the Apalachee Hill site, a late Mission period farmstead, Katharine Bierce-Gedris recovered several Colono-ware sherds. The site contained several structures reflecting two or more distinct occupations during the Mission period. The most recent occupation was relatively late in the Mission period, based on the high frequency of rectilinear stamped motifs.

Bierce-Gedris found only ten sherds of Mission Red Filmed, one of which had a foot ring base (Bierce-Gedris 1981:table 14). All of the Colono-ware sherds were associated with the later occupation of the site.

Leland Ferguson (1991) has argued that production of Colono-wares by Africans in South Carolina reflects two distinct processes: unconscious resistance by African slaves and maintenance of cultural continuity. Terry Weik (1997:89) asks the perceptive question, "When does the reproduction of cultural difference in material culture, be it old-world continuity or new-world adaptation, become resistance and not cultural resiliency?" In a similar vein, we can ask whether the failure to adopt Colono-wares by the Apalachee reflects resistance or cultural resiliency. In either case, the result was some measure of opposition to Spanish hegemony and some measure of maintenance of Apalachee identity.

Diet

During the Mission period, Spaniards introduced numerous Old World and exotic New World (Caribbean and Mesoamerican) foods to Apalachee province (Reitz 1993; C. M. Scarry 1993b). However, it appears that there was only a limited adoption of these foods by the Apalachee. Since the foods were available in the province and the Apalachee had the knowledge to raise them, the lack of use must be a function of Spanish actions or decisions by individual Apalachee.

Margaret Scarry has analyzed plant remains from several Mission period sites ranging from the provincial capital at San Luis to outlying farmsteads like Apalachee Hill. The two outlying sites that produced plant remains yielded only indigenous foods. Scarry identified corn, hickory, acorn, and persimmon from the Spanish Hoe site (Bryne 1989; C. M. Scarry 1993b:364). From the Apalachee Hill site, she identified corn and hickory (Bierce-Gedris 1981; C. M. Scarry 1993b:364).

The quantity of plant remains recovered from secondary mission sites is much larger and includes European domesticates. La Concepción de Ayubale (Griffin and Smith 1951:175) and San Juan de Aspalaga (Morrell and Jones 1970) yielded abundant corn and bean remains (the bean may include both indigenous common bean and the Old World cowpea). They also yielded remains of the Old World domesticates wheat and peach. Finally, there were persimmon and acorn, with an occasional hickory, grape, maypop, palm, plum, and bramble (C. M. Scarry 1993b:366).

The best samples of plant remains come from the recent excavations at San Luis. Two pits in the Apalachee residential area at San Luis yielded corn, hickory, acorn, and persimmon. Plain remains from the Spanish village at San Luis included corn, bean, wheat, chickpea, peach, water-melon, hazelnut, hickory, acorn, persimmon, maypop, grape, and palm (C. M. Scarry 1993b:363). Excavations of the council house (a civic struc-ture used for public meetings, the lodging of native and European guests, and perhaps some men's activities) produced a diverse assemblage. Corn, bean, sunflower, wheat, peach, hickory, acorn, and miscellaneous wild fruits were recovered from the floor. The hearth yielded hickory, corn, bean, sunflower, wheat, and wild fruits. Smudge pits under the benches that lined the walls of the structure contained corn and a much lesser quantity of squash, sunflower, wheat, watermelon, hickory, acorn, and wild fruits (C. M. Scarry 1993b:364).

Elizabeth Reitz has analyzed animal remains from San Luis and has contrasted the patterns at San Luis with those other Mission period sites (1993). The animal remains from Mission period sites in Apalachee prov-ince are limited. From outlying sites, we have only a small assemblage from the Apalachee Hill site. Bierce-Gedris (1981:232) reported bowfin, turtle, and bird bones. No European domesticates were identified. At La Concepción de Ayubale, Smith recovered cow and pig bones along with deer bone and oyster shell (Griffin and Smith 1951:175).

The best samples of animal remains from Mission period Apalachee are those recovered from the Spanish village area at San Luis (Reitz 1993). Elizabeth Reitz analyzed faunal remains from four features associated with the Spanish occupation of the site: three trash deposits from the Spanish village and a set of overlapping features from the fort. She found that the remains were dominated by European domesticates. Cattle ac-counted for about 78 percent of the total biomass, and pigs accounted for an additional 16 percent. Noncommensal wild animals accounted for only 5 percent, with deer accounting for the bulk of the biomass derived from wild fauna (1993:381). She notes that while fish remains were recovered, they were a trivial part of the assemblage. Reitz also notes that many of the domestic animals were slaughtered as juveniles. From this fact, she in-ferred that they were raised for food rather than as sources of secondary products (1993:383), not surprising given the importance of the ranches in Apalachee province in the late 1700s.

Evidence of Resistance Related to Social Identities

Social identities are difficult to discern in the archaeological record, par-ticularly at the individual level. However, mortuary data from Mission period sites do provide some clues regarding the ways the Apalachee viewed individuals. We can also derive some clues about identities from evidence of activity patterns related to labor and peoples' public visibility. Finally, the historic documents also provide information about identities and how they were constructed in Apalachee society.

It is possible to interpret the patterns in domestic life in relation to patterns of labor within Apalachee society and to the social identities of Apalachee men and women. The nature of residential sites and the composition and spatial structure of local communities is clearly related to the identities of the people living at those sites and of the groups who made up those local communities. Maintenance of the structure must have contributed to the continued production of those identities. Residential architecture helps structure the organization of domestic space and labor. As the organization of space in turn affected the visibility of domestic tasks and of the people who performed them, it may have been linked to the production of gender (Scarry and McEwan 1995). Domestic pottery is related to practices of food preparation and consumption. Pottery may also have been linked to the social identities and group affiliation of the people (probably women) who made the vessels (McEwan 1992b). Finally, diet is closely related to identity, particularly ethnic identity (see Kalcik 1984).

Mortuary Practice

There were significant changes in mortuary patterning associated with the establishment of the Apalachee missions. In pre-Columbian times, the highest elites were interred in Mound 3 at the Lake Jackson site. Great riches accompanied the few individuals buried in the mound. Grave goods included artifacts bearing iconography associated with the supernatural. There were also material symbols of political or military status, such as crownlike headdresses and stylized weapons. Many of the artifacts must have been obtained from distant sources. Commoners appear to have buried their dead in simple graves near their homes (B. C. Jones and Penman 1973).

In the Mission period, the Apalachee faithful were buried beneath the floors of the mission churches. However, there was one aboriginal pattern that appears to have been maintained: many of the dead were buried with material possessions. For example, Mitchem describes a single juvenile from San Luis who was accompanied by 659 glass beads, 23 possible rosary beads, at least 11 glass pendants, a quartzite pendant, 3 Busycon columella beads, and a brass cross (Mitchem 1993:404).

Ball Game Rituals

One important area of dispute between the Apalachee and the Spaniards concerned the Apalachee ball game (Bushnell 1978; Hann 1988). The Spanish religious authorities made several efforts to have the ball game banned during the Mission period. They argued that the rituals associated with the ball game were idolatrous and that the ball game interfered with productive labor.

In the 1650s several individual friars banned the game within their communities. However, the Apalachee protested to Governor Rebolledo during his visitation of the province in 1657. Rebolledo then expressly forbade the banning of the game. Bishop Calderón again banned the game in 1675. However, Juan de Paiva, the priest at San Luis, persuaded the bishop to rescind his ban. Ultimately, Father Paiva changed his mind and wrote an extensive treatise on the ball game that argued for its banning. Despite continued opposition within the Apalachee community, the game was banned and the ban upheld by the lieutenant governor Domingo de Leturiondo in his visitation of the province in 1677 (Hann 1988:73–74; 1993b).

During Leturiondo's visitation, the Apalachee caciques agreed to the ban. At Thomole, the cacique of Ivitachuco and the other caciques present stated: "They considered it as well done that it had been extinguished because they considered it to be certain that it contained the abuses that his excellency alluded to, because of its being suspect for those who profess to be Christians and that it should remain as extinguished for the rest of time. That those who raised such outcries that it should again be permitted to be played comprised [only] the interested players, who had the said game as a profession [and] that they [the rest of them] had already forgotten about it" (Hann 1993b:103). This acquiescence to the banning of the game was repeated at all of the assemblies held in Apalachee during the visitation.

The Apalachee believed that the ball game arose as the result of a conflict between two mythological chiefs. It seems clear that the rituals surrounding the ball game served to link the elite with those mythological beings and were a part of the discourse that created and maintained elite identities. For example, one complaint that Juan de Paiva made was that the Apalachee paid reverence to the ball pole and the cacique in the same manner they had to idols before they were converted.

I would argue that the ball game also served to produce community and ethnic identities within Apalachee society. The game was played between Apalachee communities. All the members of the community participated in the ritual preparations for the game. The cacique and the usinulo (chief's son) had important roles in these rituals, but the ballplayers and even the nonplaying members of the community maintained vigils and performed acts intended to improve their community's chances of victory (Hann 1988:78). These included groups of men and women who raised the pole that served as the goal and a dance held the night before the game. Father Paiva complained that at this time rules regarding sexual practices were suspended. He specifically stated that the community head exhorted the women not to defend themselves against the touching and fondling associated with the ceremony lest their team lose (Hann 1988:80).

Finally, we can see resistance to Spanish ascendancy in two areas that relate to personal identity or self-image. Hann notes that the Mission period Apalachee continued to use Apalachee family (or clan) names to a much greater degree than did the neighboring Guale and Timucua (Hann 1994:344). They did, however, adopt Spanish first names. Second, the Apalachee continued to dress in a distinctive fashion through much of the seventeenth century. They did so to such an extent that in 1675, Bishop Calderón claimed to have (finally) persuaded 4,081 Apalachee women to wear long tunics that covered their breasts instead of a knee-length skirt (Hann 1994:342). This was two generations after the founding of the first of the Apalachee missions. Hann also cites a description by a friar in St. Augustine that when they went to war, the Apalachee "[d]ress themselves elaborately, after their usage, painted all over with red ochre and with their heads full of multicolored feathers" (Hann 1986a:200).

Apalachee Accommodation to Spanish Hegemony

The Apalachee did not uniformly oppose Spanish efforts. There was cooperation and accommodation, at least on the part of some of the Apalachee. We can see this accommodation in three areas: religious practice, political practice, and economic practice.

Perhaps the most dramatic example of Apalachee accommodation can be seen in the widespread conversion to Catholicism on the part of the Apalachee. Following the establishment of the first missions in 1633, great numbers of Apalachee were converted and baptized. A 1638 parish census numbered the Apalachee at 16,000, and two estimates from 1675 gave numbers of 8,220 and circa 10,520 (Hann 1988:table 7.1). These are remarkable numbers, given that the pre-Mission population was probably around 25,000 and there were substantial population declines in the seventeenth century.

It appears that the conversion was real, at least by the end of the seventeenth century. Following the destruction of the Apalachee missions in 1704, some Apalachee fled to the French colony at Mobile. They settled in two communities near the French colony, and the first child baptized in the parish of Mobile was an Apalachee. Father Alexandre Huvé remarked that the Apalachee were constantly asking for sacraments (Higginbotham 1977:193; cited in Hann 1988:306). Other Frenchmen also noted the sincere adherence to Catholicism on the part of the Apalachee (Hann 1988:306–307). But, religious conversion was not the only area in which the Apalachee accommodated Spanish ascendancy.

A second major area of Apalachee accommodation can be seen in the actions of the Apalachee elite redefining their identities (J. F. Scarry 1999). While they were constrained by the structures and underlying meanings of elite identity that were generated in the past, they did modify details within a general framework. In particular, they adopted Spanish titles and names (e.g., Don Patricio). They converted to Christianity and swore allegiance to the Spanish Crown (indeed, some actively solicited missionaries in 1608). They used symbols derived from the Europeans to demonstrate their status to others, replacing symbols derived from other Mississippian societies that were associated with pre-Columbian Apalachee elites (such as the elite burials at the Lake Jackson site [B. C. Jones 1982, 1994]). While accommodating Spanish ascendancy, these acts also served to help maintain elite identities in novel contexts.

The elite became vassals of the king and followed the directions of priests in their religious observances, but they retained their elite status and their positions within Apalachee society. They also maintained identities that were in broad outline equivalent to those of earlier chiefs. That is, their identities were based on a recognition of a fundamental distinction between elites and commoners, a linkage of the elite to the other (Todorov 1984), and a role as mediators between the common Apalachee and those others (J. F. Scarry 1999). The nature of the other changed from foreign Mississippian elites and the supernatural to the Spanish religious and secular authorities.

A third area in which the Apalachee accommodated Spanish ascendancy was economic. In the seventeenth century, many Apalachee men began to work outside their local communities. Wage labor and the *repartimiento* took many men away from their homes (Hann 1994:344–345). Apalachee men worked as contract laborers, ranch foremen, personal servants, carpenters, and other tradesmen (Hann 1994:340). Historical records suggest that Apalachee men manufactured leather goods

(Hann 1994:341) and constructed houses in the Spanish style (for Spaniards), although we have not found the material evidence of such manufacturing at Apalachee sites. This accommodation was not welcomed by all of the Apalachee. In the visitation record of 1694, there were numerous complaints made on behalf of the wives of Apalachee men who were absent laboring for Spaniards on ranches or at St. Augustine (Hann 1993c:164–166).

Variation in Apalachee Responses to Spanish Ascendancy

When we examine the Apalachee responses to Spanish ascendancy in the sixteenth and seventeenth centuries, several patterns appear. The responses depended on the social identity or position of the individual Apalachee involved. Thus, the responses of the elite were different from the responses of commoners. Further, within the elite group, responses varied, perhaps depending on relative status within the elite group or on membership in political factions. At an even more fundamental level, the responses of men differed from those of women (see Sullivan and Rodning, this volume).

More specific patterning also occurred. We see more evidence of resistance in activity spheres where women may have been involved to a greater extent than men, such as domestic life, pottery production, and food preparation. We see more evidence of accommodation in activity spheres where men may have been involved to a greater extent than women, such as nondomestic labor and public (political) action. In general, there appears to have been more opposition to change in domestic life than there was to change in religious practice or economic activities beyond the household.

Resistance was greater at rural (commoner) sites than at political (elite) centers. Traditional diets were maintained to a much greater degree at smaller sites. This can be seen in the foods consumed (especially the absence of European foods at farmsteads) and in the patterns of food preparation and consumption reflected in ceramic assemblages. European foodstuffs have been recovered from elite residential debris and public (council house) contexts at San Luis, while they appear to be absent at the two rural sites we have investigated (although they were grown in the province). There was a much greater frequency of European serving wares (Colonowares) in elite contexts at San Luis than has been found at any other site (the frequency is only exceeded by the frequencies in Spanish contexts at San Luis).

We also see evidence of resistance to changes in the social identities of individuals and groups within Apalachee society. In particular, I think we can see efforts to maintain elite identities, women's (gender) identities, and community/ethnic identities (see, in this volume, Saunders's consideration of identity creation among the Mission period Guale and other groups farther east). Thus the elites were very resistant to changes that would reduce their status vis-à-vis commoners. They lobbied strenuously for elite prerogatives (such as exemptions from corporal punishment). The elites were also concerned with the maintenance of inheritance, particularly of political office (for example, the Faltassa usurpation [Hann 1988:103– 104; 1993b]). The Apalachee also strongly resisted Spanish attempts to ban the ball game and its associated rituals (although they apparently acquiesced to the abandoning of other rituals).

If resistance were greater in areas of special concern to the Apalachee, or groups within Apalachee, accommodation was greater in those areas seen as essential by the Spaniards. The two most important of these were allegiance to the Crown and conversion to Christianity. Finally, the patterns of resistance and accommodation varied over time. The Apalachee became more Hispanicized over time. While their dress was distinctive over much of the seventeenth century, they apparently dressed in the European fashion by the beginning of the eighteenth century. French observers at that time described the Apalachee who were living near Mobile as wearing cloaks and skirts of cloth (for the women) and cloth overcoats (for the men) (Hann 1994:342). The Apalachee who moved to Mobile spoke a mixture of Spanish and Apalachee (Hann 1994:343). At least some members of the elite were literate.

Conclusions

We must not oversimplify our reading of resistance and accommodation into the colonial experience. The Apalachee did not simply react to Spanish actions. Nor did they resist all Spanish actions or attempts to achieve social ascendancy or domination. The Apalachee were active participants in the colonial experience. They were not passive objects (J. F. Scarry 1999; Scarry and Maxham 1999).

The Apalachee were also individuals who had individual goals and expectations. While prior practice and the constraints of the material world may have shaped and limited their responses, like all actors, they were capable of improvisation when confronted with novel situations (Holland et al. 1998). The improvisations of the protohistoric and Mission periods provided precedents for later Apalachee actors. Not surprisingly, the actions of the Apalachee in response to the ascendancy of the Spaniards varied. They varied from individual to individual. They varied between groups within Apalachee society, for example, between elites and commoners or women and men. They also varied over time as improvisations became past practice. A more nuanced reading of Apalachee colonial history must take this variation into account.

Resistance to hegemonic ascendancy differs in several important respects from resistance to domination based on coercive or economic force. I would argue that it is likely to be less deliberate or intentional. In fact, it is likely to be what Giddens would call an unintended consequence of action rather than an achieved goal. I think we can see this in the Apalachee case.

The Apalachee did consciously resist Spanish attempts to achieve social ascendancy and domination—in the 1647 revolt, for example, and their appeals to authorities for relief from oppressive labor demands. It may well be that the Apalachee also made conscious efforts to maintain their identity as Apalachee. However, the resistance seen in the maintenance of domestic ceramic traditions, in architectural traditions, and in diet by commoners may not have been consciously motivated by a desire to resist Spanish political, economic, and religious domination. Regardless of intent or lack of intent, resistance to hegemonic ascendancy seems likely to take the form of discourse, rather than the kinds of deliberate acts that Scott (1985, 1990) describes. Resistance is likely to be counter-hegemony.

Resistance and accommodation are useful concepts for understanding patterns of cultural stability and change among the Apalachee in the early historic period. In order to make the best use of these concepts, however, we need to focus our attention on individuals and individual decision making. Rather than think of resistance as a single thing, we need to look at practice and the creation of cultural patterns. We need to look at processes and the consequences of those processes. We also need to focus on both resistance and accommodation, and the contexts in which each occur.

Samuel Wilson and Daniel Rogers (1993:13–14) argue that the processes of cultural change resulting from the interaction of European and Native American peoples were: complex and long-term, mediated by the cultural perceptions and values of both groups, and driven by the motivations and strategies of both groups. They note that "*the culture change undergone by Native American peoples was neither one-sided nor solely governed by European intentions and strategies*" (1993:3, emphasis original). I would echo this observation. The changes that the Apalachee (and other native peoples) experienced in the colonial period were not simply the result of European domination. The Apalachee shaped the course of their history during the Mission period (e.g., J. F. Scarry 1999; Scarry and Maxham 1999). Ignoring that fact demeans and lessens them as a people and as individuals.

Author's Note

The inspiration for my title comes from Kathy Deagan's 1990 paper, "Accommodation and Resistance: The Process and Impact of Spanish Colonization on the Southeast." The tension inherent in her choice of title has always seemed to me to be a good description of the dynamics of the colonial situation in Apalachee province.

4

Manipulating Bodies and Emerging Traditions at the Los Adaes Presidio

Diana DiPaolo Loren

Spanish colonial society was predicated on a conception of social order based upon racial difference. Individuals whose ancestries included more Spanish blood were allowed more freedoms and garnered more power than those with less, as illustrated by the *régimen de castas*—a Spanish colonial categorical system that hierarchically graded individuals by their percentage of whiteness. This social order perpetuated official traditions that were designed by the Spanish Crown, enforced through laws and strictures, and known to the general public through commonly understood notions of taste. As illustrated in the *régimen de castas*, different official traditions were applied to various racial categories—full-blood Spaniards, mixed-blood individuals, such as mestizos, who were generally categorized as *casta,* and Native Americans—and were meant to impact all aspects of colonial life, such as marriage, sexual relations, trade, dress, diet, and architectural form (see Boyer 1997; Cope 1994; R. Jackson 1999; Kicza 1997).

Racial difference served as the basis for status differences, as those with more homogenous Spanish ancestry often held a higher social status than those with less. Official traditions were designed to enforce these racial and status boundaries, forming social distinctions between "us" (high-status Spaniards) and "them" (lower-status mixed bloods and colonial "others," such as Native Americans and Africans) (see Stoler and Cooper 1997). Official traditions stand in sharp contrast, however, to local traditions that emerged from the need to create social distinctions in or along communities, households, and frontiers—yet often in opposition to official rules and strictures.

The colonial traditions that we know from historical processes are frequently the official ones (see Trouillot 1995). Official traditions were reproduced in laws, mandates, and official correspondence preserved in state and local archives. Official traditions were also illustrated in visual sources, such as casta paintings, curated in museum collections. In this process, local traditions and stories of colonial "others" slipped through the cracks of the dominant narrative. Archaeology used in concert with other sources, however, provides a lens through which local traditions—practices often poorly understood from archival and visual sources alone—can be investigated. Archaeological research on the emergence of local colonial traditions throughout North America (often interpreted as creolization or *mestizaje*) is one such avenue to examine formations of social distinction at the local level (see Crowell 1997; Deagan 1990, 1995, 1996; Lightfoot 1995; Lightfoot et al. 1998; McEwan 1991; Upton 1996; see also Saunders and Scarry, this volume).

This study probes the distinction between official and local traditions—also understood as the difference between the official discourse on social distinctions and daily practices within local households—by using archaeological, ethnohistorical, and visual sources. It is the tension between these two traditions that more clearly illustrates colonial reality for the Spanish Crown and within frontier households because it highlights racial and status differences imposed on colonial society, as well as on an ambiguous colonial population: mixed-bloods. While most colonial communities were socially diverse, as they were comprised of individuals from different racial, ethnic, religious, and political backgrounds, most were also primarily inhabited by mixed-bloods, such as mestizos, mulattos, and quadroons (see Boyer 1997; Callaway 1993; Cope 1994; Crowell 1997; Lightfoot 1995; Lightfoot and Martinez 1995; Stoler 1997). Mixed-bloods lived in an uncertain space, rarely accepted by either community, and often categorized as an "other"—neither Native American, nor European, nor African—though they almost always lived under colonial rule (Boyer 1997; Callaway 1993; Cope 1994; Deagan 1996; Stern 1998; Stoler 1991, 1997; Stoler and Cooper 1997).

Official social distinctions were often too narrow or constricting for most colonial individuals and, in particular, mixed-bloods. For example, mestizo (Native American and Spanish parentage) women in New Spain were instructed to dress in the Bourbon fashion, mimicking fashions worn by high-status Spanish women (Castelló Y. 1990:87). It was often more economically advantageous, however, for these women to dress in native fashions or in a combination of native and elite Bourbon fashions that allowed movement through groups to trade, although from an official standpoint they appeared "improper" (see Boyer 1997). Likewise, other

colonial subjects negotiated local and official traditions for personal, political, and economic reasons, to create new opportunities unique to those
contexts, as well as newly emerging identities, such as "mixed-blood"
(see, for example, Boyer 1997; Comaroff and Comaroff 1992; Cope 1994;
Klor de Alva 1996; Stern 1998; Stoler 1991, 1997; Sued Badillo 1996).

In the case I present here—the eighteenth-century Spanish presidio of
Los Adaes (16NA16)—the population was multiethnic, consisting of the
governor, officials, mixed-blood settlers and soldiers, Native Americans,
some French traders, and some refugee African slaves. The governor and
other officials at the presidio were mostly Spaniards, approximately half
of the soldiers were Spaniards while the other half were castas (such as
mestizos and mulattos), and the settlers were primarily castas (Avery
1997:32–58). Established in 1721 and situated along the eastern border of
Spanish Texas, just twelve miles from the French post of Natchitoches,
Los Adaes was the capital of Spanish Texas for fifty years. Los Adaes was
300 miles from San Antonio and more than a thousand miles from Mexico
City; the French post of Natchitoches was similarly 300 miles from New
Orleans (see Avery 1997). Thus the inhabitants of Los Adaes—the Adaesaños—lived along a largely isolated frontier with their French and
Caddo Indian neighbors. As both a capital and a frontier outpost, the
community of Los Adaes provides a particularly interesting case study for
investigating the negotiations of local and official traditions. In this essay,
I use the ethnohistorical, visual, and archaeological records to consider the
tensions between local and official traditions in colonial households at Los
Adaes. In particular, I highlight how individuals embodied different traditions in dress, architecture, diet, and trade to create social distinction in
public and private contexts.

Creating Social Distinctions

This study distinguishes between official and local traditions, or between
the official discourse on social distinction and "proper" behavior and the
daily practices of colonial subjects, often considered "improper" by colonial officials. Social distinction, whether officially mandated or locally
derived, is tied to taste (Bourdieu 1984). Taste is informed by habitus—
systems of structured, durable dispositions toward certain perceptions
and practices, such as tastes, which become part of an individual's sense of
self at an early age (Bourdieu 1977:72–78). Tastes, the indicators of lifestyle, are commonly understood in each society and fall into a pattern that

corresponds to the structure of lifestyles as they have been established (Bourdieu 1984:263).

The practices of taste are everyday social habits—what one eats, the form of one's home, or how one dresses—that serve to reproduce status and class differences (Bourdieu 1984:2). Practicing commonly understood tastes reinforces social distinctions (such as lower class) because these practices often occur in social arenas, allowing individuals to display their own status while at the same time allowing them to distinguish other individuals according to their practices of taste. It is the similarities among groups that give rise to social distinctions; for example, individuals of higher classes distinguish themselves via that which makes them members of that class—the acquisition and display of expensive and exclusive items that allow them to "keep up appearances" (Bourdieu 1984:258). Those in each class lower do the same; their daily practices are commensurate with their tastes.

While some of the practices of taste can be understood as unquestioned or "doxic" (see Bourdieu 1977:164–169), tastes can be manipulated to provide social movement. For example, appropriating practices of higher-class tastes may provide movement through social hierarchies to appear more elite. Some individuals, then, work against commonly understood taste distinctions to form their own distinctions, and thus allow them to be socially perceived as a different class (Bourdieu 1984:282). Some without the means to consistently project high-class tastes could do so in select and public venues, such as through dress.

Bourdieu's theory of taste and social distinction (1984) can be applied to colonial contexts (see Stahl 1999, 2001). Official traditions enforced through laws and strictures were projected models of behavior intimately tied to commonly understood social distinctions. How officials imagined colonial society was part of the structure that determined tastes—the ways that individuals were officially distinguished according to racial mixture and perceived status. Statements about colonial society created a discourse that resulted in official imaginings of colonial society based on racial difference—official traditions. Laws and strictures were a way to police tastes and traditions to ensure that colonial subjects stayed in their place. The maintenance of different traditions was found in sumptuary laws and mandates, presenting the Spanish Crown and its officials with the ability, at least in theory, to stabilize social and racial boundaries in colonial hinterlands.

Official traditions outlined proper practices for colonial subjects—how they should act, dress, and live. These ideals, however, were constructed in the metropole where the Crown and colonial officials tended to view tastes that constituted social distinctions as bounded or fixed. Official traditions did not exist separately from practices, however, as it was through daily practices that these traditions were to be reproduced by colonial subjects. Yet local practices were more fluid than officially imagined, enabling some to blur or negotiate social distinctions and allowing them to navigate imperial divisions of race and status. Local practices were often viewed as improper, as they occurred outside of what officials considered proper, particularly if they involved "native" or uncivilized practices.

The practices of taste were the embodiment of social traditions—official and local, proper and improper. Occurring in both public and private, practices of taste not only allowed one to communicate who one was to the community at large but also could mean the difference between elite or plebian, colonized or colonizer, free or enslaved. The practices of taste were often politically charged, as marginalized individuals seeking to gain status may have embodied local traditions, while elites seeking to confirm their status along the frontier may have done so by embodying official traditions. Thus the dissemination and policing of the practices of official traditions underscored the needs and anxiety of the Crown to maintain the status quo and keep "others" in their place.

Official traditions as they applied to various racial and status distinctions were defined through different media and fill colonial archives. Laws and taste distinctions were outlined in official correspondence (decrees, laws, strictures) and visual representations, including a genre of eighteenth-century Mexican art called casta paintings. Colonial officials also described traditions in narratives and descriptive accounts (see, for example, DePagés 1791; Morfí 1935; O'Crouley 1972). The recognition that the intended audience of these representations was Spanish elites in New World centers and Spain suggests that these traditions emerged from the imperial discourse on race and status. It is important to note, however, that the creation of laws and decrees was ongoing because the Spanish Crown and its officials believed that official traditions were not followed in frontier regions. The emergence of local traditions led to the creation of more official traditions in an attempt to further police the actions of subjects within colonial communities, resulting in the continual negotiation of traditions throughout the colonial period (for similar examples see Sassaman, this volume).

In particular, Spanish laws regarding dress, diet, trade, and architecture represent important material avenues for understanding the extent of colonial control in local contexts (see Boyer 1997; Comaroff 1996:21; Deagan 1990, 1995; Hendrickson 1996:8; Lightfoot et. al 1998; Shannon 1996; Stern 1998; Stoler and Cooper 1997; Upton 1996; see also Scarry, this volume). These laws illustrate how official traditions were supposed to be incorporated into daily routines; the proper forms of material culture to be used by colonial subjects following official traditions.

One important overarching official tradition imposed on both full-blood and mixed-blood subjects was that they should adhere to Spanish practices, rather than Native American practices. The anxiety over subjects "going native" is found in the accounts of Spanish officials who described this as akin to losing one's civility and becoming "savage" (e.g., Morfí 1935; O'Crouley 1972; Solís 1931). For example, copying Native American dress or combining it with a soldier's uniform was of particular offense to Spanish officials, as it signaled to them that the population had gone native. Official discouragement of adopting Native American ways was common to many colonial contexts, applied to all levels of subjects (elite to plebian), and referenced not only dress but also diet and architectural form (see Crowell 1997; Deagan 1990, 1996; M. Hall 1992; Lightfoot 1995; Lightfoot et al. 1998; Stoler 1997).

Laws regarding dress were defined in official decrees and illustrated in casta paintings. Philip V, the first Bourbon king of Spain, stated in the early eighteenth century that one should be clothed "so that his dress bespeak his profession, and nobles not be confused with plebeians, nor rich with poor" (Katzew 1996:20–21). Spaniards and even mixed-bloods were instructed to dress in the Bourbon fashion (Castelló Y. 1990:87), despite infrequent shipments of clothing to frontier outposts. Indigenous dress styles—such as shell jewelry and fringed deerskin clothes covered with white seed beads—were prohibited for Spaniards and mixed-bloods (see Morfí 1935:46; Solís 1931:43).

A genre of eighteenth-century Mexican art known as casta paintings allows us not only to visualize different dress styles in New Spain but also suggests what can be considered proper dress artifacts (García Saíz 1989:80; O'Crouley 1972). These paintings should not be interpreted as pictures of the eighteenth-century past but rather should be understood as images and conceptualizations of proper practices for colonial subjects that were produced for an elite audience (in Spain and Mexico City) and that were informed by official discourse. Casta paintings were completed in a series, depicting racial mixtures to be found in the New World from the highest race (Spanish) to the lowest mixture, *zambaigo* (*coyote* [mestizo and Native American] and mulatto parentage). Typically, each painting in the series depicted and labeled a mother and father of different races, such as a Spanish man and a Native American woman, with their child, a mestizo. While casta paintings portrayed the complex color code of the régimen de castas, they also illustrated behavior appropriate to one's race. For example, unions of individuals with more Spanish blood were scenes of domestic tranquility complete with a properly dressed family; unions of individuals perceived as further down the racial scale were often a violent, lazy, poorly and/or partially dressed group. For example, in the higher-status household of an Español and a morisca (Spanish and mulatto parentage), the man is depicted as wearing cut-away jacket and vest of fine cloth with filigree buttons (see fig. 4.1). The wife is wearing a combination of Native American and European garb: hand-woven and European fabrics with European and native jewelry. In a lower-status household of an Indio and a mestiza (Spanish and Native American parentage), both the man and the woman are wearing hand-woven and ripped clothing, missing buttons and buckles (see fig. 4.2). In this way, casta paintings depicted not only skin color, but also official traditions—visualizations of proper ways to dress, eat, work, and live bred from discourses on race and social distinction. Dress artifacts recovered from household contexts then may be indicative of the practices of dress by Los Adaes residents.

Settlers in Spanish Texas were prohibited from trading with neighboring Native American groups as well as the French at Natchitoches, and they were to obtain all dry goods—including clothes, ammunition, ceramics, glassware, and shoes—from Mexico City. As the French author François Dion Deprez Derbanne (plantation owner and warehouse keeper of Fort St. Jean Baptiste) explained in his short "Report of the Post of Natchitoches," dated 1723, the Spanish settlers did not trade with the French because "they obtain their merchandise in Mexico as cheap as they can at Natchitoches" (Bridges and DeVille 1967:253). Prohibitions on external trade ensured that Spanish settlers had items that visually identified them as Spanish. The presence of Spanish, French, and Native American goods in household assemblages could then suggest the extent to which residents followed official traditions.

Diet was not a simple matter of preference but was structured according to social hierarchy, as some foods, such as reptiles and shellfish, were not to be consumed by enlightened individuals; eating them signaled the loss of civility (see Pagden 1982:86–87). Although local availability impacted choices, certain foods were clearly undesirable. In his account of the eastern Texas missions, Fray Gaspar José de Solís of Zacatecas noted

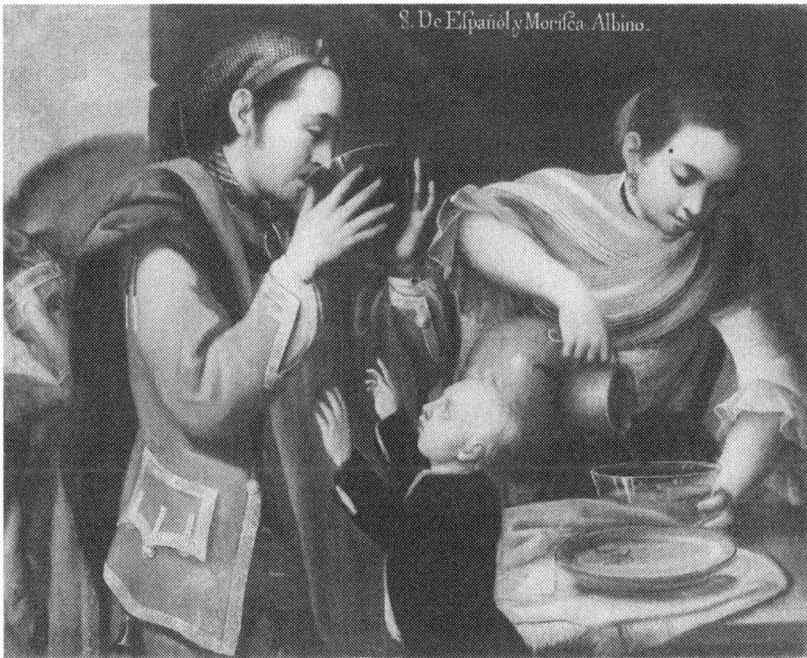

Fig. 4.1. Unknown artist [Mexican], *De Español y Morisca, Albino,* ca. 1760–1770. Philadelphia Museum of Art, gift of Mrs. Richard Drayton.

Fig. 4.2. Unknown artist [Mexican], *De Indio y Mestiza, Coyote,* ca. 1760–1770. Philadelphia Museum of Art, gift of Mrs. Richard Drayton.

in 1767 that Native Americans—not Christians—ate shellfish and horse (Solís 1931:46–47). Visiting high-status officials often indicated, however, that all Christians living along the frontier were going native. For example, Nicolas de Lafora, captain of the Spanish Royal Engineers and part of the military inspection of northern New Spain presidios led by Field Marshal Marqués de Rubí in 1767, noted in his field diary that Spaniards along the eastern Texas border were forced to eat like Native Americans and only ate fish as a last resort (Kinnaird 1958:172). Casta paintings reinforced these notions in that proper foods were depicted for colonial subjects. For example, the lower-status individuals depicted in figure 4.2 eat root vegetables from a common plate rather than domestic meat from individual dishes. Thus, the presence or absence of certain foods in faunal assemblages is significant. While consuming horse or shellfish was symbolic of losing one's status and even one's civility, the presence of these remains in the faunal assemblage could suggest the ability and desire of subjects to maintain and follow official traditions.

Spanish presidios were comprised of a central complex: a palisade that enclosed the governor's house, barracks for the soldiers, and storehouses. Outside this enclosure were usually settlers' homes, the mission, the priests' homes, and the homes of Native Americans. Houses for settlers in eastern Spanish Texas were, in theory, different from Caddo houses, which were round, made of cane and bark, and covered in grass (Bolton 1914:378). Proper Spanish house form in eastern Texas followed French forms—a rectangular post-in-ground (*poteaux-en-terre*) with *bousillage* (mud-and-animal-hair daub walls) structure. Most comments made by Spanish authors regarding local architecture were directed toward the interior complex rather than the surrounding community. From the ethnohistorical record we know that by the end of the eighteenth century, there were up to 500 settlers at Los Adaes and no less than fifty settlers' homes; however, the ethnohistorical record is vague about spatial relationships and architectural forms.

Ethnohistorical accounts and paintings discussed here provide examples of official traditions for different groups. Despite the proliferation of these traditions and the rigid social and racial hierarchy in colonial New Spain, colonial subjects (especially mixed-bloods) had the ability to change their racial label through the conscious manipulation of practices of taste in dress, lifestyle, or language (see Cope 1994:53–54). While narratives provide a sense of how official and local traditions diverged, the details of local practices are lost in silence. For example, while improper dress was discussed, there is little information on what constituted improper dress (see DePagés 1791). Houses were often described as unsuitable, but again without detail. For example, in 1728, military Inspector General Pedro de Rivera noted that the presidio of Los Adaes "did not deserve its honored name, not only because it consisted of only a few huts of sticks and grass badly put together, but also because . . . its garrison has not served for anything whatsoever" (Hackett 1934, 4:149). We can assume that colonial officials were remarking on traditions that were not official, but rather local. The archaeological record is needed to examine how different traditions played out along the frontier.

Archaeological Investigations

Traditional approaches to colonial sites are inadequate for investigating the colonial traditions outlined in this chapter. Although archaeologists have recently begun to construct theoretical approaches for interpreting colonial sites as multiethnic (see for example Deagan 1990; S. Jones 1996, 1997; Lightfoot 1995; Lightfoot et al. 1998; Upton 1996), traditional methodologies continue to be used that assume a one-to-one relationship between material culture and ethnicity. Material culture is typically categorized as either "native" or more "European," and percentages of "native" and "European" material designate the ethnicity of people residing at the site as well as their degree of acculturation (Lightfoot 1995; Lightfoot et al. 1998). A recent critique of this kind of interpretation is that a *category* of material culture is supposed to indicate ethnicity (see M. Hall 1992, 1994; Lightfoot and Martinez 1995; Lightfoot et. al. 1998; Upton 1996). But categories of "native" and "European" material culture alone relate almost no information on the ways in which colonial individuals used material culture in seemingly inconsistent combinations in processes that formed new social traditions. As Upton (1996:5) notes, the relationship between identity and material culture is not straightforward, but rather ambiguous, because colonial individuals chose different kinds of material (in this case, French, Spanish, *and* Native American) to use in daily practices. The purpose of this research is not to assign ethnicity or race to households but rather to examine the ways in which people negotiated different traditions within households and in the outside community. The use of different kinds of material resulted in confusing or overlapping images of colonial actors and their "fit" with official social and racial hierarchies. An interpretation of material culture within colonial contexts must then include a consideration for what was considered to be officially proper, as well as local availability and, most importantly, local social, economic, and political contexts.

Two household contexts from the site of Presidio Nuestra Señora del Pilar de Los Adaes (16NA16) provide information on the practices of traditions—the Spanish Texas governor's residence located inside the presidio palisade and the residence of a presumed low-status soldier or settler's family, located outside the presidio palisade. Gregory excavated the two Los Adaes households between 1967 and 1982 (Gregory 1973, 1980, 1984). Of the two households, it is assumed that residents of the governor's house should uphold and maintain official traditions, particularly as these residents were probably seen as an example of the "official" to the presidio community. The occupants of the southeast residence are unknown, but it is assumed that a mixed-blood settler or soldier's family occupied the structure, as these were the most common inhabitants of the community (Gregory 1983).

The architectural form of the governor's house conformed to official Spanish tradition for the area: a rectangular structure of *poteaux-en-terre* with *bousillage* construction. The southeast structure, however, was built using both poteaux-en-terre with bousillage construction and Native American post-in-ground construction. Outwardly, these two residences appeared very different to the community—the official governor's house displayed the established Spanish tradition (which was expected), while the southeast house broke with official traditions to mix architectural forms.

A comparison of dress artifacts suggests that residents of both structures may have broken sumptuary laws to mix Native American and European (or Bourbon) dress styles. The governor's house contained more elite goods than did the southeast house, such as matched filigree buttons (n=2), patterned buttons (n=3), patterned belt buckle (n=1), rings (n=4), and a bracelet (see table 4.1). The presence of a crochet hook and embroidery scissors (n=3) suggests leisure activities such as crocheting and embroidery, rather than the business of making clothes. A small number of glass seed beads (n=4) found at the residence suggests some influence of Native American dress, while the presence of French fabric seals (n=2) implies that individuals within this official residence may have also relied on French sources to obtain fabric, a trade that was prohibited under law.

The southeast house also yielded artifacts that conformed to Spanish sumptuary laws, such as Spanish fabric seals (n=1), a scrap of gold lace, holy medals (n=2), a copper brooch, an earring, several rings (n=4), neck-

Table 4.1. Dress artifacts from Los Adaes houses

	Governor's house	Southeast house
Thimble	1	0
Small/embroidery scissors	3	1
Large scissors	3	1
Crochet hook	1	0
Straight pins	0	6
French lead seal	2	2
Spanish lead seal	1	1
Needle	0	1
Copper brooch	1	1
Earrings	0	1
Tack plate/shirt stay	0	3
Gold lace	0	1
Tinkler	0	3
Crucifix	0	1
Holy medal	0	2
Griffon medal	0	1
Brass ring	2	1
Copper ring	2	3
Brass bracelet	1	0
Necklace beads	7	94
Seed beads	4	26
Plain buttons	5	0
Filigree buttons	2	0
Patterned buttons	3	2
Glass buttons	0	1
Plain belt buckle	3	3
Patterned belt buckle	1	1
Plain shoe buckle	0	1

lace beads (n=94), and patterned buttons (n=2; see table 4.1). A large number of seed beads (n=26) and brass tinkler cones (n=3) recovered from the house suggests lower-status and perhaps native dress. Spanish and French fabric seals recovered from the residence (n=3) as well as a needle, large scissors (n=1), and straight pins (n=6), suggest that residents were often making clothes, an activity of lower-class and native subjects as illustrated in casta paintings. While it is possible that household residents were making Bourbon-style clothes, homemade clothes were usually depicted as being worn by lower-class castas and Native Americans.

The combination of artifacts recovered from the governor's house implies some mixing of dress styles; however, the overall pattern suggests that residents were wearing elite Bourbon-style fashions. The relative lack of sewing materials at the residence suggests that individuals at the governor's house were obtaining ready-made clothing from proper sources, such as Mexico City. Thus, the overwhelming amount of European dress artifacts at the governor's residence indicates that the inhabitants often presented themselves "officially"—elite, Spanish, and even extravagant—to the rest of the Los Adaes community and along this frontier. The few native dress artifacts in the assemblage indicate minimal mixing of dress styles. Artifacts from the southeast structure, however, suggest that residents mixed Spanish, French, *and* Native American fashions. The dress styles of individuals at the southeast residence incorporated both the Spanish—elaborate and proper, as suggested by the gold lace, medallions, and other jewelry—and the native and improper, as suggested by brass tinklers and seed beads used for beaded clothing. This combination of dress artifacts at the southeast residence in combination with the presence of sewing materials suggests that residents were making and mixing different fashions—European and native, the proper with the improper—and consciously manipulating different traditions, most likely for public contexts (cf. Comaroff 1996). Given that the Spanish Crown did not condone mixing different dress styles or dressing native, what then was the benefit in breaking with this official tradition at Los Adaes? Since Los Adaes was a relatively isolated community that often relied on local French and Native Americans, it is likely that dressing native or playing up one's native identity may have allowed individuals from both the southeast residence and the governor's residence, despite their status or race, to move into forbidden territory in daily life; they thus could establish local social and economic relations with French and Native American neighbors denied to them by Spanish law.

Trade goods and imported ceramics were used not only in household activities, but also in the communication of social status, as casta paintings depict these items in use and on display. As Bourdieu (1984:281) notes, the display of taste occurred in both public and private contexts, in that the display of certain goods reinforced perceived taste and status to those living inside the household and those visiting the household. Ethnohistorical documents and casta paintings illustrate which items were considered proper and should be found in assemblages of households following official traditions: Spanish trade goods, Chinese porcelain, and Spanish majolica and olive jars. Because of the ban on external trade, both plain and decorated French faience (or tin-enameled wares) and Native American plain and decorated ceramics were considered undesirable and should, in theory, be a small percentage in households practicing official traditions.

Table 4.2. Ceramics from Los Adaes houses

Sherds	Governor's house		Southeast house	
	N	%	N	%
Chinese porcelain	34	10	90	10
Spanish majolica	81	24	130	14
Olive jar	10	3	0	0
Mexican redwares	9	2	33	4
French faience	52	16	241	27
Delft	10	3	54	6
Native American decorated	146	42	349	39
Total	352	100	897	100

The ceramics and trade goods recovered from the governor's house suggest that household residents practiced official traditions. Although this structure yielded a relatively large percentage of locally produced decorated wares (42 percent), the residence also contained the largest percentages of porcelain, Mexican ceramics, and Spanish olive jars and majolica (39 percent) of all other households at Los Adaes (see table 4.2). The percentage of trade goods at the governor's house was also predominately Spanish (31 percent; see table 4.3). This kind of assemblage was expected for the governor's residence, where the display of expensive, elite goods would have been used to constitute high-status identity and proper behavior. Ceramics at the southeast residence were mostly Native American (39 percent) and the next highest percentage was French ceramics (27 percent;

Table 4.3. Trade goods from Los Adaes houses

	Governor's house		Southeast house	
	N	%	N	%
Spanish cloth seals	1	2	1	1
Spanish horsegear	9	17	12	7.5
Spanish gunparts	3	6	3	2
Spanish swords	0	0	4	2.5
Spanish knives	3	6	5	3
Necklace beads	18	34.5	94	61
French folding knife	5	9.5	3	2
French gunparts	0	0	3	2
French cloth seals	2	4	2	1.5
Seed beads	11	21	26	16
Mirror fragments	0	0	2	1.5
Total	52	100	155	100

see table 4.2). Majolica was present but in a smaller percentage than at the governor's house, suggesting that individuals at this residence traded for French ceramics more than for Spanish ceramics. Trade goods—such as gun parts and knives—show a similar split between French and Spanish goods (see table 4.3).

Both household assemblages are then marked by a combination of goods from French, Native American, and Spanish sources, but the combination of artifacts recovered from the southeast structure suggests that residents frequently negotiated traditions in the use and display of different kinds of material. The large percentage of Spanish trade goods at the governor's residence is especially significant if one considers that sources for these materials were hundreds of miles away by land. Given the rarity of shipments from Mexico City to Los Adaes, it is not surprising that the majority of ceramics at both residences were Native American. Yet the relatively high percentage of Spanish goods at the governor's residence suggests that the inhabitants owned and displayed a relatively large amount of what could have been considered luxury goods along the frontier, an important component of constructing elite identity (see Mann and Loren, n.d.). At the same time, the overwhelming percentages of Native American ceramics at both residences speak to the daily importance of officially restricted social and economic relations between French, Native Americans, and Spanish along this border.

An examination of the faunal material from the two households also suggests the impact of official traditions within the household. As discussed previously, a proper diet should include mostly domestic meals and poultry, some wild mammal (deer), and some wild bird (turkey)—a pattern common to other areas of New Spain (see Deagan 1995). Undesirable foods were those eaten by the uncivilized—most fish, all shellfish, horse, amphibians, and reptiles.

The faunal assemblage is the clearest indication that while appearing official from the exterior, residents of the governor's house were practicing tastes and embodying traditions that were not officially proper. Faunal material from this residence suggests that individuals in this structure ate what would have been considered an improper diet. Domestic mammal constituted 44 percent of the total assemblage, and wild game (mostly white-tailed deer) constituted the next highest percentage (22 percent). Most striking, however, is that freshwater mussels constituted 15.5 percent of the total assemblage (see table 4.4). Ethnohistorical and visual sources clearly illustrate that a proper Spanish diet should not include shellfish, fish other than haddock, or amphibians, yet these are all present

Table 4.4. Faunal remains from Los Adaes structures

	Governor's house			Southeast house		
	NISP[a]	MNI[b]	%	NISP	MNI	%
Domestic mammal	137	4	44	913	13	65.5
Wild mammal	71	2	22	204	6	14.5
Domestic bird	32	5	10	13	4	0.9
Wild bird	17	2	5	58	7	4.1
Fish	6	3	2	78	4	5.5
Amphibian	0	0	0	2	1	0.1
Reptile	5	3	1.5	74	6	5.2
Shellfish	50	-	15.5	59	-	4.2
Total identified	318		100	1401		100

a. NISP = Number of identified specimens.
b. MNI = Minimum number of individuals.

in the faunal assemblage of the governor's residence. The large amount of shellfish suggests that although shellfish was considered an uncivilized food, household members regularly consumed it whether out of preference or because desired foods were unavailable.

The faunal material recovered from the southeast residence suggests that household members ate a diverse diet, much like residents of the governor's house. Although much of the assemblage from the southeast residence was domestic mammal (65.5 percent), the faunal assemblage also included wild birds, amphibians, reptiles, and fish (see table 4.4). Lafora noted that civilized people only turned to fish as a last resort (Kinnaird 1958:172); however, the quantities of fish from this assemblage bespeak the importance of this food in diets and suggest that fish were a preferred food.

Reitz (1985, 1992) has discussed how Spanish colonists in Florida were flexible in their diet to the point that the foods they consumed included fish and amphibians, probably because they relied on local Native Americans for their food. While the ethnohistorical record for Los Adaes indicates that certain foods—such as shellfish—were undesirable, the faunal record suggests that individuals along this border, like the Spanish in Florida, ate a diet that was similar to that of Native Americans. Whether by choice or out of necessity, their diet was for the most part hidden from the public; so while the practices of taste that distinguished high-status Spaniards could not (or were not) followed at home, they could still be practiced in other, more public venues.

Conclusions

The residents of the governor's residence were often more publicly official, as indicated by dress artifacts and architectural form, than the residents of the southeast house; this suggests that residents of the governor's house were attempting to display and establish elite identity to other elites in the community while simultaneously distinguishing themselves from lower-class others, highlighting the notion that the construction of self began and was reinforced at home. Yet trade goods, ceramics, and faunal material consumed in the relative privacy of the household indicate the importance of embodying local and official traditions. The negotiations of different traditions led to the emergence of new local traditions, as evidenced by the mixture of material culture from the governor's residence—faunal material, trade goods, ceramics, and, to some extent, dress artifacts—and by the trade goods, faunal material, dress artifacts, and ceramics from the southeast structure, as well as its architectural form. It is likely that the governor and his family did not have the means along the frontier to practice traditions commensurate with their tastes and practiced official traditions only in more public venues, but the household assemblage suggests that traditions were actively negotiated both in public and in private. The mixture of material found in the governor's house suggests a movement away from the practice of official traditions to embody the traditions of the surrounding mixed-blood population.

In discourses on social distinction, colonial subjects were accused of "going native"—highlighting an official anxiety about keeping colonial subjects in their place. Official traditions were an attempt by the Spanish Crown and their officials to "fix the fluid." In practice, however, the *Adaesaños* often embodied different traditions in dress, diet, and architectural form, suggesting that the manipulation and recreation of traditions was part of everyday practice (see also Pauketat 2001). The mixing of different kinds of material culture in a community of mixed-bloods may have allowed not only these officially lower-status individuals but also elite Spaniards to move across colonial boundaries, in order to establish and maintain social, economic and political relationships with French and Native American neighbors—evidence of the tension between official and local traditions. Individuals at the community of Los Adaes employed material culture in specific ways that enabled their survival along the frontier both in public (dress, architectural form) and private (diet, ceramics, and the display and use of trade goods). These new traditions indicate a change in consumption in tension with official imaginings: the choice of

Native American, French, and Spanish goods combined to create and embody social distinctions. The use of these combinations of different materials in daily practices may have indicated knowledge of language, customs, and politics that was the source of local power and status, rather than merely a few Spanish buttons or a silk jacket.

One must consider, however, how these individuals must have appeared along the frontier. While the Adaesaños may have embodied different traditions along the frontier to break out of social hierarchies, it is likely that vertical movement through the casta system was impossible even in the colonial hinterlands. These individuals may have always appeared as poseurs in the eyes of local and visiting government officials and Spanish elites. So although they embodied certain traditions to create social distinction, it was perhaps not in the way that they wished—the result was only their ability to move horizontally through the category of mixed-blood, and thus still lower status. The artifact assemblage from the governor's house, however, may point to the contrary, as it suggests that local traditions were important in the eyes of officials, at least to the extent that they practiced some of them in the privacy of the household.

Official traditions—the dominant voice that emerges from the historical process—does not tell us how individuals embodied new traditions fashioned by personal visions of resistance, race, power, and status (see Paynter and McGuire 1991; Scott 1990; Trouillot 1995; see also Sassaman, this volume). Although some might interpret these newly emerging social traditions as acts of resistance by a colonized population, resistance alone cannot capture the complexity of these processes (see Pauketat 2001). Emerging traditions were multilayered in local contexts, as deeply textured as the colonial population itself. At Los Adaes, the embodiments of local traditions in architectural form, diet, dress, and trade were meaningful in that context of plurality. The mixture of material culture from two households at Los Adaes suggests that official power over colonial subjects in this region may have been limited, as the Adaesaños negotiated different traditions in both public and private. Even the Spanish governor's family embraced local traditions in order to put on different faces inside and outside the household; in this case, official traditions appear to have been practiced publicly, while local traditions were practiced privately.

The details of these local traditions, in relation to what was envisioned in colonial accounts, become clearer with the use of archaeological data. Local traditions are often lost in silence, while official traditions were curated and reproduced in the historical process (see Trouillot 1995). The archaeological record can be used to tease out local practices; however, as Galloway (1991:457) notes, the archaeological record is often used simply to confirm the historic record. In this study, visual, ethnohistorical, and archaeological sources were placed into what Martin Hall (1992, 1994, 1996) describes as a productive tension to draw out social contradictions in colonial contexts. Although seemingly disorganized, the Los Adaes household assemblages suggest that individuals from different backgrounds embodied social traditions that existed in tension with official distinctions, personal tastes, local concerns, and the desire to move beyond rigid social hierarchies.

Acknowledgments

I am especially grateful to Hiram F. Gregory of Northwestern State University and George Avery, station manager for Los Adaes, for their help with the Los Adaes archaeological and archival collections. Thanks to Malcolm Vidrine of Louisiana State University at Eunice for conducting the mollusk analysis. I am grateful to Ann Stahl for her guidance in understanding and articulating concepts of taste and social distinction. Special thanks also go to Lewis Loren, Tim Pauketat, Rob Mann, Charlie Cobb, Sergio Ireugas, and several anonymous reviewers who read earlier drafts of this manuscript and who gave excellent suggestions for its improvement.

5

Negotiated Tradition?

Native American Pottery in the Mission Period in La Florida

Rebecca Saunders

When the Spanish began colonization of La Florida in 1565, they did so with a set of tools honed through 700 years of territorial recovery on the Iberian peninsula and 70-odd years of settlement in the New World.[1] One principal tool used for the pacification of the countryside was missionization. Ideally, missions were to be established first in native population centers where conversion of local leaders guaranteed the submission of the rest of the population. After the establishment of this beachhead, missions were to be located at intervals of a day's walk along supply roads between Spanish population centers.

These missions, located by definition on the frontiers of Spanish control, had a number of functions. Not only were they loci of conversion, but they also served as labor centers—friars and chiefs allocated personnel for agricultural and construction projects on the local mission, in St. Augustine, and elsewhere (Bushnell 1994; Worth 1995). Some missions became literal breadbaskets for the non-agriculturally oriented Spanish settlers in the few Spanish towns. In addition, missions, especially those with an attached garrison, were expected to be the first line of defense against predations or outright invasions of Spanish territory by unconverted Native Americans and competing European powers. After intensive indoctrination into Catholicism and an infusion of the work ethic ascribed to the European peasantry, Native Americans were to *become* Spanish peasants, living in *poblaciones* (*sensu* McAlister 1984:108–109) and contributing docilely to the sustenance and general well-being of the Hispanic elite. At that point, the missions would be secularized, the mission community would become a village with a parish priest, and the missionaries would move on to a new frontier.

This program had greater or lesser success in the New World depending on a number of factors, many of which were recognized early in the study of New World contact situations and acculturation (see especially Spicer 1961). In La Florida it failed. In the middle sixteenth and seventeenth centuries, the Spanish were spread too thin to post adequate personnel in all Spanish territories. The new nation-state of Spain, with a population of eight million people (many of whom of course remained in Spain), was attempting to control what would become Latin America, the Caribbean, Florida and Georgia, the American Southwest, and the Philippines. In La Florida, a relative backwater with a poor supply of even the most basic essentials, there were not enough soldiers or priests to effectively hold the countryside. Further, the weak hierarchical social system of the coastal southeasterners made it more difficult to control the native populations, as compared to the highly stratified sociopolitical hierarchies of Mexico or Peru.

This same flexible social system allowed for more effective resistance against Spanish hegemony (*sensu* Emerson 1997a:22). From 1565 to circa 1600, the Native Americans along the Florida and Georgia Atlantic coast fought against the Spanish, either by passive resistance, harassment of colonial settlements, or outright revolt. Conditions improved, or at least violence abated, along the coast after 1600, probably due to the cumulative effects of disease on the native population and the political maneuvering of the native elite. Spanish movement into the Florida interior in the 1600s was often at the request of elites, but the concomitant labor and defense demands of the Spanish also produced revolts. Throughout this time, those natives who wanted nothing to do with the Spanish could flee to relatives in the vast interior, out of the reach of Christianity and away from the epicenter of disease.

British settlement of Charleston changed the balance of power in the interior. While the Spanish controlled most trade with natives through the missions and kept a more-or-less tight leash on the trade in guns, the British encouraged such trade with their native allies. This brisk business fostered the incipient deerskin trade and advanced the flourishing trade in native slaves, many of whom were captured from Spanish missions. Native American alliance with one European power or the other was inescapable (Saunders 1998). Flight from the missions to the British milieu grew more popular as it became clear to native converts that the Spanish could not protect them. Concerted attacks against the missions by the South Carolinians and their native confederates between 1702 and 1704 destroyed the mission system.

But missions did function, if not flourish, for several generations and did so only because Native Americans agreed, with their presence and their labor, to support them. Why some individuals and families left while others stayed remains obscure.[2] To some degree, those that remained colluded with the Spanish to exchange, or at least modify, their identities and become, if not strictly more Hispanic, then at least less southeastern Native American. This chapter explores this "negotiated identity" and how it was expressed.

The discussion revolves around one aspect of material culture, utilitarian pottery, and specifically the series of pottery that originated in late pre-Columbian times as Irene pottery and became, fairly quickly after contact, Altamaha pottery made by ethnohistorically documented Guale Indians allied with the Spanish (see fig. 5.1). It is proposed that Altamaha pottery represents a "negotiated tradition," a compromise in the selection of pottery attributes that incorporated both Guale and Spanish considerations.

Further, Altamaha pottery became *emblemic* (*sensu* Weissner 1983, 1985) of natives allied with the Spanish. These included the Guale and the Yamassee, a "multiethnic" confederacy resolved out of the disintegration of interior chiefdoms previously located along the Piedmont Oconee and Ocmulgee Rivers in Georgia. Altamaha pottery, a blend of the Irene tradition, Mission period Guale sensibilities, and Spanish functional preferences, ultimately blanketed the Spanish domain west of Apalachee. It appears to have been made and used by most if not all the various Native American groups affiliated with the Spanish around St. Augustine and was the principal utilitarian ware of the Spanish as well.

Theoretical Issues

A number of current theoretical issues are embedded in the foregoing summary. The first is the thorny issue of ethnicity. Were the Guale (and other named groups like the Yamassee, Mocama, and the fourteen or fifteen distinct Timucua "tribes") an ethnic group—a self-conceptualized, bounded entity existing in opposition to other groups?[3] If so, how were such identities constituted? A second issue, and related to the first, is whether or not, in historic (and pre-Columbian) contexts, material culture can be expected to correlate in any way with such an entity, and why it might. Third is the concept of a "negotiation" of identity and of tradition. Fourth, and finally, is the aspect of style theory that incorporates active and passive roles for both technology and style in the definition of social boundaries.

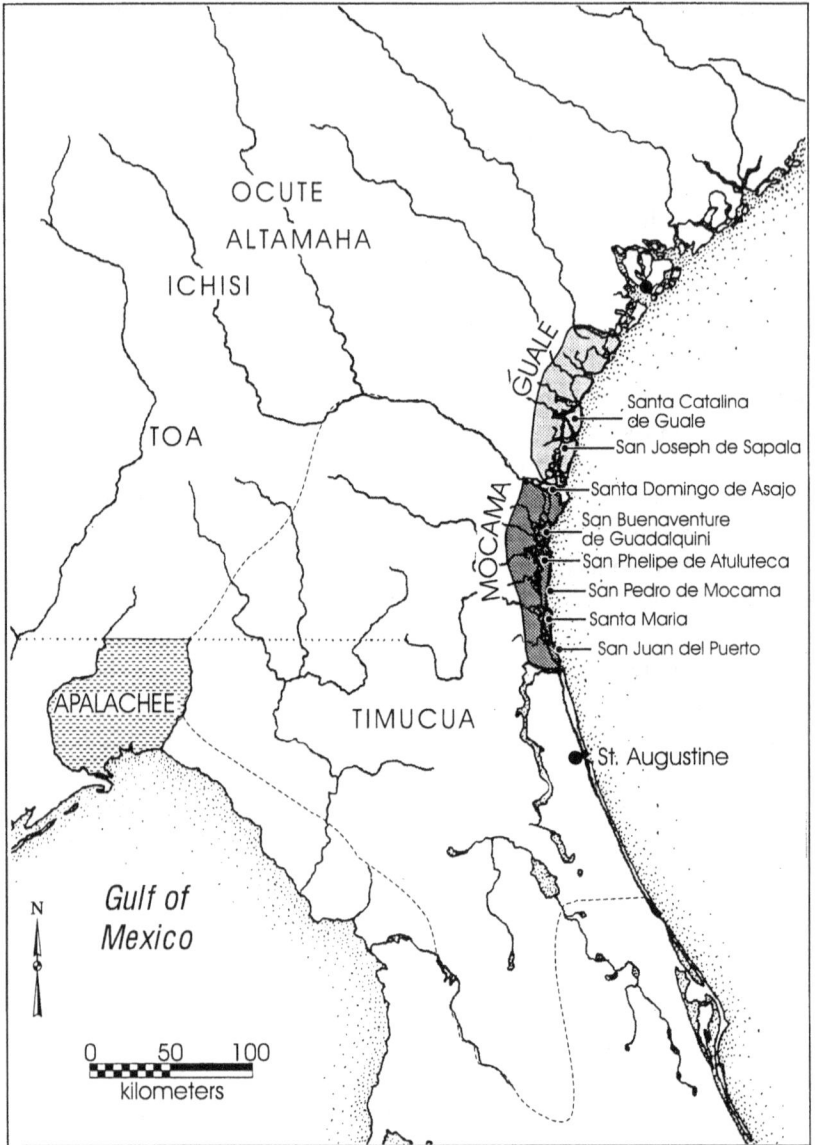

Fig. 5.1. Location of Native American groups and missions, ca. 1660.

Ethnic Groups and Material Correlates

Were the Guale and the other ethnohistorically documented groups along the lower Atlantic coast ethnic groups?[4] I have defined ethnicity based on Jones's 1997 "contextual/analytical framework" (see also discussions of ethnicity in Sassaman, and Emerson and McElrath, this volume). The question of Guale ethnicity has not been explicitly investigated; to address the question, the ethnohistoric situation must be briefly reviewed. The discussion that follows concentrates on the Guale, but conclusions for the Guale can be extended to the Timucua and to the Mocama, a linguistic division of the eastern Timucua.

Early French and Spanish explorers referred to both a chief and a town as Guale (French Oade), one of a number of interacting groups of matrilineally related, simple and complex chiefdoms along the coast (see G. D. Jones 1978; D. H. Thomas 1993). For unknown reasons, the name Guale (as opposed to that of one of the other chiefs) was adopted by the Spanish to refer to a linguistically distinct administrative province originally bounded on the south by the Altamaha River, on the north by the Savannah River, and to the west by the sparsely populated Pine Barrens.[5] This territory was more-or-less coextensive with late pre-Columbian Irene ceramics. Irene ceramics, in turn, constitute a geographically restricted variant of the larger Lamar (or South Appalachian Mississippian) ceramic tradition of the lower Southeast (Williams and Shapiro 1990a). This tradition covered a broad area that crosscut a number of physiographic units and geological and environmental zones. The defining features were curvilinear and rectilinear paddle stamping of utilitarian wares, along with applique rims that usually bore punctations made with a variety of tools. Incising under the rim on otherwise plain vessels was added to the repertoire around A.D. 1400.

No one studying the prehistory of ceramics in the Lamar area would argue that the ceramic tradition represented an ethnic group, no matter how ethnicity might be defined. Instead, as Williams and Shapiro (1990:6) observe: "We assume that shared pottery styles reflect other shared aspects of culture. Although we do not know the extent to which this is true, it is certain that the relative uniformity of pottery styles within this broad region indicates some degree of social interaction among these people." This interaction had deep roots that appeared in shared techniques and designs as early as 500 B.C.

On the one hand, design elements (in the design hierarchy, see Carr and Neitzel 1995; Redman 1978) of the Irene variant likely represent a more inclusive aspect of this interaction. On the other, design motifs very probably contained information. Pre-Columbian Irene phase design motifs are restricted to variations of the filfot cross (see fig. 5.2), which was a standardized depiction of southeastern cosmology (Saunders 1992a, 1992b, 1998, 2000a). Whether this restricted motif pool was also consciously considered to represent "Irene ethnicity" is unknown. Indeed, whether the peoples who created Irene wares conceived of themselves as a unified group distinct from their southern and northern coastal neighbors or how they envisioned their relationship to the interior Lamar groups is not clear and may never be known. In the relatively large body of primary documents from the early contact period, no Native Americans make reference to such a group.

Instead, the primary allegiance and identity of the Guale, most of whom lived in a dispersed settlement pattern, was with the village that served as the chief's residence and area ceremonial center.[6] There is no indication that pottery varies on any technological or stylistic basis by village; pottery was presumably produced by each household.[7]

In sum, though we do not know if there was a pre-Columbian self-conceptualized unit conceived in opposition to other Lamar or adjacent pottery tradition groups, an "etic" proto-Guale can be isolated using a pottery style, Irene, that was created by interaction (including intermarriage) among chiefdoms along the Georgia coast.[8]

Incorporation of Irene ware producers into the Spanish bureaucracy created a social division called Guale. However, it is still unclear from documents the extent to which the historic Guale considered themselves a coherent group. The chiefdoms did coalesce to a certain extent during the rebellions of 1576 and 1597, but they were defeated. In the 1597 Juanillo rebellion, the inhabitants of the first Mocama village they encountered repulsed the Guale. This may suggest that the Guale were a somewhat cohesive sociopolitical unit, however fragile, and possessed an allegiance to each other not shared by the Mocama. (However, the Mocama, being closer to St. Augustine, had more to lose if defeated than the Guale.) Nevertheless, in the absence of preexisting sociopolitical mechanisms to support long-term alliances, the Guale never made another concerted effort against Spanish hegemony. The scorched-earth retaliations by the Spanish, and the attendant famine and disease, also may have militated against the formation of ethnic groups in the future. The multitude that fled the mission system was said to have joined the Yamassee, who will be discussed in more detail later.

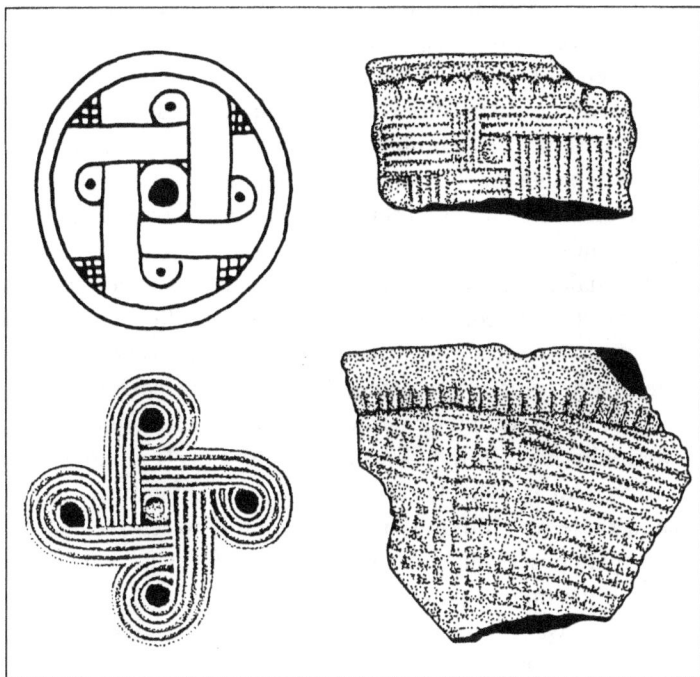

Fig. 5.2. Design motifs: *top left,* world symbol on shell gorget; *bottom left,* Irene filfot cross; *top right,* Altamaha world symbol design on sherd; *bottom right,* Altamaha sherd with overstamping.

As noted, the Guale that stayed within the system seemed to have maintained more allegiance to a town—at this point in time, a mission—than to any larger group. This appears to hold true even when missions were moved and populations were aggregated for defensive purposes (see Worth 1995:30). The Spanish reinforced these loyalties, recognizing (and thereby empowering) chiefs of each town, even chiefs who had no more subjects. Indeed, by the mid-1600s, Guale chiefs "depended on Spanish legitimization and support in retaining political control" over their subjects (Worth 1995:73).

The reinforcement of local leaders was a strategy that the Spanish used throughout La Florida. While bolstering traditional polities, at least in the short term, this strategy may have had a centripetal effect on the Guale over the long term, reducing the chances of the creation of a larger polity and an ethnic consciousness (and reducing the possibility of alliance against the Spanish).[9] It should be noted, however, that as the missions

were moved, each coastal group—Guale, Yamassee, and Mocama—
settled close to preexisting villages of its group. There were dialectical or
language differences between all three, and, because many Yamassee did
not convert to Catholicism, differences in religion. These social factors
may be as responsible for community preferences as "ethnicity," or they
might be used to argue for the existence or development of ethnic groups
at this time. It should be noted in this context that intermarriage between
the groups was not uncommon.

Unlike the Guale, there is clear evidence that the Yamassee conceived of
themselves as a discrete sociopolitical unit. Also unlike the Guale, who
had deep roots as a society, the Yamassee were a creation of the historic
period. The best information to date indicates that the core groups of the
Yamassee were remnants of the chiefdoms of Ocute, Altamaha, Ichisi, and
perhaps Toa, who lived in the Georgia piedmont or "La Tama" (Green
1991; McKirvergan 1991).[10] De Soto visited these chiefdoms in 1540. A
century later, there was intermittent interaction between the Tama area
and the Georgia coastal missions (Green 1991:19–21); this may reflect
pre-Columbian interaction patterns.

In 1662, Tama was attacked by a small contingent of British soldiers
allied with a large force of "Chichimecos," a general term used by the
Spanish to designate any warlike or nomadic natives.[11] The interior
peoples were terrorized (Worth 1995:18) and fled to the province of
Escamaçu on the lower coast of South Carolina. There they established a
number of settlements and began to attract other remnant or otherwise
disenfranchised groups, including the Salchiches and Tulafina of the
coastal plain, along with disaffected Guale.

The first mention of a social entity called "Yamassee" by the Spanish
came in 1663 in reference to the aforementioned settlements. As Worth
(1995:22) observes: "Although at first (ca. 1663) these refugees apparently endeavored to take advantage of their proximity to the Spanish without actually entering the mission provinces, continued hostilities from the
nearby Chichimeco soon forced many groups to flee southward, and peti-
tion the Spanish for permission to settle within the then largely depopu-
lated provinces of Guale and Mocama."

While the mission system was imposed upon the Guale, the Yamassee
were encouraged to settle by the Spanish because, as Worth indicates, the
Georgia mission provinces were experiencing severe labor shortages. The
Yamassee entered La Florida as pagans and were allowed to live as pagans,
as long as they provided *repartimiento* labor. Their relationship with the
local mission natives was uneasy (see Worth 1995:35), and their relation-

ship with the Spanish was not much better. All 300 or so (Worth 1995:37) Yamassee left La Florida, en masse, in 1683, after the pirate Grammont raided the coastal missions. They defected to the British sphere of influence, where, in 1715, they would perpetrate one of the most significant native uprisings in the history of the southeastern United States (Green 1991:49–52).

Ironically, there is more documentary evidence that this society of refugees conceived of themselves as a coherent, bounded group than there is for the much more deeply rooted Guale (but see Green 1991:36). Indeed, the Yamassee decision to leave La Florida together, while the Guale vacated in dribs and drabs, is telling. More direct is the evidence from the 1695 visitation of the province of Guale. In that visitation document, Santiago, a native of the "Yamazi nation," proclaimed that "out of all his nation none have remained in this province except for him alone, because out of all of such a great number of his said nation both Christian and pagan that there were in them, they all have gone to the English and he alone has remained for the love he has had and has for the Christians and for the king" (Hann 1986c: 22, 23). The development of a Yamassee consciousness from a disparate group of refugees is consistent with current theories on ethnogenesis and the development of tribal societies in the historic Southeast (e.g., Galloway 1994a, 1995).

Historic Ceramic Expressions

Virtually simultaneously with the effective missionization of the Guale, a new pottery type appeared that is associated with the Guale in mission contexts. The type is called Altamaha in Georgia and San Marcos in Florida.[12] In a recent study (Saunders 1992a, 1992b, 2000a), I compared ceramic attributes in several discrete contexts to describe and track the changes in Irene and Altamaha pottery through time. These contexts included late pre-Columbian; possible contact period native; and Early Mission and later Mission contexts in Georgia and Florida. Results indicated that while the paddle design of Altamaha was still based on the Irene filfot cross (a four-field design that represented the basic concepts of southeastern cosmology), the curvilinear elements of the cross dropped out; lands and grooves of the paddle stamping were significantly wider and deeper; and the rim strip was abandoned in favor of the folded rim. Rim elaborations, however, were similar to pre-Columbian examples, both in the tools used for punctation and in the relative frequency of the type of punctations. Altamaha pottery was also fired at a higher temperature than its predecessor. This suite of changes appeared in the earliest Mission contexts (ca. 1595–1597) at Santa Catalina de Guale on St. Catherines Island, Georgia. Irene wares—dark-bodied wares with fine lands and grooves and applique rim strips—were completely absent from the earliest and later (1604–1680) contexts. To all appearances, Altamaha wares sprang fully formed into the system; there were no discernible transitional steps in the late pre-Columbian or early historic contexts studied.[13]

Elsewhere (Saunders 1992a, 2000a, b), I have suggested that the Spanish were responsible for a number of these changes. Poor support for and supply of the colony created a need for a locally produced utilitarian ware, and in some places, particularly missions, a Colono-ware that functioned for serving vessels. In general, the Spanish set up potting industries wherever they settled (Deagan 1983:234). Along the lower Atlantic coast, with no history of craft specialization, the Spanish worked within the traditional native parameters of pottery production, the household, to ensure a supply of vessels that conformed to their functional and stylistic preferences. At missions, presumably, each mission village (or village household) provided the friars with the vessels needed as part of their routine obligations, though this is not clear from the documentary record (for these obligations, see Bushnell 1994:111–124).

Altamaha can be considered a "negotiated" tradition in the sense that there were tacitly agreed-upon technological and stylistic components of both Spanish and Guale design. Most, if not all, of the Spanish changes involved functional characteristics that also have stylistic effects (see Hegmon 1998:266–271; Stark 1998:4–5). The folded rim was stronger than the applique rim and provided a better grip when a vessel was moved. Wider and deeper lands and grooves, and the absence of curvilinear aspects, would decrease paddle-carving time and provide better coil compaction and may have affected heat conductivity (Herron 1986). The more textured surface would also make the vessel easier to handle. Higher firing temperatures, which produced a lighter-bodied ware not unlike Olive Jar, also made vessels harder (Rice 1987:354). Operating within the Spanish criteria, the Guale continued to apply attributes important to them. Instead of simply carving straight lines and applying the paddle in opposite directions to produce cross simple stamped, the Guale carved a modified World Symbol—a four-field design (the four fields represented the four directions) with a central element, usually a circle, representing the sun (the central deity), or this world, or both (Fundaburk and Foreman 1957; Hudson 1976; Waring 1968; Waring and Holder 1945; Willoughby

1932).[14] The Guale also used the same tools to punctate the folded rim that they had used on applique rims. None of these changes affected paste preparation, the formation of most vessels, or the basics of surface decoration; the changes did not affect either the *chaine opératoire* of pottery production or the fundamental habitus of the pottery tradition (Dietler and Herbich 1998). This continuity may be a fundamental reason for the rapid adoption of the type among the Guale.

As a pottery type, Altamaha had remarkable stability through the turbulent Mission period. The types Altamaha Plain and Stamped, along with a great deal of subtypical variation, survived the retreat from the Guale coast in 1684 and resettlement below the St. Marys River. (Altamaha Incised survived but was produced at much lower frequencies.) The stamped ware persisted in the new missions, virtually unchanged, until those missions were destroyed in 1702 (though the central dot dropped out of many, but not all, paddles). In the context of this persistence, I have thought that the style became associated with the Guale allied with the Spanish; that it was emblemic of this association (following Weissner 1983). And I have suggested that the coherence of the tradition across time and space might indicate that, within this negotiated tradition, the Guale maintained a strong sense of their ethnic and social identity (Saunders 1992a:193).

In the context of the foregoing discussion on Guale ethnicity, however, I am now more hesitant to ascribe an ethnic Guale association with the Altamaha type, even in the early Mission period. I do think that the rapid replacement of Irene with Altamaha on mission sites indicates that the pottery was used to establish a social identity. In addition, I would now argue that, because of functional characteristics and because the type did signal affiliation with the Spanish, Altamaha was adopted by most, if not all, of the Native Americans associated with the Spanish around St. Augustine (see Rolland and Ashley [2000:41] for a similar conclusion).

I base this conclusion on additional documentary research that provides more chronological and locational control over seventeenth-century missions and more information on the groups that inhabited them (see especially Worth 1995). Beginning about A.D.1650, Altamaha wares appeared in most mission contexts throughout La Florida. Associating Altamaha with the Guale, or with their inland relatives the Yamassee, researchers attributed this appearance to the decline of local populations and gradual population replacement by the Guale and Yamassee. Worth's (1995) research now indicates that native populations were more segregated than such a scenario would permit, and that the population replacement was not gradual but controlled and fairly abrupt. The upshot of all of this is that Altamaha cannot be associated strictly with the Guale and Yamassee. The presence of large quantities of Altamaha on sites with no documented Guale occupation indicates that the type was used, and most likely produced, by Mocama and Timucua Indians as well.

To illustrate this, it may be instructive to look at the Yamassee case first. Yamassee sites in La Florida have ceramic assemblages that are, at least at the level of the type, indistinguishable from those on Guale sites.[15] The Yamassee made Altamaha. Since the Guale and Yamassee were related in language and in the Lamar ceramic tradition, this has not seemed much of a stretch. However, late pre-Columbian and early historic ceramic assemblages in the Tama region suggest a larger change. Dyar phase (A.D. 1520–1580) assemblages are characterized by "common" Lamar stamping. In the subsequent Bell phase (A.D. 1580–1670?), stamping amounts to less than 1 percent of the assemblage; incising with multiple (thirty or more) fine lines is the dominant surface decoration (Smith and Williams 1990).[16] Thus, at the time of the 1662 Chichimeco attack, the core groups of the proto-Yamassee did little paddle stamping.

Yamassee immigrants to La Florida, then, adopted a stamped pottery style foreign to many of their members. In contrast to their treatment of the Guale, the Spanish expended little effort on directing social change among the Yamassee who came to La Florida. As long as they provided labor, they were left to do more or less as they pleased. Therefore, while it might be argued that the Guale made Altamaha because the Spanish preferred the style and imposed it on mission populations (though I doubt this was the case), the same does not apply to the Yamassee (remembering that some of these Yamassee may very well have been Guale). Apparently, despite their indifference to Catholicism, and to Spanish control in general, the Yamassee were sufficiently impressed by the pottery—or perhaps they were just astute enough—to adopt a style that indicated allegiance. In any event, the heterogeneous Yamassee began to produce a homogeneous ware, Altamaha, which they took with them when they abandoned the Spanish.

Sometime after about 1650, possibly before the Yamassee immigration, Altamaha spread to other Native American groups—groups never affiliated with the Lamar tradition—in La Florida. In the late pre-Columbian period, the "proto" Mocama and Timucua produced Savannah or St. Johns wares, respectively, or an admixture of both (Ashley 1995; Russo

1992). St. Johns pottery has a fine-grained paste with silt and sponge spicules as the only nonplastic inclusions. The wares have strong dark cores and generally buff exteriors and interiors, and they were plain or check stamped. Savannah is a dark-bodied ware with little oxidation of the interior or exterior surface. The paste generally contains fine sand, probably a natural inclusion, and sometimes sponge spicules (Cordell 1993). Both of these wares have much finer pastes than their Irene counterparts. San Pedro, a ware with grog tempering in a sandy paste and a variety of surface finishes, appeared in parts of the Mocama area almost immediately after Spanish colonization (Ashley and Rolland 1997).[17]

San Juan del Puerto, a Mocama mission on Fort George Island, Florida, is a site that has been tested (Dickinson and Wayne 1985; Russo 1992) but lacks large-scale excavations. The ceramic assemblage there is predominantly Altamaha, both within the mission quadrangle and in the surrounding area—not San Pedro, Savannah, or St. Johns as would be expected if the ceramic assemblage was determined by pre-Columbian social group or early historic ceramic assemblages. This has been explained as a result of an in-migration of Guale (Dickinson and Wayne 1985:chap. 6, 1) or site misidentification (McMurray 1973). More recent documentary evidence indicates that the residents were Mocaman throughout the long history of this important mission site—according to Worth (1995:198–199) and Hann (1990:20), the only mission in Guale and Mocama that remained in place throughout the seventeenth century (1587–1702). Additional populations were moved to San Juan del Puerto from Santa Maria in 1665 and Guadalquini about 1696 (Worth 1995:fig. 6), but these were also Mocama. Either the priests or native residents of the site were acquiring pottery from elsewhere—a dubious proposition considering the oft-lamented poverty of the missions—or the Mocama made Altamaha.

Altamaha did not dominate only mission assemblages. The type was also present in the city of St. Augustine, where it was sold in the markets (Bushnell 1994) and probably made on a household basis by native women married to or otherwise cohabiting with Spanish men. While St. Johns pottery, the local pre-Columbian type, is more frequent in colonial contexts prior to 1600, by 1650 Altamaha pottery dominates (Deagan 1990:fig. 20–3). This might suggest that the Guale had come to dominate the native population in St. Augustine. However, significant numerical superiority over Timucuans did not occur until after 1711 (Deagan 1990:table 20–2). Thus, as in the missions, it appears that Altamaha replaced the local native ware, in this case St. Johns plain and check-stamped wares, even among the local natives. Altamaha continued to be an important utilitarian ware even after aboriginal populations declined to very low levels (Deagan 1990:figs. 20–3, 20–4).

Conclusions

The thesis presented in this paper is that Altamaha ware arose initially as a negotiated tradition between the Guale and the Spanish in the context of mission sites. The Spanish instigated, as part of their routine policy of directed change, a number of functional changes in preexisting Irene ceramics. The Guale adopted those changes but preserved a number of elements that allowed them control over the style and the meaning of the final product. Perhaps the most important of these was the continuation of the use of the World Symbol, which was a condensed symbol (David et al. 1988) representing the cosmology of the Guale (and the larger Southeast).

Whether or not Irene or early Altamaha wares were used by the Guale to signal ethnicity is unknown. Researchers do not even agree on definitions of the concept (see S. Jones 1997), or on whether ethnic groups, as they are presently defined, existed in the past (see Maceachern 1998:111–112). But I think one can argue that the Guale created Altamaha—part Spanish tradition, part Guale tradition—as a way to signal a new social identity, one that allied them with the Spanish. (Similarly, upland folks around Cahokia adopted some aspects of Mississippian pottery to "create an identity consistent with the greater Cahokian community" [see Alt, this volume]). Because Altamaha was a negotiated tradition that violated neither the traditional pottery production routine (*châine opératoire*) nor the "dispositions" (habitus) (Pauketat 2001) of Guale potters, the type displaced Irene rapidly. Early in the Mission period, the type may have been coextensive with the Guale, but later, other local groups, as well as immigrant groups, adopted the type for the same reason. Thus, in this particular historic context, social groups as they existed in the late pre-Columbian period become less visible in the colonial period (cf. Goodby 1998).

At a smaller scale, Maceachern (1998:125) proposed something similar for societies in the Mandara Mountain area of Cameroon and Nigeria: "Given the central role played by ceramics within traditional material culture, especially within contexts of sociopolitical interaction involving ritual, sacrifices, and the sharing of beer [perhaps in this case, *cassina*], adoption of local pottery by small immigrant groups would have been a valuable way of signaling acceptance of local norms, just as it is for in-marrying women today." In the case of Altamaha wares, production may have signaled to the Spanish and other native peoples such an acceptance and an affiliation and may also have provided the locals and the newcomers the sense of inclusiveness necessary to withstand the turmoil of the Mission period.

Acknowledgements

This paper has benefited from recent discussions with John E. Worth and Jerald T. Milanich.

Notes

1. For the time period under discussion, La Florida included coastal Georgia and north Florida.

2. Mission cemeteries generally contain a balanced demographic profile. In other words, men did not leave the missions for the more mobile interior while women and children stayed in the more sedentary missions.

3. This listing represents a gloss of S. Jones's (1997:128) definition of ethnic groups.

4. Theorists on the issue of ethnicity run the gamut from those who see it everywhere to those such as Harris (1997) who consider it a development occurring primarily as resistance to state-level societies. Those of the former persuasion define ethnicity as based on "primordial" social and biological characteristics acquired at birth or as "the symbolic representation of inequality" (Sassaman, this volume). Under both of these (and many other) definitions in this school of thought, ethnicity is present in all human societies (Sassaman, this volume; see also Emerson and McElrath, this volume, and literature review in S. Jones 1997:65–72). I think that the primordial definition broadens the term to the point of uselessness and risks conflation with other categories of experience such as class or gender. Overextended, it may even trivialize the ethnic experience. This definition also ignores historical circumstances—a Puerto Rican in New York City experiences ethnicity at a much different scale than a Puerto Rican in a barrio in Puerto Rico. On the other hand, Harris's definition is overly constraining.

5. The first chief in this area to convert, ostensibly anyway, and under the influence of Menendez himself, was Guale, which may have had something to do with it. Guale was not a paramount chief, however, but the leader of one of the two villages that held control over the Guale-Tolomato chiefdom, one of at least three chiefdoms present in 1597 (G. D. Jones 1978).

6. This was probably due to the instability of these matrilineal chiefdoms. Chiefs made alliances of convenience with other chiefs, but such alliances were easily dissolved. In the complex chiefdoms, the primary chief was entitled to tribute from the towns of lesser chiefs; compliance to tribute and other demands was

sanctioned by a threat of force. Though both socio-political and demographic upheavals during the contact period may have exacerbated the instability of complex chiefdoms, there is archaeological information to suggest instability in pre-Columbian times as well (Anderson 1994b; Williams and Shapiro 1990a).

7. At the Meeting House Fields site on St. Catherines Island, there was no evidence that pottery attributes varied by household midden. Note also that there is no evidence for extensive trade or craft specialization in Irene wares.

8. Given S. Jones's (1997:57) critique of the concept of "etic," better terms might include an "academic" or a "heuristic" Guale.

9. The Spanish were well aware of the principle of "divide and conquer" (Saunders 1998:410). Among other emerging tribes, however, factionalism was beneficial. According to Galloway (1994b:518), the Choctaw were able to retain their autonomy because tribal factionalism made it impossible for the English or French to control them through a paramount leader.

10. Most researchers would agree that the name Yamassee reflects an origin in La Tama.

11. According to W. G. Green (1991:21), the Chichimecos in this case were Westo. According to Worth (1995:16–17), they were Rechahecrians from Virginia. The "Chichimecos" had attacked Guale in 1661 but damage was comparatively light.

12. This geographic distinction is not absolute; the term "San Marcos" has been used in Georgia and vice versa, but few researchers discuss the reasons for applying the type names. I have contended that the two should not be considered separate types and opted for the name Altamaha (Saunders 1992a, 2000a). While I don't hope to convince anybody by doing so, I will refer to the type as Altamaha throughout this chapter.

13. Based on a correlation in the horizontal distribution of Irene and Altamaha pottery at the Bourbon Fields site, it had been believed that both pottery types were produced contemporaneously. Because most pottery came from the plow zone, I consider the evidence inconclusive (Saunders 2000a:172).

14. Many researchers have assumed this four-field design was the dominant motif and assigned all Altamaha pottery to this category without close inspection. In fairness to those researchers, it should be noted that the World Symbol design produces cross simple stamped sherds in about 94 percent of an assemblage. I have considered whether the continued production of the World Symbol design in a Catholic context might be a case of passive resistance but could not come up with testable implications (Saunders 2000a:101).

15. A comparison of Guale and Yamassee pottery based on subtypical attributes has been published (Saunders 2000a).

16. Phases are not as fine grained for the Ichisi area. Cowarts phase (A.D. 1400–1600) assemblages do not show the same shift to incising that Bell phase assemblages do; however this may be due to a lack of known sites dating to the latter part of the sixteenth century. Nothing is known about ceramic assemblages in the area

between 1600 and the Creek Ocmulgee Fields assemblages of 1685–1715 (M. Williams 1990).

17. I suspect that San Pedro represents an early attempt by the Spanish to influence local ceramics. The appearance of grog-tempered Jefferson series wares in western Florida may represent another, albeit successful, alteration of local potting traditions. However, most researchers believe that the appearance of Jefferson wares signals population migration into the area.

6

Creek and Pre-Creek Revisited

Cameron B. Wesson

[T]radition is created by societies of men and transmitted in dis-
tinctively human and rational ways, it is not fixed and immutable: it is constantly changing as society deals with ever new circumstances. Tradition makes the man, by circumscribing his
behavior within certain bounds; but it is equally true that man
makes his traditions. And so . . . "Man makes himself."
V. G. Childe, *Man Makes Himself* (1951:188)

The concept of tradition has been used widely in American archaeology
since the 1940s (Caldwell 1958; Goggin 1949; Willey 1945; Willey and
Phillips 1958:34–39). It was first applied as a colloquial description of any
cultural practice that persisted through time. Eventually the concept was
expanded and formally defined for archaeological application (Caldwell
1958:3; Willey and Phillips 1958:34–39). Unfortunately, early definitions
of "tradition" were not consonant, leading to very different applications
and understandings of the term among archaeologists. Willey and Phillips
(1958:37, emphasis original) defined tradition as *"a (primarily) temporal
continuity represented by persistent configurations in single technologies
or other systems of related forms."* At the same time, Caldwell (1958:3,
emphasis added) defined tradition as *"a main-line, areally based continuity of what would theoretically be a cultural whole."* Thus the term *tradition* was applied by archaeologists to both individual culture traits and
entire cultures (see Emerson and McElrath, and Lightfoot, this volume).

Influenced by then current theoretical perspectives, many of the archaeologists who first defined and used the concept of tradition drew directly
from functionalist and unilineal evolutionary theories. These scholars argued that culture was a homeostatic system designed to ensure sociocultural equilibrium (see Hodder 1982b and Trigger 1989a:244–328 for detailed critiques of these views). From this perspective, culture conforms to
Newton's second law of motion, remaining unchanged until acted upon

by external (most commonly environmental) forces. For archaeologists espousing this position, tradition played a vital role in securing cultural stability by encouraging conformity with preexisting social actions. Tradition thus represented the glue that held social life together, with this adhesive working best when it bound social, cultural, and political relationships in perpetual stasis.

This approach to tradition is exemplified by Charles Fairbanks's article "Creek and Pre-Creek." Using culture trait lists and ceramic attributes, Fairbanks (1952:285) identified archaeological materials that he believed united the "prehistoric" and "historic" Creek of southeastern North America. Like his contemporaries, Fairbanks considered traditions roughly equivalent to cultures and artifacts. Thus longevity in the decoration of ceramic containers was believed to represent longstanding cultural traditions and, by implication, ethnic identities.[1] The biggest problem was the loss of tradition brought about through the acculturation of the Creek during the later historic period (ca. A.D. 1750–1800). As Fairbanks (1952:299) stated, the Creek "kept many social and religious traits but have left very little in the way of aboriginal artifacts. The early acceptance of European materials by the Creek with the consequent breakdown of old styles is a recurrent facet of the old problem of [the] Creek . . . once begun it could not be abandoned as the Creek could not relearn the forgotten crafts." From this perspective the Creek are seen as having little ability to resist this loss of cultural tradition or create new traditions for themselves (Corkran 1967; Cotterill 1954; Crane 1928; C. Martin 1978; Mason 1963; Morris 1993; M. T. Smith 1987:145).

In contrast to this view, other archaeologists advocate understandings of tradition that rely on active, agent-centered frameworks (Cobb 1991; Dobres and Robb 2000; Lightfoot 1995; Lightfoot et al., 1998; McGuire 1992; McGuire and Saitta 1996; Pauketat 1994; Saitta 1997). Even Childe (1951) argued a generation ago that tradition is the product of human action rather than a force of cultural conservation and is a source of perpetual culture change. Within this framework, social actors possess the ability to shape their behaviors to existing practices ("tradition," in one sense of the word) and simultaneously alter their actions to produce new practices and meanings. Through this continual reworking of action and meaning, traditions are created, defined, enacted, and altered (Bourdieu 1977, 1990, 1998; Giddens 1979, 1984, 1995).

Influenced by larger theoretical developments within the social sciences (particularly the works of Bourdieu, Foucault, Giddens, and Gramsci), archaeologists increasingly have come to recognize the plurality of social meanings inherent in traditional practices (McGuire and Paynter 1991; Pauketat 1994, 1997a, 2001; Sassaman 2000). Because of this polysemic nature, no single pan-societal meaning for tradition is possible. Individuals and social groups participate in and define their relationship to traditions differently. Thus, traditions can be simultaneously resisted (both actively and symbolically), co-opted, and subverted (Dirks 1992; S. Jones 1996; Shennan 1989; Tilley 1989; Wetherell 1982). This alteration of day-to-day practices by individuals in their enactment of (or resistance to) cultural traditions is ultimately responsible for the longer-term patterns of change with which archaeologists work (Bintliff 1991b; Cobb 1991; Deagan 1990; Galloway 1997a; Lightfoot 1995). The challenge for archaeology is accommodating shifting social and political agendas enacted in the short term with longer-term patterns of change.

Drawing from these practice-centered definitions of tradition, this chapter examines the archaeological definition and interpretation of tradition for the Creek. Through an analysis of archaeological data from prehistoric, protohistoric, and historic Creek households, the role of social action in longer-term processes of culture change is explored. As Loren (this volume) analyzes "official" and "local" traditions at the Los Adaes Presidio, I attempt to reveal the dissonance between the local, lived experience of the Creek and the official, colonialist doctrine that has promoted a normative perspective of their traditions. I show that rather than being the result of acculturation to Euro-American influences, social changes among the Creek were the results of individuals fashioning their own social identities through the enactment and redefinition of varied cultural traditions.

Archaeology and the Construction of Creek Traditions

As already argued, previous archaeological approaches to cultural tradition placed a priority on defining relationships between prehistoric and historic Native American cultures. Much of this research was directed toward the use of direct historical analogies that demonstrated long-standing cultural continuities (traditions) between these groups (Fairbanks 1952; Mason 1963; Swanton 1928). One of the most important sources for these analogies was the Creek Confederacy. Given the large body of ethnohistoric data readily available for the Creek, they were used as a source for pan-regional interpretations of Mississippian cultures (Howard 1968; Hudson 1976; Knight 1986, 1990; J. H. Moore 1994; Swanton 1922, 1928, 1946; Waring 1968; Waring and Holder 1945). This

expansive use of Creek models for regional cultural reconstruction is surprising, given the cultural diversity represented by the Creek themselves.
The central problem is that the Creek were not a single group, but a confederacy of peoples from numerous distinct ethnic groups, each with a
different language (Bartram 1958; Hawkins 1980; Swanton 1922, 1928,
1946; J. L. Wright 1986).

The name "Creek" was first applied by European traders to Native
American groups living near their trading posts, with use of the term continually expanding to include an ever increasing number of native peoples
(Crane 1928). J. W. Martin (1991:8) maintains that the name "was not a
neutral term but a colonial signification that concealed and rendered invisible a tremendous diversity of peoples and enabled Georgians to rational-
ize violence." Consistent with this view is Whitehead's (1992) contention
that state expansion necessitates the "tribalization" of colonized peoples.
From this view the growth of Euro-American influence in the Americas
meant that culturally diverse societies were "reduced to relatively homogenous, territorially discrete, bounded 'tribal' cultural identities" (Hill
1998:151). In essence, Euro-Americans created the Creek out of a number
of distinct Native American groups through this process of "tribalization." This process collapsed the variability of these individual cultures
into a monolithic "Creek tradition."

The cultural diversity of the Creek Confederacy also has been obscured
through an overreliance on the ethnohistoric accounts of John Swanton
(1922, 1928, 1946). Swanton's work has been extremely influential; however, recent criticism (Galloway 1993, 1997a) has focused on his uncritical
distillation of accounts from more than 400 years of Native American
culture history into a single, timeless, and almost completely normative
description. Galloway (1993, 1994a, 1997a) demonstrates that Swanton's
research was biased by his a priori belief that cultural traditions were
naturally unchanging. Additional analysis reveals that there is little to link
Swanton's (1922, 1928, 1946) grand syntheses with the archaeological
and historical reality of culture change (J. W. Martin 1991; J. L. Wright
1986). This reliance on Swanton, coupled with normative, unilineal, and
functionalist theoretical perspectives, resulted in a longstanding view that
Native American traditions were static and that change was brought
about by external Euro-American influences rather than internal sociopolitical factors.

Archaeologists built upon this theoretical framework by constructing
interpretations that placed the ultimate cause of culture change among the
Creek with Euro-American-introduced diseases and material goods

(Borah 1964; Dobyns 1983; Dunnell 1991; Fairbanks 1952; C. Martin 1978; Mason 1963; Morris 1993; Phillips et al., 1951:419–421). Many of these studies see the superiority of Euro-American goods as unavoidably attractive to Native Americans, with the acquisition of these items leading to material dependency and acculturation (Cotterill 1954; Crane 1928; Fairbanks 1952; Mason 1963; Morris 1993). These studies seemingly place the impetus of culture change in Euro-American material goods themselves, without adequate consideration for Native American perceptions and uses of these items. Euro-American goods are often discussed as animate social actors, capable of coercing Native Americans into the abandonment of longstanding traditions. For example, C. Martin (1978:8) states, "European hardware and other trade items were immediately perceived by the Stone Age Indian as being far superior in their utility to his primitive technology and general material culture." Ultimately, we are presented with an image of Native Americans without the ability to shape social phenomena, caught within and governed by forces outside their control or comprehension.

This position holds that the introduction of European goods through market economies based on the deerskin trade forever altered political, social, and economic relationships. The end result was considered to be the loss of longstanding indigenous traditions. Studies developed out of this perspective stress the use value of these artifacts for Native Americans without adequately assessing the social contexts in which these items were used. They also emphasize material traits without consideration of the cultural factors that mediate the social nature of Euro-American-introduced artifacts. From this perspective Creek culture change is merely one more example of acculturation, where primitive peoples succumb to the dominant Western "conquest culture" (Foster 1960:11–12; C. Martin 1978; Morris 1993; J. R. White 1975). Such approaches to the past, and the nature of the archaeological record, cannot acknowledge nonmaterial aspects of material items or the roles of these goods within networks of local social relations. As Knight (1985:169–170) notes, such views not only are built on normative anthropological theory, but also are overly reliant on colonial accounts: "Standard historical treatments concerning Indian trade in the Southeast are written for the most part, from the European point of view. To the European trader, Indian motives and cultural background were of little interest as long as their behavior as consumers remained consistent."

Recent research on Native American and Euro-American interactions demonstrates that indigenous peoples were selective in their adoption of trade items. Native peoples were capable of refusing goods that were both technologically and materially superior to their indigenously produced counterparts (Fitzhugh 1985; Hugill and Dickson 1988; Knight 1985; Linton 1940; Rogers 1990; Trigger 1976, 1985; Turnbaugh 1993; Waselkov 1993; Wolf 1982). As Rogers (1990:11) states, "It may not be assumed that native peoples automatically want to acquire the technologically exotic Euro-American trade goods, or, for that matter, accept the self-proclaimed superiority of Euro-American customs." Thus, individual Native Americans may be seen as shaping the nature and terms of trade through conscious decisions about which objects they would bring into their homes.

By shifting emphasis away from the use value of these goods to their social meanings, more detailed interpretations of southeastern traditions and culture change emerge. M. T. Smith (1987) explores these perspectives through an examination of both the archaeological distribution of these items and their positions in trade relations, as well as mechanisms of social reproduction that predate European contacts. Native Americans were not simply the passive consumers of European-introduced goods, but savvy consumers who exerted a great deal of control over cross-cultural trade and exchange (Turnbaugh 1993). Native peoples selected items based on a complex network of traditional practices. The primary criterion for selection of Euro-American trade goods may not have been the uniqueness of these items, but their correspondence to preexisting categories of prestige goods necessary for social reproduction and the cultivation of symbolic capital (Ekholm 1972; Frankenstein and Rowlands 1978; Knight 1985; Peregrine 1992).

The advancement of one's position through the manipulation of prestige goods is a means of social reproduction thought to have been in place in the Southeast long before Native American contacts with Euro-Americans (Anderson 1990, 1994a; Barker and Pauketat 1992a; J. A. Brown et al., 1990; Helms 1992; Pauketat 1994; Peregrine 1992; Rogers 1996; J. F. Scarry 1990, 1996a; Welch 1991, 1996). The exact goods fueling these systems varied between societies, but major elements of southeastern prestige goods economies are thought to have been objects of copper, shell, pearls, exotic stones, and goods embellished with supernatural iconography (Peregrine 1992). Elite exchange of these goods reinforced existing social and political hierarchies and helped establish new social relationships. Steponaitis (1986:392) contends that "valued craft items probably served as tokens in social transactions. Displayed as possessions, these tokens enhanced social prestige; presented as gifts, they could be used to build alliances and inflict social debts. Exchanges of such items, especially among budding elites, were instruments of political strategy as much as, if not more than, purely economic activities."

Southeastern peoples used prestige goods to enhance their social status through display and exchange. When displayed, these items were often seen as powerful *sacra* with supernatural and religious connections (Knight 1986; Steponaitis 1986). When exchanged, they often inflicted debts that the recipient could not repay in kind, establishing and reinforcing hierarchical social relationships. Debtors were often forced to repay these gifts with loyalty, work, or services, which the recipient could then use to create new relationships of obligation (Bourdieu 1977:195). Such interactions and the symbolic capital they produced enabled certain social groups and individuals to amass considerable power. They also gave rise to an ideology promoting elite hegemony as central to cultural continuity. Peregrine (1992:7) contends that this was made possible because "individuals . . . intensified production to support their elites in competitive exchanges with others so that they would have had more access to prestige goods, and hence a better opportunity to socially reproduce themselves at acceptable levels."

However, those denied the goods necessary for their own social reproduction would not have been content with the status quo for long. Challenges to the control of socially desired goods were ever present. Individuals circumvented the control of trade in efforts designed to build both economic and social capital for themselves and their kin (Knight 1985; Waselkov 1993; Wesson 1997). These actions were not confined to the postcontact period but are endemic to prestige goods systems (Frankenstein and Rowlands 1978; Peregrine 1992). Resistance to prestige goods systems is identified archaeologically by assessing the number of these goods circulating in society at any one time, and the ability of social elites to control their within-group circulation. The introduction of new goods or the heightened circulation of existing stocks made additional resources available to aspirant social groups and represented direct threats to the elite claims to power (Beaudry at al. 1991; Ekholm 1972; Friedman 1982; Kleppe 1989; McGuire 1992; McGuire and Paynter 1991; Williams and Shapiro 1990a). As Peregrine (1992:31) states: "If a system is flooded with prestige goods, the control of them is meaningless. Alliances with individuals who have control of prestige goods are not necessary if individuals have easy access to them." Much of the chiefly cycling identified by Anderson (1990, 1994a, 1994b, 1996a, 1996b) and others (Blitz 1993a, 1999; Hally 1996; Scarry 1996a, b; Williams and Shapiro 1990b) in the Southeast can be viewed as a response to the inability of social elites to control prestige goods (see Helms 1996:438).

Thus, the increased circulation of Euro-American goods in Native American societies precipitated increased social competition. Individuals were no longer dependent upon the trickling down of prestige goods from their social superiors; they were free to trade for these goods with Europeans directly. As Ekholm (1972:144) notes for similar exchanges in Africa, the "arrival of Europeans gave every chief career possibilities otherwise not available under the traditional system. Earlier the path to glory often went via a vassal relationship with one of the political centers, but afterwards, in principle, anyone with the ambition and military strength could compete with the traditional authority over local hegemony." Thus, rather than signs of acculturation, Euro-American trade goods were used to reinforce traditional mechanisms of social reproduction dependent upon the importation and exchange of exotic finished goods and raw materials.

Understanding these processes of social reproduction and tradition making cannot be adequately addressed on large social formations like the Creek Confederacy. As Hally (1971:62) argues, we cannot "make much progress in correlating archaeological and ethnohistorical data in the Southeast as long as we continue to concern ourselves with . . . large scale political alignments such as Creek and Apalachee." What is suggested is that we instead focus on the individual communities and cultural traditions at work on the local level (Hally 1971:62). Although the diversity of southeastern traditions will continue to be elusive, our understanding of variation can be advanced through research directed at local traditions and small-scale social changes. An examination of local uses for Euro-American trade goods within the household context provides a glimpse into the traditions that Creek enacted and altered during their interactions with Euro-Americans.

Although prestige goods entered Creek villages through new mechanisms after Euro-American contact, there is ample evidence that in addition to being functional objects, many trade goods served as status markers (Knight 1985; M. T. Smith 1987:11–53; Waselkov 1989, 1993; Wesson 1997). Native Americans certainly recognized the functional value of the objects for which they traded, but, rather than serving primarily as functional goods, many of these items were more valuable as tools of social ranking. For the Creek, efforts to circumvent existing exchange networks and advance their own social claims are manifest within a variety of contexts. In this study I present the results of an analysis of archaeological remains from Creek household contexts at several Creek sites in central Alabama. Through an examination of localized distributions of Euro-American goods I attempt to contextualize trade goods within local traditions of social reproduction. In addition, I contend that these goods were used in traditions enacted to resist social domination.

Archaeological Evidence

Households are excellent units of analysis because they actively reflect and simultaneously construct traditions (Bourdieu 1977; Cunningham 1973; Norberg-Schulz 1971, 1980; Rapoport 1969). They are superb arenas in which to evaluate the nature of traditions (Bourdieu 1977), since they are "culture[s] in microcosm . . . [where] individuals are brought to an awareness of their culture's rules, and conversely, where those rules are frequently expressed in physical form" (Deetz 1982:719). Ashmore and Wilk (1988:1) see households as "fundamental elements of human society" that "serve as sensitive indicators of . . . [social] change." This reflection of larger social changes in the household context is based on the intimate articulation of households with larger cultural processes (Wilk and Rathje 1982:618).

Analysis of archaeological data recovered from household contexts at the Creek sites of Fusihatchee (1EE191), Tukabatchee (1EE32), Hickory Ground (1EE89), Childersburg (1TA1), Jere Shine (1MT6), Tin Chaw Way (1CS148), and Jackson (1BR35) provides information on sixty-four completely or partially excavated Creek domestic structures. The vast majority of the structures used in this study are from Fusihatchee (1EE191), where more than fifty prehistoric and historic Creek domestic structures were excavated. Features associated with these structures reflect a wide range of domestic activities, but those with the most direct bearing on the present topic are burials.

The Creek practiced subfloor inhumation, with the deceased placed in a large pit excavated beneath their sleeping benches in the corners of the house (Bartram 1958; Swanton 1928). The placement of prestige goods in burial contexts serves as an estimate of the density of these goods circulating in society during a particular period and the ability of elites to control their distribution. The analysis of burial goods as status indicators is problematic (O'Shea 1984; Pearson 2000; Tainter 1975). We cannot be certain that burial goods were the personal property of the individuals with whom they are interred; however, given the domestic nature of Creek burials, there is good reason to presume that these goods were most likely the property of households members or closely related kin.

Bourdieu (1977:179–180) suggests that the cultivation of symbolic capital is not an individual enterprise but is instead a corporate activity that includes larger social relations. Thus, status claims were not based on the ability of individual actors to marshal prestige goods, but the ability of their social segment to use these goods to cultivate symbolic capital (Bourdieu 1977:179; Helms 1988, 1993; Kleppe 1989). In essence, all members of the social group shared the status won through competitions for control of prestige goods. Because of this corporate nature, prestige goods placed with deceased family members can be seen as a representation of the relative status of the social group to which the deceased belonged.

Analysis of burials from the pre-Columbian Creek Shine II period (A.D. 1400–1550) demonstrates a general paucity of burial goods, with 27 percent of individuals buried with goods (Wesson 1997). All of the goods interred with these individuals are considered prestige goods (Peregrine 1992), including shell beads, shell buttons, and a "spaghetti-style" engraved shell gorget. In addition, the nature of these high-status interments differs from that of interments without burial goods as well, with all of these high-status burials (n=4) placed within a mound. The argument that social status is corporately based is supported by the distribution of high-status goods with both adult and subadult burials.

Burial goods became much more common—found with 65 percent of individuals buried—in the Atasi Phase (A.D. 1600–1715). This shift in burial practice suggests a change in the nature of interments for the Creek and the heightened importance of burial furniture. In addition to the increasing number of individuals buried with goods, the overwhelming majority of those with burial furniture possessed prestige goods (79.4 percent). This pattern demonstrates both the availability of Euro-American material goods and the use of these items in the development of increasingly elaborate burial rites. These data suggest the use of Euro-American goods as high-status markers (principally decorative items and firearms). Although the delineation of Euro-American items functioning as prestige goods within Creek society is problematic, there is a rough correlation between indigenous status items intended for display and their Euro-American counterparts (Knight 1985; M. T. Smith 1987).

During the historic Tallapoosa phase (A.D. 1715–1830), almost all individuals (91 percent) received burial goods. Thus, the elaboration of burial practices begun in the Atasi phase continued into the historic Tallapoosa phase. Of those Tallapoosa phase burials receiving burial goods, a large percentage (83 percent) contained prestige goods. What is most remarkable about the assemblages from these burials is the ubiquity of both common trade goods and high-status goods. Small numbers of prestige goods apparently no longer sufficed for burial, with many Tallapoosa burials with goods (32 percent) possessing very large caches (n>10) of high-status items.

This pattern is entirely consistent with status emulation within burial contexts (Cannon 1989; Little et al., 1992; McGuire 1988). As Little et al. (1992:415) note, "A direct and invariable relation between rich graves and high social status cannot be assumed. A consideration of the social necessity of maintaining status and power helps in interpreting the meaning of that display by connecting it with ideology and social control." Dominant social groups periodically alter traditions (particularly burial practices) to distance themselves from other social groups. I interpret the large numbers of prestige goods placed in high-status burials as representative of an inflationary spiral in status displays. Since other social groups could afford to inter high-status goods with their dead, only ostentatious burial rituals, replete with large caches of goods, could successfully demonstrate social superiority. Thus conspicuous consumption of prestige goods in funerary rites became a principal mechanism for the maintenance and establishment of social position.

The general impressions that emerge from the Shine II, Atasi, and Tallapoosa phase burial data are increasing numbers of burials receiving goods, a widening dispersal of prestige goods within Creek society, and expanding numbers of high-status goods placed with the very richest burials. In addition, analysis of burials from the Atasi and Tallapoosa phases indicates the use of a wide range of Euro-American goods as status markers. By the Tallapoosa phase, European goods are placed with almost every burial, demonstrating their importance as social currency. Such similarities across the entire social spectrum suggest that elites were no longer able to control access to prestige goods.

Such actions are consistent with the theoretical expectations of prestige goods systems, where social groups circumvent rigid controls on high-status goods to increase their ability to expand their opportunity for social reproduction (Frankenstein and Rowlands 1978; Kleppe 1989). When claims to social position are based on the control of nonlocal prestige goods, the ability of individuals to secure these items for themselves encourages additional mechanisms of social reproduction and acts to limit the domination of nonelites by the aspiring elite. These actions were also consonant with traditions of resistance to domination, as individuals and groups placed themselves in opposition to existing social hierarchies. In addition to burial evidence, food storage facilities, public and private architecture, and Colono-ware ceramic production support the conclusion that the historic Creek practiced traditions favoring the advancement of the household's social status (Wesson 1997, 1999).

Through these and similar acts, the Creek engaged in social contests that pitted aspirant groups against each other in competitive status displays. These actions eventually resulted in the factionalization of Creek society and an inability to limit the territorial expansion of the United States (Hassig 1974; Waselkov 1993). These processes of change reveal a subversion of traditional elite authority, and an increasingly household-based focus in the Creek political economy. Thus changes in Creek traditions were responses to internal desires to alter existing social inequalities. Creek enacted traditions that reinforced their social ties with their lineage and encouraged the accumulation of high-status material goods. Such actions created inflationary cultural spirals, where an ever increasing number of prestige goods were necessary to reinforce claims to heightened social and economic status. Thus, the Creek were not dependent upon Euro-American trade goods because these were functionally superior, or because the Creek were becoming acculturated to Euro-American lifeways, but because Euro-American prestige goods were essential capital for developing social status and prestige. In the end, these items became necessary for social reproduction.

Conclusions

Three centuries of interaction between the indigenous peoples of the Southeast and Euro-Americans resulted in a series of changes in Native American traditions. Although changes in indigenous cultures during the historic period have been addressed frequently, too little research has addressed the exact nature of these changes and the role of individuals in shaping these larger processes. Unlike much previous research (Cotterill 1954; Debo 1941; Mason 1963; Morris 1993), this work argues that although Euro-American influence fostered changes in Creek culture, the major sources of change were the Creek themselves. As Knight (1985:182) states: "The nature and character of the traffic in European goods among the Creek was not wholly imposed by Europeans. It was actively shaped by Creek individuals behaving according to an entirely indigenous moral code, a code whose origins predate the arrival of Europeans. It was a code modified at times by the history of contact with the external world, but in the end it must be comprehended as an internal social force. It was not simply a case of the primitive passively yielding to an overwhelming exposure to superior technology and culture."

During the protohistoric and historic periods, the Creek underwent a series of changes in domestic economy, sociopolitical organization, and household structure. These changes were, in many respects, directly related to interactions with Euro-Americans, but they were internally driven and shaped by Native American peoples.

Acknowledgements

I wish to thank Tim Pauketat for inviting me to participate in the "Resistant Traditions" symposium and for his comments on previous drafts of this paper. I would also like to thank Maria Aviles and two anonymous reviewers for their helpful suggestions on ways to improve the clarity of my arguments. I am particularly indebted to John Cottier of Auburn University and Craig Sheldon of Auburn University at Montgomery for their assistance.

Note

1. Many of the material traits believed to securely link prehistoric archaeological materials with historic groups have been demonstrated to be relatively poor indicators of cultural identity (McGuckin 1997; Shennan 1989:5–17). Such approaches fail to address the complexity of social identities and the ability of individuals and social groups to actively engage in the production and alteration of identities and traditions (Barth 1969b; Conkey 1990; S. Jones 1997; J. Thomas 1996).

7

Gender, Tradition, and the Negotiation of Power Relationships in Southern Appalachian Chiefdoms

Lynne P. Sullivan and Christopher B. Rodning

Traditions are those cultural practices and perspectives that are passed from generation to generation, always with some revision or conscious manipulation, but commonly with references to the perceived past of a people. Tradition affects the ways that people actively create their own social identities, their roles within their communities, and their relationships with other people and other groups (Hobsbawm 1983:9–12; Peacock 1986:4–7). Gender and the place of men, women, and children within families and communities is one aspect of identity for which most if not all societies have cultural conventions or traditions (Brumfiel 1992:554–555; Conkey and Gero 1991:16–23; Conkey and Spector 1984:6–7; Hodder 1992:258–259; S. Jones 1997:134–135; Joyce and Claassen 1997:2–8; Kent 1998:15–20; S. M. Nelson 1997:15–17; Spielmann 1995; Whelan 1995). Leadership roles likewise are tied to traditions. Gender conventions and other traditions guide the pathways of aspiring leaders to power and prominence in their communities. Aspiring leaders can materialize their status through the display and exchange of prestige goods (Dye 1995; Emerson 1997a; Pauketat 1994; Steponaitis 1991), through competitive feasting and the hosting of other kinds of public events (Blitz 1993b; VanDerwarker 1999; Welch and Scarry 1995), by mobilizing tribute and hoarding surplus resources and wealth goods (Anderson 1994a; Pauketat 1994; Wesson 1999), by building and preserving monumental architecture and other kinds of landmarks (Hally 1996; Knight 1986; Rudolph 1984; M. T. Smith and Williams 1994; Williams and Shapiro 1996), and by creating whole landscapes that communicate differential social standing and claims to power (Earle 1997; Knight 1998; Wesson 1998). Gender conventions shape the ways that people achieve different kinds of power and prestige through these or other activities.

These traditions and their effects on power and leadership can become visible in the landscape in which people live.

Our main goal in this chapter is to outline the ways that perceptions of traditional gender and power relationships within native communities shaped cultural landmarks and landscapes of the greater southern Appalachians from the fourteenth through eighteenth centuries. Our thesis is that different kinds of power within the native chiefdom societies of this region were vested within the male leadership of towns and female leadership of kin groups. Relationships between gender groups would have been continually negotiated and renegotiated by women and men, drawing from their distinct and complementary sources of power and status. This gender ideology formed an abiding regional tradition that structured social dynamics and community leadership throughout the southern Appalachians and influenced mortuary ritual and the relationships between people and their surrounding landscapes.

This chapter offers some comments about the interrelationships of tradition, power, gender, and the spatial arrangements of burials and buildings. We first review ethnohistoric evidence about traditional gender roles within native societies of the southern Appalachians. We then reconstruct the ancient history of these gender distinctions with reference to archaeological evidence from different areas of the greater southern Appalachians. Our conclusions apply this evidence toward an outline of the relationship between gender and power in the history of native societies in this region, with an interest in spurring further study of this relationship in chiefdoms elsewhere.

Gender and Architecture

Architectural landmarks can become associated with different groups within communities, and they can serve as spatial referents to these community members and their access to different kinds of power. Quite often monuments are related to ancestors, demarcating mortuary spaces or other kinds of sacred space, and aspiring leaders often try to claim different forms of ownership and connection to them to legitimate their status and to differentiate themselves from other people or groups (Charles 1992, 1995; Goldstein 1980, 1995; Hodder 1984; Knight 1989a). As are power relations, gender is an axis along which people and groups are differentiated from and bound to each other, and gender can structure spatial arrangements within communities (Gilchrist 1994:150–152; Spain

1992:26–29; Spector 1993:67–77). This last point is fundamental to our study of mortuary programs in southern Appalachian chiefdoms.

Distinct spatial domains can offer members of different gender groups visible architectural anchors for their roles, identities, and status within their communities.[1] If certain architectural spaces are widely known as spaces reserved at times for activities of one or another gender group, this local knowledge likely would attach itself to architectural forms visible in the cultural landscape. Across the cultural landscape of the Mississippian period, for example, both platform mounds and menstrual huts would have served as architectural reminders of the very different kinds of rites conducted within them, even when there were not ritual events underway in those spaces (Anderson 1994a; Galloway 1997b; Knight 1989b).

Gender ideologies can thus become embedded within landscapes and architecture, as can other kinds of ideologies.[2] Visible architectural forms of course can preserve and communicate ideas about how different members of communities should relate to each other, especially when there are certain kinds of events and activities that take place within them. Such is the case in the history of medieval English monasticism—monks and nuns tended to develop different relationships with people in surrounding communities, and these contrasts became visible in the architecture of monasteries and nunneries and their placement within landscapes of town and countryside (Gilchrist 1994).

One premise of our argument here is that the placement of graves in architectural spaces that serve as dwellings, ceremonial places, or both, represents the deliberate connection of ancestors to living members of the community associated with those architectural spaces.[3] Individuals and their grave goods obviously were not visible after being placed in the ground, but related architecture served as a landmark for people given ancestral status through mortuary ritual and interment.

Another of our premises is that social structures and power relationships are embedded in the landscapes in which people live and interact with each other. Landmarks and monuments reflect attempts to establish ownership or other relationships to landscapes and ancestors (Earle 1997:161–166; Goldstein 1995; Mainfort and Sullivan 1998:13–16). Architecture also can serve as a prominently visible reminder of social differentiation and power relations within communities (Knight 1998; Pauketat 1994:105–107; Pauketat and Emerson 1997a:10–18). The structure of power relationships within communities is visible through individual landmarks and their associations to broader cultural landscapes that encompass houses, mounds, palisades, poles, henges, and mortuary spaces.[4] The manifestation of such relationships in architecture and landscapes shapes the ways that people interact with each other in ritual and routine settings, and the ways that traditions are passed from one generation to younger generations.

In sum, we would argue that gender traditions, social structure, and power relationships are visible in cultural landscapes to the people who create, interpret, and live in them. With this in mind, we now turn to ethnohistorical and archaeological evidence of gender and power within native chiefdoms of the southern Appalachians.

Traditional Gender Roles in Southern Appalachian Chiefdoms

Ethnohistoric evidence of gender traditions among the Cherokee and among more northern Iroquoian speakers, as well as some Muskogean groups of the eighteenth century in the greater southern Appalachian region, indicate that native men and women lived rather different lives. Some scholars have even wondered if men and women spoke different languages or at least knew some words that were specific to either gender group (Bell 1990:332; Perdue 1998:4). They certainly seem to have lived much of their lives in different social spheres and to have moved through different spatial domains (Braund 1993:14; Fenton 1978:309; Hudson 1976:260; Trigger 1978:802). Children almost certainly were introduced to these gender distinctions at a young age. From that point forward many people followed one of several tracks toward social prestige in their communities. Men gained status primarily as warriors, traders, hunters, and diplomats—outwardly negotiating with their peers in other towns or other chiefdoms and tribes and spending considerable lengths of time away from their own hometowns (Braund 1993:14–16; Gearing 1958, 1962; Hudson 1976:260–269). Women gained status primarily through farming, performing dances and other communal rituals, and most significantly, through controlling access to the resources of and membership within matrilineal kin groups (including households, more extensive matrilineages, and clans), and so providing the social glue that bound communities together (Hatley 1991:37–40, 1995:8–10; S. H. Hill 1997:27–34; Sattler 1995:221–229).

The circumstances of matrilineal kinship and matrilocal residence made the male presence in Cherokee households in southeastern North America irregular and unstable. Men often were found in council houses or other communal spaces within their towns, in the presence of other men (see Perdue 1998:45–46; Schroedl 1986:219–224). Houses and households were the domain of Cherokee women (see S. H. Hill 1997:27–28; Perdue 1998:42–45). Gardens and other resources associated with a Cherokee household may well have been managed primarily if not solely by women who were members and leaders of that household. It is worth noting that this distinction between the social spheres navigated by native southeastern men and women is not at all comparable to European distinctions between public and private sectors of society (see S. M. Nelson 1997, 1998, 1999; Rodning 2001; Sullivan 2001). There evidently was a different kind of balance among gender roles in native southeastern societies that offered complementary tracks to social prominence and influence for men and women, rather than placing some gender groups necessarily subordinate to others (see Levy 1999; Sattler 1995; Trocolli 1999). Women's control over domestic matters stemmed partially from male abdication of authority in this realm, but matrilineality also gave women the sole ability to convey the kinship ties "essential to a Cherokee's existence," and indeed to being Cherokee (Perdue 1998:46).

This balance is not unique to native North Americans in the Southeast. Women seem to have held comparable status within Iroquois households and villages in northeastern North America during the seventeenth century and likely well before that (Prezzano 1997:99). Women's power derived from their influential roles as heads of households and kin groups. Men's power meanwhile derived from their roles as relatively mobile hunters and warriors. This gender distinction in Iroquoia strikes us as comparable to the distinction between leadership of Cherokee towns and clans (Perdue 1998:159). This distinction also was present in historic Choctaw communities in the lower Southeast (Galloway 1989:255–256) and may well have been present in many Mississippian societies long before the arrival of Europeans (Levy 1999:70–74). Women in many Native American societies also are considered to have been tradition bearers and, as such, central to the spiritual well-being of everybody within their communities (Bataille and Sands 1984:18–24). Women in native North American societies were prominent as leaders within their families—in many different kinds of family structures—and, significantly, families represented the heart of these native communities, not a social entity subordinate to the structures of tribal and chiefdom leadership by warriors and traders (Klein and Ackerman 1995:14–15).

We do not argue that gender roles were static or that individual native men and women in southern Appalachian chiefdoms were restricted to specific sets of activities and relationships during different stages of their lives. For example, there are numerous accounts of female chiefs and warrior women (L. Thomas 2000; Trocolli 1999; White 1999). Nonetheless, we do argue that traditional gender roles typically allowed native women to claim significant authority within their communities by referencing their relative status in kin groups, if indeed these kin groups were matrilineal, as were eighteenth-century Creek and Cherokee clans. Men usually found room to advance their own social standing through the structures of town governance, in which male warriors and traders were predominant, much as they were in eighteenth-century Creek and Cherokee communities. These conventions, although flexible and malleable though time and in individual circumstances, formed long-held traditions that continue to shape and structure gender and power relationships in native communities of this region.

The social spheres in which men and women were prominent were not necessarily superordinate or subordinate to each other. The distinction between them may have been one in which the power associated with each social domain complemented and perhaps in some cases contested the other. Archaeological evidence of mortuary practices in this part of the Southeast allows us to consider the antiquity of these gender distinctions.

Archaeology of the Southern Appalachians

Southern Appalachia includes contiguous areas in eastern Tennessee, northern Georgia, and the western part of the Carolinas (see fig. 7.1). The Cherokee and several groups of Muskogean speakers lived in these areas in the eighteenth century (Booker, Hudson, and Rankin 1992; Braund 1993:3–10; S. H. Hill 1997:67–69; Hudson 1976:3–14, 1990:67–109, 1997:185–218; Levy, May, and Moore 1990; Muller 1997:61–62; M. T. Smith 1987:20–22). The interrelationships of pre-seventeenth-century archaeological phases in northern Georgia and eastern Tennessee with these post-seventeenth-century tribal groups are in some cases unclear (Hally 1994:173; Schroedl 1998:64; Sullivan 1995:100).

In northeastern Georgia, eighteenth-century Lower Cherokee towns often were located at earlier Mississippian mounds, including Tugalo and Chauga (Anderson 1994b:205–217, 302–307). In eastern Tennessee, eighteenth-century Overhill Cherokee towns often were built in the same localities as earlier Mississippian settlements, including Toqua and Citico (Schroedl 1986:548). Native residents of southwestern North Carolina from the eleventh through fifteenth centuries lived in villages spread across river valleys in which there were often one or more mounds (Dick-

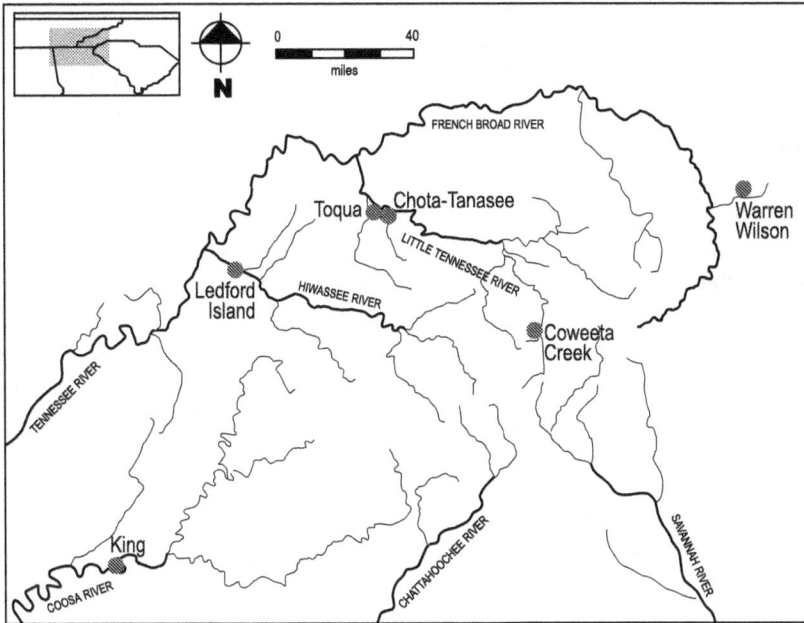

Fig. 7.1. Selected archaeological sites in the greater southern Appalachians.

ens 1976:205–206; Keel 1976:217–218; Ward and Davis 1999:158–178). These areas were home to Middle Cherokee towns as well as the Cherokee Out and Valley towns during the eighteenth century (Dickens 1976:99–101; Keel 1976:215–216; Ward and Davis 1999:178–190). Mortuary patterns visible at significant sites in these areas are described in the archaeological literature and are only briefly outlined here for the purposes of our argument about gender and power in southern Appalachian chiefdoms.

Hally and Kelly (1998) have reviewed the architectural layout of the King site along the Coosa River in western Georgia (see also Hally 1994:156; Hudson 1997:226). King dates to the sixteenth century. The site includes dwelling houses placed around a central plaza and communal buildings. The residential houses and public area were surrounded by a wooden stockade. Clusters of burials are placed within and beside both communal and residential buildings. Of interest here is the fact that eight of ten burials associated with the pair of communal buildings are the resting places of relatively old men with a variety of mortuary goods. These men likely were interred in these public buildings because their gender roles were related to the community significance of this architecture.

Members of all age and sex groups are represented in the graves placed beside or within residential houses. Hally and Kelly (1998:60–61) have not been able to identify the significant family or clan member whose death may have occasioned the rebuilding of these houses. They (Hally and Kelly 1998:61–63) nevertheless argue convincingly that the placement of graves within and beside households at King served to preserve and communicate household identity and membership to the broader community. The mortuary spaces at the King site—which are embedded within the architecture of household and communal space—serve to create a link between ancestors and the buildings associated with them.

Schroedl (1998) has described six significant characteristics of Mississippian town plans in eastern Tennessee: (1) a general town plan including a communal building with or without a mound and a village nearby; (2) a conscious partitioning of space within a town; (3) a shift through time from spatially discrete burial mounds to placement of mortuary spaces within and beside different kinds of buildings; (4) through time, the decline in the number of buildings placed atop a mound summit; (5) through time, the construction of communal council houses away from mounds altogether; and (6) fundamental changes in the social structure of the communities represented by these archaeologically known towns. Schroedl (1998:86) argues that burials associated with households reflect a public acknowledgement of the ancestors linked to certain household groups, and that this Mississippian pattern reflects a significant change from earlier communal burial mounds placed at the outskirts of Woodland period villages.

Sullivan (1995) has compared and contrasted the plans of different Mississippian towns in eastern Tennessee: (1) fifteenth-century Dallas phase towns such as Toqua include mounds, courtyards, and paired seasonal residential structures often enclosed within wooden stockades; (2) sixteenth-century Mouse Creek phase towns such as Ledford Island are comparable in their delineation of communal and residential space but are not built around mounds; and (3) Overhill Cherokee towns show a much looser spatial structure than their predecessors but nevertheless include a clearly visible communal council house distinct from household pairs of winter lodges and summer houses. Sullivan (1987, 1995:119, 2001) notes the widespread associations of male burials with "public architecture" and female burials with "residential architecture," although there are some differences in the composition of grave clusters associated with these architectural spaces through time.

This patterning is especially clear at the neighboring archaeological sites representing the historic Overhill Cherokee towns of Chota and Tanasee in the lower Little Tennessee Valley (Schroedl 1986:203–204; Sullivan 1987:26–28, 1995:115–123). The majority of graves in household cemeteries are those of women and children. The graves within and beside the council house are those of men (see fig. 7.2).

An earlier form of this patterning is apparent at Toqua and other Mississippian sites in the upper Tennessee Valley (Hatch 1987:10–12; Polhemus 1987, 1990:128–132; G. Scott and Polhemus 1987; Sullivan 2001). The majority of burials close to and within the platform mounds at these sites were adult male graves (see Claassen 1997:70–71). Rather than reflecting male dominance within the chiefdoms centered at these and other mounds, this pattern may instead reflect the relationship between men and the specific kinds of power related to those architectural spaces within the cultural landscape. Concentrations of female graves in village spaces, on the other hand, may reflect their access to different kinds of power anchored to those architectural spaces within their communities.

Spatial arrangements of burials and buildings are archaeologically visible at the Warren Wilson and Coweeta Creek sites in the Appalachian Summit region of western North Carolina (Dickens 1978:123–131; Ward and Davis 1999:162–163, 184–186; H. Wilson 1986:61). Warren Wilson represents a fifteenth-century palisaded village along the Swannanoa River; houses and the surrounding stockade were rebuilt several times. Graves of old women are most commonly placed within household cemeteries, as at the King and Toqua sites. Graves placed in the ground between houses at Warren Wilson are commonly those of men who died as young adults during what was probably the prime of their lives, although there is not a communal building at the site. Coweeta Creek includes a protohistoric period communal council house and associated village and town plaza at the confluence of Coweeta Creek and the upper Little Tennessee River. Rodning (2001) has argued that most of the graves in the council house are the resting places of male town leaders, and that adult women tend to be buried in graves associated with what are probably clan buildings in the village (see fig. 7.3).

This trend may characterize archaeologically visible mortuary programs at other southern Appalachian sites. Rudolph (1984:43–44) hints at this gender distinction in the placement of graves in the platform mound at Beaverdam Creek in the upper Savannah Valley, although the pattern is not characteristic of burials associated with the earth lodge that preceded the fourteenth-century platform mound. Anderson (1994b:217–218) like-

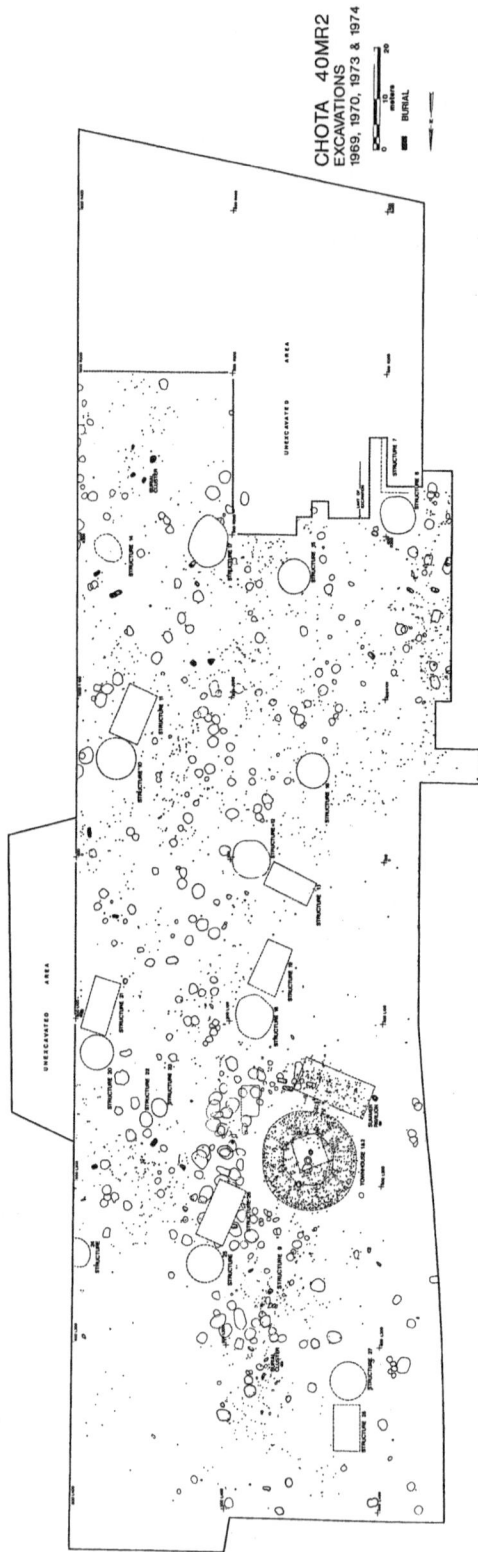

Fig. 7.2. Archaeological map of the Overhill Cherokee settlement at Chota-Tanasee, A.D. 1700–1800. From Schroedl 1986:36–37 (see also J. Chapman 1985:111 and Sullivan 1995:106).

CHOTA 40MR2
EXCAVATIONS
1969, 1970, 1973 & 1974

BURIAL

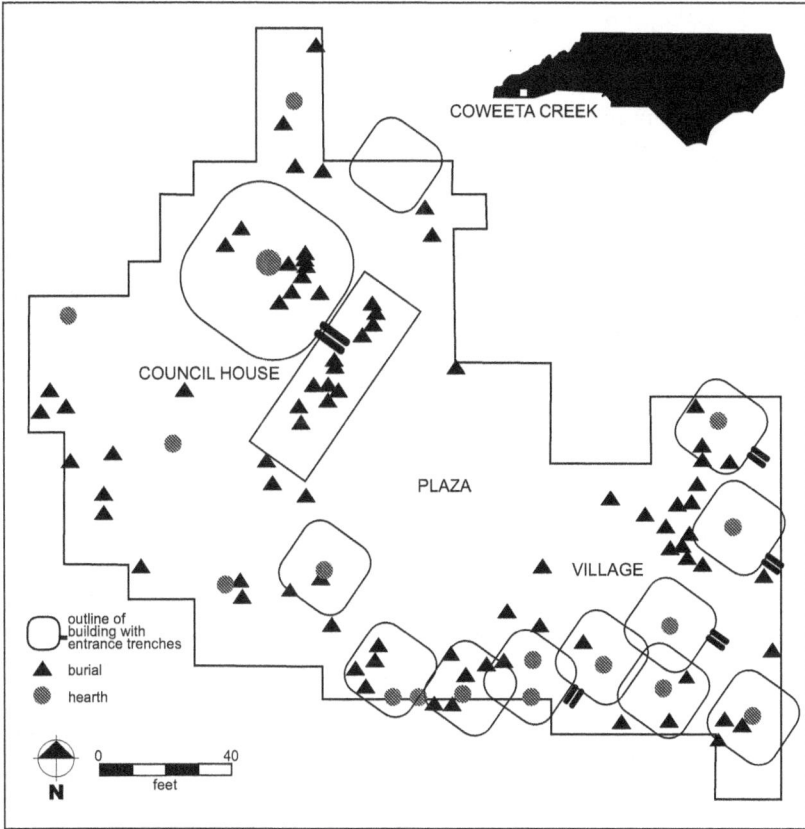

Fig. 7.3. Archaeological map of the Coweeta Creek site, A.D. 1600–1700. From Rodning 1996 (see also B. J. Egloff 1967:9 and K. T. Egloff 1971:44). Map courtesy of the University of North Carolina Research Laboratories of Archaeology, Chapel Hill.

wise hints at this kind of patterning at the I.C. Few site near the headwaters of the Savannah River, where burials in a fourteenth-century mound were primarily those of men and burials in the adjacent village were mostly adult women. Our suggestion from all this evidence is that gender distinctions in the spatial dimension of mortuary patterns have an ancient history in southern Appalachian cultures.

Our further argument is that these gender distinctions at death relate to comparable gender distinctions made during the lifetimes of native people, forming cultural traditions that persisted for several centuries in the greater southern Appalachian region. The consistency of the general spatial pattern outlined here at several southern Appalachian sites and the ethnohistoric evidence about gender ideologies in native societies of this region both support this conclusion.

Gender distinctions are thus a major dimension of the social identities that are communicated through mortuary ceremonialism at late pre-Columbian and early post–contact period sites in eastern Tennessee, northern Georgia, and western North Carolina. This phenomenon is most clearly visible at the archaeological site representing the historic Cherokee towns of Chota and Tanasee in the lower Little Tennessee Valley of eastern Tennessee. Historic accounts of eighteenth-century Cherokee culture also allow us to infer connections between observed, contemporary behavior with these archaeological patterns.

Architecture and Power in Southern Appalachian Chiefdoms

Our proposal is that the spatial relationships between different kinds of architecture and the graves of men and women reflect traditions of complementary gender domains within the social structure and cultural landscape of southern Appalachian chiefdoms. Many men were buried in association with council houses, which were sometimes built atop older mounds. Graves of women commonly were associated with buildings that likely served residential and other purposes, including housing the local members of certain matrilineages and clans, and the resting places of ancestral kin group leaders. These architectural forms represent the spaces associated with leaders of southern Appalachian towns on one hand, and kin groups on the other. People in southern Appalachian societies were members of both a matrilineal kin group and of one town or another. These different social entities within southern Appalachian communities were represented in the cultural landscape by different architectural forms.

Reconstructing the social dynamics and rituals centered at these landmarks can lead to an understanding of how town and kin group leaders negotiated their own power and status within southern Appalachian chiefdoms. Our vision of gender and power within southern Appalachian societies compares favorably with ideas about heterarchy—the presence of multiple hierarchies within communities (Brumfiel 1992:554–555, 1995:129–130; Crown and Fish 1996:811–812; Crumley 1979:157–165, 1987:163–165, 1995; Crumley and Marquardt 1987:612–615; Earle 1997:210–211; Levy 1995:46–49, 1999:74–75; Marquardt and Crumley 1987:11–12; S. M. Nelson 1999:188; Trocolli 1999:53). Gender identities within these societies connoted *differential* access to *different* kinds of power. Gender traditions empowered men to become town leaders and women to become leaders and lynchpins in the social fabric of their kin groups, creating dynamics that would have served to keep the power of the other in check.

Did men actively resist the traditional kin-based power of women by building council houses on or beside platform mounds, as refuges from architectural domains over which women presided? How did women resist the power of male warriors, hunters, and traders, who moved relatively freely across broad geographic and cultural provinces?

We think the answers to these and other questions about the diversity of Mississippian and protohistoric chiefdoms in eastern North America relate to the ways that men and women attached themselves to traditional gender groups and gender ideologies, and through which they actively negotiated the differences and common ground between them. We also think the role of gender as a structuring principle in Mississippian chiefdoms in other parts of eastern North America is worth exploring further, through studies of mortuary contexts and other facets of the abundant archaeological record. We suspect that a gendered tradition of complementary pathways to social status, prestige, and political influence within southern Appalachian societies is one significant social aspect that may differentiate them from more rigidly hierarchical chiefdoms elsewhere across the late pre-Columbian and postcontact Southeast.

Acknowledgements

Our thanks go to Tim Pauketat for the opportunity to contribute to this book and the symposium from which it originated. We appreciate his recommendations for our paper, as well as comments from Vin Steponaitis, Greg Wilson, Tiffiny Tung, Brian Billman, Bram Tucker, Steve Davis, Trawick Ward, David Moore, Tony Boudreaux, Celeste Gagnon, Jane Eastman, Cheryl Claassen, Nancy White, Michelle Schohn, Margie Scarry, Peter Whitridge, Elizabeth Driscoll, Mintcy Maxham, Amber VanDerwarker, Danny DeVries, and Carole Crumley. We also are grateful for feedback from anonymous reviewers and from the symposium discussants, Kathleen Deagan and Kent Lightfoot.

Notes

1. Gender identities are the ways that individuals relate to gendered expectations of their place within communities (Conkey and Spector 1984:15; Gilchrist

1994:8); people can follow, resist, and creatively bend these expectations in a variety of ways.

2. Gender ideologies are the meanings attached to the ways that members of different gender groups within a community relate to each other (Conkey and Spector 1984:15; Gilchrist 1994:8); these ideologies are closely related to structures of political power, economic power, and kinship networks.

3. Several archaeologists have argued convincingly that there is considerable cultural meaning embedded in the spatial arrangement of burials and more visible architectural monuments to the past at pre-Columbian and protohistoric localities in North America—whether rows or clusters of graves for clan or kin group members (Howell and Kintigh 1996:552; Mainfort 1985:558), clusters of graves associated with household architecture (Hally and Kelly 1998:58; Sullivan 1987:28), or placements of graves in or near courtyards and council houses or mounds (Beck 1995:183; Charles 1995:88; Goldstein 1995:114; Schroedl 1998:91; Sullivan 1995:119; Tainter 1978:134).

4. In his comparative study of chiefdoms in Hawaii, Peru, and Neolithic Denmark, archaeologist Timothy Earle (1997:174–182) has shown that whole landscapes can reflect the structure of hierarchical relationships within a chiefdom, especially through his description of the monuments, canals, and fields comprising the cultural landscape of chiefdoms in the Hawaiian Islands.

8

Historical Science or Silence?

Toward a Historical Anthropology of Mississippian Political Culture

Mark A. Rees

Many archaeologists would today probably agree that understanding chronology, historical variation, and context are prefatory steps in addressing problems of broader anthropological or scientific relevance. Building on earlier classificatory-historical foundations, archaeologists search for process, systems, or patterned variation with the ultimate goal of making comparative generalizations about the past (Willey and Sabloff 1980). Classified and all too neatly periodized as the culture historical approach, historical perspectives are regarded by some archaeologists as inadequate or unscientific (e.g., Leonard 1993). Yet history and social theory are complementary, comparative pursuits (Burke 1992:23). The untimely fall of culture history has been greatly exaggerated (cf. Lyman et al. 1997).

Anthropological explanation, and archaeology in particular, is historical (see Wolf 1982:21). Cultural traditions, the archaeological record, and the past itself are "historical precipitates," representations of human actions, events, and processes through time (Trigger 1991:559). Although the connection between process, human agency, and history was recognized long ago by political anthropologists (e.g., Bailey 1969; Swartz 1958, 1968; Swartz et al. 1966a:8; 1966b), decades of disagreement have seemingly hardened the rift between science and history in archaeology. The prospect of archaeology as a comparative historical science may at first glance, then, seem contradictory.

Historical perspectives are not easily reducible to caricatures of culture history, regardless of periodizations that portray the history of archaeology as the triumph of a modern, scientific approach. In contrast, the rapprochement of archaeology and historical anthropology holds considerable promise in contributing to a comparative, historical science (Light-foot 1995). The theoretical groundwork for such an approach is already being laid, based on the realization that both history and historical production are permeated by social relations of authority (Trouillot 1995:28–29). An anthropological critique of history reveals the distribution of power to be an intrinsic part of this process (Burke 1992:75–79; Wolf 1990, 1999).

The connection between history and authority ensures that the production of history is not simply a matter of assembling chronologies or sequences of facts. Archaeology as a historical science is not reduced to a narrative of events (Pauketat, this volume). Archaeologists can instead strive to discover the ways in which cultural traditions and identities were politically engaged and transformed through practice. These transformations constitute a *historical process,* challenging and making previous anthropological concepts such as tradition, culture, and culture change problematic (Ohnuki-Tierney 1990:6–18; Pauketat, this volume; Wolf 1984:396). Failure to account for the pre-Columbian, Native American past in terms of historical process disregards the agents of historical production and effectively segregates the past, silencing the histories of the inarticulate as "prehistoric" (Trouillot 1995:26).

In order to shed light on the misappropriation and polarization of science and history, I begin with a brief reexamination of changing archaeological perspectives. The relevance of anthropology in the production of history is then considered, with the goal of forwarding archaeology as a historical science. Lastly, the connection between tradition and authority is examined, encompassing practices that were simultaneously political and symbolic. The Mississippian Southeast provides the backdrop for understanding how the crafting of cultural traditions was interrelated with the production of identity and authority, what can be referred to as political culture. The development and decline of regional polities in southeastern North America can be understood in terms of this historical process, as demonstrated through a contextual analysis of engraved ceramics and effigy vessels. A historical anthropology of Mississippian political culture underscores the importance of archaeology as a comparative, historical science.

Archaeology Confronts History

The estrangement of history and science in archaeology was due not merely to the ascendance of neoevolutionary anthropology, but to the perceived inadequacy of culture history as an explanatory framework (e.g., Binford 1962, 1968b). Kluckhohn (1940:50) regarded the "flashes of intuition" of historians as inferior to the "inductive generalizations of science," influencing Taylor's indictment of the culture historical approach. Taylor (1948:202) provided further impetus for the divergence of history and science in American archaeology, suggesting that history was limited to the construction of cultural contexts, while anthropology was the comparative study of culture. According to Taylor, archaeologists should aspire beyond data collection, description, and chronology, the subject matter of ethnography and historiography. If an anthropological archaeology was to be attained, archaeologists should follow the example of cultural anthropologists and study "the nature of culture and cultural dynamics" (Taylor 1948:202).

In defining history as "mere scissors-and-paste chronicle," the potential for archaeology as a comparative, historical science was overlooked (Hudson 1973:112; Trigger 1989a:373–379). Ironically, it was this objective notion of historical facts that had been regarded by some historians as the scientific study of the past (Carr 1961:5–6). Historians who objected to this view on epistemological grounds nevertheless hoped to broaden the scope of history as the "science of men in time" (Bloch 1953:47; cf. Berlin 1961). While Taylor's portrayal of history was overly restrictive, a later generation of archaeologists rejected historical perspectives as fundamentally ideographic, particularistic, and unscientific (e.g., Binford 1968b; Flannery 1967; Longacre 1964).

From the standpoint of cultural process, it was thought by many that "historical causality is important only in that it has to be eliminated from the equation" (Willey and Phillips 1958:71). In its more extreme, positivist renderings, advocates of the New Archaeology attributed causality and cultural process to "genuine" science, seemingly uninterested in the potential for investigating culture as a *historical* process (Binford 1965; Flannery 1973; Watson et al. 1971). Cultural evolution became the paradigm for nonhistorical, ecological functionalism. Further influenced by systems theory, many archaeologists adhered to a belief that the "relative simplicity of primitive societies" could be objectively studied as cultural systems, without the "guesswork" demanded of history or humanistic disciplines (H. Muller 1943:209).

The segregation of science from history resulted in the further isolation of archaeological theory from a historically relevant anthropology, an additional irony, considering the earlier goals of the New Archaeology to be socially relevant (Flannery 1973). The "marginalization of history" entailed the search for systemic processes within the comparative generalizations of neoevolutionary anthropology, unhindered by "messy" details or native perspectives (Hodgen 1974; Thomas 1989:9–11; Trigger 1989a:312–319, 1989b). While perceived antagonisms between cultural process and historical particularism produced simplistic caricatures that could be easily criticized and dismissed, the postprocessual reaction to the New Archaeology initially contributed little to the rapprochement of archaeological science and history (McGuire 1992:145–177). The incongruity of science and history was sustained, institutionalized in the development of historical archaeology as a distinct and separate subfield. Earlier argument over whether historical archaeology was to be anthropological or the "handmaiden" of history reflected the general tenor of the debate (e.g., articles in Schuyler 1978).

Following Hodder's (1982b, 1985) earlier, more programmatic statements, there has emerged an increased appreciation for the multifaceted, cumulative nature of archaeological research (e.g., Preucel 1991, 1995; VanPool and VanPool 1999). Yet an antihistorical bias persists, despite the advancement of historical approaches in anthropology and concessions by advocates of processualism (e.g., Spencer 1997; Yoffee 1993). The stoic march toward "true science" and misappropriation of history is most conspicuous in the neo-Darwinian or selectionist school of evolutionary archaeology (see Barton and Clark 1997; Dunnell 1980, 1989; Maschner 1996; O'Brien et al., 1998). Historical variation from this perspective refers to artifact replacement instead of human agency, fitness and selection instead of political dynamics or social interactions. Nondirectional, evolutionary archaeology is based largely on inappropriate biological analogies (O'Brien and Holland 1990:32–35). History *is* directional and cumulative, however, but not merely in an evolutionary sense (Gould 1996:220–224).

During the past decade, historical archaeologists have advanced the study of political dynamics, political economy, and social identity in colonial and pluralistic contexts (e.g., Deagan 1990; Ferguson 1992; Orser 1996; Ruhl and Hoffman 1997). Pre-Columbian Native America is nonetheless viewed through the lens of European contact as both a cultural and biological watershed (e.g., Dunnell 1991; Ramenofsky 1990). The application of historical sources and perspectives has consequently remained largely incidental, limited primarily to analogies (Feinman 1997; Galloway 1993; Lightfoot 1995). Lightfoot (1995:204) points out that archaeologists have tended to partition off the Native American past from the

historical archaeology of European colonialism. This is even more problematic in terms of protohistoric research, due to the long interval between
initial European exploration and more substantial documentation (e.g., J.
A. Brown 1990:2; Hudson and Tesser 1994). In calling for "an integrated
approach to prehistory and history," Lightfoot (1995:211) argues against
the production of this segregated past.

The false dichotomy between science and history need not enervate
archaeological practice (Feinman 1997:374; Trigger 1989a:372–379,
1989b:19). As Peebles (1991:113) notes, in order to expand on our understanding of the past, "it is important to remove the stigma applied to
history by some archaeologists." Yet the common ground between archaeology and history has only gradually been recognized as a productive field
of inquiry. Deetz (1977) and Leone (1984) were among those who presented anthropological critiques of history, in which archaeology was
brought to bear on historiography. Reviewing Taylor's A Study of Archeology, Deetz (1983, 1988) suggested that history is not at odds with archaeology, but that both can be combined in a comparative, humanistic
science. Leone (1986) demonstrated that historical archaeologists are not
confined to writing narrative histories but can pursue a critical reexamination of social relations of production, structure, and ideology (cf. Paynter
and McGuire 1991). Historical archaeologists are not unique in being able
to "do" both history and anthropology, or in pursuing an interdisciplinary, historical science (Mrozowski 1988).

Hodder (1987) was an early advocate of archaeology as "long-term
history." Hodder (1986:77–102, 118–146) argued for a contextual approach, concerned largely with the interpretation of recursive meanings,
as represented by the "inside of the event" and its connection to long-term
structural constraints. Archaeology from this perspective emphasizes particular historical contexts and meaningful actions, in which self-knowl-
edge is a central goal (Hodder 1986:77–102; 1987:2). It is no surprise
then, that this interpretivist epistemology raised such an outcry among
those interested in making archaeology a cultural science. Hodder (1991,
1999) subsequently modified his interpretive approach as grounded in
material culture and a reflexive, critical discourse (cf. Shanks and Hodder
1995). Yet archaeologists need not resolve the debate between interpretivist and realist (or constructionist and positivist) philosophies of history
(e.g., Hobart 1989; Nowell-Smith 1977). Instead, we should begin to redress the disconnect between historical anthropology and archaeological
practice.

Anthropology and the Production of History

Since the 1980s, history has emerged as a major focus of anthropological research (e.g., Comaroff 1982; Ohnuki-Tierney 1990; Sahlins 1985; Wolf 1982). Historians have meanwhile sought to incorporate anthropological and comparative social theory in their explanations of the past (e.g., Burke 1990a, 1992, 1997; W. A. Green 1993). The resurgence of historical perspectives in anthropology has in turn revitalized ingrained anthropological constructs such as culture and tradition (Faubion 1993:40–44; Sahlins 1985:72). The development of ethnohistory was prominent early on in this interdisciplinary discourse in which archaeologists were to play a major role (Brain et al. 1974; Cohn 1968; Galloway 1993; Sturtevant 1966; Trigger 1982, 1986). It has become apparent however, that relegating non-Western, indigenous pasts to "ethnic histories" tends to reinforce many of the earlier theoretical contradictions (Ohnuki-Tierney 1990). For an increasing number of scholars, the question is no longer whether anthropology should be historical, but what sort of histories it should produce.

Historical anthropologists have been influenced to varying degrees by Annales, beginning with the works of Lucien Febvre and Marc Bloch, and the founding of the journal *Annales d'Histoire Economique et Sociale*. Popularized through the seminal works of Braudel (e.g., 1972, 1981), *Annaliste* scholars advocated a comparative, interdisciplinary approach to the underlying geographic, social, and ideological milieu of the past. Annales also encompasses a wide range of studies concerning historical consciousness and cultural production (*mentalité*), human agency and political economy, and an ongoing critique of political histories and events (Burke 1990b, 1992:14–21, 1997; Stoianovich 1976).

In contrast to the "history of events" (*l' histoire événementielle*), Braudel (1972:20–21, 1980:25–52) viewed long-term geographic and environmental trends (*la longue durée*), medium-term social and economic factors (*conjuncture*), and short-term events as interrelated cycles in which the *longue durée* represented unequivocal continuity and constraint. Following Febvre and Bloch, Braudel (1972:21, 1980:11) was critical of traditional narrative history that chronicled the actions and misfortunes of "great men." It is this notion of history as the objective assembling of facts, forwarded by Leopold von Ranke during the nineteenth century as "scientific historiography," that some archaeologists continue to criticize as overly idiographic and particularistic (Breisach 1983:234; e.g., Leonard 1993:33). In contrast, Braudel (1980:50, 205–

206) argued that the underlying structures of the *longue durée* provided a productive link between history, anthropology, and science. Braudel's structural history found a widespread audience in the social sciences (see Frank 1995), to the extent that a unified Annales school is often misconstrued from his work. Following Hodder (1987), Annales has drawn only sporadic interest among archaeologists. A major emphasis has been placed on the relevance of Braudel's historical structures to archaeological explanation (e.g., articles in Bintliff 1991b and in Knapp 1992). Braudel has in turn been criticized for overemphasizing long-term geographic and environmental influences to the exclusion of human agency and consciousness (Bintliff 1991a; Last 1995:142–143). Yet he maintained that the various structures of history were interdependent, to be combined and contrasted as a heuristic (Braudel 1980:48).

Braudel (1980:91) also addressed recurrent demographic, economic, and political trends, what has been called "serial history" (Burke 1992:34). He examined the connections between changes in population, foodways, material culture, technology, and urban development during the centuries of European global exploration. In comparison to his companion studies of capitalism and the world economy, Braudel (1981) demonstrated how the innumerable variables and constraints of everyday life (*"les structures du quotidien"*) could be brought together and juxtaposed over the *longue durée*. He correlated the production of maize in Mesoamerica (and other staple crops elsewhere in the world) with political development and decline in which the *historical* circumstances of certain crops proved to be a decisive yet contingent factor (Braudel 1981:161, 172–174). Braudel (1981:333) argued that stylistic changes in architecture and clothing, the "realities of material life," should similarly be understood in the context of previous customs and conventions. Technological innovation and changes in craft production were just as easily constrained as facilitated by preexisting practices (Braudel 1981:432). In short, the material necessities of everyday life are not simply the causes of change, but represent a historical process of innovation, accommodation, and resistance.

For archaeologists, the relevance of Annales lies not merely in a rapprochement between history and science (or structure and process), but also in coming to terms with the ambiguities involved in "making history" (Blok 1992). Trouillot (1995:24) refers to this as the "two sides of historicity": the process of historical production in the first instance, and the practice of historical representation in the second. History in both instances articulates with power through representations of authority and authenticity (LeGoff 1992:182–184, 201; Trouillot 1995:28–29; Wolf 1999). Simply put, it is the distinction between history as past experience, and history as a process of coming to know the past. Before examining the former, it is worthwhile to consider how the dismissal of historical representation impacts archaeology as a historical science.

As a practical engagement beyond academia, history involves the production of narratives concerning past social existence. Such discourse occurs within the context of present social realities and often crosscuts, reaffirms, or resists the reinterpretation of political and ethnic identities. In fact, it has long been recognized that the ability to interpret history entails power, and that the power of historical representation appears, at times, indisputable (Comaroff and Comaroff 1991:13–32; Wolf 1990:590). These "alternative histories" are negotiated in the context of everyday life through political-symbolic actions (Kertzer 1988:181–182, 1996:84–122; Schmidt and Patterson 1995; Wylie 1995). A central problem for archaeology is how it will participate in the ongoing production of Native American histories (Trigger 1980, 1989b). History in these terms is a collective or contested transaction, in that "how history works" is more relevant to the people involved (Trouillot 1995:25).

As Trouillot (1995) points out, the making of history also involves the production of silences through omission and ambiguity, an issue even more pertinent to archaeologists. Silence enters into historical production at various intervals, most tangibly in the creation of sources (Trouillot 1995:26). Given the virtual absence of written documents in pre-Columbian contexts, disregard for historicity and promotion of an evolutionary science (in implicit or explicit opposition to history) has been particularly effective in the extension of silences. "Prehistory" in such instances is not merely an absence of textual sources or omission of *l' histoire événementielle,* but the negation of historical consciousness and all "retrospective significance" (Trouillot 1995:26).

Such representations of the past also enter into historical narratives received with the authenticity (or disrepute) of Western science (Schmidt and Patterson 1995:10–11). The repercussion for archaeology is that it risks being irrelevant to the people who might benefit most from its body of knowledge (Trigger 1980). Worse still, it contributes to the obsolescence of past indigenous experience in collective representations of American history (e.g., McGuire 1994:180–181). Comaroff and Comaroff (1991:17) make a similar point in their study of colonialism and the politics of conversion in South Africa, in that anthropologists (and archaeologists, in particular) must come to terms with "the importance of treating the writing of histories as a generic mode of making both the past and the present." Archaeology as a historical science can address this process of representation through an internal and external critique of power (LeGoff 1992:179–216).

The second dimension of historicity refers to the "participatory process" of cultural construction (Pauketat, this volume; Trouillot 1995:24). Sahlins (1981:8) has similarly argued that the goal of historical anthropology is "not merely to know how events are ordered by culture, but how, in that process, the culture is reordered." This involves socially negotiated practices that have been characterized in less critical terms as "cultural traditions"—what might instead be understood in terms of political culture. Political culture as used here combines a concern for power as multiple overlapping and interdependent social relations (Wolf 1999:4–5), with everyday practices, symbolic actions, and the negotiation of ideological legitimacy (e.g., Cohen 1974; Earle 1997; Gellner 1988). Wolf (1990:586–587, 590) in particular, argued that a historical perspective calls for a comparative study of the unfolding relationships between structure and agency, what he referred to as structural power, strategic (or organizational) power, and social action.

Political, economic, and ideological sources of power are "intertwined and interdependent" not only in terms of the development and decline of regional polities (Earle 1997:207), but in the practical enactment of traditions. Political culture is consequently not wholly dependent on social stratification or on an economic surplus, nor should it be conflated with political socialization (Burke 1992:77; cf. Earle 1997:206). The intersection of political economy, ideology, and human agency in political culture emphasizes a range of collective actions and social relations of authority, rather than structural or systemic determination (Ortner 1984; Roseberry 1988). Recognition of the indeterminacies in social interaction requires that the simultaneously ideological and material dimensions of power be considered relationally, as part of a historical process (Wolf 1999:66–67). Archaeology as a historical science should account for contrasting trajectories of political culture as both the deliberate and "unintended consequences of human interaction" (Blok 1992:121).

Political culture as a historical process pertains to the abilities of certain individuals and groups to orchestrate social relations of production through representations of authority and ideological legitimacy. This includes compliance with certain social relations and practices, as well as the usurpation of historical consciousness, the "invention of tradition" through political-symbolic actions, factional competition, coercion, and resistance (Hobsbawm and Ranger 1983). Yet none of these practices should be regarded as determinative structures. Factional competition may either be heightened by, or ultimately contribute to, coalition building (Brumfiel 1989, 1994). Coercion is similarly related to ideological legitimacy and the creation of legitimate authority. Resistance may involve outright rebellion or take on everyday "silent" forms such as "foot dragging" or inadequate compliance (J. C. Scott 1985:29, 1990). These are "performative structures," or practices and traditions that constitute the cultural production of history (Sahlins 1985:26–31; Wolf 1990, 1999:290).

The uneven or open-ended nature of this historical process shifts the focus of attention from culture as a normative construct to social heterogeneity, as involving both hierarchical and heterarchical inequalities (Blau 1977:77; Wolf 1999:289). Heterarchy refers to social relations that are not intrinsically ranked but linked by variable distributions of authority and meaning (Brumfiel 1995; Hannerz 1992). Crumley (1995:3) thus refers to heterarchy as "unranked" yet potentially "counterpoised" social relations. Consideration of heterogeneity calls into question "layer-cake" models of cultural evolution and complexity, suggesting instead that historical production involves contested views of structural power and a wide range of opportunities for compliance, accommodation, coercion, and resistance (McGuire 1983:99–100; McGuire and Saitta 1996:200–201). Like political culture, heterogeneity in itself does not explain the development and decline of regional polities. It instead focuses the anthropological lens on a range of political-symbolic actions and consequences, in essence historical and processual questions: how a political culture was consolidated, held together, or overcome.

Political Authority and Tradition

The historical connections between authority and tradition are central to an understanding of regional political development and decline. This is increasingly apparent in the archaeology of southeastern North America, where a culture historical approach has already contributed to explanations of Mississippian political dynamics as a historical process (Barker and Pauketat 1992a:3; cf. Dunnell 1990). One avenue of investigation explored in detail by Anderson (1990 ,1994a, 1994b) focuses on factional competition within sociopolitical hierarchies, and the seemingly episodic recurrence of regional centralization. Another, more theoretically diverse approach has dealt with the political-religious symbolism of Mississippian societies and the relationship between power, agency, and tradition in social relations of production (e.g., Emerson 1997a, 1997b; Knight 1986, 1989b, 1998; Pauketat 1992, 1994, 1998b; Pauketat and Emerson 1991, 1997b). What these perspectives share is a critical reevaluation of Mississippian culture as a series of historically related, politically integrated societies. An investigation of political culture is facilitated by combining elements of both approaches, recognizing that factionalism was only one potential component in a range of political-symbolic actions that contributed to political consolidation, regional centralization, decentralization, and decline.

Building on earlier critiques of sociopolitical evolution and ecofunctionalist anthropology, regional polities are thought to have been fraught with conflicts and political instabilities, resulting in cyclical developmental trajectories (Anderson 1994b; Friedman and Rowlands 1978:213). Drawing on a wide range of evidence from the Savannah River Valley, Anderson (1994b) describes cycling as fluctuating levels of political-administrative complexity. His analysis is based on structural distinctions between simple and complex chiefdoms (cf. Steponaitis 1978:420; Wright 1977:381, 1984:43). Defined by "changes in administrative levels in the chiefdom," political cycling involved "shifting power relations" between rival interest groups or elites, the "fragmentation of complex chiefdoms," subsequent reestablishment of political control at another regional center, and formation of a new simple or complex chiefdom (Anderson 1994b: 48–50). While the causes of cycling are described as interrelated and widespread, Anderson (1994b:12, 49) concludes that factional competition or "competition for prestige and power between rival elites" was ultimately "what initiates and drives cycling in chiefdom societies." According to Anderson (1994b:50), "the process is cyclical because this very pattern of competition precludes the development of stable organizational structures capable of maintaining a two-level decision-making hierarchy indefinitely."

Applied more broadly throughout the Mississippian Southeast, Anderson's research calls into question the unit of analysis, or the sociopolitical structures (simple and complex chiefdoms) that are described as cyclical. It also undermines the underlying mechanisms of factional competition. Historical production is situated in the hands of a few elite, yet factionalism is regarded as inevitable, even structurally determined. This Machiavellian view of self-aggrandizement and interest-group politics underestimates the pervasiveness of ideological compliance, as well as the potential for coercion and resistance (Brumfiel 1989, 1994; Bujra 1973; Pohl and

Pohl 1994). Repetitive, cyclical structures do not account for political-symbolic practices on the local level, or for the divergent trajectories of regional polities (Blitz 1999). The histories and traditions of disparate and often geographically distant regions are conflated in order to portray the development and decline of Mississippian polities as inherently cyclical. Authority and tradition must be approached as a cumulative process, in "historical time" (Swartz et al. 1966a:8).

Portrayal of factionalism as an intrinsic characteristic of chiefdoms misconstrues history in terms of a particular sociopolitical type and does not explain how or why some regional polities experienced a more rapid development or protracted decline (e.g., Knight 1997; Steponaitis 1991). Brumfiel (1994:4) defines factions as "structurally and functionally similar groups which, by virtue of their similarity, compete for resources and positions of power or prestige" (cf. Bujra 1973:136). As Brumfiel (1994:12) notes however, factionalism should not be regarded as a determinative, historical structure: "Although factional competition provides a common impetus to political development, any particular sequence of development is uniquely complex and contingent." Since factionalism presented opportunities for political consolidation, as well as constraints to regional centralization, it is merely one "informal" aspect of a historical process (Bujra 1973:132). From this perspective, the encompassing field of political-symbolic actions also entailed the building of coalitions through the negotiation (or inventing) of traditions.

The historical trajectories of regional polities in the Mississippian Southeast unfolded in a series of political-symbolic negotiations, everyday practices, and interactions. Through a comparative analysis of regional political culture, attention can focus on understanding this multiscalar historical process, without reifying the contradiction between structural determination and stochastic events. As a dialectic of authority and tradition, this involved the "practical realization of the cultural categories in a specific historical context" (Sahlins 1985:xiv). Representations of authority were a pervasive aspect of cultural traditions, including the ways in which ostensibly mundane practices were implicated in transforming a social order and, in the process, were transformed (Giddens 1984:14–28, 162–206). Mississippian traditions entailed a wide range of negotiations, from compliance and accommodation to coercion and resistance (see Alt, this volume).

Authority and identity were negotiated through the enactment of traditions, in social relations of production, so-called utilitarian objects, crafted items, the social landscape, and built environment. Of particular interest are those representations of authority manifested in the abstract symbolism of ceramic traditions (Knight 1986, 1989b; Pauketat 1997b; Pauketat and Emerson 1991). Stylistic variation and iconographic representation in craft goods are accessible to archaeologists as indicators of authority and identity (Costin 1998; Earle 1990; Sassaman 1998a; Spielmann 1998). Style and tradition are in this sense not simply passive or functional, but active and historical (Conkey 1990; Dietler and Herbich 1998; Hegmon 1998; Sackett 1990). In the remainder of this chapter I examine the implications of this historical process through a comparative analysis of noncontemporaneous political dynamics in two different regions, the Black Warrior and central Mississippi Valleys. The production and distribution of engraved iconography and ceramic effigies serve as a useful point of departure for understanding the development and decline of Mississippian political culture.

Winged Serpents and Fish Effigies

It is apropos to contrast the historical trajectories of Mississippian political culture in the Black Warrior and central Mississippi Valleys (see Pauketat, this volume, fig. 1.1), as at one time it was thought that an eastward migration from a Mississippian heartland had resulted in more direct historical connections (B. D. Smith 1984). Since the expeditions of C. B. Moore, among the most intriguing aspects of Mississippian symbolism has been the representational art in ceramics, interpreted as exemplifying a southern cult, Southeastern Ceremonial Complex, and sacra or "iconic family" (Knight 1986:677; Waring and Holder 1945). The Moundville site in particular has been studied extensively, making it one of the most well-known regionally centralized polities in the Southeast. Moundville has consequently served as a comparative example for contrasting political development in other regions, whether or not more direct historical relationships have been inferred (e.g., Knight 1997; Peebles 1987; Steponaitis 1991).

Greater chronological and spatial definition of the Moundville phase as originally defined by McKenzie (1964, 1966) has been accompanied by a more precise understanding of the regional political dynamics involved in its development and decline (Peebles and Kus 1977; C. M. Scarry 1993a; C. M. Scarry and Steponaitis 1997; Steponaitis 1983, 1991; Welch 1991, 1996). While less work has been conducted at outlying mound sites and farmsteads, research during the past decade has led to the further refinement of a regional chronology (Knight and Steponaitis 1998; C. M. Scarry 1995; Steponaitis 1998; Welch 1998).

Knight and Steponaitis (1998) present a detailed political history of Moundville based on a reinterpretation of ceramic refuse, burials, and recent investigations of mound construction (see also Steponaitis 1998). The construction of Moundville as a highly formalized political-administrative center was relatively rapid, during the late Moundville I phase (Knight and Steponaitis 1998:14–17; cf. Peebles 1987). Within the first few decades of the thirteenth century, the mounds and plaza at the ceremonial center were part of a transformed social landscape or "sociogram" that reflected the legitimate authority of an elite-mediated political culture (Knight 1998:47–53; Knight and Steponaitis 1998:17). Elite authority was manifested in public and domestic architecture, mortuary differentiation, political symbolism or prestige goods, and differential access to foods, as in the mobilization of tribute (Peebles and Kus 1977; Welch 1991; Welch and Scarry 1995). This was paralleled by regional political consolidation, as indicated by mound construction at four secondary centers (Knight and Steponaitis 1998:16; Rees 1998; Welch 1998:150–155).

The distinctive authority of Moundville's elite was perhaps made most obvious and abstruse through the engraving of pottery. As containers for serving food, making mortuary offerings, or presenting tribute, pottery vessels were at the center of ritual transactions that legitimized and enacted an elite-inspired social order (Pauketat and Emerson 1991; Welch and Scarry 1995:410–413). The exteriors of burnished vessels were engraved with geometric, zoomorphic, and anthropomorphic motifs (Steponaitis 1983:58–63, 129). Among the more striking yet common examples of this representational art is the winged-serpent motif on Moundville Engraved (*variety Hemphill*) vessels, what Knight (1989a: 209) has referred to as the "*deliberately* obscure symbolism" of Mississippian monsters (see fig. 8.1). Although the specific meanings are lost, the esoteric knowledge associated with the production and distribution of such abstract iconography may have been tied to claims of supernatural authority (Helms 1979:70–108). Pauketat and Emerson (1991) describe a similar process for the polity of Cahokia, in which an elite-mediated cosmological order was symbolized and disseminated through Ramey Incised vessels.

Most of the engraved, iconographic pottery from Moundville postdates a period of political consolidation (A.D. 1200–1300), when the ceremonial center was sparsely inhabited and at least seven outlying mound sites were

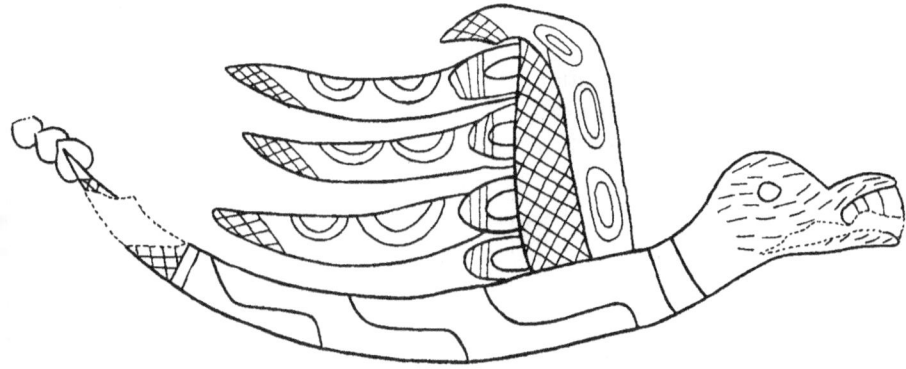

Fig. 8.1. Winged-serpent motif on a Moundville engraved bottle. From Moore 1907:372.

being constructed as far as thirty-five kilometers away (Knight and Steponaitis 1998:20; Steponaitis 1983:129; Welch 1998:163–164). Resistance to the authority imposed at Moundville may have increased during the next century and a half (ca. A.D. 1300–1450), hence the need to continually reinforce the social order through the abstract political symbolism of cosmological referents. Attempts by an elite to sustain their authority at greater distances from the center might have resulted in the heightened embellishment and distribution of engraved iconography, what Knight (1986:682) describes as the "communalization" of chiefly symbolism (Knight 1997:240; Knight and Steponaitis 1998:17–21). Despite injunctions of supernatural authority, increased factional conflicts and resistance within a decentralized polity appear to have contributed to the ultimate decline of regional political culture by the mid–sixteenth century (Rees 1999).

In contrast to Moundville, considerably less is known about the Nodena phase in the central Mississippi Valley, due in some measure to the piecemeal destruction and widespread looting of sites. Furthermore, there have been fewer systematic studies of well-provenienced artifacts, monumental architecture, craft goods distribution, and subsistence remains in specifiable archaeological contexts. With only the most cursory data on site occupation, there is relatively less information with which to construct a more precise regional chronology.

D. Morse (1990:76–83) has stated that the Nodena phase dates from approximately A.D. 1400 to 1650, and has suggested three principal site clusters (cf. Mainfort 1996). Many of these sites are single-component late Mississippian, suggesting a dramatic change in regional settlement. In fact, D. Morse and Morse (1983:280–284, 1996:128) attribute the Nodena phase to a migration of people into the eastern lowlands and subsequent demographic nucleation at around A.D. 1400. Many of these sites had one or more earthen platform mounds and were enclosed by a palisade (D. Morse 1989, 1990). Combined with the relative lack of ar-chaeological data, overlap between ceramic type frequencies used to de-fine the various phases has called into question the usefulness of the phase concept, and whether Nodena even represents a regional polity (see Fox 1998; O'Brien 1994:352–365; cf. P. Phillips 1970:930–935).

Without more detailed information on individual sites, settlement pat-terns, monumental architecture, and mound construction and use epi-sodes, it is difficult to distinguish a political history of the Nodena phase from broader stylistic and demographic trends. Present knowledge of the Nodena phase has benefited enormously, however, from the availability of narratives of the mid-sixteenth-century de Soto expedition (e.g., Dye 1994; Hudson 1997:284–303; D. Morse and Morse 1990). Whether or not the Nodena phase is recognized as the province of Pacaha, the narra-tives reference a series of unique historical events among regional polities in the central Mississippi Valley. Factional conflicts and warfare character-ized a highly contested political culture that, by A.D. 1541 at least, had not led to regional integration or lasting political consolidation (Dye 1990, 1995).

The spatial distribution of sites in the central Mississippi Valley indi-cates that political-administrative hierarchies had in places emerged (e.g., P. Morse 1981, 1990). Nonetheless, the numerous clusters of mound and village sites throughout the eastern lowlands contrasts starkly with the smaller, geographically isolated settlement hierarchy of Moundville. In comparison to the 40–55 kilometer stretch of floodplain thought to have comprised the Moundville polity at its height, at least four different poli-ties in the eastern lowlands are thought to have extended over more than 200 km of the much broader central Mississippi Valley (Hudson 1997: 271–309; Steponaitis 1978; Welch 1998:134). Lack of unambiguous evi-dence for a single ceremonial center with unrivaled monumental architec-ture attests to the factional conflicts and interpolity warfare described in the provinces of Casqui and Pacaha (e.g., Gentleman from Elvas 1993: 113–120). By introducing contagious Old World diseases, the de Soto expedition may have in fact truncated the political integration of regional polities, a historically unprecedented yet seemingly recurrent event with far-reaching demographic consequences.

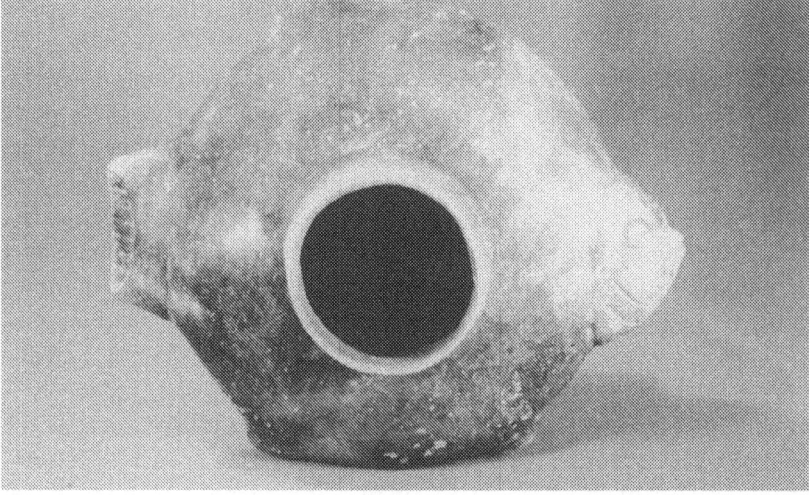

Fig. 8.2. Fish effigy vessel from the Campbell site. Courtesy of the Center for Archaeological Research, Southwest Missouri State University.

Although functional and stylistic similarities between the ceramics of Nodena and Moundville have long been noted (e.g., Holmes 1903:80–101; P. Phillips et al. 1951:127–129), it is through contrasting representational themes that distinct differences begin to emerge. The pottery most comparable to Moundville Engraved at Nodena phase sites is Walls Engraved (*variety Walls*). However, there is little stylistic similarity in representational motifs (Dye 1998:84; P. Phillips and Brown 1978:198–202; Rands 1956).

Abstract (supranatural) zoomorphic and anthropomorphic iconography is relatively uncommon on Walls Engraved vessels, which were usually decorated with geometric bands and scrolls (Dye 1998:83, 95–97; P. Phillips et al. 1951:127–129). This may be due in part to the lack of a representative sample of Walls Engraved sherds and vessels, although Moore (1908:483) also noted the relative scarcity of burnished, engraved pottery in comparison to collections from Moundville. Zoomorphic and anthropomorphic representation in the form of effigy vessels are in contrast well-known for Nodena phase sites. Among the most common of all motifs are fish, frog, and bird (Chapman and Anderson 1955:46–48; D. Morse 1989:108, 1990:90; P. Phillips et al. 1951:162–163; Price and Price 1980:36–40). Fish effigies comprise by far the largest percentage of effigy forms at sites associated with the Nodena phase (see fig. 8.2). Animal effigies such as fish were often crafted in sufficiently naturalistic form to allow for the identification of species (Mainfort and Carroll 1996). The significance of fish as political currency and symbolic offerings of food is indirectly suggested in the de Soto narratives (Rees 1997:116–118).

The contrast between the supranatural, "*deliberately* obscure symbolism" of Moundville Engraved iconography, as seen in the winged-serpent motif, and naturalistic representation of animal effigies should not be lost on account of geographic differences (Knight 1989a:209). Nor should it be attributed to ecological variations or the selective fitness of design elements. P. Phillips and Brown (1978:202) suggested that there may be a "temporal" reason for stylistic differences in engraved representations, which can more precisely be referred to as a historical explanation.

Walls Engraved vessels were generally produced later than Moundville Engraved, from the late fourteenth to seventeenth centuries, and incorporated some aspects of a Mississippian chiefly cosmology, such as the winged-serpent motif (Dye 1998:98; P. Phillips and Brown 1978:199–201). A variety of effigy vessels have in turn been found at Moundville, yet fish and frog motifs postdate the production of most engraved iconography, probably after A.D. 1400 (Steponaitis 1983:125, 131). The people who crafted pottery in the Black Warrior and central Mississippi Valleys were thus to some extent aware of both representational themes yet made deliberate choices subsequently reflected in different ceramic traditions.

Broad similarities between the ceramic traditions of these regions have been described in terms of macroregional, historical connections. Yet this stylistic variation can be fully explained only through a historical explanation that takes into account the crafting of authority and tradition in the context of regional political culture. While the esoteric knowledge and authority of Moundville's elite were ultimately embodied through supranatural, cosmological referents, such representations of authority would have been largely ineffective or openly contested in the central Mississippi Valley. The communalization of such abstract referents might have similarly been resisted. Among polities in the central Mississippi Valley, factional conflicts, warfare, and coercion were associated with less orthodox symbolism, with meanings that could be readily appropriated and imposed as a form of political currency. In both instances, the crafting of pottery vessels was a seemingly mundane practice that acknowledged a legitimate authority. Yet within these regional political cultures, quite different political histories emerge.

Conclusion

The contrasting historical trajectories of Mississippian polities do not eas-ily conform to the "stepladder" of sociopolitical evolution (Feinman and Neitzel 1984). Recent research has emphasized the seemingly inherent structural instabilities characterized by factional competition and political cycling. Yet factionalism was not an invariant attribute of Mississippian societies. A comparative analysis of political culture suggests that the con-solidation of legitimate authority was successfully pursued through coali-tion building and the regional centralization of political economy. Along with other large mound centers such as Cahokia, the polity of Moundville represents an archetype for Mississippianism (Pauketat and Emerson 1997a). Social heterogeneity was at times subsumed by the shared refer-ents of cultural accommodation and compliance. In contrast, polities in the central Mississippi Valley at the time of initial European encroachment appear to have been fraught with conflict and coercive tactics, with less emphasis on a comparable elite iconography of engraved ceramics.

The differences in these regions may be attributed in part to incommen-surate sources, especially the lack of historical documentation for Moundville. However, the fortification of nearly every town associated with the Nodena phase contrasts starkly with that of Moundville, in which the center was palisaded only during the height of political consoli-dation (Knight and Steponaitis 1998:15–18). Political culture in the cen-tral Mississippi Valley thus appears to have involved highly contested and coerced social relations of authority, while Moundville, for a time at least, dominated the surrounding Black Warrior Valley. Even after it was virtu-ally abandoned, Moundville may have continued to serve as a referent for legitimate authority in a decentralized polity. In contrast, there is no clearly comparable site associated with the Nodena phase.

Regional differences in ceramic traditions, also represented in the con-struction and fortification of ceremonial centers, reflect a historical pro-cess in which authority and ultimately identity were actively negotiated. In this light, tradition is no longer simply an archaeological unit that refers to cultural persistence, what Willey and Phillips (1958:37) defined as "tem-poral continuity represented by persistent configurations in single tech-nologies." Traditions were transformed as representations of legitimate authority, within the changing historical contexts of political culture. In order to explain the contrasting trajectories of regional political culture, the conceptual framework of the culture historical approach must be re-vised.

Archaeology as a historical science can contribute a unique source of data and theory to the advancement of historical anthropology (Lightfoot 1995). Archaeologists must accordingly develop the techniques and methods to approach culture and tradition as an open-ended process. Cultural traditions were politically engaged and transformed through practice. The production of identity and authority involved a wide range of accommodations, compliance, coercion, and resistance, which should ultimately be accounted for through a historical perspective of power relations (Wolf 1999:67). That cultural traditions were negotiated and that issues of power pervade the production of history is to acknowledge the centrality of political-symbolic action (Kertzer 1988:181–182). The ceramic traditions discussed here provide only preliminary indication of how Mississippian political culture articulated with the historical trajectories of different polities. Based on the ongoing refinement of regional chronologies, future research should consider alternative avenues for examining this historical process.

As argued earlier in the context of Annales, the debate over the "nature of history" is no longer simply a matter of particularism versus science, or *l' histoire événementielle* versus anthropological concepts of structure (Trouillot 1995:25). Instead, it concerns how the production of history and historical representation articulate with power. As Trouillot (1995: 28) states, "[P]ower is constitutive of the story." As a consequence, it is important to consider the ways in which archaeologists may contribute certain omissions or ambiguities in distancing their subject matter from a historical perspective. This final point is crucial in addressing the political culture of inarticulate or preliterate societies. As a historical science, archaeology is uniquely equipped to address authority and tradition as a historical process, in the past as well as the present.

9

Cahokian Change and the Authority of Tradition

Susan M. Alt

Cahokia, located in the American Bottom portion of the Mississippi River floodplain, is the largest pre-Columbian center in North America (see fig. 9.1). Home to more than 100 flat-topped and pyramidal mounds, it is also considered the most complex political phenomenon in pre-Columbian North America (Fowler 1997; Kelly 1990; Pauketat 1994; Pauketat and Emerson 1997b). It was during the Lohmann phase, the earliest Mississippian phase for the American Bottom (*cal* A.D. 1050–1100), that a process of political consolidation termed the "Big Bang" saw its fruition (Pauketat 1994, 1997a). This process saw the initiation of monumental construction, in the form of mounds and plazas, and the movement and resettlement of large numbers of people. This process also brought about a more overt system of social inequality and profound changes in the local settlement patterns as well as in material culture for the people of this region and beyond (Emerson 1997a, 1997b, 1997c; Pauketat 1994, 1998b).

This transformation was accomplished in a very short period of time, grounded in the actions of the people living in and around Cahokia (Pauketat and Emerson 1999). Evidence from Cahokia suggests that residential zones were shifted, with those once used for daily living transformed into spaces for massive public works such as the Grand Plaza. At the same time, new, seemingly preplanned, residential areas were established (see Dalan 1997; Pauketat 1994). Along with these residential changes came new technologies. There were new ways to construct houses and new ways to make pottery.

Outside of Cahokia proper, villages shifted locations, with new settlements such as Halliday—which I will discuss later—suddenly appearing on the landscape. Within these settlements were domestic areas that provide evidence of more intensive craft production than had been seen in the preceding Emergent Mississippian period (see Alt 1999; Pauketat 1997b; Yerkes 1991). Yet in some ways the situation for these villages in the rural

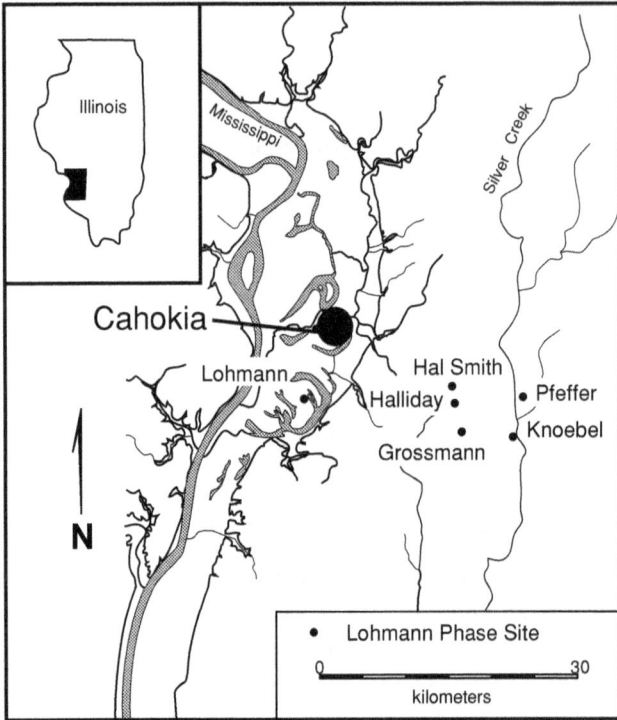

Fig. 9.1. Select sites within the greater Cahokia region.

uplands just ten miles away from Cahokia appears to have been distinct. Rather than being caught up in all of the events taking place at Cahokia and in the surrounding floodplain—that is, the American Bottom—it seems that change came more slowly and in a more piecemeal fashion for the upland people (Alt 1998).

It is this disjunction in the way change occurred at Cahokia versus the way change occurred in the uplands that presents an opportunity to view the process of changing traditions in detail. Cahokia is believed to have accommodated a population in all probability too large to be sustained by local floodplain resources yet perhaps too small to have easily accomplished the massive landscape alteration that occurred at this site (Pauketat 1997a; cf. Milner 1998). Thus, it is impossible to look at settlements near Cahokia without considering the relationships between Cahokians and those living in other settlements (*contra* Mehrer 1995). Investigations addressing such considerations have suggested that nearby settlements both in the American Bottom and in the uplands are best understood as dispersed parts of a single "greater Cahokian" community (Pauketat 1998b). Nevertheless, recent investigations have also uncovered many differences between the settlements.

I argue that the variability at two upland settlements discussed in this paper, Halliday and Knoebel, is representative of some deeper processes involving the maintenance and alterations of traditions and community identities. Given a new political order, new social practices, and the introduction of new technologies at Cahokia, it may seem reasonable to expect lag in the participation of the more distant parts of a community in those new social practices or in the adoption of the new technologies. However, it would be more satisfying to *explain* the variable adoption of practices between settlements. It is the actual processes of change, and the resistance to change in traditional practices, whether overt or inadvertent, that need to be examined. The evidence from the Halliday and Knoebel sites, now seemingly reinforced by two more recently excavated sites, Hal Smith and Pfeffer,[1] suggest that this lag should not simply be attributed to the uplanders' ignorance of the new ways of doing things at Cahokia (see fig. 9.1). It is better explained as the result of choices made by people negotiating the recognized authority of the past (as exercised in traditional lifeways) and the newly risen religious and political authority of Cahokia.

Changing Traditions

How do traditional practices change? The perspective I adopt here is that change is inherent and inescapable in the maintenance and enactment of day-to-day practices and traditions. As presented by Bourdieu and Giddens in terms of "doxa" or "structuration" (Bourdieu 1977; Giddens 1984), changes in everyday practices are a necessary consequence of day-to-day living. The actions of individuals are bounded by specific structures such as group interests and expectations, as well as know-how and habits; those structures are, at the same time, created and maintained by the actions of those individuals. It is this tension between the enactment and creation of structure in the process of daily living that ensures change; this is also a process that often occurs outside of the awareness of most participants. To them, traditions are being practiced much as they always have been, not an uncommon view in many societies. Shils (1981) has noted that traditions can undergo great changes and these changes can go unnoticed by actors, especially if they occur over time or if they occur while the core of such traditions remains intact.

However, the magnitude of the changes emanating from Cahokia, in the time frame when they are posited to have occurred, suggests a more sudden and conspicuous series of modifications than the type of everyday change often associated with doxa and structuration. The movement of populations, the sudden coordination of labor to create monumental architecture, the reorganization of community structure, the introduction of new architectural forms, and the manufacture of new vessel types and other material goods—particularly when taken as a whole—seem to suggest that people in the American Bottom were not only very aware of the changes occurring at Cahokia but must have been active participants in those alterations.

This is not to say that all of the changes that did occur were planned or even anticipated by the people of the American Bottom. Presumably, the differences between Cahokia and the upland villages were embedded in the day-to-day practices of the people living in either location. Shennan (1993:55) has pointed out that the "practices of which archaeology provides a record are two extremes: on the one hand, important 'events' which affect the way social space was structured, on the other, and much more frequent, at least in non-state societies, the routinized activity of individuals going about their daily round." The archaeological record consists of the material remains of day-to-day living, and this material can be considered as an integral component of those practices (McCall 1999; Shennan 1993). Such practices include the technological choices made by those who produced the artifacts, and such choices reflect and construct the identities of these individuals.

Cahokian Changes

The changes that came with the Big Bang can be seen in many of the material aspects of life during the Lohmann phase in the American Bottom proper and at Cahokia (Kelly 1990; Pauketat 1994; Pauketat 1998b). Most noticeably, mound and plaza construction began, forcing the movement of people into and out of residential districts (Dalan 1997; Pauketat 1994). The spatial arrangements of these residential districts also underwent a clear transformation. In the pre-Mississippian period, structures were smaller and arranged in courtyard groups, each residential area comprised of multiple courtyards (Kelly 1990). However, with the advent of the Lohmann phase, the courtyard groups were replaced by less formalized clusters of houses, which were no longer organized around a central space (see Collins 1990; Mehrer and Collins 1995; Pauketat 1998a). The smaller, more intimate communal space of the courtyard was translated into massive public space for the community in the form of plazas (Alt 1998).

In addition, houses at Cahokia were no longer built using single-post technology but were constructed using wall trenches and were now somewhat larger.[2] This probably produced buildings that were visibly distinct, owing to the concomitant alterations in wall angle and roof type. More importantly, a change (from single post to wall trench) would have required a new construction technology and plausibly altered labor practices. The Lohmann phase residents at Cahokia also developed new house forms, such as circular, T-shaped, and L-shaped structures, arranging these in ways that suggest special uses and meanings for the new building types.

An equally dramatic transition in style and technology is expressed in ceramic vessels, with changes seen in temper preferences, vessel surface treatments, and vessel form (Holley 1989; Milner et al. 1984; Pauketat 1998a). For instance, the use of shell temper more than doubled in vessel pastes after Cahokia's abrupt beginning, with the use of slips and burnishing techniques greatly increasing at the same time and at the expense of lip notching and cord marking on vessel surfaces (see Pauketat 1998a). New vessel forms appeared, such as bottles and beakers, and vessel shapes changed, with jars being constructed with more pronounced shoulders and lip modifications (see also Vogel 1975).

Upland Sites

The Halliday site is located approximately ten kilometers southeast of Cahokia on the edge of an upland prairie (see fig. 9.1).[3] During the excavation of Halliday, it became apparent that—although clearly identifiable as an early Cahokian Lohmann phase site—there were obvious deviations from expected Lohmann phase patterns as identified in the American Bottom. Likewise, another upland site with a Lohmann phase component, Knoebel, appears to be clearly similar to and yet unlike the Lohmann phase sites in the American Bottom.

Radiocarbon dates confirm that Halliday was occupied during the Lohmann phase, with occupation beginning early in the phase; ceramic and architectural evidence suggests that the occupation ended not long after A.D. 1100. Knoebel, excavated in the late 1960s by Charles Bareis and recently reanalyzed by myself, was occupied during the entire Lohmann sequence, based in part on the existence of earlier and later occupations at the site. Cahokia's Tract 15A and the Lohmann site also were occupied throughout the entire Lohmann phase. In short, then, temporal considerations as a cause for variation in the evidence should be minimal in these data sets.[4]

Space and Architecture

According to Thomas Emerson (1997a, 1997c), there is a characteristic architecture and spatial arrangement for nodal farmsteads (settlements where special political and religious activities occurred). This architecture is not present at Halliday or Knoebel. Although special structures are often associated with mounds (Bareis 1972; Collins 1990; Pauketat 1993), circular, T-shaped, and L-shaped structures also appear in residential precincts at Cahokia, and at settlements in the Bottom (see Collins 1990; Emerson 1984; Pauketat 1998a). Beyond having specialized structures related to new ceremonial activities at Cahokia, space and architecture in residential districts at Cahokia indicate that new social relationships had emerged. Space and architecture at the upland sites do not reflect these same relationships.

Halliday appears to have been founded at about A.D. 1050 as a Lohmann phase village without Cahokian-style Lohmann phase houses or settlement organization. Based on the Cahokia and Lohmann sites, the expected village arrangement for this phase would consist of wall-trench houses in clusters, often associated with a single village plaza. Instead, at Halliday, construction methods and settlement configurations exhibit the typical pre-Mississippian style single-post houses arranged around cleared oval courtyards, often marked by central posts (see fig. 9.2). Of the total of fifty-one excavated structures (in the 1995–1996 sample), only twelve are of wall-trench construction. At Cahokia's Tract 15A, 86 percent of the Lohmann phase structures were built with wall trenches, and 83 percent of structures at the Lohmann site consisted of wall-trench construction (see fig. 9.3; see Esarey and Pauketat 1992; Pauketat 1998b).[5] The superpositioning of wall-trench structures over single-post structures at Halliday and Knoebel suggest that wall-trench construction was introduced later in the Lohmann phase at upland villages than in the American Bottom. The mean floor area of the houses at Halliday, however, is not consistent with the pre-Mississippian standards in the American Bottom. Instead, it conforms closely to the mean for Lohmann phase house sizes at Cahokia and the Lohmann site and exceeds the mean structure size at Knoebel (see fig. 9.3). Pre-Mississippian Edelhardt phase structures at Cahokia's Tract 15A average a mean of 7.7 square meters, an average that

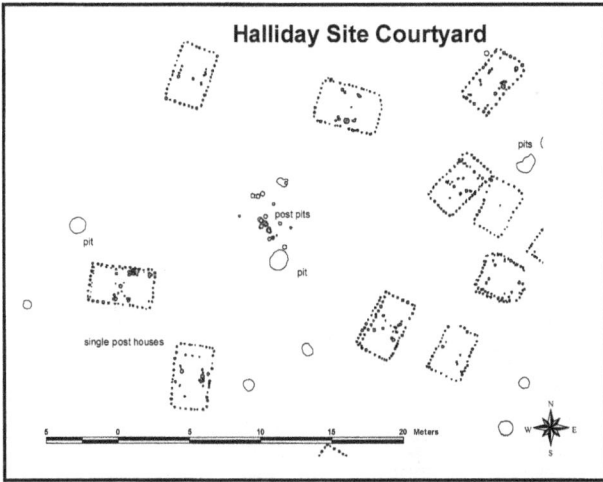

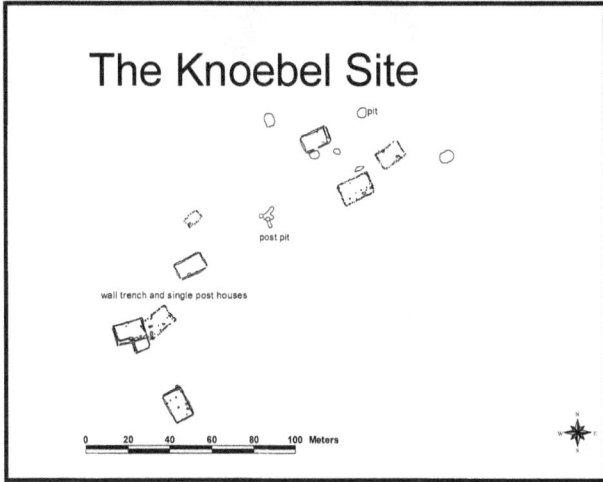

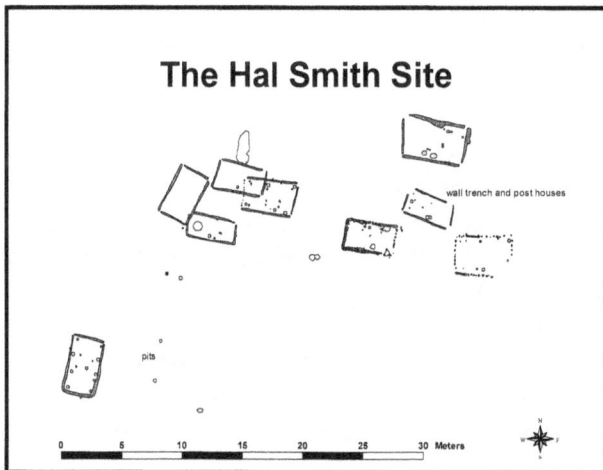

Fig. 9.2. Upland Mississippian site plans.

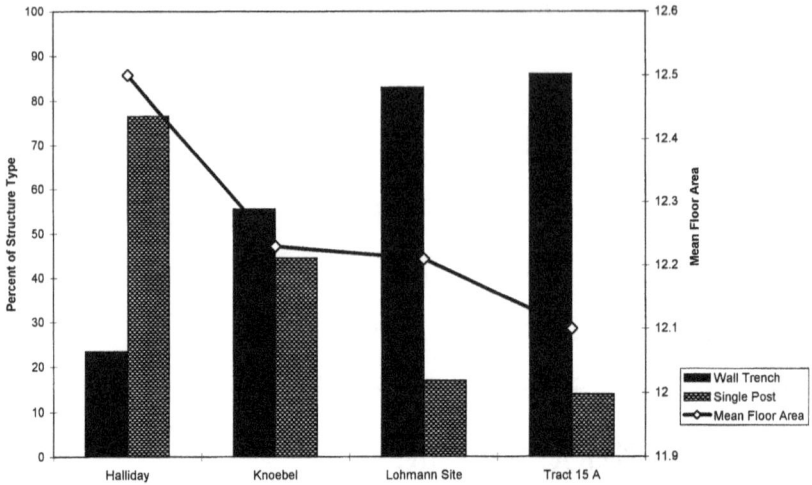

Fig. 9.3. Comparison of structure type and size.

jumps to 12.1 square meters in the Lohmann phase (Pauketat 1998a). Halliday structures average 12.5 square meters.[6] In summary, wall construction and community organization persist in a traditional mode in the uplands, while house size increases, as it does in the wall-trench houses in the American Bottom.

Knoebel was occupied before, during, and after the Lohmann phase. During all of this time, settlement configuration and structure size did not significantly change. At any given point in time, a few structures coexisted on either side of an open space (too few to form a full courtyard but situated similarly). House construction methods did change however. While the residents of Halliday preferred single-post construction for almost all dwellings, residents at Knoebel retained fewer single-post structures. At Knoebel, 55 percent of the Lohmann phase structures were of wall-trench construction, a figure closer to that seen in the American Bottom. Although a trend to larger structures over time has been noted elsewhere (Mehrer 1995; Pauketat 1994), at Knoebel, structure size varied considerably over time. Pre-Mississippian (Edelhardt phase) structures have a mean floor area of 11.23 square meters (much greater than the size of contemporaneous structures in the Bottom), while the mean size of Knoebel's Lohmann phase structures is only slightly larger, at 12.06 square meters; this size conforms with that seen at Halliday and Cahokia.

At Halliday, the walls of a few structures seem to have been constructed as a hybrid of wall-trench and single-post construction. When viewed in plan, these structures appear to be of wall-trench construction. Upon the excavation of only a few centimeters of soil from the trenches, however, these "wall trenches" resolve into the typical Halliday (and pre-Mississippian) pattern of post holes. This pattern is also very clearly seen at the nearby Hal Smith site (see fig. 9.2).[7] The Hal Smith site appears to be an early Stirling phase (A.D. 1100–1150) village containing several houses with hybrid walls. Of the nine excavated wall-trench structures, four contained at least one hybrid wall.

The Hal Smith site also helps confirm the impression of a later use of wall trenches at some upland sites. At this site, individual houses were built using wall-trench and single-post construction. Other later structures had wall trenches conforming more closely to the typical wall construction technology seen at Cahokia, where hybrid walls have yet to be reported. The pattern of hybrid walls at the Hal Smith and Halliday sites, that is, may be evidence of people learning or experimenting with a new technology rather than whole-heartedly adopting a new form.

Perhaps, with the movement of people in and around Cahokia at the start of the Lohmann phase, wall-trench construction may have been developed to enable more houses to be built more quickly, digging out a trench with a hoe being less labor intensive than digging forty to fifty individual post holes. It has also been suggested that wall-trench houses were built with prefabricated walls and so entailed a new organization of labor (Pauketat 1994). On the other hand, a single individual could have constructed single-post structures; placing and securing an entire wall as suggested by the wall trench would have required more hands. In addition, there may have been less pressure to build new houses quickly in the uplands, unlike Cahokia with its abrupt restructuring. In the uplands, there may have been less need to radically change traditional patterns of construction, as well as less pressure to alter the social relations related to construction efforts. Hybrid walls may be more a result of people attempting to introduce a new house type without actually altering the traditional practices of building a house.

There are differences in the variability of structure types at the sites as well. As might be expected, neither the Halliday nor the Knoebel site has as much variability in structure type as is seen at or around Cahokia. Presumably, this is reflective of the more limited activities or architectural know-how at the upland sites. While Cahokia gives every indication of hosting complex political, religious, and ritual functions, the upland villages were for daily living. As indicated by the huge quantities of chert hoe-blade resharpening flakes recovered, the upland villages were also the location of intensive farming (Pauketat 1998b). For example, an L-shaped structure form, while uncommon, has been reported at pre-Mississippian and early Mississippian sites with single-post and wall-trench construction, respectively (for a pre-Mississippian example, see the Robinson Lake site [Milner 1984]). At Cahokia, there are rectangular, circular, and L-shaped structures. In contrast, Halliday has only rectangular and square forms, with no L-shaped buildings. The contemporaneous settlement of Knoebel, on the other hand, has L-shaped structures as well as the typical rectangular forms (fig. 9.2).

It is common at Lohmann phase settlements at Cahokia, and in both the American Bottom and the uplands, to find very small, often nearly square structures in addition to the common rectangular structures. I interpret these as storage structures. While Halliday has at least one of these structures for each courtyard group, Knoebel has only one, despite the fact that the other houses were rebuilt several times. However, it is possible that the L extension on Knoebel's L-shaped houses is simply a version of the storage structure but in this case attached to an existing building rather than left freestanding.

The implication then, is one of change entering the upland settlements, with each village adopting different pieces of the new Cahokian forms and neither village adopting the full suite of changes seen at Cahokia. What is important is the type of changes that first came to the uplands. In both upland settlements examined here, people retained traditional settlement organization. Halliday people retained the courtyard, just as Knoebel residents retained some semblance of the courtyard. Halliday people maintained pre-Mississippian domestic spatial relationships and house construction technology; wall-trench structures appeared later, even though larger houses appeared right away. Knoebel people retained pre-Mississippian organizational patterns and house sizes (although the average Knoebel pre-Mississippian house was larger than its average American Bottom contemporary) but seem to have adopted wall-trench construction more quickly, at the same time that they utilized L-shaped additions (a rare but seemingly traditional form). Halliday residents opted for free-standing storage buildings.

Ceramics

A pattern of differential change at the upland settlements similar to that seen in space and architecture may be observed in ceramic assemblages. As with architecture, a greater variability in type characterizes Cahokia's ceramic assemblages, and a mixed adoption of new Cahokian styles and technologies seems to characterize the uplands. The upland settlements shared many stylistic and technological similarities with Cahokia and with each other, but the changes that were adopted were specific to each settlement.

During the pre-Mississippian period, most ceramic vessels in the American Bottom were tempered with grog or grit (Pauketat 1998a); shell and limestone tempers also commonly occur (Kelly et al. 1984). With the advent of the Lohmann phase, the use of shell temper dramatically increased. During the Edelhardt phase, 15 percent of the jars at the BBB Motor site, a small settlement near Cahokia, and 28 percent at Cahokia's Tract 15A were shell tempered (Emerson and Jackson 1984; Pauketat 1998a). In contrast, more than 50 percent of all Lohmann phase ceramic vessels are shell tempered (Holley 1989; Pauketat 1998a).

The use of shell temper in ceramics (thought by many to be a technological innovation) is considered one of the hallmarks of the Mississippian period. As expected, Cahokia and nearby sites saw an increase in shell temper use with time, with nearly all ceramics being made with shell temper by the end of the Lohmann phase. At Halliday, shell temper is used in 87 percent of all vessels. At Knoebel, this figure is 73 percent.[8] This is interesting in that, for the same period of time, only 58 percent of Cahokian vessels and 67 percent of the Lohmann site vessels were shell tempered (Esarey and Pauketat 1992; Pauketat 1998a). It would seem that shell-tempered ceramic technology was adopted for use in the uplands with an enthusiasm that surpassed even that of the American Bottom communities, despite the fact that this temper does not appear to have been the best choice for use in the pottery clays available to upland people.[9] Indeed, the extraordinarily large quantities of broken sherds, the poor quality of the upland ceramics, and the many visible breaks and poorly welded coils in shell-tempered vessels from the upland sites would seem to support this claim. Given this situation, why did the uplanders so readily adopt shell temper?

The surface treatments of pottery vessels were also altered in the Lohmann phase; cord marking became much less common, while the use of slip increased at Cahokia. These innovations were adopted at different

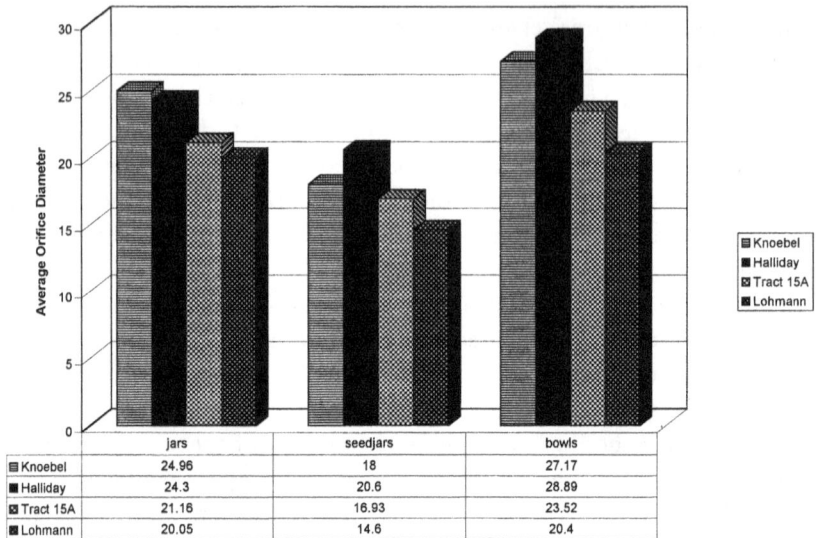

	jars	seedjars	bowls
▤ Knoebel	24.96	18	27.17
■ Halliday	24.3	20.6	28.89
▨ Tract 15A	21.16	16.93	23.52
▧ Lohmann	20.05	14.6	20.4

Fig. 9.4. Selected vessel type mean-diameter sizes.

rates in the uplands. Cahokia and Halliday have nearly identical proportions of slipped vessels but nearly twice as many as at Knoebel, which (at
15 percent) had fewer slipped vessels than has been reported for pre-Mississippian Edelhardt phase sites in the American Bottom (for example, 26
percent of the jars are slipped at BBB Motor [Emerson and Jackson
1984]). On the other hand, Knoebel potters reduced the use of cord marking to the same proportion as is seen at Tract 15A, while Halliday pots
show cord marking more than twice as often as is found at the other sites.

Although the surface appearance of ceramic vessels changed, it seems
that the basic methods for making pots did not. Ground shell rather than
grit was being used as a temper additive, yet bowls and jars were still
constructed with coils of clay, scraped to adjust wall thickness, and
paddled into final shape. Cord marking was achieved by winding cordage
around a paddle, and then the cord marking would be applied as the vessel
was shaped. Interestingly, many Lohmann phase vessels that appear to
have smooth surfaces show telltale marks of having been constructed with
cord-wrapped paddles, the cord marking itself smoothed over after the
fact. This means the surface appearance was often achieved by adding a
step to the *châine opératoire*, a counterintuitive step for those with a func-

tionalist viewpoint. That is, some analysts have suggested that cord marking produces a more efficient vessel: the uneven surface heats faster, holds heat longer, and is less likely to slip out of the hands (see Deal 1983; Henrickson and McDonald 1983). The use of shell temper and smooth surfaces, then, are both "innovations" that are not necessarily technologically "superior" choices but are nonetheless the choices made by the upland villagers.

In a comparison of vessel size, it appears that the upland sites contain somewhat larger jars and fewer but much larger bowls than those found at Cahokia's Tract 15A or at the Lohmann site (see fig. 9.4). Since it is now well accepted that there were no major changes in food use with the advent of the Mississippian period at Cahokia, changes in vessel type and size cannot be attributed to the accommodation of new foods (see Lopinot 1997). However, vessel size may be considered indicative of changes in the meanings of pots and cooking practices. The greater number of larger vessels may indicate communal living related to the courtyards at Halliday. These vessels would have been made to feed and serve larger groups of people, while the more restricted size range of vessels and the use of smaller bowls at Cahokia may be derivative of the dissolution of these communal groups.

Conclusion

At around A.D. 1050 profound changes occurred in domestic and public practices at Cahokia and nearby settlements in the American Bottom, changes that were reflected in settlement reorganization, as well as in stylistic and technological innovations. In part, these changes can no doubt be explained as the unintended results of political events and as the result of the simultaneous appearance of more overt social inequality in the immediate Cahokian landscape. The wide range of styles and material goods at Cahokia during the Lohmann phase is missing in the uplands at the same time. But the upland settlements also provide no evidence for the political and social complexity, at least that which is expressed in public architecture and ceramic styles, of Cahokia proper. Lacking this complexity, some practical changes did not occur in the uplands. Instead, the styles and technologies adopted are those that villagers incorporated into their traditional community life, not those that would be more closely associated with more profound changes in political and social life.

The spatial organization of villages in the uplands did not change at the same time that spatial arrangements changed at Cahokia. Different aspects of construction techniques did change in the uplands. The first changes to arrive in the uplands, such as those associated with pottery technology, were those potentially least connected to social relations. While spatial relations cannot be decoded as if they were a specific text, they do speak to what people do and think. Bourdieu, Giddens, and Foucault have all theorized about relationships between space or architecture and day-to-day activities, as well as cosmological beliefs. Space conditions sensibilities; sensibilities in practice shape space (Bourdieu 1977; Foucault 1973, 1979; Giddens 1984). Spatial relationships at Cahokian residential tracts suggest more complexity than is found until much later in the uplands. At Cahokia's Tract 15A, larger-than-normal structures were grouped near specialized circular structures and located on higher ground, while smaller structures are located at a distance, across a plaza, and are not associated with specialized structures (Pauketat 1998a). This suggests differences in social status, or in activities carried out in different parts of Cahokia's residential neighborhoods. This architectural segregation is not seen at the upland villages. These differences in space are related to differences in practices.

A settlement consisting of several courtyards would have projected a specific set of social and familial relationships, a set of relationships that must have been altered in those places where the courtyard was dissolved into smaller clusters of houses without a communal space (as at Cahokia). Likewise, the enlargement of a structure or the alteration of wall type may have presented less of a threat to extant social relationships than the alteration of the spatial relationship of dwellings and workspace (although the delay in adopting wall trenches is no doubt related to the need to adopt new labor relations in order to construct a house). In any case, the alterations that were accommodated at the upland Lohmann phase settlements did not define changes in relationships in the same way as the alterations of space and architecture did at Cahokia. Those changes that were accommodated in the uplands seem to be those that permitted a surface likeness to events at Cahokia but that did not substantially alter social relations.

While the change to shell temper must have altered the steps in pottery making, the greater reliance on shell temper, the alteration of lip treatments and shoulder angles, and the changes in vessel surface treatments are all choices that themselves had little effect on social relations. The matter of vessel size does, however, speak directly to social relations. Both jars and, especially, bowls were larger in the uplands. This fact, in combination with the courtyards at upland Lohmann phase sites, paints a picture of upland peoples engaged in pre-Mississippian communal practices. The smaller clusters of houses, the smaller vessels, and the larger number of smaller serving bowls at Cahokia all suggest that the extended groups (families?) found at the upland settlements no longer existed as such at Cahokia during the Lohmann phase. This difference may be explained in part by the differences between the social, political, or economic practices at Cahokia as compared to the upland settlements; however, the cause and the result were evidently rejected at the upland settlements.

Maintaining some similarities with Cahokia does seem to have been an important concern for the upland villagers. Although several changes were made in ceramic construction and style, and any change in technology will involve changes in day-to-day practices, these are innovations that could have been implemented with the least effect on daily routines. Those ceramic changes that were adopted seem to have been, if anything, demonstrably deleterious. The shell temper was added to upland clays not suited to shell temper (see Porter 1964); vessel surfaces were smoothed, although this requires an extra step in the construction process that does not improve vessel performance. While not necessary, the adoption of such things would serve to create in a practical sense an identity consistent with the greater Cahokian community.

In sum, there seem to be two levels of change represented at the upland Mississippian sites coeval with early Cahokia: large-scale sociopolitical changes (seen in mounds, plazas, and community restructuring) and smaller-scale technological and stylistic changes (such as those seen in rim and temper changes in jars). Wall trenches and house sizes may not pose or reflect the same order of change in the built environment, and so in the social environment, as might the dissolution of the courtyard. Shell temper and surface treatment may not in this case be as indicative of changes in how people were interacting with each other as are the size and type of vessels commonly used at the various settlements.

In other words, upland people appear to have been willing to adopt— or perhaps it would be more correct to suggest that they actively sought— those changes that maintained an affiliation with the currents of change at Cahokia, while they resisted those changes that would have altered social life. The upland people apparently rejected the sociopolitical authority of Cahokia and retained more traditional patterns of living and doing.

Notes

1. These sites are still undergoing analysis at the University of Illinois Urbana-Champaign.

2. With single-post construction, individual posts are set into the ground and then the wall is constructed using the upright posts. With wall-trench construction, a trench is dug into the ground and then a preformed wall is placed into the trench and set up complete.

3. Halliday was partially excavated from 1995 to 1999 under the direction of Tim Pauketat. Another portion of the site was dug by the Illinois Transportation Archaeological Research Program in 2000. All materials are being analyzed at the University of Illinois under Pauketat's direction, but the present sample includes only those remains excavated before the 2000 season.

4. I use published data from the Lohmann site and from Tract 15A at Cahokia to represent the Lohmann phase in the American Bottom, a phase defined as limited in time to A.D. 1050–1100 (Esarey and Pauketat 1992; Pauketat 1998a, 1998b). Published data from the BBB Motor site are also used for pre-Mississippian patterns (Emerson and Jackson 1984).

5. Another tract at Cahokia, the ICT-II, contains no structures with single-post construction in the Lohmann phase occupation, but occupation there began a bit later in the Lohmann phase than at the other locations (Collins 1990).

6. For further comparison with another American Bottom settlement, the BBB Motor site, Edelhardt phase structures have an average floor space of 7.5 square meters (Emerson and Jackson 1984).

7. The Hal Smith site was partially excavated in 1999 as part of Pauketat's Richland Archaeological Project.

8. Notes on file at the University of Illinois Urbana-Champaign.

9. As discussed by Porter (1964), not all clays benefit from the addition of shell temper. Clays suitable for use with shell were available in the bottomlands, but not in the uplands.

10

The Historical-Processual Development of Late Woodland Societies

Michael S. Nassaney

In a recent review of current theoretical trends in anthropological archaeology, Pauketat (2001) touted the importance of historical processes in archaeological interpretation. He rightly noted that such a "historical-processual" approach constitutes a synthesis of old and new ideas that have coalesced to inform a new vision of the relationships between cultural tradition, history, human agency, power, and the material world. Practitioners of this new historical-processual paradigm appreciate the necessity of sound space-time systematics, while trying to balance the generalizing scientism of the old processual archaeology with the particulars of historicism. From this perspective, the archaeological record serves as a laboratory to evaluate models of cultural change and simultaneously expresses a meaningfully constituted chronological sequence of material history writ both large and small.

An arena in which historical-processualism can excel is the American Southeast, where archaeologists have shifted their preoccupation with chronology building to deriving sociopolitical inferences from the material remains that litter the floodplains, terraces, and uplands of the region (see Barker and Pauketat 1992b; Blitz 1993a, b; J. Brown 1971; Peebles and Kus 1977; Welch 1991; Widmer 1988). Over the past two decades, the neoevolutionary models of earlier practitioners have become increasingly challenged by a much more nuanced, stochastic, and somewhat chaotic understanding of global historical development in general, and Late Woodland societies in particular (see Cobb and Nassaney 1995; Fortier, this volume). Social structure and historical process are actively created and reproduced by human agents who have different political aspirations and views of the world. This perspective likely illuminates social reality better than normative views which held "that cultures were distinct sociopolitical entities comprised of members that shared sets of values, beliefs, behaviors, and customs" (Nassaney and Sassaman 1995:xxi). Despite this theoretical refocusing, there still remains considerable disagreement about what people did and how or why they did it in the past.

For example, one of the thorniest issues that continues to challenge archaeologists is an understanding of the historical conditions that gave rise to social asymmetries, or the factors that leveled differences between individuals that occur in all human groups. Some anthropologists have suggested that people worldwide tenaciously held on to egalitarianism and only reluctantly yielded to more centralized sociopolitical structures (Lee 1990). Others maintain that egalitarianism is not the natural order of human society; rather, it must be actively asserted to counter the hierarchies that are based on inevitable social and physical differences (Sassaman 1998a; Sassaman, this volume). Issues surrounding the exercise and institutionalization of power are at the heart of these concerns. (And suffice it to say that any single model that can explain these processes globally is probably much too generalized to attract more than mere anecdotal interest.)

While archaeologists once focused their efforts on the identification of conspicuous material markers of social ranking, stratification, and the state, some have shifted their attention to the daily activities of nonelites as a means of examining the making of history (e.g., Ferguson 1992; Lightfoot 1995; Sassaman 1998a). Indeed, traditions are continuously being enacted and reenacted, and the earliest evidence of social classes or state bureaucracies may be merely the reified outcomes of our analytical framework. This explains, to a great extent, why the materially rich archaeological manifestations of the Middle Woodland and Mississippian periods have been the focus of interest at the expense of the Late Woodland period until recently (see Emerson et al. 2000). Perhaps unencumbered by the explicit political maneuvering of highly public and publicized leaders, the Late Woodland is a useful frame for examining the ways in which social life—history—was created, reproduced, and transformed on the southeastern landscape.

In the remainder of this chapter I examine some domestic material remains at the scale of the household and dimensions of the regional built environment to explore the conditions that gave rise to the emergence of social inequality and its resistance in the Late Woodland Midsouth. When viewed against the backdrop of the last two millennia, a picture emerges of a fragmented sociopolitical landscape that was only sporadically integrated in a spatially uneven and temporally cyclical fashion. Political frag-mentation, reintegration, and ethnogenesis appear to characterize much of the Eastern Woodlands prior to the colonization of the New World by the English, French, and Spanish beginning in the seventeenth century. Yet, the particular historical configuration of the Late Woodland is only superficially reflected in its predecessors and descendants. Nevertheless, the Late Woodland cannot be understood without a working knowledge of its antecedents. Perhaps it is more than ironic that at a time when some have declared the end of history, history is reemerging as a central organiz-ing principle in anthropological archaeology (Pauketat 2001; Stein 1998).

Where Does History Take Us?

An integrated theory of cultural history that transcends Archaic, Amish, and antebellum societies is slowly emerging, though it remains poorly articulated (Hunt 1989; Sassaman, this volume; Ulin 1996:26). Efforts to move inquiry in this direction will require anthropologists to pay more attention to history, as Wolf (1982) urged us to consider. The type of history he advocated is written on a global scale, takes into account the major transformations associated with significant world events (the adop-tion of agriculture, the age of discovery, the rise of capitalism, and so on), and traces connections among human groups and regions that anthro-pologists have often separated and reified (Roseberry 1989:125). Such efforts are poised to recapture the spirit of an older anthropology that attempted to grasp developmental—that is, historical—processes (Rose-berry 1989:125). Most early attempts failed to confront questions of power and domination, however, or to embed their subjects in the eco-nomic and political processes associated with the making of history. Glo-bal perspectives often ignored the local and, in doing so, failed to grasp the importance of actions associated with individual agents. While historical processes are not confined to the modern world, it is ill-advised to conflate the study of the margins of the modern world with kin-ordered societies in pre-state settings. Noncapitalist social relations shaped, and in some cases continue to shape, the lives of most of the communities that anthropolo-gists have studied (Roseberry 1989:144).

Anthropology must take history into account because history matters. It provides the structural possibilities for human action—a blueprint for how to act. Yet these inherited structures are seldom reproduced un-changed, because individual agents act according to perceptions that are differentially shared with members of a group (Bender 1985). Thus, the potential for change is present in every act that contributes toward the reproduction of social life, because practice is always a creative opportunity (Giddens 1976:102).

While all people participate in traditions, a dominant tradition is a selection from a people's history and does not represent it in its totality (R. Williams 1961, 1977). The selection process is tied to relations of domination and subordination, so that a dominant culture is by definition a selective tradition. Because no order of domination is total, "there are always sets of relationships and experiences that are excluded [but] may serve as points around which alternative, perhaps oppositional, cultural forms can emerge" (Roseberry 1989:75–76). The resulting tensions that emerge through practice give rise to cultural change, as individuals see their own interests as the interests of the group at large. The actions that serve to promote these interests, moreover, always have unintended consequences that are independent of, and perhaps even contrary to, the motives of individual agents. Thus, historical outcomes remain unpredictable. For example, although the bow and arrow may have been adopted by hunters in the eastern woodlands to increase productivity in the mobilization of surplus, it was also used as a weapon of warfare and a means to increase self-sufficiency (see Nassaney and Pyle 1999). Thus, it could have simultaneously challenged the relationships it was meant to reinforce. One could make a similar argument for the use of guns by early-nineteenth-century African captives in the American South. Whereas guns were provided to African Americans to allow them to supplement their subsistence base, these same tools were sometimes turned against the slaves' legal owners in rebellion. The social outcome of technological adoption is always contingent and is neither politically neutral nor knowable in advance (see Nassaney and Abel 2000).

In technological, economic, and political decision making, individuals throughout history have struggled over the right to control the creation of their own identities and against the imposition of economic and social values as a means of exercising power. These issues seldom go uncontested in human groups. Such contestation takes the form of alternative contextual uses of material objects, which, in turn, imbue them with new meanings. The challenge for archaeologists is to delineate how the meanings of material culture were created at multiple scales from the perspectives of different individuals if we are to understand how the material world served to reinforce or transform social relations.

In this chapter I use a political-economic framework that views tradition as historically shaped to interpret the spatial and temporal patterns of domestic material remains and the built environment in the Late Woodland Southeast.

A Late Woodland Southeast Primer

Any attempt to characterize Late Woodland societies across the entire Southeast requires gross generalizations about communities that were in reality historically and culturally diverse. In fact, recent regional syntheses underscore the broad variation in subsistence, settlement and demography, exchange, and social organization for societies that occupied the Southeast during the latter half of the first millennium A.D. (Cobb and Nassaney 1995; Nassaney 2000; Nassaney and Cobb 1991a, 1991b). Let me summarize some of these data.

There is well-documented evidence for subsistence intensification in the use of native and tropical cultigens by Late Woodland times (e.g., Cowan 1985; Fritz 1990; Keegan 1987; C. M. Scarry 1993d; B. D. Smith 1989; Watson 1985, 1988; Yarnell and Black 1985). However, maize apparently played a very minor dietary role in the Southeast prior to A.D. 800, and subsistence was probably dependent upon horticultural systems based on other cultigens, supplemented by opportunistic hunting and gathering. Archaeobotanical records from most areas of the Southeast suggest that indigenous plants yielding oily and starchy seeds were manipulated to varying degrees by human agents during the Late Woodland period, "from encouraged weeds, through cultivation, to domesticated status" (B. D. Smith 1986:74–75).

A differential commitment to cultigens characterizes Late Woodland subsistence. C. M. Scarry (1993b) noted that maize production was grafted on to reasonably large-scale agricultural systems in the Mississippi Valley, while in the interior Southeast, Late Woodland populations were dependent on foraging and small-scale crop production. These differing historical trajectories have implications for understanding the multiple reasons why maize agriculture was adopted throughout the greater Southeast, and why univariate models are inappropriate for addressing this problem on a panregional scale. Likewise, the timing of the adoption and intensification of indigenous cultigens is not synchronous throughout the Southeast, and these processes often pre-dated the Late Woodland period by many centuries. It seems likely that different groups were intensifying subsistence strategies at different times due to social and political alliances and indebtedness, as well as to demographic and environmental factors that contributed to resource unpredictability (see Nassaney 1987). In some cases, horticulture may have been adopted, subsequently intensified, and later diminished or even abandoned (Nassaney and Lopinot 1986:216–217). This seemingly random variation also indicates that horticulture and sociopolitical complexity are not simply correlated. The current evidence suggests that maize was a significant factor in the emergence of centralized hierarchical organizations during the Emergent Mississippian period *north* of the Ohio-Mississippi River confluence (see Muller 1987) and in east Tennessee. However, maize was neither a sufficient nor a necessary cause for the emergence of incipient ranking in the Southeast or anywhere else in eastern North America.

Subsistence is inextricably linked to settlement patterns and demography. It follows that there is considerable variation in population distribution and settlement organization during the Late Woodland period, ranging from nucleated to dispersed populations occupying diverse environmental and geopolitical settings. Movements appear to occur within restricted territories on a seasonal basis, although the clinal distribution of raw materials and stylistic elements argues for open social networks lacking rigid political boundaries (but see Hargrave et al. 1991). Settlement hierarchies rarely occur, though they are present (Kriesa and Stout 1991; Nassaney 1991).

Mound construction continues to be an important activity on the Late Woodland landscape, and earthworks occur in many regions of the Southeast. Some mounds continued to serve as mortuary facilities, whereas others were transformed into substructures for important buildings associated with ritual events (Ford 1951; Milanich et al. 1997; J. E. Miller 1982). The shift from a private, lineage-based burial location to a more public site of feasting and other ceremonial acts marks an important transformation in the meaning of earthworks on the landscape, perhaps reflecting their appropriation by supralocal leaders. Mound placement began to structure the world on a routine basis through periodic use, but mounds had yet to become integrated into daily life (Cobb and Nassaney 2000). Coles Creek period mound centers such as Lake George, Insley, and Toltec in the Lower Mississippi Valley appear to have been points of regular visitation and cyclical ritual rather than long-term occupations, giving rise to the popular term "vacant centers" (Belmont 1982; Rolinson 1990; S. Williams and Brain 1983).

Interestingly, Late Woodland population concentrations seldom coincide with earlier (Middle Woodland) and later (Mississippian) settlement patterns. Instead, there appears to be spatial discontinuity and temporal cyclicity in the distribution of southeastern populations during the Woodland and early Mississippian periods, and perhaps even extending back into the Archaic (Fortier, this volume; Kowalewski 1995; Nassaney and Cobb 1991a, b). The settlement and demographic data suggest conditions of political instability and uneven sociohistorical development. This is the result, I would argue, of the ability of individual agents to maintain political autonomy and the failure of leaders to mobilize surplus to underwrite and legitimate their claims to authority. A picture emerges of a rather fragmented social and political landscape composed of relatively small, locally integrated social groups brought into contact by short-term alliances, only to be disintegrated by irregular (though perhaps frequent), short-distance movements of individuals and groups (see Davis 1984:230–231; Fortier, this volume; McElrath and Fortier 2000). Under these conditions it would have been very difficult to institutionalize mechanisms for surplus accumulation or to reinforce social differentiation, because individuals and groups would have had ample opportunity to avoid demands placed on their labor.

The dampening of surplus accumulation is also expressed in the cessation of extensive exchange involving such exotic goods as copper, marine shell, galena, and mica. Numerous southeastern localities that had been involved in the earlier expansive Hopewellian exchange system (e.g., Brose and Greber 1979; Ford 1963; Goad 1978; Seeman 1995) subsequently witnessed the attenuation of the widespread movement of scarce and exotic objects at the close of the Middle Woodland period. Rather than the movement of high-status objects under the control of lineage heads, more utilitarian goods and ideas including the bow and arrow, expedient core technologies, and shell tempering were diffused through broad-scale interaction (Cobb and Nassaney 1995). The Late Woodland appears to be a collective response to earlier conditions. Localized self-sufficiency brought about by the intensification of cultigens and technological innovations such as the adoption of the bow and arrow made individuals less dependent on the panregional interactions of earlier times. However, these active choices also created the conditions by which individuals could attempt to elevate themselves socially and politically above their kin. This is precisely what appears to have happened, albeit briefly, in the Plum Bayou culture of central Arkansas.

Plum Bayou Culture

While one would be hard-pressed to select a "typical" Late Woodland cultural manifestation, the Plum Bayou culture of central Arkansas exhibits many of the characteristics just discussed (see Rolingson 1998). It was first defined on the basis of investigations at the Toltec Mounds site, one of the largest multiple mound and plaza complexes in the Lower Mississippi Valley. Toltec Mounds consists of eighteen mounds, ten of which were carefully arranged around a large plaza, and a semicircular earthen embankment 1.6 kilometers long that encloses the site features in an area of approximately forty-two hectares (Rolingson 1982b, 1990:fig. 7). It is the largest site in a settlement hierarchy that comprises more than Baytown–Coles Creek period components (circa A.D. 400–1100) in the Arkansas River Lowland and adjacent regions (see fig. 10.1). These sites appear to have a shared technological and economic tradition based on their material similarity (see Nassaney 1994).

Population densities were extremely low in the region prior to the establishment of Toltec Mounds and related sites along the natural levees of lakes and bayous. The region was not a hotbed of Middle Woodland activity, and it might have been undesirable for occupation until local groups began intensifying native cultigens in their subsistence pursuits (Fritz 1988, 1990; Nassaney 1991; C. Smith 1996). Maize, while present in several contexts at Toltec Mounds and in a pit at the Ink Bayou site, does not appear in any appreciable quantity. However, its recovery from a midden associated with one of the mounds adjacent to the plaza is firm evidence of its existence by the mid-eighth century A.D. (C. Smith 1996:69–71). Taken as a whole, the wide diversity of faunal and floral remains exploited by Plum Bayou peoples, together with the use of indigenous cultigens and some maize, appear to represent a broadened subsistence base aimed at producing a larger surplus.

From the archaeological record we can identify several trends that were likely causally related: an increased commitment to horticulture corresponds with the establishment of Toltec Mounds as a central place. At the same time, there is an increase in the size, density, and scale of integration of settlements that suggests the movement of people in the region and a decrease in mobility. An increase in population and settlement permanence coincided with the major period of mound construction at Toltec Mounds in the ninth and tenth centuries A.D. The maximum dispersion of Plum Bayou culture artifacts also occurs during this period; stylistically similar ceramics, lithic raw materials, and projectile point forms derived

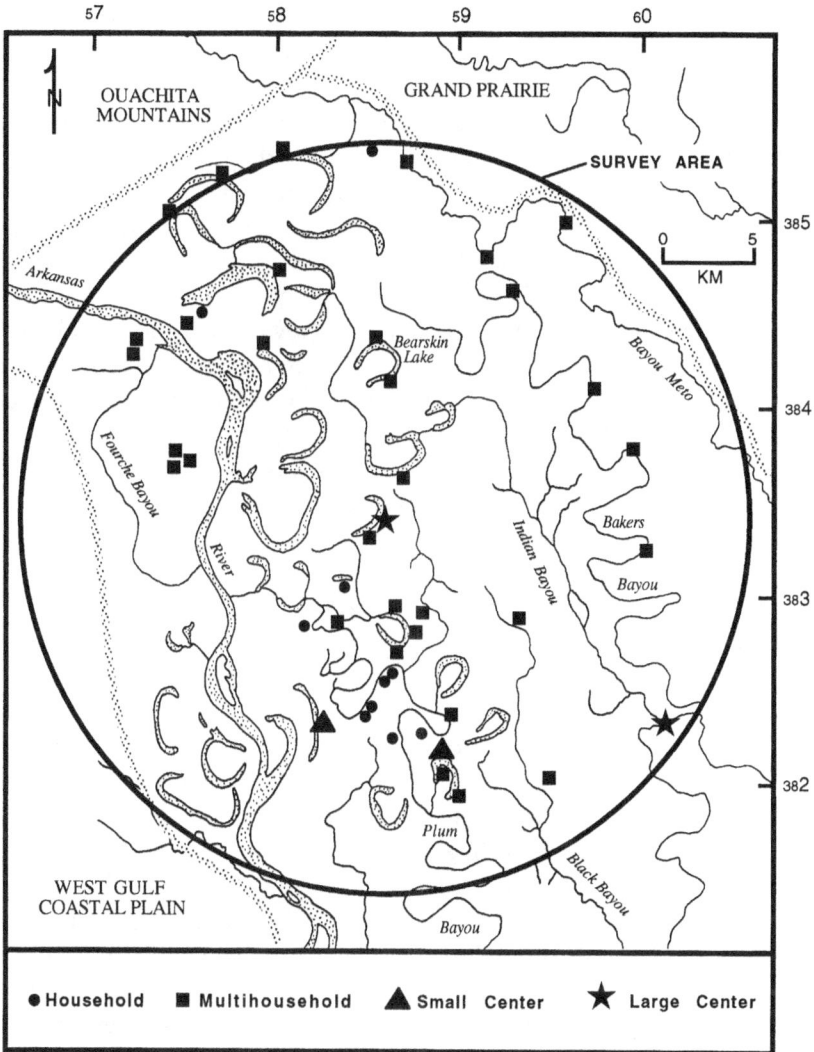

Fig. 10.1. Distribution of Baytown–Coles Creek period sites within twenty kilometers of Toltec Mounds in central Arkansas, by functional type. Adapted from Nassaney 1992a:fig. 6.8.

from central Arkansas appear in the northern Yazoo Basin east of the Mississippi River (see Nassaney and Pyle 1999). Moreover, the arrow points were found embedded in human skeletal remains, hinting at the tensions that existed along the periphery of this expanding political unit. Attempts by members of Plum Bayou culture to extend their arena of influence though intermarriage or resource exchange were clearly met with resistance.

While the broad dissemination of similar artifact forms implies an acceptance of material culture, this cannot be interpreted to mean that populations at the periphery adopted all aspects of this cultural imposition, including conditions of subordination. Other lines of evidence point to a tenuous hold on the populous by incipient elites such as lineage heads or other individuals with elevated authority and prestige, since they were apparently unable to institutionalize control over people, places, and resources essential for social reproduction, even within the heartland. For example, the settlement hierarchy that has been demonstrated for the region during the Baytown–Coles Creek period was poorly integrated and marked by few higher order centers (see fig. 10.2) (Nassaney 1991, 1992a, b, 1996b). In other words, Toltec Mounds was inordinately large and represented the only significant location on the landscape where labor was mobilized. At the beginning of the Mississippian period (ca. A.D. 1100), mound construction ceased at Toltec, the site was abandoned, and no mounds were being constructed anywhere in the region. Moreover, site density decreased dramatically, suggesting regional abandonment and a demographic hiatus that lasted several centuries. This experiment in social ranking had come to an end.

How was the domestic material assemblage implicated in this process of cultural integration and disintegration? Both ceramic and lithic artifacts provide some insight. Chert and novaculite were used predominantly for hunting and food-processing tools, whereas various igneous stones, such as syenite, and quartz crystal were fashioned into animal effigies and other objects that had symbolic meanings. The changing frequency of various raw materials through time and their spatial distribution in the archaeological record suggests that chipped stone was an important element in daily life that had implications for historical development (see Nassaney 1996b). From the Marksville through Mississippian periods, the use of local chert gravels increased in proportion to bedded novaculite, which had to be procured from the uplands to the west. Small bifacially chipped arrow points were abruptly introduced about A.D. 600 from the west for reasons that are not completely understood, though they may have served as effective implements of warfare adopted for defense against the incursions of Plains groups (see Nassaney and Pyle 1999).

There was also a dramatic increase in the frequency of quartz crystal, which reached its height of popularity during the peak period of mound construction, suggesting that this was a desirable raw material in Plum

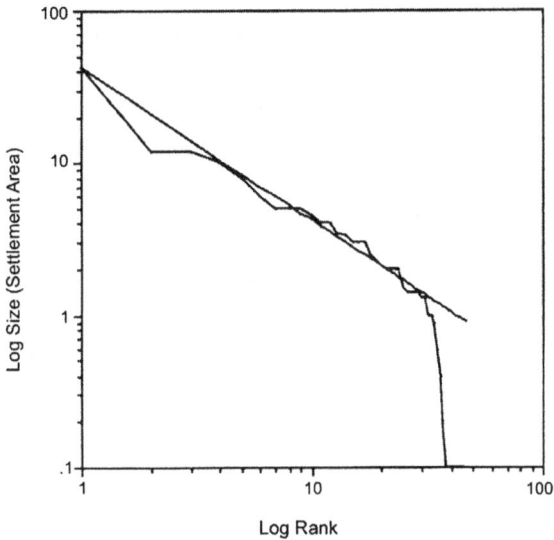

Fig. 10.2. Rank-size relation of Baytown–Coles Creek period sites in fig. 10.1 (n=46). Adapted from Nassaney 1992a:fig. 6.5.

Bayou culture (Nassaney 1996b). Crystals may have been prestige goods imbued with symbolic significance by individuals of rank. The ethnographic record provides some interesting clues regarding the role of quartz crystals in the social and ideological domains of native life throughout the Americas, including the Southeast United States (see Hudson 1976; Reichel-Dolmatoff 1979, 1981). In some societies, certain individuals used crystals for specialized purposes such as divination (Hudson 1976:166–169). The Cherokees believed that their priests and conjurers could see into the future by gazing into powerful crystals. Quartz crystals also played a role in physical and spiritual protection and could bring a man success in warfare, rainmaking, hunting, and lovemaking. In Native North American mythology generally, a woman could become impregnated by swallowing a crystal or other bright object (see also Nassaney 1992b:316–319).

Objects as powerful as quartz crystals would have been ideal materials for individuals seeking social advancement to try to monopolize. The spatial distribution of quartz crystal suggests that its processing may have been intensified or partially controlled by segments of society. For instance, the high proportion of this material in some sites nearer the source area suggest that specialized producers may have been chipping quartz crystal and passing on finished products to centralized locations such as Toltec Mounds. This does not preclude the possibility that specialists were also chipping quartz crystal at Toltec Mounds, where high proportions of the material occur in the off-plaza areas of the site (Nassaney 1992b:314).

It is unlikely that all of the lithic raw materials used by Plum Bayou peoples were obtained locally. For example, almost all of the novaculite recovered in the region lacks cortex, suggesting that novaculite was obtained from a bedded source, the closest of which is more than twenty kilometers (and probably closer to seventy-five kilometers) west of Toltec Mounds. As population mobility decreased in the Coles Creek period, people in need of this raw material would have been required to travel farther to acquire it directly or obtain it in exchange. In either event, the costs for obtaining novaculite would have increased.

In order to avoid this increased cost, local populations actively chose to make use of locally available gravel chert that could be easily procured. At the same time, this local solution would have undermined attempts by elites to formalize exchange networks designed to supply nonsource areas with lithic raw materials. Another means of avoiding these exchange relationships was to seek out "localized sources of rare stone" (see Rolingson 1982a:93). Yet another way to avoid the costs incurred by high quality, exotic raw material was the intentional thermal alteration of gravel cherts to improve their flaking characteristics. Each of these deliberate choices represents decisions made by individuals to maintain a degree of autonomy and self-sufficiency in the face of changing economic and political conditions. Some of these practices resulted from previous choices that had been made, and others were the responses to the attempts of leaders to engage in different practices aimed at monopolizing surplus to underwrite the new roles they hoped to fill in society. The archaeological record of lithic tools and debitage are tangible expressions of resistance to elite attempts to use exchange for political purposes.

Ceramics were also an important material means of social reproduction. Given the daily practices associated with container production and use, pottery is frequently implicated in political life (see E. S. Johnson 2000). Plum Bayou culture assemblages comprise vessels that were used for storing, preparing, and serving food, including burnished and unburnished bowls, flat-bottomed jars, and beakers. The predominant type—Baytown Plain—is an undecorated, grog-tempered pottery (Nassaney 1994; Rolingson 1998; Stewart-Abernathy 1982). Generally, no more than 5 percent of an assemblage is marked by the barest stylistic elaboration, consisting of one or more incised lines or punctations on the lip or rim. Overall cord marking sometimes occurs, though this is less a decorative surface treatment than it is a textured result of paddling with a cord-wrapped stick.

Grog-tempered pottery is a persistent tradition in the ceramic history of the Lower Mississippi Valley. Introduced in the early Marksville period (ca. 100 B.C.), it was employed until it was eclipsed by shell tempering more than a thousand years later in many parts of the region. The factors that led to the adoption of shell tempering are as poorly understood as the reasons that grog temper was so popular for so long (see Alt, this volume; Pauketat 2001). An attempt to better understand the technology of grog temper and its social embeddedness is being addressed in a study under the auspices of the Plum Bayou Survey project (Drake 2000; Nassaney 1999). This work involves the preparation and examination of a sample of ceramic thin-sections from a Plum Bayou culture household, the Ink Bayou site (3PU252). The thin-sections are being observed to record the presence and frequency of grog, voids, and other aplastic inclusions to determine the variability in the body of the pottery. Preliminary results indicate that the composition of grog-tempered pottery is extremely variable, perhaps more than initially expected (Drake 2000). Unlike shell-tempered pottery, which requires narrow parameters for successful production outcomes (specific amounts of shell added to the paste, a restricted firing temperature range, and so on), grog-tempered ceramic technology appears to be much more versatile and expedient. In other words, the technology could be easily taught and easily produced, and temper was always readily available. Under these conditions there would be few constraints on the control of this technology and it could be reproduced with little effort by a broad segment of the society (Drake 2000). The flexibility of the technology may explain to some extent why it persisted for such a long time in parts of the Lower Mississippi Valley and why it was an extremely long-lived ceramic tradition.

Although shell-tempered pottery was used sparingly in Plum Bayou culture, it never represented a significant proportion of the ceramic technology. Plum Bayou culture peoples did not adopt the thinner-walled containers and diversified vessel forms, such as bottles, made possible by shell temper. Despite the technological advantages that such forms may have provided, they were perhaps inconsistent with the autonomy and social flexibility that characterize Late Woodland societies in much of the Mid-south.

From these data, the social and political organization of the Plum Bayou culture remains a paradox, or at least it challenges us to rethink evolutionary ideas about complexity and inequality. For instance, the presence of goods that may have been used to mark positions of social prestige at Toltec Mounds—such as small quantities of copper, galena, mica, and conch shell obtained through long-distance exchange—could imply elite resource accumulation. Evidence of differential social status may also be gleaned from the labor mobilization embodied in the Toltec Mounds earthworks and elsewhere in the region. Yet the absence of lavish burials indicative of high rank and the poor integration of the settlement hierarchy, coupled with flexible ceramic and lithic technologies that defied easy control, suggest a model of weak leaders who had to continually negotiate their positions of rank and status. Such an interpretation is consistent with what we know about the communal nature of many native North American societies (e.g., see Saitta 1994; Trigger 1990a). Bonds of reciprocity, the need for consensus in political decisions, and other means of diffusing the exercise of power, such as maintaining local autonomy, comprise traditions that were difficult to erode. Other actions, with intended and unintended outcomes, led to subsistence intensification, technological reorganization, changing access to resources, and labor mobilization. These are potential sites of tension in small-scale societies. Although Plum Bayou culture may have severely strained the rules of communalism, the communal mode inhibits the concentration of political power so long as authority depends upon consensus among participants (see also Lee 1990:240). Moreover, "the ties of kinship set limits to the amount of social labor that can be mobilized for collective purposes" (Wolf 1982:99). If leaders cannot guarantee themselves independent power over resources, the people they strive to control may resist successfully (Wolf 1982:99). There is little evidence that segments of Plum Bayou society were able to monopolize resources, with the exception of a few nonlocal objects whose significance may be overestimated.

Further evidence for the resistance of local populations is the abandonment of Toltec Mounds and much of the region after A.D. 1100, which created a settlement vacuum or so reorganized the population that archaeologists are hard-pressed to identify any material remains from the period (Nassaney 1994:49–50). The daily practices of most of the population, which prohibited the mobilization of surplus and its concentration in the hands of a few, worked against those who tried to sustain their positions of authority in the region after A.D. 1100. Plum Bayou culture disintegrated partly because nonelites sought to pursue activities that served their own interests, including the retention of the material symbols and technologies of a communal cause. Of course, if we expand the spatial frame of analysis to the adjoining regions of the Lower Mississippi Valley and the Midsouth, we see that newly integrated polities emerged on the peripheries of Plum Bayou culture at about A.D. 1000. I am thinking particularly of the Spiro site in eastern Oklahoma and Cahokia in the Central Mississippi Valley. A generalized model of core-periphery dynamics may be too simplistic and simply inappropriate to understand historical development in pre-state societies (see McElrath et al. 2000:8–9)

The observed cyclical pattern of regional integration/aggregation and disintegration/dispersal also raises important questions about the movement of large numbers of people on the landscape (see Sassaman, Saunders, this volume). While various mechanisms can provoke migrations, displaced groups are likely to create new traditions when they settle into new areas or encounter and interact with populations that previously resided in a particular territory. For example, Rogers (1991:239) noted that early Caddoan ceremonial centers in the Arkansas Basin of eastern Oklahoma are located in places that experienced little previous use, and he proposes that this may "represent a move away from the ancestors . . . towards new sources of cosmological validation." A better theory of tradition and more detailed histories like the one I have begun to explicate for central Arkansas are needed to explore the antecedents of Spiro and Cahokia. We have already made a good start on archaeological data recovery; now we only need to think of the evidence in historical-processual terms.

Conclusion

For theories to be successful, they must elucidate the complexity of the processes that we seek to understand. As anthropological archaeologists embrace history, they soon learn that history and agency allow for a near infinite variety of social actions. But if the historical narratives and experiences of small-scale and centralized societies are so divergent, how can we hope to settle on a theoretical framework that can encompass them all?

A historical-processual approach need not completely abandon the idea of human regularities. But rather than confine ourselves to a search for laws of human behavior, human universals can serve as the moorings for an overarching framework of human history. For example, all people engage in the process of cultural construction through practice. This human activity typically implicates material culture as an active medium to create, reproduce, and transform social relations—in short, to make history on a contested terrain. Insofar as these human qualities are invariate (though, of course, their content varies tremendously), they can serve to unite historic and preliterate societies (see also Lightfoot 1995). At some level, the questions we ask about Archaic, Amish, and antebellum societies can be fundamentally the same. Thus, one of the benefits of a historical-processual approach is the way in which it transcends time and space by focusing on tradition, history, human agency, power, and the material world.

In this chapter I have tried to use a political-economic framework to illuminate the southeastern Late Woodland landscape at multiple scales of analysis. The daily practices of resource acquisition, food preparation, craft production, and mound building reinforced cultural traditions that reproduced society. Because replication is never precise, however, human actions contribute to culture change; the unintended consequences that inevitably ensue create potential contradictions in the lived worlds of different segments of society.

Plum Bayou culture consisted of hundreds of individuals who varied by age, gender, physical ability, and status. Because no two individuals occupied the same physical space or shared all of the same social experiences, each stood in a different relationship to kin, community, and polity. In seeking to reconcile conflicting demands placed on their labor by family, neighbors, and leaders, individuals made choices that led to social tensions and struggles. Thus, while some practices reinforced traditions, such as the use of grog temper, others simultaneously challenged and worked to transform traditions, such as the decreased mobility that led to increased labor costs associated with lithic resource acquisition. All of these practices were responsible for making history, and the archaeological record is the fossilized outcome of these processes.

Individuals throughout history have struggled over the rights to control the creation of their own identities and the imposition of economic and social values as a means of exercising power. Such rights are not inalienable; all human groups contest material and symbolic imposition. The Late Woodland was a particularly dynamic period, during which there were numerous threats to the social order brought about by tensions created though new productive relations and possibilities for social life. Late Woodland peoples were in the process of domesticating themselves while simultaneously resisting relationships of inequality (see Cobb and Nassaney 2000). Whereas the relations of inequality in the succeeding Mississippian period did not squelch contestation, they created an arena with a different set of cultural expectations and practices in which members of society were able to promote their interests more effectively at the expense of others. These actions, in turn, engendered new forms of resistance that emerged as part of an ongoing subordinate discourse expressed in language, material forms, and other daily media.

This model challenges us to see the historical dynamics that push kin-based societies toward inequality as a cyclical, nonlinear process (e.g., see Anderson 1996a, b; Nassaney 1992b; Zagarell 1986). The rise and fall of so-called chiefly societies is a case in point. Communal relations seem to lie immediately beneath the veneer of power and authority in incipient ranked societies (Lee 1990:232), as I have tried to demonstrate for the Late Woodland Southeast. This is not to say that egalitarianism is the natural order of humanity; rather, all forms of social relations—be they egalitarian or hierarchical—are created and reproduced through practice. Moreover, the historical processes of domination and resistance, exclusion and inclusion, are inscribed in the domestic world of material remains and the built environment of the regional landscape, which served as political instruments of expression, repression, and empowerment (see Paynter and McGuire 1991).

At the start of the twenty-first century, the general outlines of time-space systematics have been established for most areas of the world and archaeologists have moved beyond culture history, that is, merely delineating the chronological sequence of material remains (see Trigger 1989a, b). While temporal concerns will always be important to archaeologists, we can now begin to embrace a cultural history that moves inquiry toward a common concern for elaborating the meaning of contextual cultural practices and is sensitive to the peculiarities of time and space. As social scientists with an interest in long-term history, archaeologists are uniquely poised to make a significant contribution to this goal. By doing so we will have entered the realm of a truly global anthropology in which we can contribute to the debates about significant social and political issues in contemporary life.

Acknowledgments

Charlie Cobb, Eric Drake, Tim Pauketat, Ken Sassaman, Robert Ulin, and Allen Zagarell provided useful commentary on earlier drafts of this paper. Discussions with Ken Sassaman, in particular, helped me to keep sight of the ways in which my interpretations of the Plum Bayou culture exemplify a historical process of tradition and practice. I thank Tim Pauketat for inviting me to contribute to this volume and for helping to lead the way in exploring some important new reconceptualizations in the archaeological enterprise.

11

A Tradition of Discontinuity

American Bottom Early and Middle Woodland
Culture History Reexamined

Andrew C. Fortier

An evolutionary paradigm is the implicit linchpin of culture history and
has also served as a fundamental backdrop for both behavioral and processual archaeology (Dunnell 1980; Lyman et al. 1997; Schiffer 1976,
1996). The well-documented archaeological record of the American Bottom of Illinois, which contains more than thirty phases and hundreds of
excavated sites, has generally been perceived as a laboratory for the study
of accretional evolutionary process. Chronological charts deceptively portray a unilineally sequenced series of cultures and phases with embedded
diachronic linkages and local continuity (Bareis and Porter 1984:12).
Conceptual notions that cultures emerge as a result of adaptive *in situ*
processes in "wonderful" environments are based on a rather simplistic
Garden of Eden principle (see Binford 1980:19, as used in a different
context) that when applied to the American Bottom presupposes a long-
term tradition of cultural stability. Elsewhere, any observable changes in
such *in loco* traditions have generally been regarded by some as representing brief periods of punctuated equilibrium (PE) (Eldridge and Gould
1972; MacArthur and Wilson 1963; also see Farnsworth 1986:634–635;
Farnsworth and Asch 1986:438; Struever 1968:147–148).

In the Garden of Eden model, which strongly underlies the present
chronological sequencing of cultures in the American Bottom, traditional
patterns would be theoretically reestablished after each bout of PE. I have
argued elsewhere, however, (Fortier 1998:345) that for historical processes to effect so-called punctuated equilibrium, one must first establish
an equilibrium, or population stasis. In other words, to arrest or cause a
qualitative change in "tradition," there must already be a recognizable

parent tradition in place. As I shall demonstrate, the American Bottom never achieved such population stasis for much of its Woodland history, nor did it ever, prior to *cal* A.D. 650, spawn a single cultural tradition.

The punctuated equilibrium (allopatric speciation) model was developed by Eldridge and Gould (1972) to counter the more prevalent evolutionary model of phyletic gradualism in biology and paleontology. Its use in culture history was not anticipated and probably should not even be used in cultural contexts. At the basis of the PE model are local populations termed "peripheral isolates" and their parent population. "A peripheral isolate develops into a new species if *isolating mechanisms* evolve that will prevent the re-initiation of gene flow if the new form re-encounters its ancestors at some future time"(1972:94). Otherwise, biological populations mostly achieve stasis or equilibrium. Isolating mechanisms might include geologic events, such as tectonics or flooding, that might cause gene pools to be separated from the parent population, or mutations that occur within peripheral isolate populations that serve to further distance that gene pool from the parent.

It is difficult to make this kind of biological equilibrium model analogous to new culture (tradition) formation processes, since complete cultural isolation from a parental population anywhere in the Midwest probably never occurred. Identifying isolating mechanisms or specific environmental barriers in the Midwest for past cultural groups would be difficult if not impossible, especially given the high degree of mobility of people throughout pre-Euro-American history in this region. Moreover, defining a so-called parental population and homeland for any Early or Middle Woodland culture is arguable at best. Finally, I would further argue that while achieving and maintaining stasis may be characteristic of biological populations, cultural populations and human behavior in general are more dynamic and perhaps more unstable, particularly over short periods of time. In fact, one of the key themes of this volume is that traditions are formed largely as a result of perpetual renegotiation processes that are often anything but static (see Pauketat, this volume). Nowhere is this more apparent than during the Early and Middle Woodland periods of the American Bottom. In fact, neither the process of cultural gradualism, nor its proposed counter-process, punctuated equilibrium, is supported by the archaeological record in this area.

Cultural historical process does not simply involve mechanisms of stability and tradition, nor do stylistic changes in artifacts always arise from internal adaptive mechanisms, à la Struever (1968:147–148). Cultural changes of a nondevelopmental nature—for example, those induced by environmental stress (floods, drought); external human influences (migration, new trading partners); internal unpredictable conflicts involving personalities or shifts in power acquisition; unforeseen nativistic revivals or messianic cult movements; differential access to, or availability of, resources; and sudden resource depletion (crop failures or swings in faunal distribution), and so on—are equally important factors of historic process (Kelle and Kovalson 1973:75–78; see also Chesnokov 1969). In short, such aforementioned forces of chance or historical circumstance are factors that can have great influence on social relationships, as well as on social, economic, and technological development. They can also either stimulate or impede the formation of cultural tradition.

Of course, humans do not simply interact impassively with such "forces," as the mechanistic materialists of the nineteenth century suggested (Cornforth 1973), but they also respond to them in a very specific and, generally, nonpassive manner. Humans negotiate history. Sometimes, people do respond to these forces by making *in loco* modifications, as some Neo-Darwinian archaeologies (Maschner 1996; see also Pauketat 2001) have suggested. However, abandonment of territory is another option. As already noted, sometimes individuals purposively produce historical circumstances. The responses (effects) are not always predictable. Could anyone have predicted the impact that Wovoka's Far West Ghost Dance millennial cult in 1889 would have on internal Native American politics, Euro–Native American relations, ceremonial life, and social action both west and east of the Rockies (Mooney 1896), or of its long-lasting effect as a revitalistic emblem among Native Americans even within the past thirty years (Kehoe 1992:335)?

All of the aforementioned historical forces can affect tradition-forming processes and can either be construed as adaptive or nonadaptive, depending on the outcome. It becomes a question of regional scale. In the extreme case when groups abandon a region because the forces of historical circumstance leave no other option, the process of leaving may be adaptive in a survival sense, but that same process may preclude the *in situ* formation of longstanding cultural traditions. More importantly, when this pattern of response occurs repeatedly, over a given period of time, such as we observe for the Early and Middle Woodland period in the American Bottom, then a tradition of cultural discontinuity is established, not a unilineal cultural sequence.

Conceptually the word "tradition" has been used rather generically by archaeologists at both a regional and local scale and—as defined by Willey and Phillips (1958) and Haury (1956)—was intended as a fluid concept to describe both small-and large-scale interrelated material configurations that had temporal continuity (Willey and Phillips 1958:38). Hence, one can simultaneously identify Eastern Woodlands, Middle Woodland, Crab Orchard, Hopewell Zoned Rocker Stamped, blade tool, and small-tool traditions within the same temporal continuum. In this sense, "a tradition may exist for any cultural trait or combination of traits" (Haury 1956: 38). While ethnicity is implied in each term, it is also possible to have traditions practiced by more than one "ethnic" group. In short, a great deal of scalar ambiguity has been built into the term "tradition." In contrast to several other papers in this volume (for example, see Saunders, Loren, this volume), this essay takes a macrotradition approach (see Lightfoot, this volume) by diachronically examining the interplay of multiple traditions active in the American Bottom during the Early and Middle Woodland periods. As I shall argue, historical forces, often beyond the control of local populations, played a pivotal role in constantly disrupting tradition-forming processes in the American Bottom. While it is possible for microtradition studies to examine individual agents of negotiated change within relatively short-term frameworks, tracking cultural practices in the American Bottom associated with any one tradition for significant lengths of time, prior to A.D. 600, has in the past met with frustration. However, it is exactly the disjunctive nature of American Bottom historical process that makes this region so unique. Once the evolutionary conceptual baggage is discarded, then historical process, involving not one but many traditions, becomes more understandable.

An Unreticulated Tradition of Cultural Discontinuity

As we now look at American Bottom culture history, a number of major cultural discontinuities have emerged that cannot simply be explained away as episodes of PE or adaptive response. McElrath (1993, 1995; see also Emerson and McElrath, this volume) has recently reexamined the Late Archaic sequence and concluded that significant external input into the American Bottom may represent the most important historic process that accounts for cultural variability at that time. The process itself involves the periodic expansion of specific cultures into the American Bottom, and contraction back to various heartlands ("ethnic cores") in the Midsouth (Ledbetter), or to the west (Titterington) and east (Riverton).

Even in the late 1970s and early 1980s, the Late Archaic and Early Woodland transition was regarded by some (Emerson and Fortier 1986; McElrath et al. 1984) as a major cultural disjuncture, evinced by dramatic changes in material culture, community organization, and settlement positioning on the landscape. Here, again, historic processes of unknown derivation entailed abandonment of the area by Late Archaic groups and migration into, and subsequent occupation of, the Bottom by unrelated Early Woodland Marion and Black Sand cultures.

During the 500 years of subsequent Early and Middle Woodland culture history, the American Bottom served as a crossroads for numerous unlinked, mobile, and marginalized populations, including cultural entities such as Carr Creek (Marion), Ringering (Black Sand), Florence, Columbia, Morton, Cement Hollow (Havana), Crab Orchard, and Holding (Hopewell) (Emerson and Fortier 1986; Evans 1995). This was followed by the abandonment of the American Bottom and later reoccupation of it by early Late Woodland (Rosewood phase) groups after *cal* A.D. 400. McElrath and I (2000) have argued that both environmental and external social-political factors may have played significant roles in this abandonment-reoccupation process. There is an apparent abandonment of Mississippi River floodplain locales during the period *cal* A.D. 400–650 that is inexplicable without invoking ruminations of an environmental nature, such as, Was the Garden of Eden under water?

The following 600 years, characterized by relative stability and the emergence of an American Bottom cultural identity, is undoubtedly one of the few periods of time in the Bottom where *in situ* changes can be observed over a long period of time (Fortier 1998; Kelly 1990). Yet, even during this period there are major settlement shifts and movements of groups from the uplands into the Mississippi River floodplain, as well as significant *in situ* population expansion in all environmental niches (*cal* A.D. 650–850; Patrick phase) (Fortier and Jackson 2000; Kelly 1990). In addition, an incursion of Sponemann phase people from the north at *cal* A.D. 750–850 seems to mark the end of this period (Fortier et al. 1991); shortly thereafter, the possible arrival of ceramic-bearing cultures from the Lower Illinois River Valley (Late Bluff) after *cal* A.D. 850 and the appearance of lower-valley limestone-tempered traditions in the southern American Bottom is noteworthy, as is the sudden appearance and wholesale use of maize at the same time (Kelly 1990).

Near the end of this period, circa *cal* A.D. 900–1000, there is increasing evidence for Lower Mississippi River Valley interaction with American Bottom late Late Woodland groups (in the form of southern Illinois Mill Creek hoe blades, Varney Red Filmed pottery, and Lower Mississippi River Valley Yankeetown filleted and Coles Creek ware [see Kelly 1990]); finally, there is a dramatic Emergent Mississippian-Mississippian transition period, or "Big Bang" phenomenon at *cal* A.D. 1050 that heralds the Mississippian period (Pauketat 1994, 1997a, 1998b), followed several centuries thereafter by periodic Oneota incursions from the north (D. K.

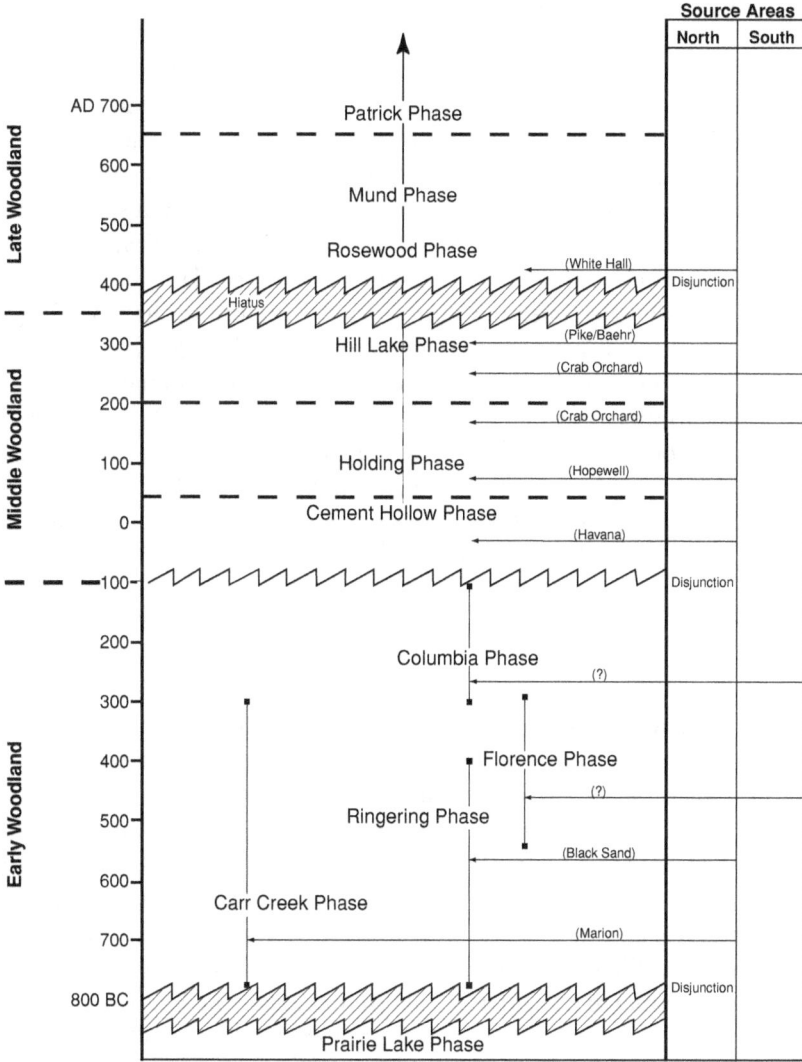

Fig. 11.1. Revised calibrated time scale for the Early and Late Woodland periods of the American Bottom.

Jackson 1998), and finally, eventual abandonment of the floodplain by all native groups after circa *cal* A.D. 1350–1450.

In effect, while we can chronologically stack a series of cultural entities, affinity between these units on this heuristic vertical edifice should not be assumed (see fig. 11.1). The sorting process is only meaningful, however, if we understand that butterflies (Leach 1968:6), once mounted for display, do not tell us much about cultural practices or historical process. Ideally each phase, period, or stage boundary relationship should be examined without the baggage of a priori evolutionary assumptions.

A tradition of discontinuity does not necessarily preclude the operation of adaptive cultural responses per se, nor does it negate evolutionary advances or cultural reticulation at the regional scale. At issue are the processes that form local traditions or obviate their formation. It simply cannot be assumed that all areas or local regimes have identical historical circumstances or resources. The repeated failure to adapt to stresses of various sorts in the American Bottom, and therefore to maintain long-term traditions of settlement, technology, and subsistence, supports a model of culture historical process that is largely discontinuous—if not, from time to time, essentially chaotic and unpredictable. What we see in the archaeological record of the American Bottom is a series of short-lived microtraditions attached either to the umbilical cords of external traditions, or to roadhouse traditions passing through the Mississippi-Illinois-Missouri Rivers confluence zone.

Early Woodland and Early Middle Woodland Traditions

Prior to *cal* 100 B.C. the American Bottom represented a kind of temporary crossroads for several distinctive Early Woodland traditions (see Emerson and McElrath, this volume), including those affiliated with the Marion, Black Sand, Florence, Morton, and Columbia cultures (Emerson et al. 1983; Emerson and Fortier 1986; Evans et al. 1999; Fortier et al. 1984). None of these groups have local origins but are derived from both northern and southern valleys or interior upland heartlands. I would regard most of these "traditions" as consisting of small band-size groups of foragers, branching out from "ethnic core areas" (see Emerson and McElrath, this volume) to procure paludal resources from the Mississippi River floodplain when conditions allowed such expansion. Small camps are typical of this period although the occupation at Florence, by Florence phase people, was more substantial and included a large circular household structure (Emerson et al. 1983). In the central and southern American Bottom, most Early Woodland settlements are restricted to low-lying, paludal floodplain environments. Marion groups are an exception and can be found in the upland creek drainages as well as the Mississippi River trench (B. Koldehoff, personal communication 1999). In the northern American Bottom along the Wood River terrace locality, Early Woodland Marion, Black Sand, and Columbia groups occupy high sandy terraces

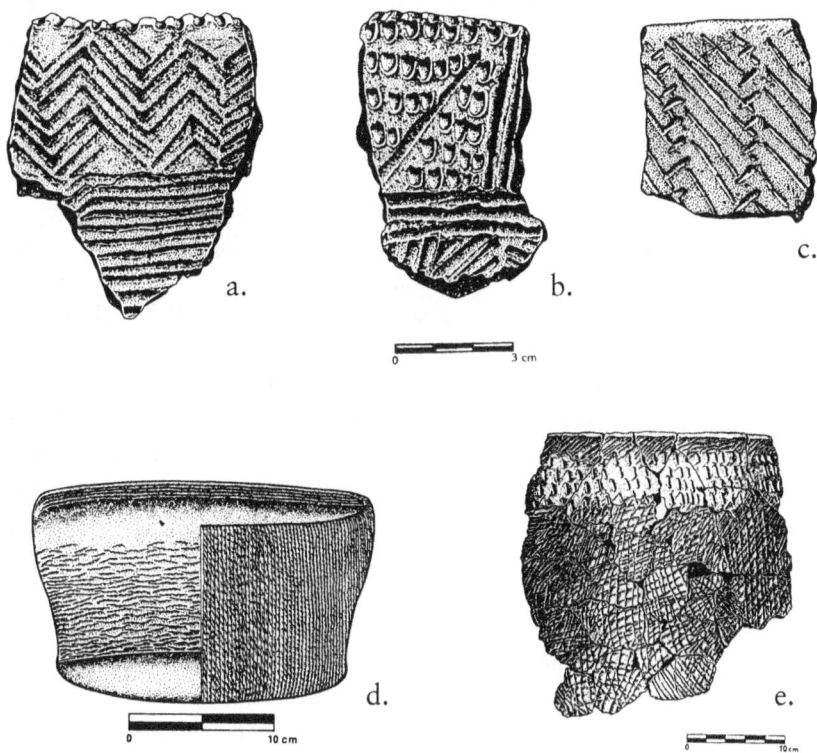

Fig. 11.2. Early Woodland ceramic traditions: a–b, Black Sand Incised; c, Morton Incised; d, Marion Thick; e, Florence.

overlooking the floodplain (Evans et al. 1999). Each of these Early Woodland groups shares a preference for sandy soils, a locational theme observed as well for early Middle Woodland settlers. There is virtually no evidence that any of the aforementioned Early Woodland groups intermingled or established long-term settlements anywhere in the American Bottom. Each practiced material culture traditions derived from outside this area. The pottery of each tradition is quite distinctive (see fig. 11.2). The grog-tempered traditions of the Florence and Columbia cultures are in stark contrast to the sand- and coarse-grit-tempered traditions of Black Sand and Marion. Although material cultural distinctions between assemblages are conspicuous, they are mostly limited to differing ceramic stylistic and technological traditions, and socially defined traits such as chert preferences.

An Early Woodland and Middle Woodland period (stage?) has been recognized for a long time in this area, but what actually distinguishes Early Woodland groups from the initial Middle Woodland occupants, other than ceramic traits, has never been considered in the literature of the American Bottom. In fact, the boundary between these two stages is arbitrarily defined. A number of artifact types, such as humpback scrapers and contracting stemmed points, as well as punctate and incised ceramic decoration, occur in both stages (Emerson et al. 1983; Finney 1983). More importantly, early Middle Woodland and Early Woodland groups share a common subsistence and settlement location strategy. Although rarely sharing the same site locations, the occupations of both are situated in low-lying, often sandy environments of the floodplain. Site densities are low in both cases, and settlements are widely dispersed throughout the floodplain, with minimal evidence for occupation in the adjacent uplands (excepting a Marion culture presence). Both Early Woodland and early Middle Woodland settlements are small and ephemeral in nature, suggesting a highly mobile way of life. Both subsistence systems are heavily oriented to the procurement of wild seeds, tubers, and nuts, and evidence for complex horticultural activity and diverse husbandry of domesticates, aspects that typify the subsequent Hopewell period in this area, is lacking. Yet, in the American Bottom a direct connection between early Middle Woodland assemblages and a specific Early Woodland tradition of material culture has never been established.

The initial Middle Woodland traditions of the American Bottom are largely the products of external influences, if not outright incursions of people. The earliest Middle Woodland expression, which we refer to as the Cement Hollow phase, dates to *cal* 100 B.C.–A.D. 50 and is directly affiliated with the Early Havana traditions of the Central Illinois River Valley. Ceramic and lithic assemblages are virtually indistinguishable. Artifact assemblages are redundant from site to site. Ceramics consist typically of large, thick-walled, sandy-grit-tempered cord-marked and plain jars, or jars with broad linear, ovate, or curvilinear dentate stamped decorations, often set within zoned fields (Fortier et al. 1984). Chevrons, deep plain impressions, cord-wrapped stick lip impressions, punctations, and occasional bossing are also observed. The use of curvilinear patterns is a new trait, one not found in Early Woodland ceramic assemblages of this area. Lithic assemblages generally include large bifacial ovate scrapers, knives, and hafted biface types, such as Snyders, Gibson, Norton, and Dickson/Waubesa. Lamellar blades are uncommon, as are the kind of extraregional exotics that typify subsequent Hopewell influences in this area after *cal* A.D. 50.

From a sociological standpoint Havana people in the American Bottom are poorly understood. They are few in number, but perhaps more numerous than their Early Woodland predecessors. At this time, it is a tradition defined by technological (ceramic and lithic) and, more recently, subsistence practices. Unlike the subsequent Hopewell tradition that is manifested throughout the midcontinent, early Havana traditions are locally based. So-called interaction sphere activities—that is, the exchange and interregional traffic of exotics—are not apparent in the initial Middle Woodland period. However, sweeping changes were afoot.

The Havana/Hopewell Renaissance

During the following two centuries after *cal* A.D. 50, fundamental changes occurred in technological, subsistence, community, ideological, and settlement systems in this area (Fortier 1995). This period, referred to locally as the Holding phase, and dating from *cal* A.D. 50 to A.D. 200, represents a significant break with the past and is associated and coeval with the emergence of Havana/Hopewell cultures throughout the Midwest. In the American Bottom the transition between early Middle Woodland and the Holding phase is clearly sharper and more defined than is the transition between the Early and Middle Woodland stages. Sweeping changes in both lithic and ceramic technology appear overnight, and smaller settlements are replaced by more extensive and nucleated horticulturally based villages (Fortier et al. 1989). Similar changes are observable throughout the Midwest at the same time. The emergence of Havana/Hopewell has generally been regarded as the culmination of a long process based in the preceding late Early Woodland and early Middle Woodland periods (Struever 1964), and this may be so at the regional level, or in so-called core areas such as the Illinois River Valley. However, in the American Bottom this emergence is better characterized as a Big Bang phenomenon.

The Holding phase evidenced a virtual renaissance in lithic technology. Assemblages are characterized by numerous formal tool types (see fig. 11.3), including chert hoes and adzes, a diverse number of disc scrapers, several new hafted biface types—for example, Manker and Ansell—a lamellar blade industry with its own subset of formal tools, and an extensive and diverse microtool industry (see fig. 11.4), including needlelike drills, perforators, gravers, end scrapers, and denticulates. The emergence of a small-tool tradition (Fortier 2000a) consisting of formal tools made on both flakes and blades appears overnight and has no precedent in the Early Woodland or early Middle Woodland traditions of this area. Numerous nonlocal cherts, especially types from the southern Illinois region, increase dramatically in Havana/Hopewell assemblages. By way of contrast, earlier Cement Hollow lithic assemblages contain fewer artifact types, are less diverse in terms of the types of technologies present, and

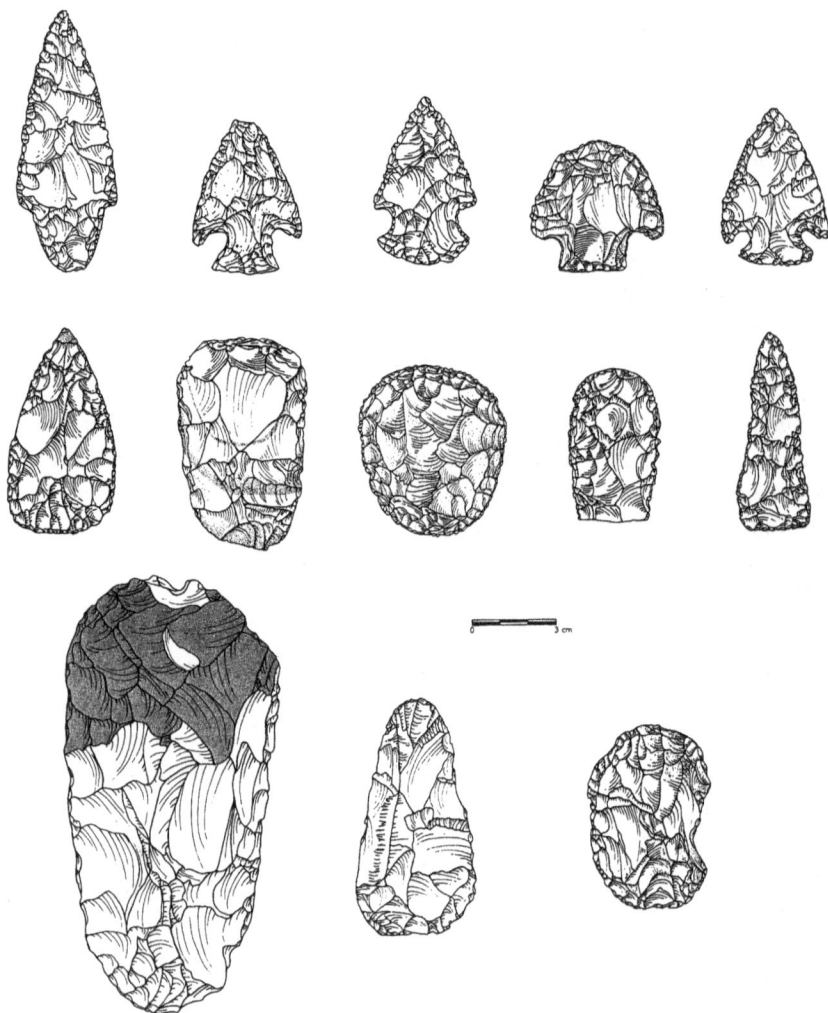

Fig. 11.3. Middle Woodland bifacial chert tool assemblage, traditional forms.

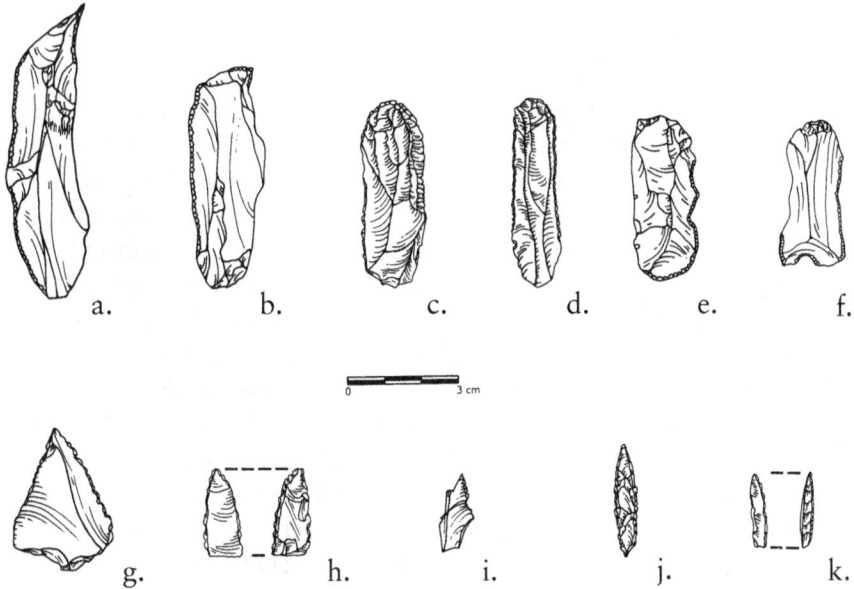

Fig. 11.4. Middle Woodland blade tool tradition: *a–b*, gravers; *c*, end scraper; *d*, side scraper/knife; *e*, denticulate; *f*, notched tool; *g*, graver; *h*, blunt-end drill; *i*, microperforator; *j–k*, microdrills.

have fewer nonlocal imports. This renaissance in lithic tool diversity during the Holding phase and Midwest in general is even more pronounced if one includes the various technologies that produced exotics, such as copper celts, tinklers, and awls, as well as stone platform pipes, and the use of such materials as mica, fluorite, and obsidian.

To be certain, some of this renaissance in lithic manipulation can be derived from the preceding Cement Hollow phase. A number of artifact types, including hafted bifaces and disk scrapers, parallel similar versions of antecedent types. However, the fact that so many new technologies are introduced at this time, and at precisely the same time that concurrent changes in ceramic and subsistence formats occur, clearly reenforces the dramatic transition that marks the emergence of the Holding phase.

In terms of ceramics the Holding phase is characterized by the appearance of elaborate design motifs, often placed in zoned fields. It is not uncommon to find multiple motifs on the same vessel, such as cross-hatching, punctating, rocker stamping, trailing, impressing, bossing, and brushing (Maher 1989). Most of these traits and their method of presentation on vessels appear overnight and unquestionably must be regarded as a form of symbolic communication (Seeman 1995), perhaps related to a kind of new cosmological remodeling that may involve the crystallization of both underworld and upper world themes. The use of these themes, particularly in repeated, predictable formats, in American Bottom ceramic assemblages speaks for strong ties with contemporary Havana/Hopewell peoples to the north. Some motifs, such as bossing or cross-hatching, always occur in the same area of the vessel. Motifs such as cross-hatching and small hemiconical punctates always occur together. Recumbent bird designs, particularly those involving aquatic diving birds, although rare in the American Bottom, are suggestive of cosmological themes. Serving bowls and ceramic earspools and figurines also appear for the first time, as do nonlocal vessel types such as partially red-slipped vessels (Hopewell Zoned Red), Marksville imitations (pots made with American Bottom pastes, but with Marksville "dot-dash" upper-rim treatment), Brangenburg vessels (bowl or jar forms with T-shaped lips), and Crab Orchard pottery (fabric-marked exterior surfaces). Tempering agents include not only sand and grit, but also, for the first time, grog and limestone. Jar size diversity increases and thin-walled types replace the thick-walled vessels of the preceding era (Maher 1996).

Grog tempering, a trait not observed in early Middle Woodland Havana assemblages elsewhere in the region, is an American Bottom identity marker. Grog temper does not occur in assemblages in the Lower Illinois River Valley with whom American Bottom peoples clearly interact and share so many other traits. Grog tempering, however, does appear in Crab Orchard tradition pottery to the south. It seems to be an expression of American Bottom cultural identity to take the design motifs of the Illinois Havana tradition and place them in the context of the grog-tempered technological traditions of southern Illinois. Limestone tempering, on the other hand, is a Lower Illinois River Valley trait and is closely associated with the finer-made Hopewell vessels found in American Bottom assemblages. Whether these vessels represent locally made imitations, or actual imports, is unclear.

Southern Illinois cherts such as Cobden, Dongola, Blair, Kaolin, and Mill Creek also find their way into Middle Woodland assemblages of the American Bottom and may represent attempts to incorporate southern Illinois traditions of chert preference into American Bottom assemblages. Overall chert color preferences, however, may prove to be a specific American Bottom identity hallmark, especially the use of local Ste. Genevieve (Root Beer, Purple, and Old Blue) cherts. It has even been suggested that such cherts were actually exported to neighboring Havana and Crab Orchard tradition regions (J. A. Williams 1989), and that a trade focusing on chert color was conducted at the highpoint of the Hopewellian Interaction Sphere (Struever 1964).

The admixture of northern and southern traditions of technology and style, as well as homegrown American Bottom color preferences, establishes a Middle Woodland American Bottom cultural identity and evidence that American Bottom people may have consciously attempted to maintain affinities to both area traditions. However, they were also expressing their own identity by making local choices in the area of technology and style, such as the use of local clay muds and cherts. I echo the thinking of others, such as Dobres and Hoffman (1999), who regard the interplay between technological practice and social identity to be closely intersected and mutually reinforcing. Closer study of American Bottom design motif combinations may also reveal local identity markers. Maher, for example, has observed that Havana cord-marked vessels from the American Bottom display exterior lip notching, while similar ceramic types from the Lower Illinois River Valley have interior notched lips (Maher 1996, 2000). A list of cultural attributes that are all found in American Bottom post–Cement Hollow phase Middle Woodland assemblages appears in table 11.1, which provides a suggested source for each.

Struever (1965) defined four Middle Woodland traditions in the southern Great Lakes region: Havana, Crab Orchard, Pike, and Scioto. He subsequently distinguished what he called four microstyle zones within the Havana tradition: Steuben, Yellow Bluffs, Snyders, and Carlyle. Microstyle zones were differentiated on the basis of area-specific ceramic decorative attributes. Although not directly expressed in Struever's 1965 article, embedded in the microstyle zone and regional tradition concepts is the presence of distinct ethnic identities, or "ethnic cores" (see Emerson and McElrath, this volume), in his view based solely on ceramic style.

The American Bottom was linked to the Havana tradition, Snyders microstyle zone of the Lower Illinois River Valley. Very little was actually known about American Bottom Middle Woodland stylistic or technological practices in the 1960s, especially their strong ties to the south. We can argue today that the American Bottom truly falls between two of Struever's regional traditions, Havana and Crab Orchard. Moreover, we can now identify nuances of technological ceramic and lithic practice that were not known forty years ago. American Bottom people drew from both southern and northern traditions of technology and style, and, perhaps in

Table 11.1. Traditional hallmarks of American Bottom Middle Woodland assemblages and their sources

Havana/Hopewell traditions of the North	Crab Orchard traditions of the South	Pan Regional Middle Woodland traditions	American Bottom traditions
Blade technology (Fulton)	Blade technology (Cobden)	Blades	Blades made on local, poor quality cherts
Limestone tempering	Grog tempering	Hoes	Use of all four ceramic tempers (grit, sand, limestone, grog)
Decorated bowls	—	Bossing	Exterior lip notching (Havana CM)
Brangenburg vessels' ceramic vessel attributes (zoning, interior lip channels, cross-hatching, rocker stamping, brushing) Hopewell zoned red, Hopewell plain, Hopewell zoned incised	Crab Orchard fabric marked Marksville ceramics xotics (fluorite) Mill Creek, Kaolin, Cobden, Dongola cherts Disk scrapers	Exotics (obsidian, mica, copper) Use of colorful cherts; Projectile point styles; Clay figurines, earspools	Use of Crescent Hills cherts and local Ste. Genevieve and Salem cherts (Root Beer, purple, Old Blue)
Log chamber tombs		Mound clusters with villages, river valley settlements, middens; Plant use diversity	Absence of mortuary mounds
Use of hazelnuts			

ways not predictable, this dual selection process generated its own identity signature. It is arguable as to whether the admixture of neighboring stylistic and technological traditions is enough to constitute an independent tradition, but since American Bottom ceramics and lithics are both predominantly made (not just used) in the American Bottom, I opine, in this case, that this unique practice should constitute tradition. In fact, the American Bottom is unique in the Midwest for its blend of northern and southern practices, and for what it does not share with neighboring traditions.

American Bottom Subsistence, Settlement, and Mortuary Practices

If there was a period of horticultural experimentation in the American Bottom preceding the Holding phase, it is not evident in the archaeological record. Food plants such as starchy seeds, wild bean, panicum type 61, as well as cucurbits, papaw, plum, persimmon, and small-seeded legumes increase dramatically after cal A.D. 50. Maize and tobacco appear for the first time (Riley et al. 1994; J. A. Williams 1993:197). The occurrence of more extensive and longer-term settlements, such as Holding (Fortier et al. 1989), Nochta (Higgins 1990), or Meridian Hills (J. A. Williams 1993), speaks for increasing reliance on a horticulturally based economic system (B. D. Smith 1992). Extensive villages, with associated middens, probably emerged for the first time as a direct consequence of the need to care for cultivated stands of plants in singularly hospitable locations. It is this kind of settlement stability that no doubt supported the grand diversity of crafts, arts, and technologies that characterizes this phase.

Despite the existence of several large Holding phase communities in the American Bottom (Fortier et al. 1989), the overall population base was relatively sparse. There are no large mound and village centers of the scale seen in the Lower Illinois River Valley or at sites such as Twenhafel in southern Illinois. Moreover, there is also no evidence for the kind of elaborate mortuary activity identified in those areas. The absence of any evidence of mortuary practice in the archaeological record is a significant American Bottom identity marker and enigmatic. It is unclear why elaborate mound burial, such as that observed in both the Havana (Buikstra et al. 1998) and Crab Orchard traditions to the north and south, respectively, should not also occur in the American Bottom. Were different mortuary formats practiced in this area, or were individuals transported for burial, in some format, to more northerly locations? In addition, the number of so-called Hopewell exotics excavated from American Bottom sites or recovered by collectors number scarcely twenty items (Maher 1996). Twice this number has been recovered from single burials in the Illinois River Valley (Ken Farnsworth, personal communication 1998). Were American Bottom communities unwilling to participate or submit their hard-won identity to the obligations associated with the Hopewellian Interaction Sphere and affiliated mortuary programs of the north and south?

Reducing Tradition and Area Abandonment

The period between *cal* A.D. 150 and 350 is known as the Hill Lake phase and is characterized by a number of notable changes in settlement, technology, and subsistence. Hopewell trickle-down artifacts disappear, and subsistence procurement patterns revert to pre–Holding phase levels, especially in terms of decreasing use of cultigens and diversity of procured plants. Ceramic design elements are now erratically executed, and free field designs replace zoned field designs (see fig. 11.5). Grog-tempered rocker-stamped and brushed jars become the predominate vessel types of this phase. Bowls disappear and lamellar blade industries occur only at the larger settlements (Fortier 2000b). There is increasing reliance on local chert resources, although colorful local cherts continue to be preferred (Fortier 1992). The only domicile from this period comes from the Truck #7 site and is relatively elaborate but probably built for one winter-based family (Fortier 1985:183–197). The existence of such small-scale homesteads at this time may represent evidence for social fissioning and be indicative of a breakdown in aggregated community life.

For nearly 150 years the American Bottom continued to be occupied by a small Middle Woodland population that was widely dispersed over the floodplain. I propose that as American Bottom communities began to establish their own identity or traditions, they also became increasingly isolated from both northern and southern traditions. The casual and even haphazard way in which older design motifs, such as rocker stamping, are applied to vessels, as well as the shift to free field design presentation and the disappearance of zoning, may reflect a desire to establish a local identity and break from the regimented and imposed northern Havana tradition styles of the preceding period. The abandonment of specialized blade industries and many formal tool types at the end of this phase may reflect a similar desire to break from Havana stylistic and technological traditions. On the other hand, rather than actively resisting those traditions,

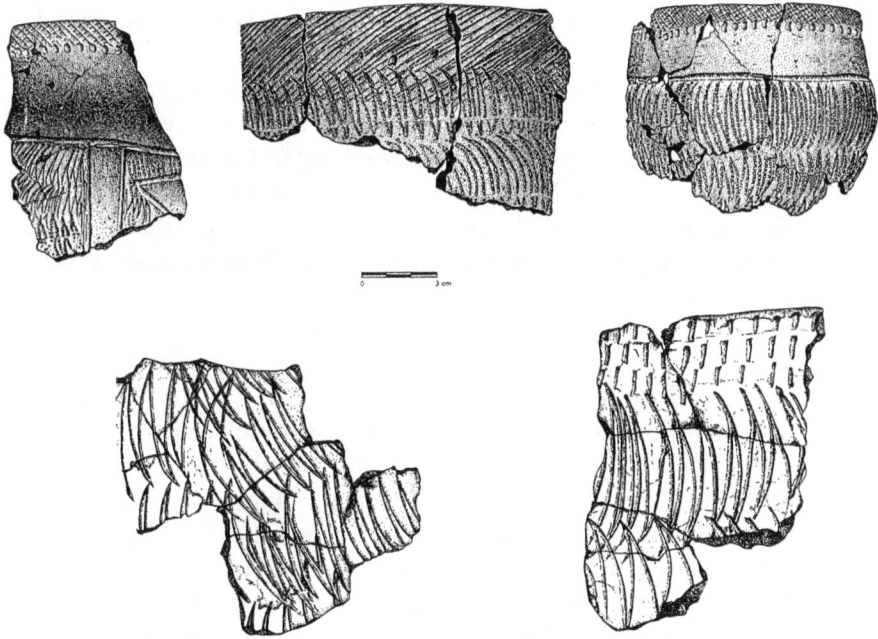

Fig. 11.5. Middle Woodland ceramic design formats: *upper*, Holding phase zoned, fixed field; *lower*, Hill Lake phase unzoned, free field.

perhaps American Bottom people were simply undergoing a process of peripheral isolation. In Haury (1956:44) terminology, this parallels, in many respects, a "Reducing Tradition" where trait loss occurs through an increasing simplification process brought about by an emergent closed value system (that is, a "lack of cultural interest" [47] in other cultures). Alternatively, with the breakdown of the Hopewell Interaction Sphere, northern and southern ethnic cores were no longer interested in maintaining traditional ties with backwater areas such as the American Bottom.

At the end of this phase, sometime around *cal* A.D. 350, the gradual process of Hopewellian collapse in the American Bottom is suspended by the apparent abandonment of the area. It is unclear what historic processes brought about this final collapse. One possibility is that the small hinterland population of the American Bottom moved back into one or more core areas, perhaps in response to collapsing religious, social, or political systems in those areas. This may have occurred for appropriational (*sensu* Polanyi 1957) reasons (Halperin 1994), for example, a desire to maintain closer social or religious ties, a practice or response that leaves no evidence in the archaeological record. Perhaps it was due to a perceived need to revitalize a rapidly disintegrating cultural tradition that still owed much to the north and south. In any case, following abandonment of the area by Middle Woodland populations, less than a century afterward, early Late Woodland populations, clearly related to Lower Illinois River Valley traditions (White Hall), reappear in the American Bottom—*but* with lithic and ceramic assemblages and settlement strategies that differ in virtually every respect from their Middle Woodland predecessors (McElrath and Fortier 2000).

Conclusion

Understanding the discontinuous nature of the culture historical process of the Woodland stage is in its infancy and still based on only a handful of excavated sites. Ironically, much of our thinking about Early and Middle Woodland archaeology has been colored by research at Cahokia and its mostly gradualistic, unilinear models of Mississippian emergence (Kelly 1990). However, the historical circumstances and cultural trajectory of that period were quite different and disconnected from the Early and Middle Woodland past. The vertical nature of chronological charts such as have been established for the American Bottom is unfortunate, for it implies connectivity. On the contrary, the American Bottom "sequence" really embodies a hodgepodge of cultural traditions, many of which are horizontally intrusive, unrelated, and short-lived. The Early Woodland, Middle Woodland, and initial Late Woodland traditions of the American Bottom are only sequential in a chronological sense. In fact, cultural period interfaces are mostly disjunctive in nature and, therefore, belie simple evolutionary interpretations.

The fact that an *in situ* population in the American Bottom never became established during this 500 to 600 year period is probably due to four important historic factors: (1) its geographic position at the confluence of three rivers, making it competitively attractive to multiple cultural traditions for short periods of time; (2) the hydrological instability and mostly inhospitable paludal nature of the Mississippi River basin; (3) the unstable mobility patterns of Early Woodland groups throughout the Midwest; and (4) its cultural position between two major Middle Woodland tradition core areas. In this sense the American Bottom may have functioned as a kind of no-man's-land or buffer zone between the Havana and Crab Orchard traditions for much of the Middle Woodland period and under these circumstances could neither establish a permanent identity of its own nor break from its northern or southern parent traditions, that is, it could not become a peripheral isolate. The development of some sort of incipient self-identity may have developed over an undefined portion near the end of this period, but unknown circumstances that accelerated the collapse of Middle Woodland traditions in the core areas, and perhaps throughout the Midwest, may have prompted this fledgling and marginalized American Bottom "tradition" to abandon the periphery for its perceived motherland. Perhaps there was a revitalistic movement at the end of Hopewell that beckoned neighboring and marginal affines back to the central arena, possibly for one last fandango (see Fortier 1998:356–358). The actual circumstances of abandonment can only be surmised. In any case, the most telling factors for the demise of the Middle Woodland stage in the American Bottom will not be found locally, but in those core areas.

Future Middle Woodland research in the American Bottom should be directed at defining the hallmarks of local identity and technological practice, such as may be found in ceramic decorative styles, projectile point types, ceramic manufacturing techniques, material source preferences, mortuary practices, settlement logistics, and community organization formats. The forces of historical circumstance also need to be better defined, especially at the boundaries of periods and phases. Models by their very natures color perceptions of our data. Models based on cultural gradualism, adaptation, punctuated equilibria, or forces of historical circumstance each carry a certain amount of theoretical baggage that prefigure how we regard cultural tradition and the means of articulating traditions in time and space.

Chronological sequences are, after all, heuristic devices that explain very little about cultural practice or historical process. In any case, recognizing the discontinuous nature of American Bottom cultural traditions during the Woodland period is a minimal first step in deconstructing evolutionary models for this period that have now outlived their usefulness in this arena of culture history.

Acknowledgments

Although I was not an original participant in the symposium that spawned this book, Tim Pauketat graciously invited me to contribute here, and that act is appreciated, as are his editorial efforts on this manuscript. I have benefited over the years, through direct conversations or writings, from a number of dedicated Early and Middle Woodland colleagues, including Thomas Emerson, Thomas Maher, Kenneth Farnsworth, John Walthall, N'omi Greber, J. Bryant Evans, Fred Finney, Kathryn Parker, Joyce Williams, Michael Wiant, and the late James Griffin. I wish to thank both Thomas Emerson and Dale McElrath for reading and commenting on the manuscript. Mike Lewis and Linda Alexander are responsible for the illustrations, which are used with the permission of the Illinois Transportation Archaeological Research Program at the University of Illinois.

12

Interpreting Discontinuity and Historical Process in Midcontinental Late Archaic and Early Woodland Societies

Thomas E. Emerson and Dale L. McElrath

Fiddler on the roof . . . every one of us is a fiddler on the roof
trying to scratch out a pleasant simple tune without breaking his
neck. . . . How do we keep our balance? I can tell you in one
word—TRADITION!
Tevye the dairyman, in *Fiddler on the Roof*

Every individual, as Tevye observes, is a "fiddler on the roof," trying to keep their balance within the shifting demands and obligations of multiple social and natural environments, oscillating between stasis and catastrophic change, negotiating between "us" and "them," and so forth. The result of the many individuals' participation in such societal balancing acts is the very reproduction and transformation of society. Acting individually, but within a social context, these individuals create "communities of practice" that in their multiple interactions we might envision as creating "traditions."[1] An important aspect of such a heuristic is the recognition that such traditions are interwoven with social reproduction and, consequently, contain many subjective and arbitrary elements of learned behavior that are transmitted in the context of the multiple "communities of practice" (cf. Lave and Wenger 1991). Traditions have many material facies and multiscalar expressions ranging from narrow technologies to their broadest guise as panregional cultural correspondences. But we suggest that, at least at the level of a region, thinking of traditions in terms of "ethnic cores" may be useful for conceptualizing the past.

In this study we focus on the recognition of a number of historically and spatially defined local traditions in Terminal Archaic and Early Woodland cultural assemblages in the restricted area of the Mississippi River floodplain known as the American Bottom region of Illinois. At this period in pre-Columbian America, cultural histories are often seen as marked by evolutionary change encouraged by the addition of domesticates and ceramic technology to the cultural repertoire. Many archaeologists have viewed such changes as reflecting underlying environmentally conditioned, functional adaptations by stable in situ populations. However such interpretive models have an inherent functionalist and evolutionary bias that validates continuity and gradual change while obscuring evidence of variation and discontinuity, thus confirming their interpretations (e.g., Caldwell 1958; J. B. Griffin 1964; Willey 1966). By specifically recognizing independent local traditions, we recognize disjuncture in the archaeological sequence that may reflect changing and interacting communities of practice. In this regard we evaluate inferences derived from proposed evolutionary schemes for western Illinois Terminal Archaic and Early Woodland populations and provide alternative interpretations to explain observed variations in local cultural patterns (also see Fortier, this volume).

Abandoning strictly functionalist and adaptationalist interpretations, we reexamine the cultural-historical framework that archaeologists have created to characterize the groups occupying the American Bottom from about 1400 to 150 B.C.. We revisualize these earlier constructs in the context of communities of practice, ethnic cores, and local traditions within the broader confines of practice and agency (*sensu* collectivities) theory. While some have seen culture-history and postprocessual paradigms as incompatible or at least incongruent paradigms (e.g., Dancey 1999:254–256 or Lightfoot, this volume), we do not (see Emerson 1999:267–268). In the American Bottom it is apparent that the massive data sets (including entire excavated sites with extensive chronometric, subsistence, settlement, and material culture information) organized against a cultural-historical backdrop provide the time-space-material culture dimensions necessary to study practice and agency in a pre-Columbian context. Ultimately, in this examination, we conclude that, conceptually, communities of practice and developing ethnicities prove to be strong candidates for understanding social change in pre-Colombian America (see similar conclusions by other authors in this volume, especially Sassaman, Saunders, and Lightfoot).

Traditions

Tradition is a loaded concept having a considerable history in archaeological theory, but most are familiar with it as codified in Willey and Phillips's taxonomy as "a (primarily) temporal continuity represented by persistent configurations in single technologies or other systems of related forms" (Willey and Phillips 1958:34–38). This narrower, materialist definition was an express retreat from an earlier, broader social conceptualization as "a distinctive way of life, reflected in various aspects of the culture . . . [marked by] persistent themes [that] dominate the life of the people" (Goggin 1949:17) or as a "socially transmitted cultural form which persists in time" (Haury 1956:39).

Pauketat (this volume) asks us to look to that broader earlier usage. It is a return to a commonsense tradition, defined by the 1990 *World Book Dictionary* as "the handing down of beliefs, opinions, customs, and stories, such as from parents to children, especially by word of mouth or by practice." However, this view also acknowledges that the reproduction of tradition is its transformation. This is a "historical" and "processual" tradition that is both grounded in the past and transformed through practice into a revitalized, reformulated, and living tradition. Such an interactive vision of tradition relies heavily on, and might be considered a synonym for, the post-structuralist agency-and-practice-centered concept of social reproduction (e.g., Bourdieu 1977, 1990; Foucault 1979; Giddens 1979, 1984).

The renewed archaeological interest in a socially centered archaeology is encouraging, especially as it is one that includes historical process as an integral aspect of its interpretive schema (cf. Lightfoot et al. 1998; Lightfoot and Martinez 1995; Pauketat 1998a, 2001; Shennan 1993; Stein 1998; Trigger 1989a, b). In anthropology in general there has been increasing disquiet concerning the suitability of monolithic ahistorical analytical units such as "culture" and "society" for investigating human interaction (cf. Marcus and Fischer 1986). In part this is due to recognition of the multiscalar nature of societies and the analytical potential of factions and other communities that comprise virtually any social collectivity. In archaeology, the shift in attention, as well as a renewed historical perspective, has made the identification of communities an important issue. The recognition of factional and community interaction also means we must cope with "social resistance" as a force operating within and between collectivities.

An important aspect of the foregoing approaches is the recognition that social continuance and transformation are products of the actual practices of real people, as well as the negotiations, accommodations, and resistance of various factions within the greater social collectivity. It provides us an opportunity to shift some of our attention from such external

ahistorical and asocial forces as adaptation, environmental change, population growth, and subsistence and to redirect them toward social interactions. With the recognition of diversity within what were formerly perceived as monolithic cultural entities, we can examine the applications of
power, resistance, and negotiation within and between segments of society.

The linking of tradition with a practice model of social reproduction
moves us closer toward a historical and social archaeology but is not, in
and of itself, a problem-free heuristic. Its archaeological implementation
carries with it issues of scale, boundedness, and duration that we must be
careful to define on a case-by-case basis. Tradition brings this flexibility
forward into the social arena—it allows us to consider wide-ranging issues
of technological continuity, local cultural expressions, broad ecological
and adaptationalist patterning, or something altogether different. However, if this reborn tradition is to contribute to archaeological understanding, we need to delimit its parameters and to conceptualize it in a socially
meaningful way. We suggest that an approach incorporating the concepts
of communities of practice and ethnic cores addresses these problems, and
we examine their utility using the Terminal Archaic–Early Woodland archaeology of the American Bottom as an example.

Ethnicity

Studies of Eastern Woodlands cultures have long been dominated by interpretive models that rely heavily on adaptation and evolution as key causative themes (see the summaries in B. D. Smith 1986 and Steponaitis
1986). These studies commonly incorporate evolutionary models of progressive social organization, such as bands to states (*sensu* Service 1962),
concepts of economic rationality, such as optimal foraging, and a more
general viewpoint that material culture is adaptationalist (*sensu* L. White
1959). These approaches are especially prevalent in hunter-gatherer research. Archaic people are usually depicted living as small family or band-
level mobile hunters and gatherers marked by logistical or foraging subsistence and settlement patterns. Understanding the past is essentially
reduced to understanding the relationship of people with their environment. Such studies are seldom concerned with specific social collectivities,
and variation is usually attributable to environmental variations and adaptations. These studies outline one way of approaching the past (see
papers in Winterhalder and Smith 1981; Bettinger 1991).

The recognition of local traditions may, however, provide us a different perspective on the microscale social, economic, and political interactions that shaped the various Terminal Archaic and Early Woodland societies in the American Bottom. In fact, we suggest that tradition, when incorporating communities of practice, ethnogenesis, and ethnic differentiation, may be a useful conceptual heuristic.[2] Such social categories are dynamic, fluid, and subject to change. Consequently, ethnic identification is fundamentally crafted by a group vis-à-vis "others" and requires the "objectification" of *social and material differences* through a system of classification for its existence, reproduction, and transmission (S. Jones 1997:84). The importance of ethnicity is that it may provide a social boundedness that we believe can, in certain circumstances, be equated with the archaeological recognition of local traditions.

Such a characterization is sympathetic to an agency and practice theory approach, since ethnogenesis, in a sense, works in the active creation and maintenance of cultural boundaries, through community interaction, as an active component of the social system (S. Jones 1997:28). Ethnogenesis also must, of necessity, incorporate a spatial, contextual, and historical approach to material culture, since it is primarily a creation of a historical trajectory of practices that operate within communities of practice and of the recognition of ethnicity as a problem of archaeological contexts. We see ethnicity as a way of conceptualizing and operationalizing the concept of tradition at the level of the community, in this case, at the level of a band- or tribal-level society. We also find it useful because it incorporates, in its very definition, factors of scale, boundedness, resistance, and group and material differentiation.

Ethnicity also provides a way to understand how local traditions can come into being as forces of differentiation through the creation of group "consciousness."[3] The strength of such collective consciousness (that is, ethnicity) is most dramatically expressed in culture contact situations involving asymmetrical power relations (cf. S. Jones 1997:96–100). The creation of "ethnic" minorities is maximized by the "resistance" of disenfranchised groups interacting with strong centralized societies (e.g., Brass 1985; Emberling 1997; Shennan 1989). Ethnicity appears less strongly expressed in situations of interaction between groups roughly comparable in terms of power. Many researchers looking at the mechanisms involving "ethnogenesis" note that environmental, social, or political stress, and warfare are important and perhaps even necessary accelerating factors (see Creamer and Haas 1985; R. B. Ferguson 1990; Fried 1975; Haas 1990b; Hodder 1979; Kimes et al 1982; Shennan 1989). Primary sources of social, political, and economic stress are the boundaries between societies with markedly different sociopolitical patterns, especially where conditions of asymmetrical power relations exist (cf. Champion 1989). Clearly, an important factor in the formation of local tradition and ethnicity is intercommunity interaction.

Since ethnogenesis is specifically promoted by recognition of difference—that is, by "we/they" oppositions—it is encouraged in situations that bring the prevailing *doxa* (which supports the naturalization of the existing social order) into confrontation with a different reality. Such confrontations most readily come into play where subordinated or socially differentiated groups encounter a new social reality through their relations with dangerous or powerful neighbors (see Scarry, Loren, this volume). However, the recognition of *difference* is a key aspect of all group interaction and consequently plays a role in social formation throughout history (see Sassaman, this volume).[4]

Ethnicity can be seen as a critical factor in the social landscape of the earliest hunting and gathering groups (see especially Van den Berghe 1981). Such a view stems from a "primordialist" concept of ethnicity (e.g., Emberling 1997; Geertz 1963; S. Jones 1997) that defines it as "deeply rooted" in human interactions. This conceptualization operates on the premise of ethnic groups as "collectivities" that incorporate integrative mechanisms, provide corporate definition and boundedness, structure intergroup interaction, and create the "us-them dichotomy" (Jenkins 1997: 10–19). To some extent, such a perspective is a reaction to the "social superfluidity" models of Barth and others that seem to project ethnicity as a totally amorphous social entity present only in the reflected light of resistance. Both Jenkins (1997) and Van den Berghe (1981) stress the "structuring" force of ethnicity and its critical cohesive function. It is possible that this fluidity of ethnicity may be a modern phenomenon linked to its existence primarily in the shadow of powerful states. In earlier ethnic groups, group cohesion rather than resistance may have been the critical generative factor. At all levels, however, ethnicity is simply kinship writ large, and in this context it can be seen as a structuring factor in all societies from the smallest bands to the largest states.

Van den Berghe (1981:22–39), in a very functionalist and adaptationalist interpretation, located ethnic origins in early human societies in the practices of small breeding populations' need to maintain internal cohesion and peace, preferential endogamy, common (real or putative) ancestry, and physical propinquity (or territoriality), that is, the gemeinschaft of German scholars. He saw such integrative forces, as expressed both through biological and social themes, as the basis for ethnic expressions that led to the establishment of the critical "us-them" dichotomy. One does not have to accept Van den Berghe's causative interpretations to value his point that ethnicity may have been a factor in the earliest human societies. Ethnic identities are created and reinforced through patterns of intergroup competition and interactions, sociocultural environments, and adaptational adjustments to varying environmental niches. While not denying that such ethnic groups have a certain fluidity to them, Van den Berghe (1981:22, 39) argues they are maintained primarily by preference and isolation and partially by the mechanism of territoriality, which serves to reduce competition. The strength of these identities is likely directly correlated with the strength of the challenges to those identities. This correlation explains the relatively low level of ethnic identity encountered among comparatively equal, low-density, contemporaneous hunter-gatherer groups versus the marked ethnicity just noted here in marginal groups within powerful states.

If we focus on ethnicity à la tradition as a cohesive and integrative force in early hunting and gathering societies, then we might expect that the patterning of archaeological material cultures should reflect that same cohesiveness. Unfortunately anthropologists and ethnoarchaeologists have been unable to demonstrate this in modern situations (cf. Emberling 1997; S. Jones 1997:106–127). To some extent the problem reflects the fact that ethnic markers are derived from a group's material configuration through an internal process of accentuating or diminishing selected cultural traits (Bentley 1987; S. Jones 1997:115–122; Shennan 1989:14–17). While we may have difficulty recognizing this subset we should still be able to identify the material culture of the larger group vis-à-vis others (see Lightfoot and Martinez 1995:478–482). This recognition must be performed in each specific case because the material world obtains meaning from the wider context and can shift both message and significance as that context changes. However, the use of the material world in the active creation of ethnic identity is not random but emerges, instead, from "particular sociohistorical contexts" and "the existing cultural practices and modes of differentiation" (S. Jones 1997:125). In essence, the historical context and technological trajectory of the material remains of past communities of practice provide clues to the production of the material world in the present.

Consequently it seems possible to recognize ethnic groups in the archaeological record, perhaps not as tightly circumscribed, impenetrable material clusters, but as ethnic cores (cf. Van den Berghe 1981) with permeable bounds and as communities of practice that have a material dimension (cf. Lightfoot and Martinez 1995:481–482). It is a conceptual shift by archaeologists to a focus on a community's internal practices of self-definition vis- à-vis the other that will allow us to examine the interactions and historical trajectories of pre-Columbian societies, that is, their traditions. Whether one frames this research in terms of communities of practice, ethnic cores, boundaries, or other models of group interaction, to identify them we must look across broad social and spatial regimes within well-defined chronological and spatial parameters. This requires that archaeologists build strong historical sequences in those areas in which we seek to understand the developments, interactions, and transformations of historical and cultural traditions.

Adaptational Models of Late Archaic–Early Woodland Lifeways

In this discussion we explore Late Archaic and Early Woodland communities of practice within the confined space of the American Bottom. A precept of this study is that this period involved multiple and diverse groups, most often categorized in politicosocial terms as bands or, possibly, tribes. It is a time filled with socially and politically heterogeneous contemporaneous societies—societies we believe are most appropriately modeled as ethnic groups. Such collectivities should be reflected in the overall archaeological record but, we argue, are often obscured by present-day archaeological practice. We believe that a careful examination of the archaeological contextual evidence for such collectivities, seen within a historical trajectory, can supply new insights into the formation and dissolution of pre-Columbian societies.

Most discussions of Archaic lifeways in the midcontinent, however, follow Binford's new archaeology "materialist paleoecological" paradigm (e.g., Binford 1968a, 1980; cf. Watson 1991). We think that such research (which we have labeled "adaptationalist" earlier in this chapter) often incorporates underlying and unexpressed determinant assumptions of economic rationality, environmental functionalism and adaptationism, and notions of unilinear social evolution that undermine its achievements and limit the value of its interpretations of Archaic societies. We are especially concerned with the latent evolutionary frameworks that are revealed through *in situ* gradualist, adaptational interpretations of Archaic culture change. These perspectives encourage interpretations in which society is epiphenomenal and all variation is generated by environmental change. Regrettably, the ecofunctionalist demarcation of research boundaries restricts our ability to focus on society and explore its workings, because society is not reducible to one-to-one relationships with the "environment," "function," or "economy" (see Shennan 1991, 1993, among many others). While we view adaptational variables as important in setting the outer limits for community practice, we believe those limits are so broad that they do little, in and of themselves, to explain social change.

Furthermore, regional approaches to chronology and sequence building typically include long periods of cultural stasis conjoined within a model of gradualist change to present an impression (false, we would argue) of a smooth, unbroken sequence of evolutionary transformation of *in situ* populations (cf. Fortier, this volume; Sassaman, this volume, points out similar concerns in his discussions of the Southeast). Such continuous taxonomic sequences are often supported by sparse data and by significant unstated presumptions. The most pervasive presumption includes the unspoken rule that there cannot be culturally differentiated (whether these are "cultures," "phases," and so on) groups occupying the same point within the space-time continuum—contemporaneity is not allowed. This presumption is logically consistent within an adaptational model. If material culture is a result of environmental adaptation it is not possible to have functionally differing material assemblages within the same environment. Contemporaneity of differing cultural assemblages is also precluded if environmental change is the driving force in cultural change. An adaptational model of change seeks adaptational answers to shifts in material assemblages, which occur even in periods of environmental stability. We do not deny that the land-human relationship is important in understanding past societies, but such a single-minded focus obscures other equally interesting questions, such as those related to social interaction and change, that are embedded in the archaeological record.

Adaptational models are dominant in two compendiums on Archaic period societies, *Archaic Hunters and Gatherers in the American Midwest* (Phillips and Brown 1983) and *Foraging, Collecting, and Harvesting: Archaic Period Subsistence and Settlement in the Eastern Woodlands* (Neusius 1986). Perhaps this agenda is nowhere more clearly expressed than in the writings of James A. Brown (1985:166; Brown and Vierra 1983) in his Archaic period model "linking environmental history, ecology, subsistence, and settlement in the lower Illinois Valley."[5] The earliest research (Brown and Vierra 1983:167–169) was specifically based on a consensus that the significant subsistence and settlement changes that occurred during the Archaic period were due to environmental change. Furthermore, that shift in subsistence and settlement was seen as directional, trending toward agriculture and sedentism. To investigate this hypothesis Brown applied hunter-gatherer settlement and subsistence models based on optimal foraging theory to the available limited samples from the Koster site in the lower Illinois Valley. He interpreted these data as supporting an increasing utilization of riverine resources and an increasingly sedentary lifestyle, which he accounts for as follows: "In our view, the key factor in this development was the growth of the food-rich slack-water environment of the valley to the point where the valley pulled hunter-gatherer subsistence and settlement strategies predominantly toward this area to the exclusion of alternatives. With increasing floodplain productivity, this zone came to dominate, and with this came sedentism and economic intensification" (Brown and Vierra 1983:190).

James Brown (1985) revisited this issue a few years later as he discussed the appearance of sedentism and complexity among hunter-gatherers in the Midwest. He begins by observing that the development of *in situ* sedentism is very long and very gradual and that it is best observed within an evolutionary framework. While still emphasizing environmental change and resource adaptation as primary causal factors in social change, Brown has now incorporated social factors into his explanation of changes via risk management theory. Sedentism and complexity become the unintended results of mobile hunter-gatherers (1) responding to subsistence risk, (2) shifting mobility strategies, and (3) minimizing territorial overlap with competing groups. The independent variables of environment and population change can act to upset the equilibrium and create risk factors that discourage hunter-gatherer risk strategies and encourage those that lead toward sedentism.[6]

In the end we are presented with an interpretation in which ahistorical, unbounded human societies are understood as the result of economic rationalism and increasingly functional environmental adaptations, all within a framework of gradualist change. We believe that such adaptational models do not explain all aspects of the archaeological record.

Crossroads and Boundaries, 1400–1150 B.C.

Nowhere, in our view, does the adaptationalist model seem less applicable than to the discontinuous and dynamic American Bottom cultural sequence in the Terminal Late Archaic through the Early Woodland periods (Fortier, this volume, fig. 11.1). At no time prior to the emergence of Cahokia does the region display more diversity and heterogeneity in the lifestyles of its inhabitants. This approximately 1200-year-long period reveals the American Bottom as a place where many peoples come together or pass through—it is truly a place of crossroads, boundaries, and interaction. Our understanding of this cultural diversity is a result of the extensive research performed as part of the FAI-270 project and various other cultural resource, management-driven projects carried out by the University of Illinois (e.g., Bareis and Porter 1984). As this research continues, the archaeological evidence becomes increasingly difficult to fully comprehend within the limits of either a cultural historical or adaptational model. In the following paragraphs we will attempt to summarize that evidence (although recognizing that such a summary by phase somewhat obscures and structures the richly detailed American Bottom archaeological record) and to demonstrate why an approach incorporating tradition and ethnicity better accounts for the empirical data of the archaeological record.

Archaeological research in the last two decades has altered our understanding of Late Archaic peoples' use of the American Bottom floodplain and adjoining uplands. The Terminal Late Archaic Prairie Lake phase in the American Bottom has been thoroughly studied (Emerson 1980, 1984; Emerson and McElrath 1983; Emerson et al. 1986, 1991; Fortier et al. 1998; McElrath and Fortier 1983; McElrath et al. 1984; Yerkes 1987). It extends, in a limited way, to the north in the Mississippi River Valley and Lower and Central Illinois River Valley. However, the real origins of the Prairie Lake point styles lie in the straight-stemmed points of the Mid-south and Lower Mississippi River Valley (Emerson and McElrath 1983: 227). In essence, the American Bottom is on the northern frontier of this larger southern Late Archaic tradition.

Chronologically we have twenty ^{14}C assays ranging from *cal* 771 B.C. to *cal* 1494 B.C., with the majority of dates between *cal* 900 B.C. and cal 1410 B.C. More than 1,400 features including hearths, deep and shallow pits, occasional structures, stains, postmolds, and diffuse scatters of charcoal and calcinated bone have been excavated from two restricted locales, one around the Prairie Lake Meander scar (Emerson 1984; McElrath and Fortier 1983) and one about the base of the Wood River Terrace near Grassy Lake (Evans 1999). The dominant projectile point styles fall into categories of straight-stemmed, barbed, and triangular blade forms that go under the labels of Dyroff, Springly, Mo-Pac, Floyd, and Kampsville Barbed points. Artifact inventories (Emerson and McElrath 1983; Emerson et al. 1991; Evans 1999) for Prairie Lake sites include grinding and nutting stones, axes, and numerous chert unifacial and bifacial cutting, scraping, and drilling tools, as well as more unusual objects such as cloudblower pipes, gorgets, beads, hematite pestles, and plummets. Local

Burlington cherts comprise the majority of the chert used (70–80 percent). There is a focus on expedient flake technology with hafted bifaces as the dominant tool form. Heat treatment of chert is typically in the 40 percent range. Subsistence is poorly understood because of preservation problems. While no mortuary facilities have been located in the American Bottom, in the Lower Illinois River Valley Kampsville phase cremation, flexed, and bundle burials have been found in small cemeteries, usually on bluff tops (Farnsworth and Asch 1986).

Emerson (1980, 1984; Emerson and McElrath 1983) argues that Prairie Lake peoples followed a residentially stable lifeway clustered within large base locales (Emerson 1980:163) surrounding the resource-rich bluff-base bottomland oxbow lakes that are found in the American Bottom. Base locales often covered many hectares and contained high densities and diversities of artifacts, with structural remains that possibly include dwellings, various types of pit features, and perhaps burial zones. We see base locales as arguing for macroband aggregations and "as strongly suggestive of territorialism and possibly even of tribalism" (Emerson et al. 1986:251). These large Prairie Lake gatherings must have been undergoing the kind of social and political shifts that facilitated large group stability (cf. Keeley 1988). Prairie Lake settlement also includes campsites that represent the seasonal movement of small groups to take advantage of differentially distributed resources on the broad floodplain and nearby upland woods and prairies (Emerson et al. 1986). The validity of this model for American Bottom Terminal Late Archaic settlement that entails a few widely spaced base locales clustered about bluff-base lakes and thinly scattered extractive camps and loci has generally been supported by extensive surveys of the bottomlands and adjacent bluffs (Emerson et al. 1986:258–265). It is clear that the earlier patterns of extreme group mobility had begun to shift toward patterns of decreasing mobility and increasing residential stability in the later Late Archaic.

It has been half a century since Early Woodland became a recognized taxonomic unit in the Eastern Woodlands, but its specific nature is still subject to definition (Farnsworth and Emerson 1986). Certainly, based on our American Bottom investigations, we would have to reject the common aphorism that "Early Woodland cultures are simply Late Archaic peoples with pottery," nor do we see much evidence for gradualist *in situ* evolution. In fact, there are significant differences between the Terminal Late Archaic inhabitants of the American Bottom and those of the various Early Woodland phases (cf. Emerson and Fortier 1986).

The Early Woodland Carr Creek phase (the local manifestation of the

Marion culture) has five ^{14}C dates that stretch from *cal* 393 B.C. to *cal* 814 B.C.. The chronological patterning is uneven, with several dates clustered about *cal* 400 B.C. and several about *cal* 800 B.C. It is possible that Prairie Lake and Carr Creek peoples' use of the valley overlaps. The Carr Creek phase (Emerson 1986; Emerson and Fortier 1986) represents the southern fringe, perhaps even frontier, of the widespread northern Marion culture, which includes components in Michigan, Wisconsin, Indiana, northern Illinois, easternmost Iowa, and southern Minnesota.

Carr Creek sites (Evans et al. 1999; Fortier 1985) typically are small campsites marked by low-density scatters of Marion thick ceramics, stone projectile points, lithic debitage, calcinated bone, and charcoal, occasionally including *cucurbits* remains. Some of these concentrations (ca. 5x3m) of ceramics lithics, and subsistence remains have been interpreted to be the floors of lightly built structures. This first appearance of ceramics in the Midwest is marked by the presence of thick, grit-grog tempered, cord-marked, moderately large cone-shaped vessels with small flat bottoms and a smaller bowl form (Fortier, this volume, fig. 11.2). The small lithic assemblages include the diagnostic straight-stemmed, weak-shouldered Kramer point as the only recognized Marion formal tool type. Generally the lithic assemblages are primarily expedient and comprised of Burlington cherts (ca. 70 percent) showing about 30–40 percent heat treatment. A few shallow pits and scattered debris clusters comprise most campsites.

These sites have a wide distribution in the American Bottom region (Emerson and Fortier 1986) and are disbursed across the floodplain and uplands. In the floodplain the small sites are present near many low-lying physiographic zones on the edges of old marshes, meander lakes, sloughs, and the like. In the uplands they are present in significant numbers in the secondary drainages that crisscross the area. Considering the small size of Carr Creek sites, they are assumed to represent residential camps of family-sized groups of foragers. No larger sites suggesting band- or macroband-level aggregations are known. No mortuary sites are currently known, but in other areas of Marion culture both small mounds and cemetery burials are recorded (Emerson 1986).

This pattern of wide settlement dispersion across very diverse environments by many small family-sized groups is a shift from the earlier Terminal Late Archaic Prairie Lake phase macroband base locales. We have some evidence as to the possibility of external forces as causative factors in this change in settlement form. Emerson and Fortier (1986:517–518) have suggested that lowered lake levels may have made it difficult for the lakes to provide the necessary resources to support large gatherings. More recent investigation seems to suggest that increased water levels during this period may have resulted in meander lakes being cut off and filled in at a rapid rate (Evans 1999).

Some of the most fleeting archaeological signatures on the landscape are left by the Ringering phase people who are a local group related to the larger Black Sand culture that is spread across the Midsouth and Midwest. Two ^{14}C dates of *cal 768* B.C. and *cal 790* B.C. suggest a narrow window for these people's presence in the American Bottom as well as their contemporaneity with Carr Creek groups. Their ephemeral occupations are represented by a few fragments of grit-tempered Black Sand pottery with incised decorations (see Fortier, this volume, fig. 11.2a-b), some contracting stem points, and debitage showing a reliance on diverse local gravels and cherts with only a marginal use of Burlington cherts (40 percent). These remains occur as such thin scatters across the American Bottom floodplain that it is difficult to reconstruct even the nature of a single occupation or a "typical" assemblage. Evidence suggests (e.g., Evans et al. 1999; Farnsworth 1986; chapters in Farnsworth and Emerson 1986) that Ringering phase/Black Sand groups ultimately are derived from similar cultures in the Midsouth and slowly move north, reaching southern Wisconsin about a century before the time of Christ. Their sojourn into the northern American Bottom seems to be brief and may consist of small family groups foraging from larger population clusters in the Mississippi River and Lower Illinois River Valleys.

The Florence phase was first recognized in the American Bottom at the catastrophically buried Florence Street site (Emerson et al. 1983; Emerson and Fortier 1986). Located on the bank of a formerly active Mississippi River channel, ^{14}C samples yielded dates of *cal 165* B.C., *cal 381* B.C., and *cal 407* B.C., suggesting overlap with the end of the Carr Creek phase occupation of the valley. However, the lifestyle of Florence phase inhabitants must have been very different from that of other contemporary peoples in the American Bottom.

The occupation zone included a number of large activity areas (up to 60m^2) that contained massive rock hearths. These ranged up to 5.4m in length (up to 16m^2) and could include more than 1,200 limestone slabs and cobbles. Surrounding the hearths were dense debris concentrations that contained extensive ceramic and lithic materials. The site contained a number of pits, and a wigwamlike structure (7.4x5.8m) was excavated.

The material assemblage included many formal tools, including contracting stem points, distinctive humpbacked scrapers, diamond-shaped Goose Lake knives, hafted drills, numerous bifaces, scrapers, denticulates, gravers, limestone chopping tools and cleavers, mauls, pitted stones, abraders, and mineral pigments. The assemblage was dominated by high-quality Burlington cherts (97 percent debitage, 90+ percent tools) with heat treatment used on about one-half of the material. This assemblage was focused on formal tool manufacture, and less than 4 percent of the flakes show any evidence of use.

The Florence ceramic assemblage was very different from that associated with either the Carr Creek or Ringering phases (Fortier, this volume, fig. 2). The fifty-four vessels recovered represent a cream-colored, grog-tempered ware that used directional cord marking, fingernail impressions, and stab-and-drag decorative motifs on a conoidal- to subconoidal-shaped jar. This ceramic and lithic assemblage is culturally tied to the earlier Alexander and Tchefuncte groups in the Midsouth and Lower Mississippi Valley (Emerson and Fortier 1986:511–512). The Peisker site in the Lower Illinois River Valley is the known northern extent of these people (Farnsworth and Ash 1986).

All of the known Florence phase sites are located along active river channels (Emerson and Fortier 1986; Farnsworth and Asch 1986), and we suspect the inhabitants focused on the exploitation of riverine resources. They must have had access to watercraft, because large amounts of limestone were transported to the site from the bluff sources across the river. Very high percentages of black walnut shells were recovered (40 percent versus a more typical 5 percent of contemporary groups). Although they are a low-yielding food source, black walnut is the source of a well-known fish poison. Unfortunately, faunal preservation was poor and we cannot verify this focus on riverine resources.

The massive hearths and activity areas at the Florence Street site suggest multifamily use and occupation of the riverbank site, perhaps for some length of time. The Goose Lake Meander that contains the Florence Street site also contains a number of small Florence phase campsites that are marked by the presence of the distinctive lithic assemblage but seldom contain ceramics. To date, sites of this phase have not been recorded away from the river channels.

These poorly known assemblages have been recovered from only the Carbon Monoxide and the Ringering sites (Emerson and Fortier 1986; Evans et al. 1999; Fortier 1985). Each site appears to contain a small campsite consisting of a structure basin (2.4x1.7m and 5.4x3.2m) and a few hearths and pits. The ceramics are grog-tempered jars with plain or burnished surfaces. The lithic assemblage has Goose Lake knives and contracting stem points with a limited number of other formal tools and a concentration on flake production. The raw materials in the lithic assemblage include Salem chert and gravels with varying uses of Burlington sources. Accepted ^{14}C dates are *cal* 137 B.C. and *cal* 181 B.C. Given ceramic and lithic assemblage similarities to the earlier Florence phase, we assume there is a genetic relationship between the two groups, but the Columbia phase is so poorly known that it is impossible to explore the nature of this relationship.

Conclusion

The archaeological evidence recovered during the past three decades has shown that simple *in situ* unilinear evolutionary models of American Bottom Terminal Archaic–Early Woodland cultural developments are flawed (also see Fortier 1998; Fortier, this volume). Instead, this period is characterized by the presence of mutually contemporaneous groups bearing recognizably differentiated material cultures but with generally similar adaptations to the broad Mississippi River floodplain. Many variables beyond local environmental change and stability are clearly generating cultural diversity, stability, and change.

Given this emerging picture of a highly variable sequence, how do we incorporate this scenario into a cohesive, understandable perspective of the archaeological record for this area? If we accept that communities of practice, group consciousness, and ethnicity are a part of the earliest human social organization, then such factors may have an integral role to play in explaining variation among the pre-Columbian natives of the American Bottom. Given that perspective, we argue that the American Bottom sequence is best addressed within a historic framework that is sensitive to the fact that populations, as ethnic groups, have recognizable traditions and identifiable spatial and chronological parameters that vary through time and space. These local traditions are the product of unique social, material, and environmental interactions within specific communities of practice. While interaction between such communities can increase their similarities to some degree, they always are to a greater or lesser extent unique. The variation between both contemporaneous and non-contemporaneous Early Woodland groups is a product of those unique historical events. Their juxtaposition on the landscape is most often attributable to the expansion of territories or the actual movement of peoples.

It is unfortunate that Binford's (1972) early well-directed criticism of diffusion and migration theory led to the complete abandonment of such models. The result was that archaeologists treated the archaeological record as if migration, depopulation, or group expansion never occurred. This is a false and naive view because, as Seeman and Dancey (2000) point out, the most casual examination of a linguistic map of the North American indigenous groups at the time of European expansion would clearly invalidate such a position. It is abundantly clear that groups did move across the landscape, and glottochronology suggests that these movements were common, continuous, patterned, and often of great antiquity.

Because this dynamic aspect of demography could represent a significant source of change in local and regional chronologies, it is worthy of our attention. Unfortunately, the methods for recognizing these movements archaeologically have not advanced over the last four decades of the twentieth century in North American studies, and we must resort to preprocessual archaeology for relevant analytical procedures. Seeman observed that Emil Haury had established criteria for recognizing population replacement nearly fifty years ago. Haury suggested two criteria for recognizing population immigration: "(1) If there suddenly appears in a cultural continuum a constellation of traits readily identifiable as new, and without local prototypes, and (2) If the products of the immigrant group not only reflect borrowed elements from the host group, but also, as a lingering effect, preserve unmistakable elements from their own pattern" (Haury 1958:1). Additional proof of such immigration would be provided "(1) If identification of an area is possible in which this constellation of traits was the normal pattern, and (2) If a rough time equivalency between the 'at home' and the displaced expressions of the similar complexes can be established" (Haury 1958:1).

These simple criteria, forgotten, ignored, or overlooked for four decades, seem to provide an adequate framework with which to begin an examination of disjunctures in the archaeological record for the American Bottom. The American Bottom is at the intersection of four major areas (Plains, Midwest, Midsouth, Ozarks). Even minor fluctuations in populations within these areas may have an effect on this crossroad/boundary area. Indeed, we have come to recognize the American Bottom as a dynamic tension zone between numerous social groups that played a marginal role in midcontinental native history until Late pre-Columbian times (Emerson and Fortier 1986; Emerson and Jackson 1987; Fortier 1998; McElrath 1995; McElrath et al. 2000). We believe that significant long-term *in situ* evolutionary change is not evident in the American Bottom until the middle of the Late Woodland period, beginning about cal A.D.

650 (cf. Emerson and Jackson 1987). With these criteria in mind let us reexamine the American Bottom Terminal Late Archaic–Early Woodland sequence.

We have contended (Emerson and Fortier 1986; Emerson and McElrath 1983) that there is a dramatic break in the continuity of the archaeological sequence between the Terminal Late Archaic Prairie Lake and Early Woodland Carr Creek phases. In the sense of a gradualist, evolutionary model it could only be considered a devolutionary step. Prairie Lake peoples are clearly moving toward a pattern of large macroband aggregations about a limited set of floodplain lake locales for a long period of each year. This move toward decreasing residential mobility and increasing sedentism must have been accompanied by a significant number of social and political changes in the management of the resulting internal and external stresses (see Keeley 1988). Such sites also provide additional evidence for the increasing importance of ceremonial and ritual behavior, as well as the introduction of increased personal status, with the widespread presence of cloudblower pipes, hematite plummets, exotic beads, and gorgets. Perhaps such items are associated with the appearance of more stable leadership and ritual roles among larger macrobands. It seems that these peoples are moving rapidly toward an increasing social and political complexity and an increasingly sedentary lifestyle.

Yet in about the ninth century B.C. this tradition rapidly disintegrates or removes from the American Bottom to be overlapped or replaced by one that is diametrically opposed in social, political, and adaptationalist characteristics. Even the source of this new tradition differs from that of earlier groups—the Carr Creek inhabitants of the American Bottom have roots in the widespread Marion culture of the Great Lakes rather than with the Midsouth of the Prairie Lake peoples. They bring into the area a very different lifestyle based on a high degree of residential mobility and a widespread utilization of both the uplands and floodplain resources. Their mobile lifestyle also suggests that only the lowest forms of social and political integration were present. The majority of sites indicate that the typical residential unit was the family and that multifamily sites were rare or nonexistent. Subsistence patterns must have differed (based on areas of utilization), but we have little evidence of this besides the rare presence of Early Woodland squash. Technologically, except for the addition of occasional ceramic vessels, their basic tools kits are very similar to those of the Prairie Lake groups. Both groups use an expedient flake technology, with formal tools limited to ubiquitous hafted bifaces and based primarily on Burlington chert (about 30–40 percent heat-treated).

About a century or two after the Carr Creek inhabitants initially occupied the areas around the American Bottom, they had visitors. Archaeologically these visitors left ephemeral campsites that we archaeologically associate with the broadly distributed Black Sand culture. In our area these camps go under the rubric of the Ringering phase and contain only fragments of chert, distinctive incised pottery vessels, and more ambiguous contracting stem points. Their diffuse campsites show a greater dependence on local cherts and gravels for lithic tools. We know little else about them except that their major villages and occupations occur primarily to the south, west, and north of the American Bottom. We know that they occasionally utilized the area inhabited by the Carr Creek phase peoples but do not appear to have actually occupied it.

Near the end of the Carr Creek occupation of the region a very distinctive group of riverine people enter the area from the south. The Florence phase people live in large multifamily riverbank sites with extensive communal cooking areas and dense debris accumulations. Their houses are fairly substantial, and they possess a distinctive tool assemblage consisting of highly decorated grog-tempered ceramic vessels and bifacial formal tools with few flake or expedient tools. They used only the highest-quality Burlington cherts and further increased its workability with heat treatment in about 50 percent of the examples. Florence phase inhabitants are apparently residentially stable. Small sites are known along the river edge, but as yet no use of the broader floodplain or uplands has appeared. By the second century B.C., the Florence phase appears to have shifted to the very poorly known Columbia phase, which continues some of the same patterns but with the use of more localized chert sources, a generally less sophisticated ceramic and lithic technology, less attachment to the river edge environments, and a more mobile lifestyle.

The foregoing summary demonstrates the cultural "sequence" as complex and hardly represented by an unbounded, ahistorical, gradualist, unilinear, *in situ* adaptationist past (also see Fortier, this volume, for further discussions of this issue). We have evidence of multiple groups co-occupying and co-utilizing the restricted spaces of the American Bottom at various times during the Terminal Late Archaic and Early Woodland periods. Sometimes this utilization is focused on different subzones of the local environment, as with the Carr Creek peoples' use of broadly distributed upland and floodplain resources and the Florence groups' intensive exploitation of the riverine areas. In such cases one is reminded of Barth's (1969) early discussions of the linkage of ethnicity and environmental diversity in Pakistan. Only in the broadest sense can we see technological and functional improvements through time—when observed in detail, such a pattern is, at best, obscure. The increasing evolutionary efficiency of lithic technology from Prairie Lake to the Columbia phase seems difficult to substantiate, and the dominant pattern seems to be one of expedient tools with a few formal hafted bifaces. The Florence phase represents an anomaly with its formal tool assemblage, one that begins to degenerate during the Columbia phase. The famous inevitable trend toward sedentism (Brown 1985; Brown and Vierra 1983;), to loosely quote Ames (1991:108–109), seems "neither inevitable nor progressive," since Prairie Lake Terminal Late Archaic peoples appear to have been the most sedentary group, followed by various residentially mobile Early Woodland groups. Only Florence phase peoples appear to represent a break in the shift to very mobile lifestyles.

There appears to be little evidence that the various groups in the American Bottom during this period of time represent a unilinear *in situ* development of stable populations. In fact stylistic, technological, and historical evidence suggests that most of these groups are unrelated historically and are on the frontiers of larger traditions to the north, west, and south. The American Bottom, partially because of its highly variable and intensely riverine and lacustrine environment, is an "edge" zone of social interaction rather than a center during this period. It seems to represent just the kind of socially dynamic boundary zone that many researchers believe drives processes of ethnogenesis and tradition building. We suggest that the dynamic nature of the region created a setting that facilitated the interaction of the surrounding groups and brought them into close contact with diverse communities of practice—continually forcing them to confront a new reality, one differing from the prevailing doxa. This is a situation that is antithetical to social stasis, and, in and of itself, argues against adaptational views of gradualist, environmentally driven culture change. It is only after circa A.D. 600 that the areas will serve as the center for the evolutionary development of one of the greatest and most complex societies in North America (cf. McElrath et al. 2000; Pauketat 1994, 1998b).

Our own interpretation of the implications of such a sequence is derived from a historical paradigm that recognizes that multiple lifestyles are viable within any given environmental regime or geographic region. It also acknowledges that recurrent and transmittable social behavior establishes identifiable traditions that leave a recognizable imprint on material assemblages, independent of any requisite need to adapt to the physical environment. Such individual social and material signatures are expected to conform to the spatial contours of specific social collectivities of varying geographic scale that in many, but not all, instances may be recognized as ethnic cores. Such patterns of social reproduction are flexible, generative, contextually referential, and inherently capable of significant internal change independent of any exogenous stimuli from the environment or requisite need to "adapt." Furthermore, since such collectivities have expanded and contracted, and since they have interacted at differing levels or scales of connectivity, observed change in the archaeological record of a given locality (especially in boundary areas) may reflect this social condition rather than functional adaptation. These are often recognized in the archaeological record as "traditions."

This does not mean that all aspects of adaptationalist models are to be ignored in explaining the historical trajectories of societies, but it means that they cannot be considered the prime or only stimuli for change. A historical paradigm that recognizes the existence of traditions provides for other vectors of perceived change in the archaeological record in addition to that stemming from the articulation of the organization of technology and the environment. The most relevant of these vectors, from an anthropological point of view, is the internal dynamic of social self-definition linked with the external influences of intergroup interaction that are key to the reproduction and transformation of tradition and ethnicity. Although archaeologists have given some lip service to "social factors" by acknowledging the existence of other social groups as an aspect of the environment to be considered, they have in large part ignored the concept of ethnic groups and their implications for interpreting the archaeological record. We have found that an understanding of this historic process of social formation and population movement and expansion coupled with an understanding of traditions as ethnic cores is useful for interpreting the archaeological record in western Illinois.

Acknowledgments

We are grateful to Tim Pauketat for his invitation to contribute to this volume and for his cogent comments on earlier drafts of this paper. As always we have benefited from the research and discussions of our colleagues working in midcontinental archaeology, especially Andrew Fortier and John Walthall. Both Kenneth Sassaman and Janet Dixon Keller provided anthropological insights that helped us clarify our arguments. The extensive archaeological data base and nearly quarter-century of research that has been essential to this chapter has been supported primarily by the Illinois Department of Transportation with the direction and advice of John Walthall, chief archaeologist. We would also like to thank the Illinois Transportation Archaeological Research Program and the Department of Anthropology, University of Illinois at Urbana-Champaign, for additional logistical support.

Notes

1. A community of practice does not necessarily imply a "primordial culture-sharing entity. . . . Nor does the term community imply necessarily co-presence, a well-defined, identifiable group, or socially visible boundaries. It does imply participation in an activity system about which participants share understandings concerning what they are doing and what that means in their lives and for their communities" (Lave and Wenger 1991:98).

2. Ethnogenesis is intimately involved with economic and political relationships and intergroup competition and interaction. It is a "self-defining system" that focuses on a "consciousness of identity vis à vis other groups; a 'we'/'they' opposition" (S. Jones 1997:84). Barth (1969a, 1969b) described ethnic groups as originating from "categories of ascription and identification by the actors themselves" (1969b:10).

3. Bentley (1987) proposed that ethnic consciousness is a result of *practice* operating within habitus (cf. Bourdieu 1977). Consequently ethnicity is depicted as part and parcel of everyday life in all societies. While we would agree with this, it falls short of addressing one of ethnicity's most critical aspects—the "consciousness of difference" (S. Jones 1997:94). In fact, Jones (1997:94) suggests that because habitus largely works to reinforce doxic social knowledge it actually acts to naturalize differences, inequality, domination, resistance, and so on. The link between habitus and doxic forms of knowledge operates to support social stability, continuity, and stasis, since they are products of a shared lived experience (cf. Bourdieu 1977). Therefore in many instances habitus may be most readily seen as a force that acts to suppress the active definition and implementation of ethnicity (*contra* Bentley 1987).

4. Such group interactions encourage the questioning of the current doxa in the face of the emerging social reality, which may lead to a new doxa (a process that we would conceive of as *ethnogenesis*). These new patterns become part of the reformulated habitus that is recognizably associated, by both external and internal observers, with a specific ethnic identity.

5. We focus on Brown's work here because he has created the most thorough and articulate evolutionary, functionalist adaptationist, *in situ* developmental model for the region. Most scholars investigating Archaic period remains in the midcontinent have worked within these paradigms (including ourselves).

6. With this adaptational model in mind Brown reviews the Midwestern Archaic and Early Woodland record, including many excavated sites in the lower Illinois Valley and the adjacent American Bottom (Bareis and Porter 1984) within

a context that includes environmental, resource abundance, and population changes. But none of these factors is sufficient to explain his interpretations of a steady drift to sedentism. He believes this trend to sedentism can best be understood

> as the consequence of the cumulative effects of individual groups to maintain intergroup spacing in those situations in which resource abundance makes this a relatively inexpensive option requiring minimal technological innovation. . . . [C]ontinual feedback and selection for successful solutions to social problems eventually results in complete year-around residence and cultural elaboration.
>
> Although environmental change and population growth are key variables in the process of increasing sedentism, it has been argued that decision making in risk management—under the constraints of these variables—is the mechanism that promotes the shift away from residential mobility. The tempo of change thereby turns out to be a reflection of the strength and consistency of environmental and population-growth factors. Long, drawn-out processes eliminate prime mover forces from consideration. (J. A. Brown 1985:224)

13

Hunter-Gatherers and Traditions of Resistance

Kenneth E. Sassaman

More than three decades of ethnohistoric and archaeological research
have dashed any lingering hopes of treating ethnographic hunter-gatherers as evolutionary ideals of the pre-state world (Bender and Morris
1988). In virtually every case investigated to date, ostensibly isolated and
primordial human foragers have experienced histories of contact with
food-producing or industrial societies (Bahuchet and Guillaume 1982;
Blackburn 1982; Chang 1982; Denbow 1984; Gordon 1982; Grinker
1994:29; Turnbull 1961); episodes of economic exploitation, militarization, or political oppression (Hoffman 1984; Lee and Hurlich 1982;
Schrire 1984; Wilmsen 1989, 1995); campaigns of assimilation and missionization (Leacock 1954); and attempts at ethnic cleansing or forced
resettlement (Latorre and Latorre 1976; Ndagala 1988). These histories
are not often apparent, because they are encrypted in the traditions and
myths of human foragers, and in the very forms of behavior long regarded
as inevitable to people living off the land. These traditions embody not
merely histories of domination from without, but also the actions of resistance that separated human foragers from the rest of the world, fooling us
into seeing them as we thought they always were, primitive.

Revised thinking about the evolutionary validity of ethnographic foragers raises a variety of questions of relevance to archaeology. Are we
justified in ignoring the historical particulars of modern power relations to
address the emergent properties of human adaptations to environment (cf.
Yellen 1989)? Should ethnographic cases be rejected categorically as viable analogs of the past? Are the circumstances of capitalism and modernity so peculiar as to have no bearing on ancient times? Can we still rely on
uniformitarian principles to seek generalizations about historical process
that will serve as an inferential basis for prehistory?

I accept that much of what we observe among ethnographic hunter-
gatherers—from their geographic dispersion, to their generalized mode of

subsistence, to their ethos of sharing—is a consequence of marginalization, encapsulation, and domination (e.g., Headland and Reid 1991;
Keene 1991; Woodburn 1988). I suggest that these features are among the
cross-cultural regularities found among traditions of resistance. Here I
refer to resistance in its broadest sense, that is, as action in opposition to
structure, the opposite of compliance. In keeping with the theme of this
volume, I am interested in the development of collective resistance, the
establishment and negotiation of traditions or actions of noncompliance
(*real* resistance, to use J. C. Scott's [1985] term). I am most interested in
cultivating generalized knowledge about resistant traditions for purposes
of archaeological inference. My guess is that the structural parallels between ethnographic and archaeological hunter-gatherers have much to do
with similar histories of domination and resistance. Obviously, the pre-
Columbian past was free of the institutional oppression of modern na-
tions, although capitalism is hardly necessary to spawn structures of
domination or its resistant consequences. In fact, the so-called regionali-
zation of the world's post-Pleistocene hunter-gatherers bears witness to
negotiations of power and privilege as groups defined themselves in opposition to others. Such diversity is too often read as a product of isolation
and local adaptation. Historical readings of ethnographic subjects give us
reason to think otherwise.

In developing a cross-cultural perspective on resistant traditions I take
a deliberately broad approach. I trust we can agree that there is little
structural unity between a particular subsistence base and sociocultural
features such as hierarchy, kinship, or the appropriation of surplus. It
follows that hunting and gathering alone does not determine sociocultural
structures, and, conversely, that sociocultural structures among food producing or industrial economies have potential relevance in our understanding of hunter-gatherer diversity. With a historical perspective that
links everyone together in webs of domination and resistance, hunter-
gatherers can hardly be isolated conceptually as exceptional or unique.
Hunter-gatherers today exist because of modernity, not in spite of it. Similarly, hunter-gatherer diversity in the past derived from interactions, not
from isolationism.

The cases I review in this chapter go beyond examples of hunter-gatherer resistance to include ethnic and religious movements of the modern
world. I include here discussion of the Rom of Eastern Europe and the Old
Order Amish because they exemplify especially long-lived traditions of
resistance. Despite the many differences between these two cases, parallels
are apparent in the structures and actions each negotiates to create identi-

ties that are deliberately oppositional to the conditions of oppression they experienced in the past. I add a third case, that of the Mexican Kickapoo, to illustrate how similar actions of resistance are manifested in an ethnographic hunter-gatherer context.

The ultimate goal in this chapter is to build an inferential basis for examining historical processes of resistance in the pre-Columbian past. Here I draw on two examples from the Archaic period of the American Southeast because I know these best. I suspect that examples of resistant traditions are legion in the archaeological records of hunter-gatherers worldwide and trust that my approach here is sufficiently general to encourage its application elsewhere.

Persistent Resistance: Three Case Studies

The Rom

The Rom are one of several groups of Eastern European Gypsies whose origins can be traced to the subcontinent of India. The status of ancestral Rom in India's caste system is uncertain, as are the timing and circumstances of their exodus from India. However, by the fifth century A.D. they appear to have occupied portions of Persia and Syria, and southeast Europe by the fourteenth century. In the ensuing three centuries they came to occupy virtually every European country, along with large portions of North Africa, the Near East, and the New World (Kephart 1982:7–8).

The Rom have persevered under enormous persecution in the twentieth century. Nazis exterminated hundreds of thousands of Rom in the early 1940s, eliminating nearly the entire Czech population. Under Soviet domination, the Rom were subject to a systematic assimilation campaign. Since 1989, the Rom have become the "scapegoats of postcommunism" (M. Stewart 1997:3) in Eastern Europe, suffering increased oppression in the balkanized landscape of emergent capitalism and democracy.

Although there have always been a significant number of sedentary Gypsies (Sinte), especially since World War II, traveling is among the more defining characteristics of traditional Rom living. Other groups oftentimes described as "Gypsies," such as the Irish Travelers, sustain a truly mobile existence, a lifestyle accentuated in some cases by state efforts to disperse Gypsies from residential districts (see Adams et al. 1975). But even among the relatively stationary Rom there is an inherent flexibility that comes from a lack of land control. No particular preference is expressed by the Rom about where they live. Community for them is defined by interactions and sharing amongst themselves, not an objectified sense of place. Lacking land and unable to realize autonomy through labor, they seized on circulation as a way of life (M. Stewart 1997:237).

A communal ethos is also among the defining features of Rom society. In response to the hostility that has plagued Gypsies throughout their history, the Rom nurture a sense of respect and honor for one another. They represent themselves as fulfilling each other's needs, while preserving each other's autonomy. There is a continuous flow of food, tools, and services among households. Things are shared willingly without expectation of return. They reject any form of differentiation within the community stemming from interactions with outsiders. Thus there exist great pressures to level differences, and effective means for expelling uppity or greedy members.

Because members of Rom society are invariably unique individuals, the maintenance of egalitarianism requires a constant assertion of what it is to be Gypsy. This is manifested in mundane as well as ritualized aspects of Rom life. "So long as all the Gypsies did the same, looked the same, and ate the same food, they appeared as equals" (M. Stewart 1997:92). The hidden contradictions between individuality and community occasionally rise to the surface in conflict and crisis, but offsetting this tension is the encapsulation of Rom by the outside world.

The sense of being encapsulated by more powerful and hostile people is conceptualized by the Rom as a state of siege (M. Stewart 1997:40). The world outside Rom communities is regarded as dangerous and polluted, and their interactions with it are highly circumspect. They define themselves in opposition to the *gazos,* the non-Rom, whom they consider to be other than human (M. Stewart 1997:232). The Rom substitute egalitarian relations within the community for the hierarchical ones they suffer with the *gazos* and that the *gazos* endure with each other (M. Stewart 1997:234).

In a recent study of Rom identity, Michael Stewart (1997) described three contexts of cultural appropriation and self-assertion: horse trading, speech, and concepts of bodily shame. In each case the Rom have negated representations or relations from the outside world—those used expressly to subordinate and denigrate the Rom—by symbolically converting them to assert their superiority. For instance, money taken through wage labor with the *gazos* is "cleansed" by purchasing horses that are then traded back to the *gazos* at higher prices. Because the Rom live in a world where they are despised by the *gazos,* establishing a separation between themselves and others and then "policing" the boundary are integral features of their resistance to domination (M. Stewart 1997:234). The key to under-standing the remarkable persistence of the Rom "lies in the way these Gypsies have been able to take their experience of the world around them and convert or transform it into their own cultural terms, into a specifi-cally Rom sense of what it means to be human" (M. Stewart 1997:232).

The Old Order Amish

"Amish history is a history of divisions and migrations" (Hostetler 1980:36). The roots of Amish religion lie in the Anabaptist movement of sixteenth-century Europe (Hostetler 1980; Kraybill 1989). Critical of the slow pace of protestant reformation sparked by Martin Luther, a group of young dissidents held a secret meeting in Zurich in 1525, where they re-baptized one another to initiate an offshoot movement. Within five months civil authorities killed one of them for sedition. Over the ensuing decades, thousands of the religious heretics were imprisoned, tortured, and executed. Refuge by small factions was sought in increasingly remote parts of Alpine and northern Europe, and eventually in North America. In the Netherlands Menno Simons emerged as the leader of a sect that came to be known as the Mennonites. Another influential figure, Jacob Am-mann, led a group of Alsatian immigrants in the late 1600s in reforms that eventually became the Amish church. The chief divisive issue was the prac-tice of excommunication, or *Meidung*, which Ammann and his followers upheld strictly but Swiss Mennonites tended to relax (Kephart 1982:49; Kraybill 1989:6). The Old Order Amish emerged after 1693 as the conser-vative branch of Anabaptists, distinct to this day from the Mennonite Church.

A fundamental tenet of Amish religion is separation from the world. Like other sectarian movements, the defining beliefs of the Amish were consciously selected on the basis of differences with the parent group (Hostetler 1980:48). The Amish created and constantly renew separatism to maintain their order. Geographic separation has factored heavily in their histories, notably immigration to the New World, but more funda-mental is the ideological separation that was asserted in opposition to the church establishment of Europe. "The Amish contrast church versus world, Amish and non-Amish, and 'our people' versus 'outsiders'" (Kray-bill 1989:37). As a constellation of ideas consciously asserted to oppose orthodoxy, separateness is reified and reproduced through daily activity, which itself is imbued with spiritualism, as well as through distinctive material culture, such as dress, hair style, and farmhouses.

Although separation from the world is deemed necessary, geographic isolation from outsiders is neither sought after nor considered desirable (Hostetler 1980:113). Acceptable behavior in public, as well as private and ceremonial life, is guided by the unwritten code of conduct known as *Ordnung* (Kraybill 1989:95). The *Ordnung* specifies some things as simply outside the Amish world. "On such grounds business partnerships or conjugal bonds with outsiders are forbidden. Strife, war, and violence have no place in the community or in the life of the member. Members of the community cannot function as officers or caretakers of the political or world society" (Hostetler 1980:23). At the same time, the *Ordnung* evolves to accommodate changes in the world beyond Amish control, and enforcement varies among communities, some more conservative than others.

In direct reaction to their history of oppression, the Amish are fiercely egalitarian. This feature is enabled by the *Ordnung* as a communal means of managing the human tendency toward self-exaltation and manipulation (Hostetler 1980:85). Social penalities are leveled against personal power, wealth, conspicuous consumption, idleness, and stinginess. Pride is shunned, humility cultivated. Although Amish farms are largely self-sufficient, households pool labor for large-scale projects, such as barn-raising, woodcutting for the winter, fencing, and preparations for ritual. They visit one another routinely. In cases of disaster or illness, communities take action to alleviate the burden on individual families.

Whereas the Amish might be regarded as a commonwealth, their religious beliefs preclude the occupation and defense of a particular territory (Hostetler 1980:5). In the face of hostility, the Amish pick up and move without defending their rights (Hostetler 1980:78). "Without freedom of movement the Amish would encounter serious difficulties in trying to resolve and maintain the essential elements of their community life" (Hostetler 1980:364).

Ever since being pushed into rural isolation through persecution in Europe, the Amish have worked the land as farmers. They regard farming as a religious mandate, tilling the soil a spiritual endeavor. At the same time, fertile soil is a paradox, for the prosperity it enables has the potential to destroy the church with luxury (Kraybill 1989:189). Thus, Amish farming defines one's place in the community of God, but not one's relationship to the land.

Hostetler (1980:10–17) points to four features of Amish society that help to understand their persistence: distinctiveness, smallness of scale, homogeneous culture patterns, and strain toward self-sufficiency. To this list we might add the ability to adjust to a rapidly changing world without compromising longstanding values. This is made possible, arguably, by the conditions of democracy and human rights the Amish enjoy as U.S. citizens. Indeed, the Amish are often revered for their utopian ways and efficient farming. Tourists flock to Amish country each year to experience what they regard to be a quaint and simple holdover of a bygone era.

The Mexican Kickapoo

The Algonquian-speaking Mexican Kickapoo Indians are one of three extant Kickapoo tribes with common ancestry among late pre-Columbian populations of the Great Lakes region. Compared to their counterparts in Kansas and Oklahoma, the Mexican Kickapoo are particularly conservative and reclusive. They are portrayed expressly as a resistant cultural tradition by Mary Nunley (1986, 1991), whose work I draw on liberally in the following summary.

Early accounts of the Kickapoo put them in southern Michigan, where they were living among the Menomini and Winnebago as refugees of Iroquois aggression (Latorre and Latorre 1976:3). Sustained European contact began in 1634 with the French. Subsistence prior to contact was based on seasonal rounds of hunting, gathering, and limited farming. For the next two centuries after contact, the Kickapoo engaged in shifting alliances with neighboring Indians and Europeans. Western expansion led to a series of divisions and forced resettlement beginning in 1833, when a group settled permanently in Kansas. A second split in 1873 established the Oklahoma reservation nation. The third group, the Mexican Kickapoo, never accepted a fully sedentary existence, despite pressures from both the U.S. and Mexican governments. They fled to Mexico during the Oklahoma resettlement campaign, where in 1873, they were chased down by the U.S. Fourth Cavalry. Attacking while the Kickapoo men were away on the spring hunt, the U.S. troops abducted women and children and held them hostage in Oklahoma to force others to settle on reservation land. The scheme worked on some, but others resisted the campaign and were joined over the years by refugees to constitute what today is a population of several hundred Mexican Kickapoo who reside more-or-less regularly in government-allocated land in Coahuila, Mexico.

Irrespective of their access to land and resources to make an adequate living through farming, the Mexican Kickapoo choose to maintain a transhumant lifestyle that takes them from Mexico to as far as the Canadian border on an annual basis. In fact, many Kickapoo soundly reject agriculture, as they opt to lease pasture and cropland to others rather than work it themselves. Hunting is the preferred means of subsistence, although it is no longer the chief economic pursuit. Today the Kickapoo cobble together a livelihood from a combination of wage labor, welfare, foraging, and hunting. They generally spend the winter months in the major Mexican settlement of El Nacimiento, where they focus on foraging. In May they travel northward for agricultural wage labor, hunting wherever and whenever they have the chance.

Migration is consciously used by the Mexican Kickapoo to assert autonomy. They regard moving as an expression of independence and freedom. Besides the annual wage-labor trips northward, many Kickapoo make the long roundtrip drive to Texas or Oklahoma several times a week during the winter. Because of the ambiguity about citizenship with the United Sates, the Kickapoo in effect have dual citizenship and thus move unimpeded across the Mexican border. They use this dual affiliation to great advantage, for wages earned in the United States are converted to pesos in Mexico at rapidly increasing rates of exchange in recent decades.

The Kickapoo have likewise taken good advantage of welfare and charity opportunities in the United States. For decades they have used Eagle Pass, Texas, as a seasonal staging area for hiring out for agricultural labor. In the early 1970s, when the Kickapoo became aware of social services available to them, a small settlement was established near Eagle Pass to exploit these opportunities. Characterized by the U.S. news media as impoverished and homeless, the Kickapoo began to receive additional land and capital improvements without asking, largely due to public pressure. According to Nunley (1991:349), the Kickapoo "have learned that looking poor may be profitable."

Although they involve themselves in a variety of economic opportunities with outsiders, the Mexican Kickapoo are a decidedly reclusive people. They discourage foreign entry into their winter village by keeping the nineteen-mile access road in a poor state of repair. Although most Kickapoo are bilingual and some trilingual, they restrict use of Spanish and English to only necessary circumstances and otherwise use their native language in public. Marriage with non-Kickapoo is taboo, and very few outsiders are afforded lasting friendships. Cultural boundaries are consciously guarded.

Relations within Kickapoo society are strongly egalitarian. Generalized reciprocity is codified in rules for sharing food and in communal rituals of cooperation. Preserving internal cohesion is a voiced concern, as the Kickapoo regard themselves united against the hostile world. The staunch resistance they express against anything promoting assimilation is underwritten by a complex set of social sanctions to inhibit deviations from tradition. According to Nunley (1991:352), Kickapoo society has always been divided into two bands, those willing to accommodate changes imposed by the dominant society, and those committed to preservation of aboriginal values. Splits leading to the formation of the three extant groups are explained in these terms. In this manner of fissioning, "those Kickapoo who do not hold to the traditional culture are purged along with acculturative traits they may have acquired" (Nunley 1991:352).

Finally, the Mexican Kickapoo exhibit an overall opportunistic flexibility that Nunley (1991) attributes to their "foraging ethos." They expand their catchment of natural and social resources whenever and wherever possible so long as it does not undermine their autonomy. This flexibility has been enabled by preserving, even expanding, their range of mobility, as well as by maintaining a sharp division between themselves and outsiders. This latter feature helps to sustain different types of economic relationships in their dealing with the "out-group." "Whereas a generalized reciprocity requires sharing and cooperation among members of the in-group, by creating and maintaining an out-group, a social environment in which exploitation or negative reciprocity that does not threaten closer in-group relations is possible" (Nunley 1991:353).

Emergent Properties of Persistent Resistance

The three cases reviewed to this point are wildly divergent in their historical particulars and cultural content. And yet, a number of parallels exist among them. Most obvious, each has a history of oppression or domination by a nation-state that involved or precipitated events of separation, both geographic and ideological. Notably, these were events constituted by actions of resistance to the imposition of will. The cultural meanings informing these actions were constructed in direct opposition to the structures and actions of domination. As examples of culture building, these resistant actions are no different than other sorts of actions, in that all actions have significance in relational or oppositional terms.

A more interesting parallel among these cases is the role of separation (action) in reproducing and altering resistant traditions (structure). Separation in this sense is not an event, but an ongoing process of asserting difference. In the same way, the tradition to resist power to change or assimilate, coercively or otherwise, is not static but created and negotiated through routine action, little of which may be consciously regarded as resistance. Thus, separation does not result in mutually exclusive cultural traditions, each internally homogeneous and integrated. Clearly each of the cases reviewed here involved circumstances requiring individuals to decide whether to go along with the objectives articulated by a few. But this does not imply that all actors were similarly motivated, or that the resultant cultural forms remained unambiguous and self-perpetuating. With each action of every day, each actor negotiates tradition. Resistance to change is prevalent in each of the cases, but it is effective because change is accommodated, and the separation process continues to mediate change.

In the cases reviewed, egalitarianism is fundamental to separation. Asserting equality and autonomy enables a line to be drawn between those one treats as self, and those one treats as the other. The cases here suggest that when interactions across these boundaries are routine and historically adversarial, the differences between self and other are marked. Differences enable the interactions by rendering unambiguous the roles of the actors.

A variety of actions for asserting egalitarianism are exemplified in these case studies. In structural form, they bear strong resemblance to those found among many hunter-gatherer societies worldwide (Leacock and Lee 1982). Among the actions are mobility, sharing, enforced humility, and economic autonomy. They work to level differences among members and to impede conflict or exploitation. Ethos about land has this effect too, as none of the groups reviewed objectify land as inalienable property, not even the Amish, who own sizeable tracts. Limited capital investment, simple technology, and self-sufficiency among the Amish help to prevent constraints on mobility. Arguably, the Rom avoid full-time wage labor and the Kickapoo avoid agriculture for the same reason.

Ultimately, we see in these cases not the perpetuation of deeply rooted, static tradition, but continuous processes of tradition-making constituted on the power relations within and between collectivities (see also Saunders, this volume). The historical particulars that engendered cultural differences are no doubt as varied as the resultant forms, but the processes of ethnogenesis and reproduction of difference have cross-cultural regularity that is of potential value to archaeologists. What we have seen so far is that conditions of political oppression, economic exploitation, or other modes of domination are met with resistance that is made and reproduced through egalitarian social relations, mobility, and an ongoing process of separation.

Persistent Resistance in the Archaic Southeast

Emergent properties of resistant traditions bear remarkable similarity to the defining characteristics of ethnographic hunter-gatherers typically appropriated through analogy to interpret hunter-gatherers of ancient times. I suggest these similarities derive from similar historical processes. As I indicated earlier, this is not to suggest that ancient societies were enmeshed in the sorts of hegemonic forces that engendered the resistant traditions of the Rom, Amish, or Kickapoo. Rather, I am proposing simply that diversity among ancient hunter-gatherer societies can often be traced to negotiations of power and tradition in historically situated contexts of interaction (see also Emerson and McElrath, this volume). The emergent properties just reviewed provide an inferential basis for examining this proposition. Before attempting this exploration, however, some methodological and conceptual barriers must be removed.

First, we have to allow for the existence of cultural diversity among hunter-gatherer populations with histories of interaction among them. There is an inherent bias that diversity derives largely, if not solely, from isolation, and conversely, that interaction produces homogeneity or assimilation. The very methods used by archaeologists to construct cultural historical sequences perpetuate this bias (Sassaman 2000). As elsewhere, archaeological sequences in eastern North America are extrapolations of stratigraphic sequences that are inherently unilineal. The constituent cultures or phases of such sequences are thus isolated in time, one following the other, usually without hiatuses between them. In addition, sequences are generally subregional in scale, each derived from one or a few stratigraphic profiles. Clearly, some constituent phases crosscut sequences to constitute cultural horizons, but differences between two or more sequences at given points in time are never integrated at a higher scale of archaeological systematics. Here the differences are attributed to spatial isolation and the attendant consequences of local or subregional adaptations.

Beyond these methodological pitfalls lie the interpretive issues of diversity. We have in radiocarbon dating and other independent means of chronology a way around the stratigraphic conundrum. Short of dismissing absolute dates as "bad" when they demonstrate contemporaneity among two or more stratigraphically defined phases, archaeologists have the means to recognize synchronic cultural diversity. How they choose to interpret such diversity is a matter of theoretical predilection. Those reluctant to regard diversity as cultural or "ethnic" tend to explain it in ecological or functional terms. Following Marvin Harris (1997), they may regard ethnicity as a condition exclusive to state-level societies, or even to modernity. In this sense, ethnicity is the distinctive cultural identity of a group that was incorporated into a state through conquest or migration. It follows that pre-state cultural landscapes were devoid of ethnicity, so observed diversity, if not ethnic, temporal, or a product of isolation, must be functional.

A broader definition of ethnicity allows us to expand political causes for diversity to pre-state circumstances. That is, ethnicity may be defined as the symbolic representation of inequality (*sensu* Comaroff 1987). Inasmuch as cultural differences of any sort existed among pre-state societies, including hunter-gatherer societies, inequality existed. I hasten to add that inequality does not necessarily imply exploitation or oppression, only difference (McGuire and Saitta 1996). But it does necessitate the existence of power. As the late Eric Wolf (1999:67) insisted, differentiation throughout human history is a manifestation of power—power to mark off insiders from outsiders. Once such differences are demonstrated in archaeological contexts of hunter-gatherers, we are forced to either throw up boundaries of our own—that is, isolate them conceptually—or seek to understand the specific historical circumstances that caused agents to create and maintain differences in cultural identity.

In the balance of this chapter, I offer two illustrations of resistant traditions in the pre-Columbian Archaic Southeast. The case of the Morrow Mountain tradition illustrates a long-term pattern of cultural resistance. Like any long-term pattern in archaeology, it is not terribly revealing of day-to-day living, or the consequences of human agency. The example of the Mill Branch tradition is a bit more illustrative in this regard because it has been examined at much finer temporal and spatial scales. I believe it useful to juxtapose these two cases not only to examine the differences in scale, but to underscore the importance of particular historical contexts. Just like the cases described earlier, the Morrow Mountain and Mill Branch traditions are vastly different, yet like their modern-day counterparts they share certain qualities that shed insight on cross-cultural regularities in power relations, historical process, and tradition.

Morrow Mountain

A Middle Archaic cultural tradition signified by the Morrow Mountain hafted biface type (Coe 1964) is among the most widespread in eastern North America. Morrow Mountain points are distributed across most of the Southeast, the lower Midwest, and the Middle Atlantic regions. Southern New England can be added to this list if we include the virtually identical biface form known as Stark (Dincauze 1976; following Cross 1999; Cassedy 1983; Dent 1995). Either way, the enormous expanse of Morrow Mountain points obscures a great deal of interregional variation in subsistence and settlement organization, population density, and social complexity. Describing and explaining the full range of diversity in Morrow Mountain expressions is beyond the scope of this chapter. My purpose here, instead, is to highlight the persistence of certain elements of this tradition in the Southeast, particularly throughout the Piedmont province of the South Atlantic Slope, from Virginia to eastern Alabama.

Joffre Coe (1964) defined the Morrow Mountain type based on excavations at stratified sites in North Carolina designed to establish an archaeological sequence for the region. Coe considered the type intrusive to a deeply rooted Carolina Piedmont sequence, pointing to possible parent sources to the west. Radiocarbon dating has since shown that the oldest occurrences are indeed to the west, at sites in western Tennessee (Dye 1996). Morrow Mountain points and a related type known as Eva show up in the basal strata of freshwater shell midden sites on the Tennessee and Cumberland Rivers. Dating from about 7300 radiocarbon years B.P., these strata mark a dramatic change in lifestyle. For the first time in the region, groups began to occupy riverine sites repeatedly, even permanently, intensifying production to meet the rising economic and social demands of sedentism. They also regularly interred their dead in shell deposits and participated in long-distance exchange. These and other changes began a period of cultural elaboration referred to collectively as the "Shell Mound Archaic," which lasted for nearly four millennia over portions of the lower Midwest, Midsouth, and South Atlantic Slope.

Over the geographic and temporal expanse of its existence, the Shell Mound Archaic encompassed scores, perhaps hundreds of distinct cultural entities. Common among them is an intensive riverine settlement and subsistence pattern. Many locations were used repeatedly over the millennia, bearing witness to changes in material culture that bespeak a dynamic social landscape. Throughout, sites were repositories for the dead, some housing hundreds of burials. Several archaeologists have suggested that mortuaries signified corporate "ownership" of land, sacred sites that legitimated claims to territory (Claassen 1996; Hofman 1985; cf. Charles and Buikstra 1983). Examples of interpersonal conflict, scalping, and trophy taking have been documented at some sites, suggesting a marked level of intergroup competition (Walthall 1980), or avenues to prestige (C. Smith 1996). Occurrences of trade items and hypertrophic artifacts reflect other possible conduits to status and prestige (Jefferies 1996; Johnson and Brookes 1989).

The cultural boundaries created, negotiated, and redefined throughout the protracted history of the Shell Mound Archaic did more than demarcate the rights and privileges of one Shell Mound group from the next. They also categorically excluded alternative factions. Undoubtedly hundreds of cultural entities existed in the interstitial spaces of the Shell Mound Archaic landscape, but only one persisted sufficiently long and in such distinctive fashion to gain much archaeological recognition.

Throughout the Piedmont province of the South Atlantic Slope, the Morrow Mountain point continued to be made and used for at least 500 years after it disappeared from its region of origin in the Midsouth. Whereas the persistence of a simple hafted biface technology is hardly notable, the contexts in which it is found during these later centuries are decidedly antithetical to those of the Shell Mound Archaic (Sassaman n.d.). None of the thousands of Morrow Mountain components in the Piedmont or adjacent provinces contain shellfish remains, although by all indications freshwater shellfish were widely available. Riverine sites are plentiful, but none contain the sorts of organic accumulations indicative of long-term or repeated occupation, and they are eclipsed twofold by small, low-density habitation sites throughout inter-riverine zones. Nonlocal raw materials are but a trace occurrence in toolkits, and no evidence exists for long-distance exchange or the production of nonsubsistence items. Analysts working throughout the Piedmont province consistently report a lack of intersite functional variability indicative of labor differentiation or specialized land use (Anderson and Joseph 1988; Blanton and Sassaman 1989; Cable 1983; Purrington 1983). By all accounts, the Morrow Mountain pattern was one of generalized subsistence, frequent residential mobility, and small co-resident group size. The pattern fits to a tee the criteria of a forager model (Binford 1980) and an immediate return economy (Woodburn 1982). It was sustained seemingly unchanged for more than a millennium.

The specific events resulting in cultural separations between Morrow Mountain foragers and their Shell Mound counterparts are unknown to us. We can, however, surmise the circumstances that would have contributed to fissioning in the Shell Mound Archaic. The costs of participating in increasingly intensive economic and social activities were likely distributed unevenly among community members. Technologies, labor arrangements, and means of extracting social surplus may have put undue demands on certain households, kin groups, genders, or age groups. Communal labor ventures with delayed returns, objectification of place through mortuary practice, and social debts all had potential to constrain mobility, and thus individual autonomy. Increased investment in specific places and people may have had a spiraling effect on labor demands, as specialized production to offset marginal returns enabled the emergence of a group of nonproducers. As access to labor was likely mediated by the rights and responsibilities of kinship and marriage, it would not have been difficult to manipulate the flow of surplus labor ceremonially. Those unable to accumulate adequate ceremonial funds for lack of obliged labor may have had difficulty securing mates or other allies, thus exacerbating their plight. The evidence for violent confrontation in Shell Mound Archaic graves might reflect possible recourse for (or threat to) less privileged individuals or subgroups.

Whether or not these speculations about rising inequality withstand further scrutiny is not altogether relevant to our understanding of the persistence of Morrow Mountain culture. For whatever reason, a separation (i.e., fissioning) event or series of events took place in the Midsouth after 7000 B.P., constituted on the "invention" of a way of life in direct contradiction to what had come before. Its reproduction thereafter involved repeated geographic separations (i.e., migrations) eastward, perhaps in conjunction with fissioning episodes that divided communities between resistant and "progressive" elements. By the time bearers of Morrow Mountain culture came to dominate the Piedmont landscape (ca. 6900–5600 B.P.), the egalitarian relations they asserted appear to have been reproduced quite effectively by the everyday practices of mobility, generalized food getting, and expedient tool using. Perhaps a variety of less mundane rituals reinforced cooperation and humility among them, but it was probably unnecessary for them to experience regularly the very conditions that led to their separation generations before and hundreds of kilometers away. The persistence of their tradition would begin to erode only after about 5800 B.P., when the Piedmont cultural landscape was again reorganized for reasons yet poorly understood.

Mill Branch

As a local phase of Late Archaic Broadpoint cultures, Mill Branch was centered on the Middle Savannah River Valley of South Carolina and Georgia from about 4200 to 3800 radiocarbon years B.P. (Elliott et al. 1994; Ledbetter 1995). Its ancestry can be traced back several hundred years in the local area, with a regional lineage in the Carolina Piedmont sequence dating to as much as 9500 B.P. (Oliver 1985). The archaeologically defining features of Mill Branch and related Late Archaic phases are the Savannah River Stemmed point (Coe 1964), cruciform drills, the nearly exclusive use of metavolcanics for chipped stone tools, and polished stone artifacts such as winged bannerstones.

Distinguishing Mill Branch from other regional expressions is the use of soapstone for indirect heat cooking (i.e., stone boiling). This technique of cooking has great antiquity in the Eastern Woodlands, but only in the Savannah River Valley and limited adjacent areas was soapstone drafted for such uses. Because of its superior thermal shock resistance, soapstone offered not only an effective thermal medium, but a durable one at that. Several geological sources of soapstone existed within the geographic expanse of Mill Branch sites, and throughout the greater Piedmont province, but not in the adjacent Coastal Plain.

Mill Branch history in the Middle Savannah was shaped largely through interactions with their Coastal Plain neighbors, bearers of Stallings culture. Known chiefly for the oldest pottery in North America, Stallings culture had only a shallow past in the lower Savannah Valley. Local ancestry can be traced to a preceramic phase dating from 5000 B.P., perhaps a few centuries earlier. These early shell-bearing sites mark the first intensive occupations of the Coastal Plain since the Early Archaic period. From the onset of renewed occupation, preceramic Stallings groups engaged their Piedmont neighbors in exchange for soapstone cooking stones. Shallow, flat-bottomed ceramic vessels began to be made in the Coastal Plain at about 4400 B.P. They were ideally suited to indirect-heat cooking (Sassaman 1993), and soapstone continued to be acquired from Piedmont suppliers for this purpose. The Mill Branch phase coincides with a division of the Coastal Plain population into two factions: one that established permanent coastal settlement and developed pots for use directly over fire, and another that continued with traditional cooking technology, including the acquisition of soapstone.

Aside from their shared use of soapstone, Mill Branch and Stallings had little in common. A series of Mill Branch cultural traits appears to have been intended to mark their difference with Stallings. Conspicuous among them is the Notched Southern Ovate bannerstone. Elaborating on a long-standing design, Mill Branch artisans crafted large, hypertrophic bannerstones, as well as more typical ovate forms (Sassaman 1998a). Bifaces too became unusually large, and tool makers maintained a nearly exclusive preference for local rhyolites. Notably absent from Mill Branch inventories are ceramic vessels, despite ready access to knowledge and materials for making them. In fact, resistance to the adoption of pottery remained a defining feature of this culture throughout its history in the Middle Savannah and beyond. From its genesis until about 4000 B.P., Mill Branch settlement rounds included repeated, warm-season occupation of sites on the river and cold-season dispersal into adjacent Piedmont uplands. Burials of Mill Branch affiliation are numerous in strata below Stallings shell middens in the Middle Savannah (e.g., Claflin 1931; C. Miller 1949). Marine shell beads acquired presumably from Stallings partners were sometimes interred with the dead, particularly with children (Claassen 1996).

Within a century of the genesis of Mill Branch culture, bands of Stallings affiliation began to occupy Middle Savannah sites on a seasonal (apparently fall and winter) basis. Until recently, the appearance of Stallings sites in the area was considered to follow from the abandonment, assimilation, or evolution of Mill Branch culture, chiefly because that is the only story stratigraphic sequences allowed. Dozens of radiocarbon dates from several sites now confirm that Mill Branch and Stallings coexisted in close proximity for at least two centuries (Sassaman 1998b). At first, use of Mill Branch sites by Stallings bands may have been enabled by seasonal differentiation, as in the fashion of Kohistani and Gujar use of sites in the Swat region of Pakistan (Barth 1969b). But by 4000 B.P., Stallings shell middens began to form at Mill Branch riverine sites, including ones containing Mill Branch burials. Given that members of these two groups had long interacted through soapstone and shell bead exchange, it seems reasonable to suggest that they became one people via ethnogenesis (*sensu* J. H. Moore 1994b). Indeed, individuals of Mill Branch ancestry likely assimilated into Stallings culture via marriage. However, resistant factions of Mill Branch culture survived in the area for generations through their separation and reinvention in dispersed, mobile settlements of the adjoining uplands. The relationship of these dispersed factions to Stallings groups is unknown; shortly after 3800 B.P. they abandoned the area and relocated to central Georgia, perhaps elsewhere too.

Mill Branch abandonment of the Middle Savannah coincides with marked changes in Stallings pottery. The plain, flat-bottomed vessels of early Stallings times were thoroughly replaced by highly decorated pots technologically suited for direct-heat cooking. Remarkably, pots were still used as containers for stone boiling with soapstone (Sassaman 1993) and would be until Stallings residents abandoned riverine sites in the Middle Savannah some 150 years later. Stallings culture during these waning years appears to have become increasingly insular. Interactions with coastal groups and other Coastal Plain factions are evident in the panregional repertoire of surface decoration on pottery. But at the same time, the highly localized nature of technological design, as in vessel wall thickness and temper type (Sassaman et al. 1995), as well as traditions of pottery function, suggests there were limited transfers of personnel, at least among those (women?) involved in pottery manufacture and use. Persons of Mill

Branch affiliation may have been altogether excluded from alliances with Stallings members, perhaps contributing to Mill Branch motives for abandonment.

The history of Mill Branch culture away from its homeland in the Middle Savannah shows a remarkable turn of events. Having arrived in present-day central Georgia by 3600 B.P. (Stanyard 1997), Mill Branch descendents began to acquire and use soapstone vessels. Interestingly, this new technology combined the raw material of tradition (soapstone) with the form of innovation (pottery vessel). Archaeologists have long assumed that soapstone vessels were the technological precursors of pottery. AMS-dating of soot from soapstone vessel sherds from throughout the Southeast demonstrates just the opposite—that pottery predates soapstone vessels virtually everywhere in the greater region (Sassaman 1997). Still, as the Mill Branch case shows, soapstone vessels were not used because of a lack of knowledge about pottery, but in spite of it. After about 3500 B.P., groups with direct access to the largest quarries in Georgia began to funnel soapstone into the trading routes that led to Poverty Point in Louisiana (B. W. Smith 1991). To the extent descendents of Mill Branch culture were involved in these ventures—an involvement that is all but certain—they had succeeded in reinventing tradition yet again. Their actions would continue to inhibit the adoption of pottery, this time on a much grander scale. Poverty Point exchange and its attendant Late Archaic affiliates far and wide all disappear from the cultural landscape of the Southeast with the eventual panregional adoption of pottery some 2900 years ago.

Conclusion

Structural similarities in the actions humans take to resist domination should enable archaeologists to locate and investigate the histories of resistant traditions of the ancient past. The cases reviewed here illustrate marked differences in the historical context and cultural forms of resistance. However, in understanding the persistence of resistance it is the connection between power and ideas, between action and ideational structure, that is most relevant, not their content or form. In each of the cases reviewed, persistence was achieved by subverting domination through separation. Geographic separation was involved in each case, but more to the point is the ideological separation of tradition. Creations of identity in opposition to structures of domination empowered actors to mark difference and to assert egalitarian relations among themselves in order to guard that distinction. Ideological separation between those who do and do not adhere to tradition is continuously negotiated, hence traditions of resistance, like all culture, are always in a state of becoming.

Negotiations of power and ideas get played out in material and behavior terms through the mundane actions of everyday life. Ethos about community, humility, and autonomy are reproduced and challenged in the actions of visiting, food sharing, cooperative work, and group mobility. Little can be assumed about these simple actions without understanding the histories of power and interaction that gave rise to a group as a collective of equals. Kinship itself is an insufficient explanation, for it too is a nexus of culturally and historically constituted power relations (e.g., Collier 1988). Similarly, relationships of people to land and its resources are never ahistorical or apolitical. It may seem trite to say that environment is mediated by culture, but this truism seems to be overlooked inexcusably. Only history and culture can explain why Morrow Mountain people chose nut collecting over shellfishing and Mill Branch preferred soapstone over pottery, or why Mexican Kickapoo hunt instead of farm, the Rom trade horses instead of toil in factories, and the Amish pull manure spreaders with horses and not tractors.

The rising awareness of the importance of history to our understanding of hunter-gatherer diversity has the potential danger of merely turning the tables on ecofunctionalist doctrine. Whereas ecofunctionalist perspectives were ahistorical in their disregard for intergroup connections among ethnographic hunter-gatherers, explicitly historical approaches are sometimes deterministic about the effects of contact on hunter-gatherer organization (Bird-David 1988; Woodburn 1988:63). The "internal" and "external" relations among hunter-gatherer societies, or all societies for that matter, are mutually constitutive. The concept of resistance reminds us of this because resistance, by definition, is relational, indeed oppositional. And, to become tradition, as opposed to isolated action, it must be similarly constituted. The mere existence of domination, no matter how acute, does not explain the persistence of cultural differences. It takes an understanding of histories of interaction and power relations to understand the persistence of difference. The challenge then is to investigate the histories of interaction that contributed to hunter-gatherer diversity. I recommend that in archaeological cases of persistent traditions, particularly those constituted on egalitarian relations, mobility, and generalized economies, we consider carefully the possibility that interactions among groups of varying cultural complexity contributed to these patterns, despite the stratigraphic and geographic separations that make them appear to be isolated, self-contained wholes.

14

Traditions as Cultural Production

Implications for Contemporary Archaeological Research

Kent G. Lightfoot

My purpose in writing this chapter is to provide commentary on *The Archaeology of Traditions* from the point of view of an outsider who is not a practicing southeastern archaeologist. I appreciate very much Tim Pauketat's invitation to write this chapter after my serving as a discussant in the 1999 symposium at the Society for American Archaeology meeting in Chicago, where I heard many of the papers for the first time. In my view, the primary contribution of this volume is a renewed interest in "traditions" as an important concept for interpreting the social relations of past peoples, using archaeological remains. The authors explore multiple meanings and uses of traditions in their investigations of diverse southeastern societies ranging from early Archaic hunter-gatherers and later Woodland and Mississippian chiefdoms to postcontact Spanish missions and plantations. I find the theoretical reworking of the meanings of traditions very provocative and the overall breadth of the chapters refreshing. The volume clearly has implications for the study of traditions that resonate well beyond the southeastern United States.

From the outset, however, I want to stress that the multiple meanings of "traditions" employed in this volume differ considerably from how the term has been conventionally used by most archaeologists. Scholars trained as culture historians or processual archaeologists may question the new meanings of "traditions" and argue that the contributors are not really defining traditions per se, but something else. I begin my discussion by comparing the conventional usage of the term "traditions" with the new concepts of traditions outlined in the volume. I then consider three major implications that this new vision of traditions has for the practice of archaeology. These include how we study culture change, how we account for persistent cultural practices, and how we define alternative forms of traditions. Next, I comment upon some of the explanations proposed in various chapters to account for persistent cultural practices that focus on resistance and domination. Then I examine the advantages of employing concepts of traditions that are rooted in the study of cultural practices and highlight the array of archaeological remains (architecture, pottery, stone tools, food ways, and so on) used by the contributors to define and analyze traditions. I conclude with a discussion of the multiscalar views of traditions presented in the volume, noting that the microscale and macroscale studies are very complementary.

Multiple Meanings of Traditions

The initial concept of tradition was first commonly defined and used in American archaeology in the 1940s, although it had its genesis in earlier culture classifications such as those proposed by Gladwin and Gladwin for the American Southwest (Willey and Sabloff 1980:174). As Willey and Sabloff (1980:174–175) note, this definition of tradition was somewhat vague, but the basic meaning referred to "traditional" or "time-persistent ways of doing things." Traditions were defined as persistent cultural traits that exhibited continuity with the past and could be delineated in time-space grids. The essence of this concept is captured nicely in Wesson's chapter when he states that traditions "represented the glue that held social life together, with this adhesive working best when it bound social, cultural, and political relationships in perpetual stasis." The scales at which traditions were analyzed varied from broad-based "cultural traditions" involving the development of entire cultures to "artifact traditions" in which specific pottery types or projectile point types were traced through space and time (see P. S. Martin and Rinaldo 1951; Thompson 1956; Willey 1945; Willey and Phillips 1958). Emerson and McElrath cite in their chapter examples of traditions that range from a narrow materialistic perspective (see Willey and Phillips 1958) to a broader "social conceptualization" of the term (see Goggin 1949; Haury 1956, 1958).

In contrast, the contributors to *The Archaeology of Traditions* do not present one coherent concept of traditions, but rather a constellation of meanings that are polysemous in definition. Each author may share some of these different meanings, but they are not necessarily all employed in any one chapter. One meaning of this new conception of traditions emphasizes historical contingency and human agency. Individuals may construct different traditions based on their perceived interests, agendas, and worldviews, and based on the negotiation of social relations with other peoples. Another theme stresses that traditions are the means of continuously defining cultural production through peoples' actions. This meaning, as discussed in more detail further on, is critical because it provides a dynamic vision of traditions in which the seeds of both culture reproduction and transformation may exist. Traditions are rooted in the past, but they are constructed in the present, and as such they may be continually in the process of reconfiguration, as past actions are reinterpreted and modified to meet contemporary demands. A third meaning links the concept of traditions to a practice-centered approach. This approach, closely tied to practice theory, emphasizes the importance of day-to-day practices for understanding how traditions are created and transformed over time.

Implications of the New Meanings of Traditions

The multiple meanings of traditions, especially when taken together, differ in many respects from the previous definition of traditions. The new meanings provide an innovative theoretical and methodological structure for analyzing the creation, development, and transformation of traditions over time. The implications of this reconceptualization of traditions for the practice of archaeological research are threefold. The first is shifting the study of culture change from punctuated equilibrium models to those of continuous time flows. The second is accounting for persistent culture practices and not taking them for granted. The third is rethinking the limited range of traditions defined in the past and experimenting with alternative definitions and forms of traditions.

Study of Culture Change

Conventionally defined traditions were based on material culture that exhibited consistency and continuity through time. This perception of conservatism and stability in material culture allowed archaeologists to define traditions through time and space. Culture classification charts reified the idea that traditions were equated with long periods of cultural stasis. For example, Gordon Willey (1966) in his seminal book *An Introduction to American Archaeology* depicted various cultural traditions for North American prehistory that were characterized by long periods of relative stasis broken by short punctuated intervals of change. He showed the "Big Game Hunting Tradition" and especially the "Archaic Tradition" in the Eastern Woodlands as long-term cultural entities that eventually gave rise to later traditions, such as the "Woodland Tradition" and "Mississippian Tradition."

My mentor, Fred Plog (1973:188–190; 1974), argued that the reliance on conventional space-time grids and culture classification charts in archaeology reinforced a conceptual model of chronology as a series of successive periods or stages, each of which represented a discrete chronological unit. In this model of culture chronology, a tradition was typically equated to one or more periods or stages. The upshot was that the study of culture change was relegated to the intersections or lines that separated one period or stage of a culture tradition from another. Plog (1973, 1974) criticized this archaeological practice because it limited the analysis of change to only a relatively few chronological units rather than allowed the tracing of change through a series of continuous points through time. This practice also fostered a perspective in which traditions were treated as discrete units whose internal workings were typically not analyzed for evidence of culture change or transformation. Furthermore, this practice tended to perpetuate the conventional punctuated equilibrium model of long periods of cultural stasis divided by rapid periods of change.

Processual archaeologists of the 1960s and 1970s, while they critiqued many of the fundamental concepts of culture history, as outlined in Rees's chapter, did little to modify the conventional concept of traditions in archaeology (but see Binford 1965:208). In fact, the common perception of traditions as characterized by long periods of cultural stasis punctuated by rapid intervals of change was ideally suited for adaptational models of culture change. Adaptational models, heavily influenced by systems theory, depicted cultures as seeking equilibrium with their natural and social environments. A culture's equilibrium would remain in a steady state unless kicked out of balance by positive feedback processes stimulated by any number of factors, including ecological imbalances in people/land relationships, population growth, resource intensification, droughts, and so on (see Flannery 1972a; Glassow 1972; Zubrow 1971). The long-term stasis of cultural traditions is emphasized by Flannery (1972a:230) when he notes that "under conditions of fully achieved and permanently maintained equilibrium, prehistoric cultures might never have changed. That they did change was due at least in part to the existence of positive feedback or 'deviation-amplifying' processes."

The contributors to *The Archaeology of Traditions* question this long-held belief that traditions are characterized by long periods of cultural stasis and self-perpetuation punctuated by rapid intervals of change.

Fortier examines the problems of employing such a punctuated equilibrium model in archaeology. Rather than arguing for long periods of equilibrium or stasis, he feels that "cultural populations and human behavior in general are more dynamic and perhaps more unstable, particularly over short periods of time." Emerson and McElrath present a case example of how adaptation models have been employed in Eastern Woodlands research and consider the problems that have resulted from viewing sedentism in the Archaic and Early Woodland periods as an ahistorical and gradualistic process. All three of these authors are critical of models that assume a priori that cultural traditions are necessarily characterized by long-term continuity and *in situ* development of stable populations.

By proposing one of the new meanings of traditions as a dynamic and continuous process of cultural production, the contributors to *The Archaeology of Traditions* are redirecting the study of culture change in a way that Fred Plog would have approved. For example, Pauketat argues for a definition of traditions that is not static or the opposite of political action but rather as historical forms that are always in the process of becoming. Sassaman stresses the ongoing creative process of cultural production when he states that "with each action of every day, each actor negotiates tradition." Emerson and McElrath also underscore the dynamic character of a tradition "that is both grounded in the past and is transformed through practice into a revitalized, reformulated, and living tradition."

With this view of traditions as transformative in nature, I believe, the necessary theoretical infrastructure is now being established to implement an approach to culture change that Plog advocated some years ago. Since traditions are now viewed as the nexus of cultural production, there exists the potential for both culture change and culture persistence to take place in the creation of traditions. Thus, the study of culture change is not restricted to the interfaces of cultural traditions, nor is the study of culture persistence relegated to traditions themselves. Rather, the seeds of change and persistence may be observed in the process of creating traditions through day-to-day living, in which an individual's action may always involve aspects of both culture reproduction and culture transformation. At any point in time, cultural practices may be performed that are linked to the past but redefined or reinterpreted in order to be made meaningful in contemporary social contexts. This meaning of traditions requires archaeologists to examine change and persistence as a continuous flow of time. For any point in time, one must begin to consider why some aspects of an individual's culture practices may persist intact, why others may be modified to some degree, and why still others may be completely transformed.

Accounting for Persistent Traditions

While the potential for change is always present in the process of cultural production, there are situations in which persistent cultural practices are repeatedly performed over extended periods of time. "Persistent tradition" is the kind of tradition that will be most familiar to culture historians and processual archaeologists. However, in recognizing that change may potentially take place at any moment in the process of cultural production, one cannot take persistent traditions for granted or assume them to be part of a natural cycle of culture development over time. It is clear that one must be explicit in accounting for persistent traditions.

An important contribution of *The Archaeology of Traditions* is exploring why some people consciously choose or unconsciously follow specific cultural traditions that become routinized over multiple generations. In viewing traditions as historical processes that must be interpreted, the contributors examine power structures, identity construction, and resistance as important factors that may influence an individual's decision to reproduce cultural practices over time in direct opposition to other peoples' traditions.

In accounting for Archaic traditions in the Southeast, Sassaman observes that cultural traditions are often assumed to develop in relative isolation. He notes that the standard cultural historical sequences employed in archaeology, which are typically devised for distinct areas (valleys, physiographic regions), tend to foster this perspective. Sassaman persuasively argues that for Archaic traditions, the opposite is probably more realistic—that distinct hunter-gatherer traditions were established as a consequence of interactions and the marking of differences between "others." This point accentuates a common interpretation in *The Archaeology of Traditions* in which persistent traditions are perceived to have been created in opposition to other peoples' lifeways. Many of the contributors explore tradition building as part of a process of identity construction that may be undertaken as a strategy of resistance by oppressed peoples to cope with social relations of domination and inequality. Pauketat goes even further by arguing explicitly that "contrary practice" may be viewed as "dissidence of the latent everyday sort, done less to oppose some dominant persons and more to reproduce one's sense of tradition." A few examples from the volume illustrate this point.

Sassaman presents a classic case example of a tradition as an embedded form of cultural resistance in considering the persistent use of soapstone cooking slabs by some Archaic peoples, when they were fully aware of pottery production. This persistent tradition is argued to have been created in opposition to nearby groups who employed pottery in their day-to-day activities, and as such it is considered a latent form of resistance. Emerson and McElrath employ the concept of "ethnic cores" to define a variety of Late Archaic and Early Woodland peoples with distinct traditions who encountered and differentiated themselves from one another over time in the permeable American Bottom region of Illinois. Nassaney, in his study of the Plum Bayou culture, argues that tensions arose between the sociopolitical aspirations of elites in the Toltec Mound center and persistent traditions of communalism in outlying communities. He shows how resistance to inequality was negotiated in the production and use of ceramics and lithic tools in the daily practices of nonelite peoples. And Thomas considers various aspects of African-American slave traditions (display of property, fictive and cross-cutting kinship relations) that developed on southern plantations in direct opposition (and resistance) to the power structure established by white planters.

Alternative Forms of Traditions

The conventional concept of traditions was limited to a relatively narrow range of phenomena, primarily cultural traditions and artifact traditions defined at the scale of regions and local sites. An important contribution of *The Archaeology of Traditions* is the recognition that cultural production may involve alternative forms of traditions that vary greatly in their spatial and temporal scales. In viewing cultural production as a negotiated historical process involving individual agency, it becomes clear that individuals and groups, depending on their values, beliefs, and motivations, may instigate very different kinds of cultural practices. If the performance of these practices persists long enough to become archaeologically visible, then we may be able to define them as distinct traditions. For instance, alternative forms of traditions may be created at different scales of analysis and relate to distinct cultural entities, communities, kinship groups, political affiliations, and factional groups, or employed to demarcate gender, age, and status differences. Several examples from the volume exemplify this point.

Sullivan and Rodning describe the development of separate but equal gender traditions among males and females of late prehistoric chiefdoms in southern Appalachia. Alt considers the creation of related but still distinct traditions that developed within the Cahokia ceremonial/political center and nearby upland communities. A shared identity was perpetuated between the center and hinterland, but uplands people maintained traditional practices that Alt interprets as signaling their rejection of Cahokia political domination. Loren details the development of "local" and "official" traditions at the Los Adaes Presidio and shows how native, mestizo, and Spanish peoples employed various combinations of these traditions in private and public spaces, depending on the motivations and interests of individual actors. Scarry highlights the multifaceted and deeply layered traditions that arose when Apalachee peoples encountered Spanish colonists and implemented strategies of both resistance and accommodation.

Recognizing that an individual, single community, or broader culture may have created diverse traditions that are meaningful for understanding past social relations raises concerns about how these entities are defined by archaeologists. Conventionally defined traditions were usually based on normative assumptions concerning time-space grids and the distribution of specific projectile point and pottery types. One problem with some of the case studies is the ad hoc nature in which traditions appear to have been defined. This is not unexpected when one considers that *The Archaeology of Traditions* is breaking new theoretical and methodological ground. But future research should be directed toward the problem of how one defines alternative forms of traditions. Ultimately, archaeologists will need to consider whether all these alternative forms should be considered traditions per se or defined by some other concept.

Another potential problem concerns the application of conventional cultural traditions in very different ways than those in which they were originally defined and used. Some chapters begin with sophisticated theoretical discussions on traditions and then employ culture traditions that have been defined in the past by traditional ceramic types or stone tool types to illustrate their points. It is not clear to me how well these older archaeological entities, which are the product of a very different paradigm, will hold up under these new multiple meanings of traditions. I do not think that we will be able to translate them directly into studies of cultural production, agency, and negotiation. But since most culture historians were well versed in describing archaeological traits across space and time, my feeling is that many of these conventionally defined traditions will prove to be a good beginning point for defining new forms of traditions. I think Sassaman illustrates this point with his study of the Morrow Mountain tradition, a cultural tradition that was defined originally by a specific type of projectile point. He then considers other kinds of archaeological data (shellfish remains, nonlocal goods, mortuary practices) to define different traditions (Shell Mound and foragers) within the Morrow Mountain complex. However, I still think considerable work is needed to tease apart the cultural practices that embody these different traditions.

A Consideration of "Resistant Traditions"

With the recent focus on power relations and resistance in the anthropological and archaeological literature (see McGuire and Paynter 1991; D. Miller et al. 1989; J. C. Scott 1985), some scholars are voicing concern that domination and resistance are being overplayed at the expense of other kinds of social relations—for example, cooperation, reciprocity, and accommodation—and that resistance is now being applied to almost any historical context, a trend that undermines the analytical utility of these concepts (M. F. Brown 1996:729–730). With this growing backlash resulting from the inappropriate use of resistance and power as explanations, there are now some who are directing challenges "to prove there was resistance in the past" (Frazer 1999:5). Others are critiquing resistance arguments because they tend to deny decision making (agency) to subordinate or less powerful populations and communities by portraying them as reactionary clones responding to domination (see Frazer 1999:5).

Pauketat, Scarry, and other contributors are well aware of these critiques and are concerned about trivializing resistance in accounting for the creation of contrary traditions. There are two kinds of resistance discussed in *The Archaeology of Traditions*. The first type concerns conscious and intentional actions to resist oppression. This is the type with which most scholars are familiar. For example, R. Jackson and Castillo (1995: 73–74) in their discussion of native peoples and their encounters with Franciscan missionaries in California describe two dimensions of this kind of resistance (active and passive). Active resistance involves overt confrontations that often lead to violence by subordinated populations who initiate revolts, raids, and assassinations against their oppressors. Passive resistance, while tougher to document archaeologically, involves covert actions against oppressors such as work slowdowns, noncooperation, foot dragging, feigned sickness, and so on.

It is this second type of resistance, described by Pauketat as "any contrary practice," that is bound to raise some eyebrows among our colleagues. This is the kind of resistance that is examined to understand the creation and maintenance of "resistant traditions" in many chapters of the volume. The authors are not alone in this approach, as Singleton (1998:180) notes that it is increasingly common for archaeologists to interpret evidence of shared cultural practices as forms of resistance.

Quite frankly, I am somewhat uneasy with the growing trend of employing resistance, subordination, and inequality to explain the genesis of many social relationships. But I also see the problem inherent in previous studies of traditions that did not take power relationships, domination, and resistance into account when considering persistent traditions. As Frazer (1999:5) rightly points out, if one accepts that power differentials existed in the past, then one must acknowledge that resistance "as the other half of a dialectical relation of power" must have also existed (a point also voiced by Emerson and McElrath). I think the critical issue in employing resistance to account for persistent traditions is to consider in detail the specific historical context of interactions with "others," and to examine the interplay of other possible social factors, such as accommodation, alliance building, and negotiation (see Singleton 1998:181).

I think there are specific historical contexts where it makes considerable sense to consider resistance as part of the explanation for why people maintain separate cultural practices, and why they may maintain direct links with their ancestral past. Some years ago, Spicer (1962:578–579) identified culture contact settings in the American Southwest as social arenas where native peoples intentionally maintained persistent cultural traits and practices that set them apart from the white world. I think in the context of the oppressive power dynamics of colonial and plantation settings one must consider strategies of resistance in accounting for the traditions of the underclass. The chapters by Loren, Scarry, and Thomas provide, in my opinion, excellent examples of such resistant traditions. The rise of chiefdoms and the development of elite and commoner traditions in the Southeast is another context where it makes considerable sense to consider issues of domination, inequality, and resistance. I think that Alt and Nassaney in the volume present compelling cases for examining the development of cultural practices as resistance to sociopolitical inequality.

I am very intrigued with studies of persistent traditions in other historical contexts involving hunter-gatherer and/or horticultural interactions (see Sassaman, Emerson and McElrath, Fortier). It is not clear to me whether these social contexts can really be viewed as resistance to some dominant power per se (although Sassaman makes a strong case for such resistance arguments when considering historic hunter-gatherers and their relations with the outside world). Rather I see the creation of traditions among these groups as part of a process of identity marking related to alliance formations, trade ties, and religious movements, as well as facilitating the identity of friend or foe. For example, I have long been dissatisfied with traditional explanations for why native peoples in California remained hunter-gatherers and mostly nonpottery users throughout prehistory, when neighboring groups along the Colorado River and throughout the American Southwest practiced agriculture and produced some of the finest pottery in the Americas. As Sassaman outlines, the traditional explanations for hunter-gatherer perseverance are isolation, marginalization and, in the case of California, supposedly poor climatic conditions for producing native cultigens. I think it will be constructive in the future to consider persistent hunter-gatherer traditions in California as identities created in opposition to the agricultural "others," as well as identity construction that signaled a common ancestral relationship among the many hundreds of communities that dotted the California landscape.

Practice-Centered Approach

Another important contribution of *The Archaeology of Traditions* is taking a practice-centered approach to the study of traditions. Building upon such concepts as doxa, habitus, and structuration as originally conceived by Pierre Bourdieu and Anthony Giddens, the authors of the volume employ aspects of practice theory to consider how the history of traditions unfolds at the interface of structure and action. Pauketat and others emphasize how cultural categories, values, and meanings are reproduced and transformed during the process of day-to-day practices. As I have noted before (Lightfoot et al. 1998:201–202), I think this approach is tailor-made for archaeology. Daily practices are ideally suited for archaeological study because they involve the investigation of how space is structured, how mundane domestic tasks are conducted, and how refuse is disposed. The performance of daily routines produces patterned accumulations of material culture that are often among the most interpretable kinds of deposits found in archaeological contexts. By viewing traditions as the means of continuously redefining cultural production through the enactment of day-to-day practices, one can develop the necessary linkages between the theoretical construct and the archaeological database. In other words, traditions may be defined, analyzed, and interpreted using those cultural remains that are commonly found in the archaeological record.

Most of the contributors employ this practice-centered approach in their case studies. To emphasize the great diversity of cultural materials that may be employed in the study of cultural practices and traditions, I list the kinds of archaeological remains associated with specific traditions.

(a) Kenneth Sassaman. Archaic traditions (projectile points, shell-fish, nonlocal goods, mortuary practices, soapstone vessels, pottery)

(b) Thomas Emerson and Dale McElrath. Late Archaic and Early Woodland traditions in the American Bottom region of Illinois (lithic and pottery assemblages, settlement distributions)

(c) Andrew Fortier. Early and Middle Woodland cultural traditions (pottery temper, shape, and design motifs; lithic assemblages)

(d) Michael Nassaney. Toltec Mound site and hinterland community traditions (pottery, chipped-stone artifacts)

(e) Susan Alt. Cahokia and upland communities traditions (ceramic styles and temper, construction methods, settlement configurations)

(f) Mark Rees. Black Warrior(Moundville) and Central Mississippi Valleys (Nodena phase) traditions (representational themes/motifs on pottery)

(g) Lynne Sullivan and Christopher Rodning. Male and Female traditions in chiefdoms of southern Appalachia (spatial relationship of mortuary remains to the built environment)

(h) Cameron Wesson. Historic period Creek traditions (Euro-American trade goods)

(i) Rebecca Saunders. Negotiated native tradition in Spanish La Florida (pottery)

(j) Diana Loren. Diverse native, mestizo, and Spanish traditions at the Los Adaes Presidio (architecture, dress, trade goods, ceramics)

(k) John Scarry. Apalachee native traditions (settlement patterns, domestic architecture, ceramics, diet)

(l) Brian Thomas. African-American traditions in southern plantations (property of slaves such as ceramics, glass, etc.)

Traditions Through Time

The authors of *The Archaeology of Traditions* employ their multiple meanings of traditions to undertake analyses of societies that collectively span the entire Archaic, Woodland, Mississippian, and Historic periods of the Southeast. It is truly refreshing to see a collection of papers that approaches a theoretical problem employing both prehistoric and historic data, a point that Rees emphasizes in his historical overview. In particular, I appreciate Wesson's and Fortier's explicit discussion of historical processes involving the creation and maintenance of traditions that spanned prehistoric, protohistoric, and historic settings.

The multiscalar approach to the *The Archaeology of Traditions* is also refreshing, as I find the investigation of traditions at both the micro- and macroscales highly complementary. Many of the chapters are microscale analyses that detail the creation of specific traditions at the scale of individuals and groups. These studies tend to focus on how specific traditions were created by individual actions in selectively retaining and transforming cultural traditions on a day-to-day basis. For example, Saunders describes how individuals created the Altamaha pottery tradition by combining technological and stylistic components of both Spanish and Guale Indian design. Sullivan and Rodning consider how individuals were buried in relation to public architecture and residential buildings in defining the creation of gender structures in southern Appalachia chiefdoms. Loren describes the construction of diverse and overlapping traditions in the Los Adaes Presidio that were the product of individuals manipulating visible cultural practices (dress, architecture, trade goods) that related to some aspects of the Spanish elite, while adhering to some of their ancestral practices behind closed doors. Scarry details how native men and women implemented different kinds of strategies of resistance and accommodation to Spanish colonial authority, and how these different traditions may be defined among the historic Apalachee people using a wide range of archaeological materials (domestic architecture, ceramics, diet, dress).

Other chapters are macroscale analyses that consider the juxtaposition of multiple traditions through extended periods of time. Fortier takes the *longue durée* in examining cultural traditions in the American Bottom of Illinois and observes evidence of discontinuities and replacement over time. He argues that our typical view of traditions as being unilineal and gradualistic in their growth over time may be more a result of our archaeological methods, such as the vertical nature of chronological charts that imply connectivity over time, and less a realistic representation of what actually takes place. In employing a macroscale view of the American Bottom, he is able to show that this sequence "really embodies a hodgepodge of cultural traditions, many of which are horizontally intrusive, unrelated, and short-lived." Emerson and McElrath's macroscale approach to the Late Archaic and Early Woodland traditions of the American Bottom complements this perspective of cultural variation and discontinuity. At the regional scale, they define "ethnic cores" based on various lines of archaeological data as representing the cultural practices and traditions of discrete cultural groups that moved in and out of the American

Bottom region over hundreds of years. The ethnogenesis of new cultural traditions in the American Bottom may have involved the process of negotiating separate identities in a permeable boundary zone (a perspective supported by Sassaman's analysis of Archaic hunter-gatherers). Emerson and McElrath also stress that archaeologists need to revisit their theoretical and methodological approaches for defining and understanding population movements and migrations, especially in frontier areas such as the American Bottom.

Conclusion

The contributors to *The Archaeology of Traditions* present multiple meanings in redefining the concept of traditions in archaeology. This new vision of traditions stresses historical contingency, day-to-day practices, and human agency. A critical component of the new concept is viewing traditions as the means of continuously redefining cultural production through daily practices. This makes traditions come alive with the possibility that individuals may negotiate both culture persistence and change in the performance of daily life. At any point in time, some cultural practices may persist while others are transformed so that they can be made meaningful in new social contexts.

The reconceptualization of traditions has three major implications for the practice of archaeology.

•It raises questions about the common use of punctuated equilibrium models comprised of long periods of cultural stasis (traditions) that are divided by quick spurts of change (interfaces of traditions). The study of change is now conceptualized as a continuous flow of time in which cultural transformations may potentially take place at any moment.

•It requires that we no longer take persistent cultural practices for granted. Instead we must account for the development of persistent traditions that are replicated over multiple generations. The contributors to the volume explore such factors as identity construction, dominance, and resistance to account for why people created persistent traditions that arose in opposition to other nearby groups. In many of these studies, there is good evidence of unequal power relations and oppression that may have stimulated the creation of resistant traditions. However, other studies of persistent traditions took place among groups of relatively equal power, in which no one group clearly dominated the others. In these cases, it may be fruitful

in the future to expand our concepts of contrary practices beyond resistance per se, and to consider other reasons why people identify themselves in opposition to others. For instance, I think that Emerson and McElrath's discussion of "ethnic cores" is very promising.
•It forces archaeologists to consider a more diverse range of alternative traditions than those defined in the past. Individuals and groups may create very different kinds of traditions depending upon their varied interests, agendas, and worldviews. These traditions may be observable at different scales of analysis. Some may become visible only at the scale of individuals who differentiate themselves based on gender, status, and age differences. Other traditions may come into focus at the scale of kinship groups, sodalities, and factional groups, while still others may become clear at the scale of communities, polities, and broadscale cultures.

Furthermore, some of these alternative traditions may be very short-lived phenomena, while others may persist over hundreds of years. One problem that needs to be addressed in the future is a more formal method for defining these varied alternative traditions. Also, it is not clear to me whether conventionally defined traditions based primarily on projectile point and ceramic types can be translated directly into this new conceptual framework.

Another important contribution of *The Archaeology of Traditions* is employing a practice-centered approach to the study of traditions. Daily practices are ideally suited for archaeological study because the performance of daily routines produces patterned deposits of material culture that are among the most interpretable to archaeologists. Consequently, traditions may be defined, analyzed, and interpreted using remains that are commonly recovered from archaeological contexts.

Ultimately, time will tell if the multiple meanings of traditions proposed in *The Archaeology of Traditions* will be widely accepted by American archaeologists. I think some scholars will quibble that resistance and domination are overplayed as explanatory factors in the persistence of cultural practices. I also think some archaeologists will question whether some of the traditions described in the volume should really be defined as such. Should an individual's cultural practices that unfold over a generation and can be identified in the archaeological record be defined as a "tradition"? Should a specific group's aggregated cultural practices that are rapidly transformed over time and have little continuity with the past be defined as a "tradition"? Should discrete cultural practices that are used to differentiate gender, age, status, and other kinds of social distinctions be defined as one or more "traditions"? I think these are excellent questions that will undoubtedly be addressed in the future.

In concluding, I think *The Archaeology of Traditions* is an important book because it will generate renewed interest in how we define and employ traditions in archaeological practice. I also think it is important because it explores new and creative ways of defining traditions using archaeological materials. Given my recent exposure to southeastern archaeology, I am now convinced that the Southeast is the new frontier for exploring cutting-edge developments in the method and theory of American archaeology. While southwestern archaeologists once held this position in the days of processual archaeology, the Southeast is rapidly becoming the place to do innovative research in these postprocessual days, a point exemplified by the chapters in this volume.

15

Concluding Thoughts on Tradition, History, and Archaeology

Timothy R. Pauketat

[E]ach of us makes meaning out of meanings that others have already made and are making—a process that makes us *living embodiments* of the history of our relations with others.
Christina Toren (1999:125, emphasis in the original)

The Southeast offers a resolution to the conundrum of tradition. In separate but related historical cases, the authors of this volume analyze tradition by focusing on the process of tradition making at a number of different scales of analysis. This can be done in the Southeast, perhaps more than in any other part of the world, given the theoretically preadapted and well-funded archaeology of the Eastern Woodlands (Graham 1998:31; Lightfoot, this volume; Pauketat 1998b:45). The ability to measure diversity through time and within artifact assemblages, features, settlements, and regions is requisite, meaning that rich data sets are necessary.

That said, it is also the case that an archaeology of traditions before and after Columbus transcends the perceived limitations of archaeological data sets. In fact, given the principle of materiality, history in the sense that various contributors have used it is more accessible to archaeologists than to historians. Thus, it is no longer acceptable for "prehistorians" to rely on the crutch that their data sets, lacking written descriptions by Europeans, are somehow impoverished and not suitable for understanding the ways that traditions were shaped, politicized, and negotiated between persons and among peoples. At the same time, it is no longer acceptable for historical archaeologists to use the ever-biased written accounts of the literate few as substitutes for actual on-the-ground measures of how people produced history. History in this volume is not limited to certain time periods where individual agents are identified by name or where texts may be used to aid in archaeological interpretations.

The processes of cultural change in the so-called historic and prehistoric past must always be understood as *historical processes*. What people did, how they represented themselves, and how their motivations were inculcated matters in our explanations of cultural change. People's actions, representations, and dispositions are not merely consequences of cultural processes. People doing and being from day to day and year to year *are* the processes that archaeologists should seek to explain. Indeed, human agency is so closely intertwined with traditions—those patterns of doing and knowing that range from technologies (as "know-how") to ethnicities (as "know-who")—as to be inseparable.

This "historical-processual" view of traditions is not novel. Archaeologists working with diverse case material are turning to approaches that can be listed under its banner (Pauketat 2001; see references in chapter 1). However, such historical-processualism remains a minority view. The underlying principle of materiality—that the creation of culture (including material culture and the built environment) is a process directly accessible to archaeologists—is not the doxa of archaeology today. It seems that, having learned the lessons of processual archaeology—that archaeological residues provide actual measures of processes, that culture is not normative but participatory, and that variation in artifact assemblages has explanatory potential—archaeologists stopped short of building a theory (of materiality) that explains how variation in the daily lives of people brings about long-term cultural change (in the spirit of Binford 1983; but in the sense of Dietler and Herbich 1998; Dobres and Robb 2000; Shennan 1993). A commonsense adherence to the tenets of behaviorism may be largely to blame.

Divesting archaeology of behavioral tenets is a work in progress. The variable degree of acceptance of materiality as a new basis for explaining the past by the authors of this volume is revealing of the progress. In our move away from abstract laws of human behavior, however, it is true that archaeology must still confront the problem of why developmental parallels seem to exist between peoples far removed from one another in time and space. For example, few archaeologists would argue that the "state" is a completely artificial construct (see Feinman and Marcus 1998; Yoffee 1993). Likewise, few would deny that gender divisions of some sort characterized many peoples at various times and in diverse places around the world. Given this sense of regularity, archaeology must resolve what Bruce

Smith (1990) has called the "analogy-homology dilemma." Are homologies or analogies most appropriate in explaining the past? What regularities owe their origins to common historical linkages? Which owe their existence to general processes that characterize all people in all places?

An archaeology of traditions offers just such a resolution. There *are* large-scale cultural, organizational, or technological patterns that appear to have constrained what people did in the past (see R. Hall 1997). History is not chaotic, and any one person is not free to step outside of and radically alter traditions. Nor would that be something that might ever occur to most people. Then again, there is ample evidence of people supposedly altering traditional patterns and making history, so to speak. This is because traditions themselves are not static things. They are always being made and remade. Regardless, there is uniformity to the process of tradition making even if the traditions—for example, of mobile foraging groups versus colonizing armies—seem entirely unlike one another.

The resolution of the analogy-homology dilemma, then, is twofold. As the Southeast bears witness, the regional and panregional patterns that are sometimes called traditions do constrain the many and multiscaled process of tradition making and, thus, history. They constrain not because they are real things but because they are the raw cultural material from which people make tradition anew every day. Homology is therefore a critical part of an archaeology of traditions. However, the studies of tradition in this volume are also comparative. That is, analogous argumentation remains central to archaeological theories founded on the principle of materiality just as it was for a behavioral archaeology. However, genealogies of traditions, not behaviors, are the units of comparison. The results, perhaps counterintuitive to some, are generalizations about a universal process that produced diversity! The generalizations are not different for Archaic hunter-gatherers, Woodland villagers, Mississippian chiefdoms, historic-period missions and presidios, or antebellum plantations.

The generalizations also are not simply appeals to acculturation, missionization, colonization, migration, and other commonly known historical processes. Instead, we have begun in this book to investigate the commonalities of these processes. The effect is to pay considerably more attention to the historical moments wherein traditions were created, negotiated, accommodated, or resisted. This necessitates data-heavy studies and attention to the variability of the archaeological record, as contributions in this volume bear out.

Ultimately, such historically rich and archaeologically complex studies of the many kinds and multiple scales of tradition making will produce more than mere reifications of trendy concepts. The long-term goal of an archaeology of traditions is the development of theories of world historical development. Our real challenge, then, is to match the complex questions of world historical development with suitably rich and multiscaled archaeological data sets. Theorizing without them is not theorizing at all.

Bibliography

Adams, B., J. Okeley, D. Morgan, and D. Smith
1975   Gypsies and Government Policy in England: A Study of the Traveller's Way of Life in Relation to Policies and Practices of Central and Local Government. Heinemann, London.

Allison, J. R., L. A. Terzis, and B. R. Moore
1991   The Spanish Franciscan Mission of San Pedro y San Pablo de Patale: Analysis of Ceramic Scatter, Feature #136, 1990–1991. Ms. on file, Department of Anthropology, Florida State University, Tallahassee.

Alt, S.
1998   From Plazas to Courtyards in the American Bottom. Paper presented at the Fiftieth Annual Meeting of the Southeastern Archaeological Conference, Greenville, S.C.
1999   Spindle Whorls and Fiber Production at Early Cahokian Settlements. Southeastern Archaeology 18:124–133.

Ames, K. M.
1991   Sedentism: A Temporal Shift or a Transitional Change in Hunter-Gatherer Mobility Pattern? In Between Bands and States, edited by S. A. Gregg, 108–134. Occasional Paper No. 9. Center for Archeological Investigations, Southern Illinois University at Carbondale.

Anderson, D. G.
1990   Stability and Change in Chiefdom-Level Societies: An Examination of Mississippian Political Evolution on the South Atlantic Slope. In Lamar Archaeology: Mississippian Chiefdoms in the Deep South, edited by J. M. Williams and G. D. Shapiro, 187–213. University of Alabama Press, Tuscaloosa.
1994a   Factional Competition and the Political Evolution of Mississippian Chiefdoms in the Southeastern United States. In Factional Competition and Political Development in the New World, edited by E. M. Brumfiel and J. W. Fox, 61–76. Cambridge University Press, Cambridge.
1994b   The Savannah River Chiefdoms: Political Change in the Late Prehistoric Southeast. University of Alabama Press, Tuscaloosa.
1996a   Chiefly Cycling and Large-Scale Abandonments as Viewed from the Savannah River Basin. In Political Structure and Change in the Prehistoric Southeastern United States, edited by J. F. Scarry, 150–191. University Press of Florida, Gainesville.

1996b   Fluctuations between Simple and Complex Chiefdoms: Cycling in the Late Prehistoric Southeast. In *Political Structure and Change in the Prehistoric Southeastern United States*, edited by J. F. Scarry, 231–252. University Press of Florida, Gainesville.

Anderson, D. G., and J. W. Joseph
1988   Prehistory and History Along the Upper Savannah River: Technical Synthesis of Cultural Resource Investigations, Richard B. Russell Multiple Resource Area. Russell Papers, Interagency Archeological Services Division, National Park Service, Atlanta.

Anderson, D. G., D. W. Stahle, and M. K. Cleaveland
1995   Paleoclimate and the Potential Food Reserves of Mississippian Societies: A Case Study from the Savannah River Valley. *American Antiquity* 60:258–286.

Archer, M. S.
1996   *Culture and Agency: The Place of Culture in Social Theory*. Revised edition. Cambridge University Press, Cambridge.

Ashley, K. A.
1995   Grappling with Cord-Marked Pottery Sites in Northeastern Florida. Paper Presented at the Fifty-second Southeastern Archaeological Conference, Knoxville.

Ashley, K. A., and V. Rolland
1997   Grog-Tempered Pottery in the Mocama Province. *Florida Anthropologist* 50:51–66.

Ashmore, W., and R. Wilk
1988   Household and Community in the Mesoamerican Past. In *Household and Community in the Mesoamerican Past*, edited by W. Ashmore and R. Wilk, 1–27. University of New Mexico Press, Albuquerque.

Askins, W.
1985   Material Culture and Expressions of Group Identity in Sandy Ground, New York. *American Archaeology* 5:209–218.

Avery, G.
1997   Annual Report for the Los Adaes Station Archaeology Program. Department of Social Sciences, Northwestern State University, Natchitoches, La.

Baden, W. A.
1983   Tomotley: An Eighteenth-Century Cherokee Village. Report of Investigations 36. Department of Anthropology, University of Tennessee, Knoxville.

Bahuchet, S., and H. Guillaume
1982   Aka-Farmer Relations in the Northwest Congo Basin. In *Politics and History in Band Societies*, edited by E. Leacock and R. Lee, 189–211. Cambridge University Press, Cambridge.

Bailey, F. G.
1969   *Stratagems and Spoils: A Social Anthropology of Politics*. Basil Blackwell, Oxford.

Bamforth, D. B., and A. C. Spaulding
1982   Human Behavior, Explanation, Archaeology, History, and Science. *Journal of Anthropological Archaeology* 1:179–195.
Bareis, C. J.
1972   Report of 1971 University of Illinois Excavations in Cahokia Mounds State Park. Research Report 7. University of Illinois, Urbana.
Bareis, C. J., and J. W. Porter, editors
1984   *American Bottom Archaeology: A Summary of the FAI-270 Project Contribution to the Culture History of the Mississippi River Valley.* University of Illinois Press, Urbana.
Barker, A. W.
1992   Powhatan's Pursestrings: On the Meaning of Surplus in a Seventeenth-Century Algonkian Chiefdom. In *Lords of the Southeast: Social Inequality and the Native Elites of Southeastern North America*, edited by A. W. Barker and T. R. Pauketat, 61–80. Archaeological Papers of the American Anthropological Association 3, Washington, D.C.
Barker, A. W., and T. R. Pauketat
1992a   Social Inequality and the Native Elites of Southeastern North America. Introduction to *Lords of the Southeast: Social Inequality and the Native Elites of Southeastern North America*, edited by A. W. Barker and T. R. Pauketat, 1–10. Archeological Papers of the American Anthropological Association 3, Washington, D.C.
Barker, A. W., and T. R. Pauketat, editors
1992b   *Lords of the Southeast: Social Inequality and the Native Elites of Southeastern North America.* Archeological Papers of the American Anthropological Association 3, Washington, D.C.
Barrett, J. C.
1990   The Monumentality of Death: The Character of Early Bronze Age Mounds in Southern Britain. *World Archaeology* 22:179–189.
Barth, F.
1969a   Introduction. In *Ethnic Groups and Boundaries: The Social Organization of Culture Difference*, edited by F. Barth, 1–38. Little, Brown, Boston.
1987   *Cosmologies in the Making.* Cambridge University Press, Cambridge.
Barth, F., editor
1969b   *Ethnic Groups and Boundaries: The Social Organization of Culture Difference.* Little, Brown, Boston.
Barton, C. M., and G. A. Clark, editors
1997   *Rediscovering Darwin: Evolutionary Theory and Archaeological Explanation.* Archaeological Papers of the American Anthropological Association 7, Arlington, Va.
Bartram, W.
1958   *The Travels of William Bartram*, edited by F. Harper. Yale University Press, New Haven.

Bataille, G. M., and K. M. Sands
1984 *American Indian Women: Telling Their Lives.* University of Nebraska Press, Lincoln.

Beaudry, M. C., L. J. Cooke, and S. A. Mrozowski
1991 Artifacts and Active Voices: Material Culture as Social Discourse. In *The Archaeology of Inequality*, edited by R. H. McGuire and R. Paynter, 150–191. Basil Blackwell, Cambridge.

Beck, L. A.
1995 Regional Cults and Ethnic Boundaries in "Southern Hopewell." In *Regional Approaches to Mortuary Analysis*, edited by L. A. Beck, 167–187. Plenum Press, New York.

Bell, A. R.
1990 Separate People: Speaking of Creek Men and Women. *American Anthropologist* 92:332–345.

Bell, C.
1997 *Ritual: Perspectives and Dimensions.* Oxford University Press, Oxford.

Belmont, J. S.
1982 Toltec and Coles Creek: A View from the Lower Mississippi Valley. In *Emerging Patterns of Plum Bayou Culture*, edited by M. A. Rolingson, 64–70. Arkansas Archeological Survey Research Series 18. Fayetteville.

Bender, B.
1985 Emergent Tribal Formations in the American Midcontinent. *American Antiquity* 50:52–62.

Bender, B., and B. Morris
1988 Twenty Years of History, Evolution, and Social Change in Gatherer-Hunter Studies. In *Hunters and Gatherers*, vol. 1, *History, Evolution, and Social Change*, edited by T. Ingold, D. Riches, and J. Woodburn, 4–14. Berg, London.

Bentley, G. Carter
1987 Ethnicity and Practice. *Comparative Studies in Society and History* 29: 24–55.

Berlin, I.
1961 History and Theory: The Concept of Scientific History. *History and Theory* 1:1–31.
1998 *Many Thousands Gone: The First Two Centuries of Slavery in North America.* Harvard University Press, Cambridge.

Berlin, I., and P. D. Morgan, editors
1993 *Cultivation and Culture: Labor and the Shaping of Slave Life in the Americas.* University of Virginia Press, Charlottesville.

Bernbeck, R., organizer
1999 The Limits of Agency: Lebenswelt and Doxa. Annual Meeting of the American Anthropological Association, Chicago.

Bettinger, R. L.

1991   *Hunter-Gatherers: Archaeological and Evolutionary Theory*. Plenum Press, New York.

Bierce-Gedris, K.

1981   Apalachee Hill: The Archaeological Investigation of an Indian Site of the Spanish Mission Period in Northwest Florida. M.A. thesis, Florida State University, Tallahassee.

Binford, L. R.

1962   Archaeology as Anthropology. *American Antiquity* 28:217–225.

1965   Archaeological Systematics and the Study of Cultural Process. *American Antiquity* 31:203–210.

1968a   Post-Pleistocene Adaptations. In *New Perspectives in Archeology*, edited by S. Binford and L. Binford, 313–341. Aldine, Chicago.

1968b   Some Comments on Historical Versus Processual Archaeology. *Southwestern Journal of Anthropology* 24:267–275.

1972   *An Archaeological Perspective*. Seminar Press, New York.

1980   Willow Smokes and Dogs Tails: Hunter-Gatherer Settlement Systems and Archaeological Site Formation. *American Antiquity* 45:4–20.

1983   *Working at Archaeology*. Academic Press, New York.

Bintliff, J.

1991a   The Contribution of an Annaliste/Structural History Approach to Archaeology. In *The Annales School and Archaeology*, edited by J. Bintliff, 1–33. New York University Press, New York.

Bintliff, J., editor

1991b   *The Annales School and Archaeology*. New York University Press, New York.

Bird-David, N.

1988   Hunter-Gatherers and Other People: A Re-examination. In *Hunters and Gatherers*, vol. 1, *History, Evolution, and Social Change*, edited by T. Ingold, D. Riches, and J. Woodburn, 17–30. Berg, London.

Blackburn, R. H.

1982   In the Land of Milk and Honey: Okiek Adaptations to Their Forests and Neighbours. In *Politics and History in Band Societies*, edited by E. Leacock and R. Lee, 283–305. Cambridge University Press, Cambridge.

Blakey, M. L.

1990   American Nationality and Ethnicity in the Depicted Past. In *The Politics of the Past*, edited by P. Gathercole and D. Lowenthal, 38–48. Unwin Hyman, London.

Blanton, D. B., and K. E. Sassaman

1989   Pattern and Process in the Middle Archaic Period of the South Carolina Piedmont. In *Studies in South Carolina Archaeology: Essays in Honor of Robert L. Stephenson*, edited by A. C. Goodyear and Glen T. Hanson, 53–

72. Anthropological Studies 9. South Carolina Institute of Archaeology and Anthropology, University of South Carolina, Columbia.

Blassingame, J. W.

1979   *The Slave Community: Plantation Life in the Antebellum South.* Oxford University Press, New York.

Blau, P. M.

1977   *Inequality and Heterogeneity: A Primitive Theory of Social Structure.* Free Press, New York.

Blitz, J. H.

1993a   *Ancient Chiefdoms of the Tombigbee.* University of Alabama Press, Tuscaloosa.

1993b   Big Pots for Big Shots: Feasting and Storage in a Mississippian Community. *American Antiquity* 58:80–96.

1999   Mississippian Chiefdoms and the Fission-Fusion Process. *American Antiquity* 64:577–592.

Bloch, M.

1953   *The Historian's Craft.* Translated by P. Putnam. Vintage Books, New York.

Blok, A.

1992   Reflections on "Making History." In *Other Histories*, edited by K. Hastrup, 121–127. Routledge, New York.

Bolton, H. E.

1914   *Anthanse DeMézières and the Louisiana/Texas Frontier, 1768–1780.* Arthur C. Clark, Cleveland.

Booker, K. M., C. M. Hudson, and R. L. Rankin

1992   Place Name Identification and Multilingualism in the Sixteenth-Century Southeast. *Ethnohistory* 39:399–451.

Borah, W. W.

1964   The Historical Demography of Aboriginal and Colonial America: An Attempt at Perspective. In *The Native Population of the Americas in 1492*, edited by W. H. Denevan, 13–34. University of Wisconsin Press, Madison.

Borofsky, R.

1987   *Making History: Pukapukan and Anthropological Constructions of Knowledge.* Cambridge University Press, Cambridge.

Bourdieu, P.

1977   *Outline of a Theory of Practice.* Cambridge University Press, Cambridge.

1980   *The Logic of Practice.* Stanford University Press, Stanford.

1984   *Distinction: A Social Critique of the Judgement of Taste.* Translated by W. Nice. Harvard University Press, Cambridge.

1990   *The Logic of Practice.* 2d ed. Polity Press, Cambridge.

1998   *Acts of Resistance: Against the Tyranny of the Market.* New York University Press, New York.

Boyer, R.

1997   Negotiating Calidad: The Everyday Struggle for Status in Mexico. *Historical Archaeology* 31:64–73.

Brain, J. P., A. Toth, and A. Rodriguez-Buckingham

1974   Ethnohistoric Archaeology and the De Soto Entrada into the Lower Mississippi Valley. *The Conference on Historic Site Archaeology Papers*, vol. 7, 232–289.

Brass, P. R.

1985   Ethnic Groups and the State. In *Ethnic Groups and the State*, edited by P. Brass, 1–56. Barnes and Noble Books, Totowa, N.J.

Braudel, F.

1972   *The Mediterranean and the Mediterranean World in the Age of Phillip II*, vol. 1. Harper and Row, New York.

1980   *On History*. Translated by S. Matthews. University of Chicago Press, Chicago.

1981   *Civilization and Capitalism, Fifteenth–Eighteenth Century*, vol. 1, *The Structures of Everyday Life: The Limits of the Possible*, translated by S. Reynolds. Harper and Row, New York.

Braun, D. P.

1995   Style, Selection, and Historicity. In *Style, Society, and Person: Archaeological and Ethnological Perspectives*, edited by C. Carr and J. E. Neitzel, 124–141. Plenum Press, New York.

Braund, K. E. H.

1993   *Deerskins and Duffels: The Creek Indian Trade with Anglo-America, 1685–1815*. University of Nebraska Press, Lincoln.

Breisach, E.

1983   *Historiography: Ancient, Medieval, and Modern*. 2d edition. University of Chicago Press, Chicago.

Bridges, K., and W. DeVille

1967   Natchitoches and the Trail to the Rio Grande. *Louisiana History* 8:239–259.

Brose, D. S., and N. Greber, editors

1979   *Hopewell Archaeology: The Chillicothe Conference*. Kent State University Press, Kent, Ohio.

Brown, J. A.

1985   Long-term Trends to Sedentism and the Emergence of Complexity in the American Midwest. In *Prehistoric Hunter-Gatherers: The Emergence of Cultural Complexity*, edited by T. D. Price and J. A. Brown, 165–195. Academic Press, New York.

1990   Archaeology Confronts History at the Natchez Temple. *Southeastern Archaeology* 9:1–10.

Brown, J. A., editor

1971   *Approaches to the Social Dimensions of Mortuary Practices*. Society for American Archaeology Memoir 25, Washington, D.C.

Brown, J. A., and R. K. Vierra
1983   What Happened in the Middle Archaic? Introduction to the Ecological Approach to Koster Site Archaeology. In *Archaic Hunters and Gatherers in the American Midwest*, edited by J. L. Phillips and J. A. Brown, 165–195. Academic Press, New York.

Brown, J. A., R. A. Kerbert, and H. D. Winters
1990   Trade and the Evolution of Exchange Relations at the Beginning of the Mississippian Period. In *The Mississippian Emergence*, edited by B. D. Smith, 251–280. Smithsonian Institution Press, Washington, D.C.

Brown, J. E.
1977   *The Spiritual Legacy of the American Indian*. Crossroad Publishing, New York City.

Brown, M. F.
1996   On Resisting Resistance. *American Anthropologist* 98:729–735.

Brumfiel, E. M.
1989   Factional Competition in Complex Society. In *Domination and Resistance*, edited by D. Miller, M. Rowlands, and C. Tilley, 127–139. Unwin Hyman, London.

1992   Breaking and Entering the Ecosystem: Gender, Class, and Faction Steal the Show. *American Anthropologist* 94:551–567.

1994   Factional Competition and Political Development in the New World: An Introduction. In *Factional Competition and Political Development in the New World*, edited by E. M. Brumfiel and J. W. Fox, 3–13. Cambridge University Press, Cambridge.

1995   Heterarchy and the Analysis of Complex Societies. In *Heterarchy and the Analysis of Complex Societies*, edited by R. M. Ehrenreich, C. L. Crumley, and J. E. Levy, 125–131. Archaeological Papers of the American Anthropological Association 6, Washington, D.C.

Bryne, Stephen C.
1989   Archaeological Investigations at the Spanish Hoe Site (8LE667), Leon County, Florida. Ms. on file, Florida Bureau of Archaeological Research, Tallahassee.

Buikstra, J. E., D. K. Charles, and G. F. M. Rakita
1998   *Staging Ritual: Hopewell Ceremonialism at the Mound House Site, Greene County, Illinois*. Kampsville Studies in Archaeology and History 1. Center for American Archaeology, Kampsville, Ill.

Bujra, J. M.
1973   The Dynamics of Political Action: A New Look at Factionalism. *American Anthropologist* 75:132–152.

Burke, P.
1990a   Historians, Anthropologists, and Symbols. In *Culture Through Time: Anthropological Approaches*, edited by E. Ohnuki-Tierney, 268–283. Stanford University Press, Stanford.

1990b   *The French Historical Revolution: The Annales School, 1929–89.* Stanford University Press, Stanford.

1992   *History and Social Theory.* Cornell University Press, Ithaca.

1997   *Varieties of Cultural History.* Cornell University Press, Ithaca.

Bushnell, A. T.

1978   That Demonic Game: The Campaign to Stop Indian Pelota Playing in Spanish Florida, 1675–1684. *The Americas* 35:1–19.

1979   Patricio de Hinachuba: Defender of the Word of God, the Crown of the King, and the Little Children of Ivitachuco. *American Indian Culture and Research Journal* 3(3):1–21.

1994   *Situado and Sabana: Spain's Support System for the Presidio and Mission Provinces of Florida.* Anthropological Papers of the American Museum of Natural History 74. University of Georgia Press, Athens.

Cable, J. S.

1983   Organizational Variability in Piedmont Hunter-Gatherer Lithic Assemblages. In *The Haw River Sites: Archaeological Investigations at Two Stratified Sites in the North Carolina Piedmont,* assembled by S. R. Claggett and J. S. Cable, 637–688. Commonwealth Associates, Jackson, Miss.

Caldwell, J. R.

1958   *Trend and Tradition in the Prehistory of the Eastern United States.* American Anthropological Association Memoir 88, Washington, D.C.

Callaway, H.

1993   Purity and Exotica in Legitimating the Empire: Cultural Construction of Gender, Sexuality, and Race. In *Legitimacy and State in Twentieth-Century Africa: Essays in Honour of A. H. M. Kirk-Greene,* edited by T. Ranger and O. Vaughan, 31–61. St. Anthonys College, Oxford.

Cannon, A.

1989   The Historical Dimension in Mortuary Expressions of Status and Sentiment. *Current Anthropology* 30:437–458.

Carneiro, R. L.

1973   The Four Faces of Evolution: Unilinear, Universal, Multilinear, and Differential. In *Handbook of Social and Cultural Anthropology,* edited by J. L. Honigmann, 89–110. Rand McNally, Chicago.

1978   Political Expansion as an Expression of the Principle of Competitive Exclusion. In *Origins of the State: The Anthropology of Political Evolution,* edited by R. Cohen and E. R. Service, 205–223. Institute for the Study of Human Issues, Philadelphia.

Carr, C., and J. E. Neitzel

1995   Integrating Approaches to Material Style in Theory and Philosophy. In *Style, Society, and Person: Archaeological and Ethnological Perspectives,* edited by C. Carr and J. E. Neitzel, 3–20. Academic Press, San Diego.

Carr, E. H.

1961   *What Is History?* Random House, New York.

Cassedy, D. F.
1983   Middle Archaic Stemmed Points in Eastern North America. Ms. on file, Department of Anthropology, Binghamton University, Binghamton, N.Y.

Castelló Y., T.
1990   La Indumentaria de las Castas del Mestizaje. La Pintura de Castas. *Artes de Mexico* 8:74–78, 87–88.

Champion, T. C.
1989   *Introduction to Centre and Periphery: Comparative Studies in Archaeology*, edited by T. C. Champion, 1–21. Routledge, London.

Chang, C.
1982   Nomads Without Cattle: East African Foragers in Historical Perspective. In *Politics and History in Band Societies*, edited by E. Leacock and R. Lee, 269–282. Cambridge University Press, Cambridge.

Chapman, C. H., and L. O. Anderson
1955   The Campbell Site: A Late Mississippi Town Site and Cemetery in Southeast Missouri. *Missouri Archaeologist* 17.

Chapman, J.
1985   Tellico Archaeology: Twelve Thousand Years of Native American History. Report of Investigations 43. Department of Anthropology, University of Tennessee, Knoxville.

Chapman, R.
1995   Ten Years After: Megaliths, Mortuary Practices, and the Territorial Model. In *Regional Approaches to Mortuary Analysis*, edited by L. A. Beck, 29–51. Plenum Press, New York.

Charles, D. K.
1992   World Demography and Social Dynamics in the American Midwest: Analysis of a Burial Mound Survey. *World Archaeology* 24:175–197.

1995   Diachronic Regional Social Dynamics: Mortuary Sites in the Illinois Valley/American Bottom Region. In *Regional Approaches to Mortuary Analysis*, edited by L. A. Beck, 77–99. Plenum Press, New York.

Charles, D. K., and J. Buikstra
1983   Archaic Mortuary Sites in the Central Mississippi Drainage: Distribution, Structure, and Behavioral Implications. In *Archaic Hunter-Gatherers in the American Midwest*, edited by J. L. Phillips and J. A. Brown, 117–146. Academic Press, New York.

Chesnokov, D. I.
1969   *Historical Materialism*, translated from the Russian by C. Dutt. Progress Publishers, Moscow.

Childe, V. G.
1951   *Man Makes Himself*. New American Library of World Literature, New York.

Claassen, C.
1996   A Consideration of the Social Organization of the Shell Mound Archaic. In *Archaeology of the Mid-Holocene Southeast*, edited by K. E. Sassaman and D. G. Anderson, 235–258. University Press of Florida, Gainesville.
1997   Changing Venue: Women's Lives in Prehistoric North America. In *Women in Prehistory: North America and Mesoamerica*, edited by C. Claassen and R. A. Joyce, 65–87. University of Pennsylvania Press, Philadelphia.

Claflin, W. H., Jr.
1931   *The Stallings Island Mound, Columbia County, Georgia*. Peabody Museum of American Archaeology and Ethnology Papers 14(1). Harvard University, Cambridge.

Clark, J. E.
1998   The Arts and Governmentality in Early Mesoamerica. *Annual Review of Anthropology* 26:211–234.
2000   Towards a Better Explanation of Hereditary Inequality: A Critical Assessment of Natural and Historic Human Agents. In *Agency in Archaeology*, edited by M.-A. Dobres and J. Robb, 92–112. Routledge, London.

Cobb, C. R.
1991   Social Reproduction and the Longue Durée in the Prehistory of the Midcontinental United States. In *Processual and Postprocessual Archaeologies: Multiple Ways of Knowing the Past*, edited by R. W. Preucel, 168–182. Occasional Paper 10. Center for Archaeological Investigations, Southern Illinois University at Carbondale.

Cobb, C. R., and M. S. Nassaney
1995   Integration and Interaction in the Late Woodland Southeast. In *Native American Interactions*, edited by M. Nassaney and K. Sassaman, 205–226. University of Tennessee Press, Knoxville.
2001   Cultivating Complexity in the Woodland Southeast. In *The Woodland Southeast*, edited by D. Anderson and R. Mainfort. University of Alabama Press, Tuscaloosa.

Coe, J. L.
1961   Cherokee Archaeology. In *The Symposium on Cherokee and Iroquois Culture*, edited by W. N. Fenton and J. Gulick, 151–160. Smithsonian Institution, Bureau of American Ethnology Bulletin 180, Washington, D.C.
1964   *The Formative Culture of the Carolina Piedmont*. Transactions of the American Philosophical Society 5(5), Philadelphia.

Cohen, A.
1974   *Two-Dimensional Man: An Essay on the Anthropology of Power and Symbolism in Complex Society*. University of California Press, Berkeley.

Cohn, B. S.
1968   Ethnohistory. In *International Encyclopedia of the Social Sciences*, edited by D. L. Sills, 440–448. Macmillan, New York.

Collier, J. F.
1988   *Marriage and Inequality in Classless Societies*. Stanford University Press, Palo Alto.

Collins, J. M.
1990   *The Archaeology of the Cahokia Mounds ICT-II: Site Structure*. Illinois Cultural Resources Study 10. Illinois Historic Preservation Agency, Springfield.

Collins, J. M., and M. L. Chalfant
1993   A Second-Terrace Perspective on Monks Mound. *American Antiquity* 58:319–332.

Comaroff, J.
1982   Dialectical Systems, History, and Anthropology: Units of Study and Questions of Theory. *Journal of Southern African Studies* 8:143–172.
1987   Of Totemism and Ethnicity: Consciousness, Practice, and the Signs of Inequality. *Ethnos* 52:301–323.
1996   The Empire's Old Clothes: Fashioning the Colonial Subject. In *Cross-cultural Consumption: Global Markets, Local Realities*, edited by D. Howes, 19–38. Routledge, New York.

Comaroff, J., and J. Comaroff
1991   *Of Revelation and Revolution: Christianity, Colonialism, and Consciousness in South Africa*, vol. 1. University of Chicago Press, Chicago.
1992   *Ethnography and the Historical Imagination*. Westview, Boulder.

Conkey, M. W.
1990   Experimenting with Style in Archaeology: Some Historical and Theoretical Issues. In *The Uses of Style in Archaeology*, edited by M. Conkey and C. Hastorf, 5–17. Cambridge University Press, Cambridge.
1999   An End Note: Reframing Materiality for Archaeology. In *Material Meanings: Critical Approaches to the Interpretation of Material Culture*, edited by E. S. Chilton, 133–141. University of Utah Press, Salt Lake City.

Conkey, M. W., and J. M. Gero
1991   Tensions, Pluralities, and Engendering Archaeology: An Introduction to Women and Prehistory. In *Engendering Archaeology: Women and Prehistory*, edited by J. M. Gero and M. W. Conkey, 3–30. Blackwell, Oxford.

Conkey, M. W., and J. D. Spector
1984   The Archaeological Study of Gender. *Advances in Archaeological Method and Theory* 7:1–38.

Connell, R. W.
1987   *Gender and Power: Society, the Person, and Sexual Politics*. Stanford University Press, Palo Alto.

Cope, R. D.
1994   *The Limits of Racial Domination: Plebian Society in Colonial Mexico City, 1660–1720*. University of Wisconsin Press, Madison.

Cordell, A. S.
1993   Chronological Variability in Ceramic Paste: A Comparison of Deptford
        and Savannah Period Pottery in the St. Marys River Region of North-
        east Florida and Southeast Georgia. *Southeastern Archaeology* 12:33–
        58.
Corkran, D. H.
1967   *The Creek Frontier, 1540–1783*. The Civilization of the American Indian
        Series. University of Oklahoma Press, Norman.
Cornforth, M.
1973   *Materialism and the Dialectical Method*. 4th edition. International Pub-
        lishers, New York.
Costin, C. L.
1998   Craft and Social Identity. Introduction to *Craft and Social Identity*, edited
        by C. L. Costin and R. P. Wright, 3–16. Anthropological Papers of the
        American Anthropological Association 8, Washington, D.C.
Cotterill, R. S.
1954   *The Southern Indians: The Story of the Five Civilized Tribes Before Re-
        moval*. University of Oklahoma Press, Norman.
Cowan, C. W.
1985   Understanding the Evolution of Plant Husbandry in Eastern North
        America: Lessons from Botany, Ethnography, and Archaeology. In *Prehis-
        toric Food Production in North America*, edited by R. I. Ford, 205–243.
        Anthropological Paper 75. Museum of Anthropology, University of
        Michigan, Ann Arbor.
Crane, V. W.
1928   *The Southern Frontier, 1670–1732*. Seeman Press, Philadelphia.
Creamer, W., and J. Haas
1985   Tribe versus Chiefdom in Lower Central America. *American Antiquity*
        50:738–754.
Cross, J. R.
1999   By Any Other Name . . . A Reconsideration of Middle Archaic Lithic
        Technology and Typology in the Northeast. In *The Archaeological
        Northeast*, edited by M. A. Levine, K. E. Sassaman, and M. S. Nassaney,
        57–73. Bergin and Garvey, Westport, Conn.
Crowell, A.
1997   *Archaeology and the Capitalist World System: A Study from Russian
        America*. Plenum Press, New York.
Crown, P. A., and S. K. Fish
1996   Gender and Status in the Hohokam Pre-Classic to Classic Transition.
        American Anthropologist 98:803–817.
Crumley, C. L.
1979   Three Locational Models: An Epistemological Assessment for Anthropol-
        ogy and Archaeology. *Advances in Archaeological Method and Theory*
        2:141–173.
1987   A Dialectical Critique of Hierarchy. In *Power Relations and State Forma-*

tion, edited by T. C. Patterson and C. W. Gailey, 155–169. American Anthropological Association, Washington, D.C.

1995 Heterarchy and the Analysis of Complex Societies. In *Heterarchy and the Analysis of Complex Societies*, edited by R. M. Ehrenreich, C. L. Crumley, and J. E. Levy, 1–5. Archaeological Papers of the American Anthropological Association 6, Washington, D.C.

Crumley, C. L., and W. H. Marquardt

1987 Regional Dynamics in Burgundy. In *Regional Dynamics: Burgundian Landscapes in Historical Perspective*, edited by C. L. Crumley and W. H. Marquardt, 609–623. Academic Press, New York.

Cunningham, C.

1973 Order in the Atoni House. In *Right and Left: Essays on Dual Symbolic Classification*, edited by R. Needham, 204–238. University of Chicago Press, Chicago.

Dalan, R.

1997 The Construction of Cahokia. In *Cahokia: Domination and Ideology in the Mississippian World*, edited by T. Pauketat and T. Emerson, 89–102. University of Nebraska Press, Lincoln.

Dancey, W. S.

1999 The Power of Tradition in Archaeological Discourse. In *Review Feature: Cahokia and the Archaeology of Power*, by T. Emerson, W. Dancey, T. Pauketat, A. Whittle, E. DeMarrais, W. DeBoer, and A. Kehoe. *Cambridge Archaeological Journal* 9:254–256.

David, N., J. Sterner, and K. Gavua

1988 Why Pots Are Decorated. *Current Anthropology* 29:365–379.

Davis, D. B.

1975 *The Problem of Slavery in the Age of Revolution*. Cornell University Press, Ithaca.

1999 *The Problem of Slavery in the Age of Revolution*. 2d edition. Oxford University Press, Oxord.

Davis, D. D.

1984 Protohistoric Cultural Interaction along the Northern Gulf Coast. In *Perspectives on Gulf Coast Prehistory*, edited by D. D. Davis, 216–231. University Press of Florida, Gainesville.

Deagan, K. A.

1983 *Spanish St. Augustine: The Archaeology of a Colonial Creole Community*. Academic Press, New York.

1990 Accommodation and Resistance: The Process and Impact of Spanish Colonization in the Southeast. In *Columbian Consequences*, vol. 2, *Archaeological and Historical Perspectives on the Spanish Borderlands East*, edited by D. H. Thomas, 297–314. Smithsonian Institution Press, Washington, D.C.

1996 Cultural Transformation: Euro-American Cultural Genesis in the Early

Spanish-American Colonies. *Journal of Anthropological Research* 52:135–160.

Deagan, K. A., editor

1995   *Puerto Real: The Archaeology of a Sixteenth-Century Spanish Town in Hispaniola.* University Press of Florida, Gainesville.

Deal, M.

1983   Pottery Ethnoarchaeology among the Tzeltal Maya. Ph.D. dissertation, Simon Fraser University, Burnaby, British Columbia.

Debo, A.

1941   *The Road to Disappearance.* University of Oklahoma Press, Norman.

de Certeau, M.

1984   *The Practice of Everyday Life.* University of California Press, Berkeley.

Deetz, J.

1977   *In Small Things Forgotten: The Archaeology of Early American Life.* Anchor Press, Garden City, N.Y.

1982   Households. *American Behavioral Scientist* 25:717–724.

1983   Scientific Humanism and Humanistic Science: A Plea for Paradigmatic Pluralism in Historical Archaeology. In *Geoscience and Man*, vol. 23, *Historical Archaeology in the Eastern United States: Papers from the R. J. Russell Symposium*, edited by R. W. Neuman, 27–34. Louisiana State University School of Geoscience, Baton Rouge.

1988   History and Archaeological Theory: Walter Taylor Revisited. *American Antiquity* 53:13–22.

1993   *Flowerdew Hundred: The Archaeology of a Virginia Plantation, 1619–1864.* University Press of Virginia, Charlottesville.

de la Cadena, M.

1995   Race, Ethnicity, and the Struggle for Self-representation: Deindianization in Cuzco, Peru. Ph.D. dissertation, University of Wisconsin, Madison.

Denbow, J. R.

1984   Prehistoric Herders and Foragers of the Kalahari: The Evidence for 1500 Years of Interaction. In *Past and Present in Hunter-Gatherer Studies*, edited by C. Schrire, 175–193. Academic Press, Orlando.

Dent, R. J., Jr.

1995   *Chesapeake Prehistory: Old Traditions, New Directions.* Plenum, New York.

DePagés, P. M. F.

1791   *Travels Round the World in the Years 1767, 1768, 1769, 1770, and 1771*, vol. 1. Translated from the French. J. Murray, London.

Dickens, R. S., Jr.

1976   *Cherokee Prehistory: The Pisgah Phase in the Appalachian Summit Region.* University of Tennessee Press, Knoxville.

1978   Mississippian Settlement Patterns in the Appalachian Summit Area: The

Pisgah and Qualla Phases. In *Mississippian Settlement Patterns*, edited by B. D. Smith, 115–139. Academic Press, New York.

1979 The Origins and Development of Cherokee Culture. In *The Cherokee Indian Nation: A Troubled History*, edited by D. H. King, 3–32. University of Tennessee Press, Knoxville.

Dickenson, M. F., and L. B. Wayne

1985 Archaeological Testing of the San Juan del Puerto Mission Site (8Du53), Fort George Island, Florida. Report prepared for Fairfield Communities, Inc. Water and Air Research, Gainesville, Fla.

Dietler, M., and I. Herbich

1989 Tich Matek: The Technology of Luo Pottery Production and the Definition of Ceramic Style. *World Archaeology* 21:148–164.

1998 Habitus, Techniques, Style: An Integrated Approach to the Social Understanding of Material Culture Boundaries. In *The Archaeology of Social Boundaries*, edited by M. T. Stark, 232–263. Smithsonian Institution Press, Washington, D.C.

Dillehay, T. D.

1990 Mapuche Ceremonial Landscape, Social Recruitment, and Resource Rights. *World Archaeology* 22:223–241.

Dincauze, D. F.

1976 *The Neville Site: 8000 Years at Amoskeag Falls*. Peabody Museum Monographs 4. Harvard University, Cambridge.

Dirks, N. B.

1992 Colonialism and Culture. Introduction to *Colonialism and Culture*, edited by N. B. Dirks, 1–25. University of Michigan Press, Ann Arbor.

Dobres, M.-A.

1999 Technology's Links and *Chaînes*: The Processual Unfolding of Technique and Technician. In *The Social Dynamics of Technology: Practice, Politics, and World Views*, edited by M.-A. Dobres and C. Hoffman, 124–146. Smithsonian Institution Press, Washington, D.C.

2000 *Technology and Social Agency*. Blackwell, Oxford.

Dobres, M.-A., and C. R. Hoffman

1994 Social Agency and the Dynamics of Prehistoric Technology. *Journal of Archaeological Method and Theory* 1:211–258.

1999 A Context for the Present and Future of Technology Studies. Introduction to *The Social Dynamics of Technology: Practice, Politics, and World Views*, edited by M.-A. Dobres and C. R. Hoffman, 1–19. Smithsonian Institution Press, Washington, D.C.

Dobres, M.-A., and J. Robb, editors

2000 *Agency in Archaeology*. Routledge, London.

Dobyns, H. F.

1983 *Their Number Become Thinned: Native American Population Dynamics in Eastern North America*. University of Tennessee Press, Knoxville.

Doyle, B. W.
1937   *The Etiquette of Race Relations in the South: A Study in Social Control.* University of Chicago Press, Chicago.
Drake, E. C.
2000   Exploring Variations in the Use of Grog Temper at the Ink Bayou Site: A Plum Bayou Culture Site in Central Arkansas. M.A. thesis, Western Michigan University, Kalamazoo.
Dunnell, R. C.
1980   Evolutionary Theory and Archaeology. In *Advances in Archaeological Method and Theory*, vol. 3, edited by M. B. Schiffer, 35–99. Academic Press, New York.
1989   Aspects of the Application of Evolutionary Theory in Archaeology. In *Archaeological Thought in America*, edited by C. C. Lamberg-Karlovsky, 35–49. Cambridge University Press, Cambridge.
1990   The Role of the Southeast in American Archaeology. *Southeastern Archaeology* 9:11–22.
1991   Methodological Impacts of Catastrophic Depopulation on American Archaeology and Ethnology. In *Columbian Consequences*, vol. 3, *The Spanish Borderlands in Pan-American Perspective*, edited by D. H. Thomas, 561–580. Smithsonian Institution Press, Washington, D.C.
Dye, D. H.
1990   Warfare in the Sixteenth-Century Southeast: The de Soto Expedition in the Interior. In *Columbian Consequences*, vol. 2, *Archaeological and Historical Perspectives on the Spanish Borderlands East*, edited by D. H. Thomas, 211–222. Smithsonian Institution Press, Washington, D.C.
1994   The Art of War in the Sixteenth-Century Central Mississippi Valley. In *Perspectives on the Southeast: Linguistics, Archaeology, and Ethnohistory*, edited by P. B. Kwachka, 44–60. Southern Anthropological Society Proceedings 27. University of Georgia Press, Athens.
1995   Feasting with the Enemy: Mississippian Warfare and Prestige Goods Circulation. In *Native American Interactions: Multiscalar Analyses and Interpretations in the Eastern Woodlands*, edited by M. S. Nassaney and K. E. Sassaman, 289–316. University of Tennessee Press, Knoxville.
1996   Riverine Adaptation in the Midsouth. In *Of Caves and Shell Mounds*, edited by K. C. Carstens and P. J. Watson, 140–158. University of Alabama Press, Tuscaloosa.
1998   An Overview of Walls Engraved Pottery in the Central Mississippi Valley. In *Changing Perspectives on the Archaeology of the Central Mississippi Valley*, edited by M. J. O'Brien and R. C. Dunnell, 80–98. University of Alabama Press, Tuscaloosa.
Earle, T. K.
1990   Style and Iconography as Legitimation in Complex Chiefdoms. In *The*

Uses of Style in Archaeology, edited by M. Conkey and C. Hastorf, 73–81. Cambridge University Press, Cambridge.

1991   Property Rights and the Evolution of Chiefdoms. In *Chiefdoms: Power, Economy, and Ideology*, edited by T. K. Earle, 71–99. Cambridge University Press, Cambridge.

1997   *How Chiefs Come to Power: The Political Economy in Prehistory*. Stanford University Press, Stanford.

Eggan, F.

1954   Social Anthropology and the Method of Controlled Comparison. *American Anthropologist* 56:743–763.

Egloff, B. J.

1967   An Analysis of Ceramics from Historic Cherokee Towns. M.A. thesis, University of North Carolina, Chapel Hill.

Egloff, K. T.

1971   Methods and Problems of Mound Excavation in the South Appalachian Area. M.A. thesis, University of North Carolina, Chapel Hill.

Ekholm, K.

1972   *Power and Prestige: The Rise and Fall of the Kongan Kingdom*. Uppsala, Sweden.

Eldridge, N., and S. J. Gould

1972   Punctuated Equilibria: An Alternative to Phyletic Gradualism. In *Models in Paleobiology*, edited by J. Schopf, 82–115. Freeman and Cooper, San Francisco.

Elliott, D. T., R. J. Ledbetter, and E. A. Gordon

1994   *Data Recovery at Lovers Lane, Phinizy Swamp, and the Old Dike Sites, Bobby Jones Expressway Extension Corridor, Augusta, Georgia*. Occasional Papers in Cultural Resource Management 7. Georgia Department of Transportation, Atlanta.

Emberling, G.

1997   Ethnicity in Complex Societies: Archaeological Perspectives. *Journal of Archaeological Research* 5:295–344.

Emerson, T. E.

1980   The Dyroff and Levin Sites: A Late Archaic Occupation in the American Bottom. FAI-270 Archaeological Mitigation Report 24. Department of Anthropology, University of Illinois at Urbana-Champaign.

1984   The Dyroff and Levin Site. *American Bottom Archaeology, FAI-270 Site Reports*, vol. 9. University of Illinois Press, Urbana.

1986   A Retrospective Look at the Earliest Woodland Cultures in the American Heartland. In *Early Woodland Archeology*, edited by K. Farnsworth and T. Emerson, 621–633. Center for American Archeology Press, Kampsville, Ill.

1997a   *Cahokia and the Archaeology of Power*. University of Alabama Press, Tuscaloosa.

1997b   Cahokian Elite Ideology and the Mississippian Cosmos. In *Cahokia: Domination and Ideology in the Mississippian World*, edited by T. R. Pauketat and T. E. Emerson, 190–228. University of Nebraska Press, Lincoln.

1997c   Reflections from the Countryside on Cahokian Hegemony. In *Cahokia: Domination and Ideology in the Mississippian World*, edited by T. R. Pauketat and T. E. Emerson, 167–189. University of Nebraska Press, Lincoln.

1999   Review Feature: *Cahokia and the Archaeology of Power*, by T. Emerson, W. Dancey, T. Pauketat, A. Whittle, E. DeMarrais, W. DeBoer, and A. Kehoe. *Cambridge Archaeological Journal* 9:267–272.

Emerson, T. E., and A. C. Fortier

1986   Early Woodland Cultural Variation, Subsistence, and Settlement in the American Bottom. In *Early Woodland Archeology*, edited by K. B. Farnsworth and T. E. Emerson, 475– 522. Kampsville Seminars in Archeology 2. Center for American Archeology, Kampsville, Ill.

Emerson, T. E., and D. K. Jackson

1984   The BBB Motor Site. *American Bottom Archaeology FAI-270 Site Reports*, vol. 6. University of Illinois Press, Urbana.

1987   The Edelhardt and Lindeman Phases: Setting the Stage for the Final Transition to Mississippian in the American Bottom. In *The Emergent Mississippian: Proceedings of the Sixth Mid-South Archaeological Conference*, edited by R. Marshall, 172–193. Occasional Papers 87–91. Cobb Institute of Archaeology, Mississippi State University, State College, Miss.

Emerson, T. E., and D. L. McElrath

1983   A Settlement-Subsistence Model of the Terminal Late Archaic Adaptation in the American Bottom, Illinois. In *Archaic Hunters and Gatherers in the American Midwest*, edited by J. L. Phillips and J. A. Brown, 219–242. Academic Press, New York.

Emerson, T. E., D. L. McElrath, and A. C. Fortier, editors

2000   *Late Woodland Societies: Tradition and Transformation across the Midcontinent*. University of Nebraska Press, Lincoln.

Emerson, T. E., D. L. McElrath, and J. A. Williams

1986   Patterns of Hunter-Gatherer Mobility and Sedentism During the Archaic Period in the American Bottom. In *Foraging, Collecting, and Harvesting: Archaic Period Subsistence and Settlement in the Eastern Woodlands*, edited by S. Neusius, 247–274. Occasional Paper 6. Center for Archaeological Investigations, Southern Illinois University at Carbondale.

Emerson, T. E., G. R. Milner, and D. K. Jackson

1983   The Florence Street Site. *American Bottom Archaeology FAI-270 Site Reports*, vol. 2. University of Illinois Press, Urbana.

Emerson, T. E., J. Williams, and P. Cross

1991   Late Archaic Cultures on the Northern Periphery of the Mid-South. In

The Archaic of the Mid-South, edited by C. McNutt, 15–22. Archaeological Report 24. Mississippi Department of Archives and History, Jackson.

Errington, S.

1998   *The Death of Authentic Primitive Art and Other Tales of Progress*. University of California Press, Berkeley.

Esarey, D., and T. R. Pauketat

1992   The Lohmann Site: An Early Mississippian Center in the American Bottom. *American Bottom Archaeology FAI-270 Site Reports*, vol. 25. University of Illinois Press, Urbana.

Evans, J. B.

1995   Cultural Discontinuity in the American Bottom during the Late Archaic–Early Woodland Transition. Paper presented at the Sixtieth Annual Meeting of the Society for American Archaeology, Minneapolis.

1999   The Floyd Site: A Terminal Archaic Habitation in the Northern American Bottom. Ms. on file, Illinois Transportation Archaeological Research Program, University of Illinois at Urbana-Champaign.

Evans, J. B., M. G. Evans, and T. E. Berres

1999   Ringering: An Early Woodland Multicomponent Site in the American Bottom. Ms. on file, Illinois Transportation Archaeological Research Program, University of Illinois at Urbana-Champaign.

Evans, J. B., M. G. Evans, M. Simon, and T. E. Berres

1997   Ringering: A Multi-Component Site in the American Bottom. Ms. on file, Illinois Transportation Archaeological Research Program, University of Illinois at Urbana-Champaign.

Fairbanks, C.

1952   Creek and Pre-Creek. In *Archaeology of Eastern United States*, edited by J. B. Griffin, 285–300. University of Chicago Press, Chicago.

Farnell, B.

1999   Moving Bodies, Acting Selves. *Annual Review of Anthropology* 28:341–373.

Farnsworth, K. B.

1986   Black Sand Origins and Distribution. In *Early Woodland Archeology*, edited by K. B. Farnsworth and T. E. Emerson, 634–641. Kampsville Seminars in Archeology 2. Center for American Archeology, Kampsville, Ill.

Farnsworth, K. B., and D. L. Asch

1986   Early Woodland Chronology, Artifact Styles, and Settlement Distribution in the Lower Illinois Valley Region. In *Early Woodland Archeology*, edited by K. B. Farnsworth and T. E. Emerson, 326–457. Kampsville Seminars in Archeology 2. Center for American Archeology, Kampsville, Ill.

Farnsworth, K. B., and T. E. Emerson, editors

1986   *Early Woodland Archeology*. Center for American Archeology Press, Kampsville, Ill.

Faubion, J. D.
1993 History in Anthropology. *Annual Review of Anthropology* 22:35–54.
Febvre, L.
1973 *A New Kind of History.* Harper and Row, New York.
Feinman, G. M.
1995 The Emergence of Inequality: A Focus on Strategies and Processes. In *Foundations of Social Inequality*, edited by T. D. Price and G. M. Feinman, 255–279. Plenum Press, New York.
1997 Thoughts on New Approaches to Combining the Archaeological and Historical Records. *Journal of Archaeological Method and Theory* 4:367–377.
Feinman, G. M., and J. Marcus, editors
1998 *Archaic States.* School of American Research Press, Santa Fe.
Feinman, G. M., and J. Neitzel
1984 Too Many Types: An Overview of Sedentary Prestate Societies in the Americas. In *Advances in Archaeological Method and Theory*, edited by M. Shiffer, vol. 7, 39–102. Academic Press, New York.
Fenton, W. N.
1978 Northern Iroquoian Culture Patterns. In *Handbook of North American Indians*, vol. 15, *Northeast*, edited by B. G. Trigger, 296–321. Smithsonian Institution Press, Washington, D.C.
Ferguson, L. G.
1991 Struggling with Pots in Colonial South Carolina. In *The Archaeology of Inequality*, edited by R. McGuire and R. Paynter, 28–39. Basil Blackwell, Oxford.
1992 *Uncommon Ground: Archaeology and Early African America, 1650–1800.* Smithsonian Institution Press, Washington, D.C.
Ferguson, R. B.
1990 Explaining War. In *The Anthropology of War*, edited by J. Haas, 26–55. Cambridge University Press, Cambridge.
Ferguson, T. J.
1996 Native Americans and the Practice of Archaeology. *Annual Review of Anthropology* 25:63–79.
Fields, B. J.
1990 Slavery, Race, and Ideology in the United States of America. *New Left Review* 181:85–118.
Finney, F. A.
1983 Middle Woodland Cement Hollow Phase. In *The Mund Site*, by A. C. Fortier, F. A. Finney, and R. B. Lacampagne, 40–108. *American Bottom Archaeology FAI-270 Site Reports*, vol. 5. University of Illinois Press, Urbana.

Fitzhugh, W. W.
1985   Introduction to *Cultures in Contact*, edited by W. W. Fitzhugh, 1–15. Smithsonian Institution Press, Washington, D.C.

Flannery, K. V.
1967   Culture History Versus Culture Process: A Debate in American Archaeology. *Scientific American* 217:119–122.

1972a   Archaeological Systems Theory and Early Mesoamerica. In *Contemporary Archaeology*, edited by M. P. Leone, 222–234. Southern Illinois University Press, Carbondale.

1972b   The Cultural Evolution of Civilizations. *Annual Review of Ecology and Systematics* 3:399–426.

1973   Archeology with a Capital S. In *Research and Theory in Current Archeology*, edited by C. L. Redman, 47–58. Wiley, New York.

Ford, J. A.
1951   *Greenhouse: A Troyville–Coles Creek Period Site in Avoyelles Parish, Louisiana.* Anthropological Paper 44, part 1. American Museum of Natural History, New York.

1963   *Hopewell Culture Burial Mounds near Helena, Arkansas.* Anthropological Papers 50. American Museum of Natural History, New York.

Fortier, A. C.
1985   Selected Sites in the Hill Lake Locality. *American Bottom Archaeology FAI-270 Site Reports*, vol. 13. University of Illinois Press, Urbana.

1992   A People of Colors: The World of American Bottom Hopewell: Their Middens, Blades, and Other Profanities. Paper presented at the Thirty-seventh Annual Midwest Archaeological Conference, Grand Rapids.

1995   Renaissance and Disequilibrium: Middle Woodland Discontinuities in the American Bottom. Paper presented at the Sixtieth Annual Meeting of the Society for American Archaeology, Minneapolis.

1998   Pre-Mississippian Economies in the American Bottom of Southwestern Illinois, 3000 B.C.–A.D. 1050. *Research in Economic Anthropology* 19: 341–392.

2000a   The Dash Reeves Site (11-Mo-80): A Middle Woodland Village and Lithic Production Center in the American Bottom. Ms. on file, Illinois Transportation Archaeological Research Program, University of Illinois, Urbana.

2000b   The Emergence and Demise of the Middle Woodland Small Tool Tradition in the American Bottom. *Midcontinental Journal of Archaeology*, in press.

Fortier, A. C., and D. K. Jackson
2000   The Formation of a Late Woodland Heartland in the American Bottom, Illinois (cal A.D. 650–900). In *Late Woodland Societies: Tradition and Transformation across the Midcontinent*, edited by T. E. Emerson, D. L. McElrath, and A. C. Fortier, 123–147. University of Nebraska Press, Lincoln.

Fortier, A. C., T. E. Emerson, and F. A. Finney
1984 Early Woodland and Middle Woodland Periods. In *American Bottom Archaeology: A Summary of the FAI-270 Project Contribution to the Culture History of the Mississippi River Valley*, edited by C. J. Bareis and J. W. Porter, 59–103. University of Illinois Press, Urbana.

Fortier, A. C., T. E. Emerson, and K. Parker
1998 The Meyer Site: A Terminal Late Archaic Residential Camp in the American Bottom. *Illinois Archaeology* 10:195–228.

Fortier, A. C., T. O. Maher, and J. A. Williams
1991 The Sponemann Site: The Formative Emergent Mississippian Sponemann Phase Occupations. *American Bottom Archaeology FAI-270 Site Reports*, vol. 23. University of Illinois Press, Urbana.

Fortier, A. C., T. O. Maher, J. A. Williams, M. C. Meinkoth, K. E. Parker, and L. S. Kelly
1989 The Holding Site: A Hopewell Community in the American Bottom. *American Bottom Archaeology FAI-270 Site Reports*, vol. 19. University of Illinois Press, Urbana.

Foster, G.
1960 *Culture and Conquest*. Quadrangle Books, Chicago.

Foster, H. B.
1997 *New Raiments of Self: African American Clothing in the Antebellum South*. Berg, Oxford.

Foucault, M.
1973 *The Order of Things: An Archaeology of the Human Sciences*. Vintage Books, New York.
1978 *The History of Sexuality: An Introduction*, vol. 1. Random House, New York.
1979 *Discipline and Punish: The Birth of the Prison*. Vintage Books, New York.

Fowler, M. L.
1997 *The Cahokia Atlas: A Historical Atlas of Cahokia Archaeology*. Rev. edition. Illinois Transportation Archaeological Research Program, Studies in Archaeology 2, Urbana.

Fox, G. L.
1998 An Examination of Mississippian-Period Phases in Southeastern Missouri. In *Changing Perspectives on the Archaeology of the Central Mississippi Valley*, edited by M. J. O'Brien and R. C. Dunnell, 31–58. University of Alabama Press, Tuscaloosa.

Foxhall, L.
1995 Monumental Ambitions: The Significance of Posterity in Greece. In *Time, Tradition, and Society in Greek Archaeology: Bridging the "Great Divide,"* edited by N. Spencer, 132–149. Routledge, London.

Frank, A. G.
1995 The Modern World System Revisited: Rereading Braudel and Wallerstein.

In *Civilizations and World Systems: Studying World-Historical Change*, edited by S. K. Sanderson, 163–194. Alta Mira Press, Walnut Creek, Calif.

Frankenstein, S., and M. Rowlands
1978   The Internal Structure and Regional Context of Early Iron Age Society in South-Western Germany. *Bulletin of the Institute of Archaeology of London* 15:73–112.

Frazer, B.
1999   Reconceptualizing Resistance in the Historical Archaeology of the British Isles: An Editorial. *International Journal of Historical Archaeology* 3:1–10.

Frazier, E. F.
1930   The Negro Slave Family. *Journal of Negro History* 15:198–259.

Frey, S. R., and B. Wood
1998   *Come Shouting to Zion: African American Protestantism in the American South and British Caribbean to 1830.* University of North Carolina Press, Chapel Hill.

Fried, M. H.
1975   *The Notion of Tribe.* Cummings Press, Menlo Park, Calif.

Friedman, J.
1982   Catastrophe and Continuity in Social Evolution. In *Theory and Explanation in Archaeology: The Southampton Conference*, edited by C. Renfew, M. J. Rowlands, and B. A. Seagraves, 175–196. Academic Press, New York.

1989   Culture, Identity, and World Process. In *Domination and Resistance*, edited by D. Miller, M. Rowlands, and C. Tilley, 246–260. Unwin Hyman, London.

1992   The Past in the Future: History and the Politics of Identity. *American Anthropologist* 94:837–859.

Friedman, J., and M. J. Rowlands
1978   Notes Towards an Epigenetic Model of the Evolution of Civilisation. In *The Evolution of Social Systems*, edited by J. Friedman and M. J. Rowlands, 201–276. Duckworth, London.

Fritz, G.
1988   Adding the Plant Remains to Assessments of Late Woodland/Early Mississippi Period Plant Husbandry. Paper presented at the Fifty-third Annual Meeting of the Society for American Archaeology, Phoenix.

1990   Multiple Pathways to Farming in Precontact Eastern North America. *Journal of World Prehistory* 4:387–435.

Fundaburk, E. L., and M. D. F. Foreman, editors
1957   *Sun Circles and Human Hands: The Southeastern Indians' Art and Industries.* Southern Publications, Fairhope, Ala.

Furman, J.
1998   *Slavery in Clover Bottom*. University of Tennessee Press, Knoxville.
Galle, J. E.
1997   Designing Women: Social Networks and the Occupation of Seamstress at the Hermitage Plantation, Hermitage, Tennessee. M.A. thesis, University of Virginia, Charlottesville.
2001   Designing Women: Social Networks and the Occupation of Seamstress at the Hermitage Plantation, Hermitage, Tennessee. In *Engendering African-American Archaeology*, edited by A. L. Young and J. E. Galle. University of Tennessee Press, Knoxville (in press).
Galloway, P.
1989   "The Chief Who Is Your Father": Choctaw and French Views of the Diplomatic Relation. In *Powhatan's Mantle: Indians and Europeans in the Colonial Southeast*, edited by P. H. Wood, G. A. Waselkov, and M. T. Hatley, 254–278. University of Nebraska Press, Lincoln.
1991   The Archaeology of the Ethnohistorical Narrative. In *Columbian Consequences*, vol. 3, *The Spanish Borderlands in Pan-American Perspective*, edited by D. H. Thomas, 453–471. Smithsonian Institution Press, Washington, D.C.
1993   Ethnohistory. In *The Development of Southeastern Archaeology*, edited by J. K. Johnson, 78–108. University of Alabama Press, Tuscaloosa.
1994a   Confederacy as a Solution to Chiefdom Dissolution: Historical Evidence in the Choctaw Case. In *The Forgotten Centuries: Indians and Europeans in the American South, 1521–1704*, edited by C. Hudson and C. C. Tesser, 393–420. University of Georgia Press, Athens.
1994b   "So Many Little Republics": British Negotiations with the Choctaw Confederacy, 1765. *Ethnohistory* 41:513<n537.
1995   *Choctaw Genesis, 1500–1700*. University of Nebraska Press, Lincoln.
1997a   Conjoncture and the Longue Durée: History, Anthropology, and the Hernando de Soto Expedition. In *The Hernando de Soto Expedition: History, Historiography, and "Discovery" in the Southeast*, edited by P. Galloway, 283–294. University of Nebraska Press, Lincoln.
1997b   Where Have All the Menstrual Huts Gone? The Invisibility of Menstrual Seclusion in the Late Prehistoric Southeast. In *Women in Prehistory: North America and Mesoamerica*, edited by R. A. Joyce and C. Claassen, 47–62. University of Pennsylvania Press, Philadelphia.
García Saíz, M. C.
1989   *Las Castas Mexicanas: Un Género Pictórico Americano*. Olivetti, Mexico City.
Gearing, F. O.
1958   The Structural Poses of Eighteenth-Century Cherokee Villages. *American Anthropologist* 60:1148–1157.
1962   *Priests and Warriors: Social Structures for Cherokee Politics in the Eigh-*

teenth Century. American Anthropological Association Memoir 93, Washington, D.C.

Geertz, C.

1963   The Integrative Revolution: Primordial Sentiments and Civil Politics in the New States. In *Old Societies and New States*, edited by C. Geertz, 105–157. Free Press, New York.

Gellner, E.

1988   *Plough, Sword, and Book: The Structure of Human History.* University of Chicago Press, Chicago.

Genovese, E. D.

1976   *Roll, Jordan, Roll: The World the Slaves Made.* Vintage Books, New York.

Gentleman from Elvas

1993   The Account by a Gentleman from Elvas. In *The De Soto Chronicles: The Expedition of Hernando de Soto to North America in 1539–1543*, vol. 1, edited by L. A. Clayton, V. J. Knight, Jr., and E. C. Moore, 19–171. University of Alabama Press, Tuscaloosa.

Giddens, A.

1971   *Capitalism and Modern Social Theory.* Cambridge University Press, Cambridge.

1976   *New Rules of Sociological Method: A Positive Critique of Interpretive Sociologies.* Basic Books, New York.

1979   *Central Problems in Social Theory: Action, Structure, and Contradiction in Social Analysis.* University of California Press, Berkeley.

1984   *The Constitution of Society: Outline of a Theory of Structuration.* University of California Press, Berkeley.

1995   *A Contemporary Critique of Historical Materialism.* 2d edition. Stanford University Press, Stanford.

Gilchrist, R.

1994   *Gender and Material Culture: The Archaeology of Religious Women.* Routledge, London.

Glassow, M. A.

1972   Changes in the Adaptations of Southwestern Basketmakers: A Systems Perspective. In *Contemporary Archaeology*, edited by M. P. Leone, 289–302. Southern Illinois University Press, Carbondale.

Gmelch, G.

1977   *The Irish Tinkers: The Urbanization of an Itinerant People.* Cummings Press, Menlo Park, Calif.

Goad, S. I.

1978   A Reconsideration of the Hopewellian Interaction Sphere in Prehistory. *Early Georgia* 6:4–10.

Goggin, J. M.

1949   Culture Traditions in Florida Prehistory. In *The Florida Indian and His Neighbors*, edited by J. Griffin, 13–44. Winter Park, Fla.

Goldstein, L. G.
1980   *Mississippian Mortuary Practices: A Case Study of Two Cemeteries in the Lower Illinois Valley.* Scientific Papers 4. Northwestern University Archaeological Program, Evanston.
1995   Landscapes and Mortuary Practices: A Case for Regional Perspectives. In *Regional Approaches to Mortuary Analysis*, edited by L. A. Beck, 101–121. Plenum Press, New York.
Goodby, R. G.
1998   Technological Patterning and Social Boundaries: Ceramic Variability in Southern New England, A.D. 1000–1675. In *The Archaeology of Social Boundaries*, edited by M. T. Stark, 161–182. Smithsonian Institution Press, Washington, D.C.
Gordon, R. J.
1982   The !Kung in the Kalahari Exchange: An Ethnohistorical Perspective. In *Past and Present in Hunter-Gatherer Studies*, edited by C. Schrire, 195–224. Academic Press, Orlando.
Gould, S. J.
1987   *Time's Arrow, Time's Cycle: Myth and Metaphor in the Discovery of Geological Time.* Harvard University Press, Cambridge.
1996   *Full House: The Spread of Excellence from Plato to Darwin.* Harmony Books, New York.
Graham, E.
1998   Mission Archaeology. *Annual Review of Anthropology* 27:25–62.
Gramsci, A.
1971   *Selections from the Prison Notebooks of Antonio Gramsci*, edited by Q. Hoare and G. N. Smith. International Publishers, New York.
Graves, M. W.
1994   Kalinga Social and Material Culture Boundaries: A Case of Spatial Convergence. In *Kalinga Ethnoarchaeology: Expanding Archaeological Method and Theory*, edited by W. A. Longacre and J. M. Skibo, 13–49. Smithsonian Institution Press, Washington, D.C.
Gray, L. C.
1933   *History of Agriculture in the Southern United States to 1860.* 2 vols. A. M. Kelley, Clifton, N.J.
Green, W. A.
1993   *History, Historians, and the Dynamics of Change.* Praeger, Westport, Conn.
Green, W. G.
1991   The Search for Altamaha: The Archaeology of an Early Eighteenth-Century Yamasee Indian Town. M.A. thesis, University of South Carolina, Columbia.
Greenberg, J. H.
1968   Culture History. In *International Encyclopedia of the Social Sciences*, edited by D. L. Sills, 448–455. Macmillan, New York.

Gregory, H. F.

1973   Eighteenth-century Caddoan Archaeology: A Study in Models and Interpretations. Ph.D. dissertation, Southern Methodist University, Dallas.

1980   *Excavations 1979: Presidio de Nuestra Señora del Pilar de Los Adaes.*
Office of State Parks, Louisiana Department of Culture, Recreation, and
Tourism, Baton Rouge.

1983   Los Adaes: The Archaeology of an Ethnic Enclave. *Geoscience and Man*
23:53–57.

1984   *Excavations 1982: Presidio de Nuestra Señora del Pilar de Los Adaes.*
Williamson Museum, Northwestern State University, Natchitoches, La.

Griffin, J. B.

1964   The Northeast Woodlands Area. In *Prehistoric Man in the New World,*
edited by J. Jennings and E. Norbeck, 223–258. University of Chicago
Press, Chicago.

1992   Fort Ancient Has No Class: The Absence of an Elite Group in Mississippian Societies in the Central Ohio Valley. In *Lords of the Southeast: Social
Inequality and the Native Elites of Southeastern North America,* edited
by A. W. Barker and T. R. Pauketat, 53–59. Archeological Papers of the
American Anthropological Association 3, Washington, D.C.

Griffin, J. W.

1951   Excavations at the Site of San Luis. In *Here They Once Stood: The Tragic
End of the Apalachee Missions,* by M. F. Boyd, H. G. Smith, and J. W.
Griffin, 137–160. University of Florida Press, Gainesville.

Griffin, J. W., and H. G. Smith

1951   Trait List of Two Spanish Sites of the Mission Period. In *Here They Once
Stood: The Tragic End of the Apalachee Missions,* by M. F. Boyd, H. G.
Smith, and J. W. Griffin, 175–177. University of Florida Press, Gaines-
ville.

Grinker, R. R.

1994   *Houses in the Rainforest: Ethnicity and Inequality among Farmers and
Foragers in Central Africa.* University of California Press, Berkeley.

Gutman, H. G.

1976   *The Black Family in Slavery and Freedom, 1750–1925.* Vintage Books,
New York.

Haas, J.

1987   The Exercise of Power in Early Andean State Development. In *The Origins and Development of the Andean State,* edited by J. Haas, T. Pozorski,
and S. Pozorski, 31–35. Cambridge University Press, Cambridge.

1990a   Warfare and the Evolution of Tribal Polities in the Prehistoric Southwest.
In *The Anthropology of War,* edited by J. Hass, 171–189. Cambridge
University Press, Cambridge.

Haas, J., editor

1990b   *The Anthropology of War.* Cambridge University Press, Cambridge.

1934   *Pichardos Treatise on the Limits of Louisiana and Texas.* 5 vols. University of Texas Press, Austin.

Hall, M.
1992   Small Things and the Mobile, Conflictual Fusion of Power, Fear, and Desire. In *The Art and Mystery of Historical Archaeology: Essays in Honor of James Deetz*, edited by A. Yentsch, and M. Beaudry, 373–399. CRC Press, Boca Raton.

1994   Lifting the Veil of Popular History: Archaeology and Politics in Urban Cape Town. In *Social Construction of the Past: Representations as Power*, edited by G. C. Bond and A. Gillian, 167–184. Routledge, New York.

1996   Subaltern Voices? Finding the Space Between Things and Words. In *Historical Archaeology: Back from the Edge*, edited by P. P. Funari, M. Hall, and S. Jones, 193–203. Routledge, New York.

Hall, R. L.
1997   *An Archaeology of the Soul: North American Indian Belief and Ritual.* University of Illinois Press, Urbana.

Hally, D. J.
1971   The Archaeology of European-Indian Contact in the Southeast. In *Social and Cultural Identity: Problems of Persistence and Change*, edited by T. K. Fitzgerald, 55–66. Southern Anthropological Society Proceedings, vol. 8. Georgia Anthropological Society, Athens.

1994   An Overview of Lamar Culture. In *Ocmulgee Archaeology, 1936–1986*, edited by D. J. Hally, 144–174. University of Georgia Press, Athens.

1996   Platform-Mound Construction and the Instability of Mississippian Chiefdoms. In *Political Structure and Change in the Prehistoric Southeastern United States*, edited by J. F. Scarry, 92–127. University Press of Florida, Gainesville.

Hally, D. J., and H. Kelly
1998   The Nature of Mississippian Towns in Georgia: The King Site Example. In *Mississippian Towns and Sacred Spaces: Searching for an Architectural Grammar*, edited by R. B. Lewis and C. B. Stout, 49–63. University of Alabama Press, Tuscaloosa.

Hally, D. J., and J. T. Langford
1988   *Mississippi Period Archaeology of the Georgia Valley and Ridge.* Laboratory of Archaeology Report 25. University of Georgia, Athens.

Hally, D. J., and J. L. Rudolph
1986   *Mississippi Period Archaeology of the Georgia Piedmont.* Laboratory of Archaeology Report 24. University of Georgia, Athens.

Halperin, R. H.
1994   *Cultural Economies Past and Present.* Texas Press Sourcebooks in Anthropology 18. University of Texas Press, Austin.

Hann, J. H.
1986a   Translation of Alonso de Leturiondos Memorial to the King of Spain. In *Spanish Translations*, by J. H. Hann, 165–225. Florida Archaeology 2. Florida Bureau of Archaeological Research, Tallahassee.
1986b   Translation of Governor Rebolledos 1657 Visitation of Three Florida Provinces and Related Documents. In *Spanish Translations*, by J. H. Hann, 81–145. Florida Archaeology 2. Florida Bureau of Archaeological Research, Tallahassee.
1988   *Apalachee: The Land Between the Rivers.* Ripley P. Bullen Monographs in Anthropology and History 7. University Presses of Florida, Gainesville.
1990   Summary Guide to Spanish Florida Missions and Visitas with Churches in the Sixteenth and Seventeenth Centuries. *The Americas* 46(4).
1993a   Friars' Responses to the Rebolledo Visitation of 1657. In *Visitations and Revolts in Florida, 1656–1695*, by J. H. Hann, 5–30. Florida Archaeology 7. Florida Bureau of Archaeological Research, Tallahassee.
1993b   The Visitation Records of 1677–1678. In *Visitations and Revolts in Florida, 1656–1695*, by J. H. Hann, 77–146. Florida Archaeology 7. Florida Bureau of Archaeological Research, Tallahassee.
1993c   The Visitation Records of 1694–1695 and Related Documents. In *Visitations and Revolts in Florida, 1656–1695*, by J. H. Hann, 147–296. Florida Archaeology 7. Florida Bureau of Archaeological Research, Tallahassee.
1994   The Apalachee of the Historic Era. In *The Forgotten Centuries: Indians and Europeans in the American South, 1521–1704*, edited by C. Hudson and C. C. Tesser, 327–354. University of Georgia Press, Athens.
Hann, J. H., translator
1986c   General Visitation of the Provinces of Guale and Mocama made by the Capt. Juan de Pueyo. Ms. on file, San Luis Archaeological and Historic Site, Tallahassee.
Hannerz, U.
1992   *Cultural Complexity: Studies in the Social Organization of Meaning.* Columbia University Press, New York.
Hargrave, M. L., C. R. Cobb, and P. A. Webb
1991   Late Prehistoric Ceramic Style Zones in Southern Illinois. In *Stability, Transformation, and Variation: The Late Woodland Southeast*, edited by M. Nassaney and C. Cobb, 149–176. Plenum Press, New York.
Harper, C .W.
1978   House Servants and Field Hands: Fragmentation in the Antebellum Slave Community. *North Carolina Historical Review* 55:42–59.
Harré, R.
1986   *Varieties of Realism.* Blackwell, Oxford.
Harris, M.
1997   *Culture, People, Nature: An Introduction to General Anthropology.* 7th edition. Longman, New York.

Hassig, R.
1974   Internal Conflict in the Creek War of 1813–1814. *Ethnohistory* 21:251–271.
1988   *Aztec Warfare*. University of Oklahoma Press, Norman.
Hatch, J. W.
1976   The Citico Site: A Synthesis. *Tennessee Anthropologist* 1:74–103.
1987   Mortuary Indicators of Organizational Variability among Late Prehistoric Chiefdoms in the Southeastern U.S. Interior. In *Chiefdoms in the Americas*, edited by R. D. Drennan and C. A. Uribe, 9–18. University Press of America, Lanham, Md.
Hatch, J. W., and P. S. Willey
1974   Stature and Status in Dallas Society. *Tennessee Archaeologist* 30:107–131.
Hatley, M. T.
1991   Cherokee Women Farmers Hold Their Ground. In *Appalachian Frontiers: Settlement, Society, and Development in the Preindustrial Era*, edited by R. D. Mitchell, 37–51. University of Kentucky Press, Lexington.
1995   *The Dividing Paths: Cherokees and South Carolinians Through the Revolutionary Era*. Oxford University Press, Oxford.
Haury, E. W.
1956   An Archaeological Approach to the Study of Cultural Stability. In *Seminars in Archaeology: 1955*, 31–57. Society for American Archaeology Memoir 11, Washington, D.C.
1958   Evidence at Point of Pines for a Prehistoric Migration from Northern Arizona. In *Migrations in the New World Culture History*, edited by R. H. Thompson, 1–6. Social Science Bulletin 27. University of Arizona Press, Tucson.
Hawkins, B.
1980   *Letters, Journals, and Writings of Benjamin Hawkins*. 2 vols. Beehive Press, Savannah, Ga.
Hayden, B.
1995   Pathways to Power: Principles for Creating Socioeconomic Inequalities. In *Foundations of Social Inequality*, edited by T. D. Price and G. M. Feinman, 15–86. Plenum Press, New York.
Headland, T., and L. Reid
1991   Hunter-Gatherers and Their Neighbors from Prehistory to the Present. *Current Anthropology* 30:43–66.
Heath, B. J.
1997   Slavery and Consumerism: A Case Study from Central Virginia. *African-American Archaeology* 19:1, 58.
1999   *Hidden Lives: The Archaeology of Slave Life at Thomas Jefferson's Poplar Forest*. University Press of Virginia, Charlottesville.
2000   Buttons, Beads, and Buckles: Contextualizing Adornment Within the Bonds of Slavery. In *Historical Archaeology and Current Perspectives on*

Ethnicity, edited by M. Franklin and G. Fesler. Colonial Williamsburg Research Publications. Dietz Press, Richmond.

Hecht, J. J.
1968   Social History. In *International Encyclopedia of the Social Sciences*, edited by D. L. Sills, 455–462. Macmillan, New York.

Hegmon M.
1998   Technology, Style, and Social Practices: Archaeological Approaches. In *The Archaeology of Social Boundaries*, edited by M. T. Stark, 264–279. Smithsonian Institution Press, Washington, D.C.

Helms, M. W.
1979   *Ancient Panama: Chiefs in Search of Power*. University of Texas Press, Austin.
1988   *Ulysses' Sail*. Cambridge University Press, Cambridge.
1992   Long-Distance Contacts, Elite Aspirations, and the Age of Discovery in Cosmological Context. In *Resources, Power, and Interregional Interaction*, edited by E. M. Schortman and P. A. Urban, 157–174. Plenum Press, New York.
1993   *Craft and the Kingly Ideal*. University of Texas Press, Austin.
1996   Review of *The Savannah River Chiefdoms: Political Change in the Late Prehistoric Southeast* by D. G. Anderson. *American Antiquity* 61:437–438.

Hendon, J. A.
1996   Archaeological Approaches to the Organization of Domestic Labor: Household Practice and Domestic Relations. *Annual Review of Anthropology* 25:45–61.

Hendrickson, H., editor
1996   *Clothing and Difference: Embodied Identities in Colonial and Post-Colonial Africa*. Duke University Press, Durham.

Henrickson, E. F., and M. McDonald
1983   Ceramic Form and Function: An Ethnographic Search and an Archaeological Application. *American Anthropologist* 4:630–643.

Herron, M. K.
1986   A Formal and Functional Analysis of St. Johns Series Pottery from Two Sites in St. Augustine, Florida. In *Papers in Ceramic Analysis*, edited by P. M. Rice. *Ceramic Notes* 3:31–45.

Higginbotham, J.
1977   *Old Mobile: Fort Louis de la Louisiane, 1702–1711*. University of Alabama Press, Tuscaloosa.

Higgins, M. J.
1990   The Middle Woodland Occupation. In *The Nochta Site: The Early, Middle, and Late Archaic Occupations*, by M. J. Higgins, 143–157. *American Bottom Archaeology FAI-270 Site Reports*, vol. 21. University of Illinois Press, Urbana.

Hill, J. D.
1998   Violent Encounters: Ethnogenesis and Ethnocide in Long-Term Contact
        Situations. In *Studies in Culture Contact: Interaction, Culture Change,
        and Archaeology*, edited by J. G. Cusick, 146–171. Center for Archaeo-
        logical Investigations, Southern Illinois University, Carbondale.
Hill, S. H.
1997   *Weaving New Worlds: Southeastern Cherokee Women and Their Bas-
        ketry*. University of North Carolina Press, Chapel Hill.
Hingley, R.
1996   Ancestors and Identity in the Later Prehistory of Atlantic Scotland: The
        Reuse and Reinvention of Neolithic Monuments and Material Culture.
        World Archaeology 28:231–243.
Hobart, M. E.
1989   The Paradox of Historical Constructionism. *History and Theory*
        28(1):43–58.
Hobsbawm, E.
1983   Inventing Traditions. Introduction to *The Invention of Traditions*, edited
        by E. Hobsbawm and T. Ranger, 1–14. Cambridge University Press, Cam-
        bridge.
Hobsbawm, E., and T. Ranger, editors
1983   *The Invention of Traditions*. Cambridge University Press, Cambridge.
Hodder, I.
1979   Social and Economic Stress and Material Culture Patterning. *American
        Antiquity* 44:446–454.
1982a   *Symbols in Action*. Cambridge University Press, Cambridge.
1982b   Theoretical Archaeology: A Reactionary View. In *Symbolic and Struc-
        tural Archaeology*, edited by I. Hodder, 1–16. Cambridge University
        Press, Cambridge.
1984   Burials, Houses, Women, and Men in the European Neolithic. In *Ideol-
        ogy, Power, and Prehistory*, edited by D. Miller and C. Tilley, 51–68.
        Cambridge University Press, Cambridge.
1985   Postprocessual Archaeology. *Advances in Archaeological Method and
        Theory* 8:1–26.
1986   *Reading the Past: Current Approaches to Interpretation in Archaeology*.
        Cambridge University Press, Cambridge.
1987   The Contribution of the Long-Term. In *Archaeology as Long-Term His-
        tory*, edited by I. Hodder, 1–8. Cambridge University Press, Cambridge.
1989   This Is Not an Article about Material Culture as Text. *Journal of Anthro-
        pological Archaeology* 8:250–269.
1991   Interpretive Archaeology and Its Role. *American Antiquity* 56:7–18.
1992   Gender Representation and Social Reality. In *Theory and Practice in Ar-
        chaeology*, edited by I. Hodder, 254–262. Routledge, London.
1999   *The Archaeological Process: An Introduction*. Blackwell, Oxford.

Hodgen, M. T.
1974   *Anthropology, History, and Cultural Change.* University of Arizona Press, Tucson.

Hoffman, C. L.
1984   Punan Foragers in the Trading Networks of Southeast Asia. In *Past and Present in Hunter-Gatherer Studies,* edited by C. Schrire, 195–224. Academic Press, Orlando.

Hofman, J. L.
1985   Middle Archaic Ritual and Shell Midden Archaeology: Considering the Significance of Cremations. In *Exploring Tennessee Prehistory: A Dedication to Alfred K. Guthe,* edited by T. Whyte, C. Boyd, and B. Riggs, 1–21. Report of Investigations 42. Department of Anthropology, University of Tennessee, Knoxville.

Holland, D. C., and M. A. Eisenhart
1990   *Educated in Romance: Women, Achievement, and College Culture.* University of Chicago Press, Chicago.

Holland, D. C., W. Lachicotte, Jr., D. Skinner, and C. Cain
1998   *Identity and Agency in Cultural Worlds.* Harvard University Press, Cambridge

Holley, G.
1989   *The Archaeology of the Cahokia Mounds ICT-II: Ceramics.* Illinois Cultural Resources Study 11. Illinois Historic Preservation Agency, Springfield.

Holmes, W. H.
1903   Aboriginal Pottery of the Eastern United States. *Bureau of American Ethnology, Twentieth Annual Report, 1898–99,* 1–237. Washington, D.C.

Hostetler, J. A.
1980   *Amish Society.* 3d edition. Johns Hopkins University Press, Baltimore.

Howard, J. H.
1968   *The Southeastern Ceremonial Complex and Its Interpretation.* Missouri Archaeological Society Memoir 6, Columbia.

Howell, T. L., and K. V. Kintigh
1996   Archaeological Identification of Kin Groups Using Mortuary and Biological Data: An Example from the American Southwest. *American Antiquity* 61:537–554.

Hudson, C. M.
1973   The Historical Approach in Anthropology. In *Handbook of Social and Cultural Anthropology,* edited by J. L. Honigmann, 111–141. Rand McNally, Chicago.

1976   *The Southeastern Indians.* University of Tennessee Press, Knoxville.

1990   *The Juan Pardo Expeditions: Explorations of the Carolinas and Tennessee, 1566–1568.* Smithsonian Institution Press, Washington, D.C.

1997   *Knights of Spain, Warriors of the Sun: Hernando de Soto and the South's Ancient Chiefdoms.* University of Georgia Press, Athens.

Hudson, C. M., and C. C. Tesser
1994   Introduction to *The Forgotten Centuries: Indians and Europeans in the American South, 1521–1704*, edited by C. M. Hudson and C. C. Tesser, 1–14. University of Georgia Press, Athens.
Hugill, P. J., and B. Dickson, editors
1988   *The Transfer and Transformation of Ideas and Material Culture.* Texas A and M University Press, College Station.
Hunt, L., editor
1989   *The New Cultural History.* University of California Press, Berkeley.
Ingraham, J. H.
1860   *The Sunny South: or, The Southerner at Home, Embracing Five Years Experience of a Northern Governess in the Land of the Sugar, and the Cotton.* G. G. Evans, Philadelphia.
1968 *The Southwest: By a Yankee.* 2 volumes. 1830. Reprint, Negro Universities Press, New York.
Jackson, A., Jr.
1845–77 A. Jackson II Account Books, 1845–1877, MSS 1880. Microfilm Edition, Western Reserve Historical Society, Cleveland.
Jackson, D. K.
1998   Settlement on the Southern Frontier: Oneota Occupations in the American Bottom. *Wisconsin Archeologist* 79(2):93–116.
Jackson, R. H.
1999   *Race, Caste, and Status: Indians in Colonial Spanish America.* University of New Mexico Press, Albuquerque.
Jackson, R. H., and E. Castillo
1995   *Indians, Franciscans, and Spanish Colonization: Impact of the Mission System on California Indians.* University of New Mexico Press, Albuquerque.
Jefferies, R. W.
1996   The Emergence of Long-Distance Exchange Networks in the Southeastern United States. In *Archaeology of the Mid-Holocene Southeast*, edited by K. E. Sassaman and D. G. Anderson, 222–234. University Press of Florida, Gainesville.
Jenkins, R.
1997   *Rethinking Ethnicity: Arguments and Explorations.* Sage, London.
Johnson, E. S.
2000   The Politics of Pottery: Material Culture and Political Process Among Algonquians of Seventeenth-Century Southern New England. In *Interpretations of Native North American Life: Material Contributions to Ethnohistory*, edited by M. Nassaney and E. Johnson. University Press of Florida, Gainesville.
Johnson, J. K., and S. O. Brookes
1989   Benton Points, Turkey Tails, and Cache Blades: Middle Archaic Exchange in the Southeast. *Southeastern Archaeology* 8:134–145.

Johnson, M.

1989   Conceptions of Agency in Archaeological Interpretation. *Journal of Anthropological Archaeology* 8:189–211.

1996   *An Archaeology of Capitalism*. Blackwell, Cambridge.

Jones, B. C.

1982   Southern Cult Manifestations at the Lake Jackson Site, Leon County, Florida: Salvage Excavation of Mound 3. *Midcontinental Journal of Archaeology* 7:3–44.

1991   Apalachee Mission Architecture at Patale: The Archaeological Evidence. In *San Pedro y San Pablo de Patale: A Seventeenth-Century Spanish Mission in Leon County, Florida*, by B. C. Jones, J. H. Hann, and J. F. Scarry, 25–57. Florida Archaeology 5. Florida Bureau of Archaeological Research, Tallahassee.

1994   The Lake Jackson Mound Complex (8LE1): Stability and Change in Fort Walton Culture. *Florida Anthropologist* 47:120–146.

Jones, B. C., and J. T. Penman

1973   Winewood: An Inland Fort Walton Site in Tallahassee, Florida. *Bureau of Historic Sites and Properties Bulletin* 3:65–90.

Jones, B. C., J. Hann, and J. F. Scarry

1991a   *San Pedro y San Pablo de Patale: A Seventeenth-Century Spanish Mission in Leon County, Florida*. Florida Archaeology 5. Florida Bureau of Archaeological Research, Tallahassee.

Jones, B. C., J. F. Scarry, and M. Williams

1991b   Material Culture at Patale: Assemblage Composition and Distribution. In *San Pedro y San Pablo de Patale: A Seventeenth-Century Spanish Mission in Leon County, Florida*, by B. C. Jones, J. H. Hann, and J. F. Scarry, 59–107. Florida Archaeology 5. Florida Bureau of Archaeological Research, Tallahassee.

Jones, G. D.

1978   The Ethnohistory of the Guale Coast through 1684. In *The Anthropology of St. Catherine's Island: Natural and Cultural History*, by D. H. Thomas, G. D. Jones, and R. S. Durham, 178–209. Anthropological Papers of the American Museum of Natural History, vol. 55, pt. 2, New York.

Jones, S.

1996   Discourses of Identity in the Interpretation of the Past. In *Cultural Identity and Archaeology: The Construction of European Communities*, edited by P. Graves-Brown, S. Jones, and C. Gamble, 62–80. Routledge, New York.

1997   *The Archaeology of Ethnicity: Constructing Identities in the Past and the Present*. Routledge, London.

Joyce, R. A., and C. P. Claassen

1997   Women in the Ancient Americas: Archaeologists, Gender, and the Making of Prehistory. In *Women in Prehistory: North America and Mesoamerica*, edited by C. P. Claassen and R. A. Joyce, 1–14. University of Pennsylvania Press, Philadelphia.

Joyce, R. A., and J. A. Hendon

2000   Heterarchy, History, and Material Reality: "Communities" in Late Classic Honduras. In *The Archaeology of Community: A New World Perspective*, edited by M. A. Canuto and J. Yaeger, 143–160. Routledge, London.

Kalcik, S.

1984   Ethnic Foodways in America: Symbol and the Performance of Identity. In *Ethnic and Regional Foodways in the United States*, edited by L. Brown and K. Mussell, 37–65. University of Tennessee Press, Knoxville.

Katzew, I.

1996   Casta Painting: Identity and Social Stratification in Colonial Mexico. In *New World Orders: Casta Painting and Colonial Latin America*, edited by I. Katzew, 8–29. Americas Society Art Gallery, New York.

Keegan, W. F., editor

1987   *Emergent Horticultural Economies of the Eastern Woodlands*. Occasional Paper 7. Center for Archaeological Investigations, Southern Illinois University at Carbondale.

Keel, B. C.

1976   *Cherokee Archaeology: A Study of the Appalachian Summit*. University of Tennessee Press, Knoxville.

Keeley, L. H.

1988   Hunter-Gatherer Economic Complexity and Population Pressure: A Cross-Cultural Analysis. *Journal of Anthropological Archaeology* 7:373–411.

Keene, A. S.

1991   Cohesion and Contradiction in the Communal Mode of Production: The Lessons of the Kibbutz. In *Between Bands and States*, edited by S. A. Gregg, 376–394. Occasional Paper 9. Center for Archaeological Investigations, Southern Illinois University, Carbondale.

Kehoe, A. B.

1981   Revisionist Anthropology: Aboriginal North America. *Current Anthropology* 22:503–517.

1992   *North American Indians: A Comprehensive Account*. 2d edition. Prentice-Hall, Englewood Cliffs, N.J.

Kelle, V., and M. Kovalson

1973   *Historical Materialism: An Outline of Marxist Theory of Society*. Translated from the Russian by Y. Sdobnikov. Progress Publishers, Moscow.

Kelly, J. E.

1990   The Emergence of Mississippian Culture in the American Bottom Region. In *The Mississsippian Emergence*, edited by B. D. Smith, 113–152. Smithsonian Institution Press. Washington, D.C.

Kelly, J. E., S. J. Ozuk, D. K. Jackson, D. L. McElrath, F. A. Finney, and D. Esarey
1984   Emergent Mississippian Period. In *American Bottom Archaeology: A Summary of the FAI-270 Project Contribution to the Culture History of the Mississippi River Valley*, edited by C. J. Bareis and J. W. Porter, 128–157. University of Illinois Press, Urbana.

Kelso, W. M.
1984   *Kingsmill Plantations, 1619–1800: Archaeology and Country Life in Colonial Virginia*. Academic Press, New York.

Kemble, F. A.
1984 *Journal of a Residence on a Georgian Plantation in 1838–1839*. 1838–39. Reprint, edited, with an introduction, by J. A. Scott. University of Georgia Press, Athens.

Kent, S.
1998   Gender and Prehistory in Africa. In *Gender in African Prehistory*, edited by S. Kent, 9–21. Alta Mira Press, Walnut Creek, Calif.

Kephart, W. M.
1982   *Extraordinary Groups: The Sociology of Unconventional Lifestyles*. 2d edition. St. Martin's Press, New York.

Kertzer, D. I.
1988   *Ritual, Politics, and Power*. Yale University Press, New Haven.
1996   *Politics and Symbols: The Italian Communist Party and the Fall of Communism*. Yale University Press, New Haven.

Kicza, J. E.
1997   Native Americans, Africans, and Hispanic Communities During the Middle Period in the Colonial Americas. *Historical Archaeology* 31:9–17.

Kidder, T. R.
1992   Coles Creek Period Social Organization and Evolution in Northeast Louisiana. In *Lords of the Southeast: Social Inequality and the Native Elites of Southeastern North America*, edited by A. W. Barker and T. R. Pauketat, 145–162. Archeological Papers of the American Anthropological Association 3, Washington, D.C.

Kimes, T., C. Haselgrove, and I. Hodder
1982   A Method for the Identification of the Location of Regional Cultural Boundaries. *Journal of Anthropological Archaeology* 1:113–131.

Kinnaird, L.
1958   *The Frontiers of New Spain: Nicolas de Laforas Description, 1766–1768*. Quivira Society, Berkeley.

Kirch, P. V.
1990   Monumental Architecture and Power in Polynesian Chiefdoms: A Comparison of Tonga and Hawaii. *World Archaeology* 22:206–221.
1991   Chiefship and Competitive Involution: The Marquesas Islands of Eastern Polynesia. In *Chiefdoms: Power, Economy, and Ideology*, edited by T. K. Earle, 119–145. Cambridge University Press, Cambridge.

Klein, L. F., and L. A. Ackerman
1995   Introduction to *Women and Power in Native North America*, edited by L. F. Klein and L. A. Ackerman, 3–16. University of Oklahoma Press, Norman.

Kleppe, E. J.
1989   Divine Kingship in Northern Africa: Material Manifestations of Social Institutions. In *The Meaning of Things: Material Culture and Symbolic Expression*, edited by I. Hodder, 195–201. Unwin-Hyman, Winchester, Mass.

Klor de Alva, J.
1996   Mestizaje from New Spain to Aztlán: On the Control and Classification of Collective Identities. In *New World Orders: Casta Painting and Colonial Latin America*, edited by I. Katzew, 58–72. Americas Society Art Gallery, New York.

Kluckhohn, C.
1940   The Conceptual Structure in Middle American Studies. In *The Maya and Their Neighbors*, edited by A. M. Tozzer, 41–51. Appleton-Century, New York.

Knapp, A. B., editor
1992   *Archaeology, Annales, and Ethnohistory*. Cambridge University Press, Cambridge.

Knight, V. J., Jr.
1985   *Tukabatchee: Archaeological Investigations at an Historic Creek Town, Elmore County, Alabama, 1984*. Office of Archaeological Research, Report of Investigations 45. Alabama State Museum of Natural History, Tuscaloosa.

1986   The Institutional Organization of Mississippian Religion. *American Antiquity* 51:675–687.

1989a   Some Speculations on Mississippian Monsters. In *The Southeastern Ceremonial Complex: Artifacts and Analysis*, edited by P. Galloway, 205–210. University of Nebraska Press, Lincoln.

1989b   Symbolism of Mississippian Mounds. In *Powhatan's Mantle: Indians in the Colonial Southeast*, edited by P. H. Wood, G. A. Waselkov, and M. T. Hatley, 279–291. University of Nebraska Press, Lincoln.

1990   Social Organization and the Evolution of Hierarchy in Southeastern Chiefdoms. *Journal of Anthropological Research* 46:1–23.

1997   Some Developmental Parallels Between Cahokia and Moundville. In *Cahokia: Domination and Ideology in the Mississippian World*, edited by T. R. Pauketat and T. E. Emerson, 229–247. University of Nebraska Press, Lincoln.

1998   Moundville as a Diagrammatic Ceremonial Center. In *Archaeology of the Moundville Chiefdom*, edited by V. J. Knight, Jr., and V. P. Steponaitis, 44–62. Smithsonian Institution Press, Washington, D.C.

Knight, V. J., Jr., and V. P. Steponaitis
1998   A New History of Moundville. In *Archaeology of the Moundville Chief-dom*, edited by V. J. Knight, Jr., and V. P. Steponaitis, 1–25. Smithsonian Institution Press, Washington, D.C.

Kolchin, P.
1993   *American Slavery, 1619–1877*. Hill and Wang, New York.

Kowalewski, S.
1995   Large-Scale Ecology in Aboriginal Eastern North America. In *Native American Interactions*, edited by M. Nassaney and K. Sassaman, 174–204. University of Tennessee Press, Knoxville.

Kraybill, D. B.
1989   *The Riddle of Amish Culture*. Johns Hopkins University Press, Baltimore.

Krech, S., III
1991   The State of Ethnohistory. *Annual Review of Anthropology* 20:345–375.

Kreisa, P. P., and C. Stout
1991   Late Woodland Adaptations in the Mississippi and Ohio Rivers Confluence Region. In *Stability, Transformation, and Variation: The Late Woodland Southeast*, edited by M. S. Nassaney and C. R. Cobb, 212–148. Plenum Press, New York.

Kroeber, A. L.
1935   History and Science in Anthropology. *American Anthropologist* 37:539–569.
1963a   *An Anthropologist Looks at History*. University of California Press, Berkeley.
1963b   *Anthropology: Culture Patterns and Processes*. Harcourt, Brace and World, New York.

Ladies' Hermitage Association
1817–32 *Hermitage Farm Journal and Account Book, 1817–1832*. Ladies' Hermitage Association, Hermitage, Tennessee.

Last, J.
1995   The Nature of History. In *Interpreting Archaeology: Finding Meaning in the Past*, edited by I. Hodder, M. Shanks, A. Alexandri, V. Buchli, J. Carman, J. Last, and G. Lucas, 141–157. Routledge, London.

Latorre, F. A., and D. L. Latorre
1976   *The Mexican Kickapoo Indians*. University of Texas Press, Austin.

Lave, J., and E. Wenger
1991   *Situated Learning: Legitimate Peripheral Participation*. Cambridge University Press, Cambridge.

Leacock, E.
1954   *The Montagnais Hunting Territory and the Fur Trade*. American Anthropological Association Memoir 78. Washington, D.C.

Leach, E. R.
1968   *Rethinking Anthropology*. Monographs on Social Anthropology, London School of Economics, University of London, 1961. Reprint, Athlone Press, London.

464
444
464
444

Leacock, E., and C. W. Gailey
1992   Primitive Communism and Its Transformations. In *Dialectical Anthropology: Essays in Honor of Stanley Diamond*, vol. 1, *Civilization in Crisis: Anthropological Perspectives*, edited by C. W. Gailey, 95–110. University Press of Florida, Gainesville.

Leacock, E., and R. Lee
1982   Introduction to *Politics and History in Band Societies*, edited by E. Leacock and R. Lee, 1–20. Cambridge University Press, Cambridge.

Lears, T. J. J.
1985   The Concept of Cultural Hegemony: Problems and Possibilities. *American Historical Review* 90:567–593.

Lechtman, H.
1977   Style in Technology: Some Early Thoughts. In *Material Culture: Styles, Organization, and Dynamics of Technology*, edited by H. Lechtman and R. S. Merrill, 3–20. American Ethnological Society, St. Paul, Minn.

Ledbetter, R. J.
1995   *Archaeological Investigations at Mill Branch Sites 9WR4 and 9WR11, Warren County, Georgia*. Technical Report 3. Interagency Archeological Services Division, National Park Service, Atlanta, Ga.

Lee, R.
1990   Primitive Communism and the Origin of Social Inequality. In *The Evolution of Political Systems: Sociopolitics in Small-Scale, Sedentary Societies*, edited by S. Upham, 225–246. Cambridge University Press, Cambridge.

Lee, R., and S. Hurlich
1982   From Foragers to Fighters: South Africa's Militarization of the Namibian San. In *Politics and History in Band Societies*, edited by E. Leacock and R. Lee, 327–345. Cambridge University Press, Cambridge.

LeGoff, J.
1992   *History and Memory*. Translated by S. Rendall and E. Claman. Columbia University Press, New York.

Lemonnier, P., editor
1993   *Technological Choices: Transformation in Material Cultures since the Neolithic*. Routledge, London.

Leonard, R. D.
1993   The Persistence of an Explanatory Dilemma in Contact Period Studies. In *Ethnohistory and Archaeology: Approaches to Postcontact Change in the Americas*, edited by J. D. Rogers and S. M. Wilson, 31–47. Plenum Press, New York.

Leone, M. P.
1984   Interpreting Ideology in Historical Archaeology: Using the Rules of Perspective in the William Paca Garden in Annapolis, Maryland. In *Ideology, Power, and Prehistory*, edited by D. Miller and C. Tilley, 25–35. Cambridge University Press, Cambridge.

1986   Symbolic, Structural, and Critical Archaeology. In *American Archaeology Past and Future*, edited by D. J. Meltzer, D. D. Fowler, and J. A. Sabloff, 415–438. Smithsonian Institution Press, Washington, D.C.

Levy, J. E.
1995   Heterarchy in Bronze Age Denmark: Settlement Pattern, Gender, and Ritual. In *Heterarchy and the Analysis of Complex Societies*, edited by R. M. Ehrenreich, C. L. Crumley, and J. E. Levy, 41–53. Archeological Papers of the American Anthropological Association 6, Washington, D.C.

1999   Gender, Power, and Heterarchy in Middle-Level Societies. In *Manifesting Power: Gender and the Interpretation of Power in Archaeology*, edited by T. L. Sweely, 62–78. Routledge, London.

Levy, J. E., J. A. May, and D. G. Moore
1990   From Ysa to Joara: Cultural Diversity in the Catawba Valley from the Fourteenth Through Sixteenth Century. In *Columbian Consequences*, vol. 2, *Archaeological and Historical Perspectives on the Spanish Borderlands East*, edited by D. H. Thomas, 153–168. Smithsonian Institution Press, Washington, D.C.

Lewis, R. B., and C. Stout
1998   *Mississippian Towns and Sacred Spaces: Searching for an Architectural Grammar*. University of Alabama Press, Tuscaloosa.

Lightfoot, K. G.
1995   Culture Contact Studies: Redefining the Relationship Between Prehistoric and Historical Archaeology. *American Antiquity* 60:199–217.

Lightfoot, K. G., and A. Martinez
1995   Frontiers and Boundaries in Archaeological Perspective. *Annual Review of Anthropology* 24:471–492.

Lightfoot, K. G., A. Martinez, and A. M. Schiff
1998   Daily Practice and Material Culture in Pluralistic Social Settings: An Archaeological Study of Culture Change and Persistence from Fort Ross, California. *American Antiquity* 63:199–222.

Lincoln, B.
1989   *Discourse and the Construction of Society: Comparative Studies of Myth, Ritual, and Classification*. Oxford University Press, New York.

Linton, R., editor
1940   *Acculturation in Seven American Indian Tribes*. Appleton-Century-Crofts, New York.

Little, B. J., K. M. Lanphear, and D. W. Owsley
1992   Mortuary Display and Status in a Nineteenth-Century Anglo-American Cemetery in Manassas, Virginia. *American Antiquity* 57:397–418.

Longacre, W. A.
1964   Archaeology as Anthropology: A Case Study. *Science* 144(19):1454–1455.

Lopinot, N. H.
1997   Cahokian Food Production Reconsidered. In *Cahokia: Domination and Ideology in the Mississippian World*, edited by T. R. Pauketat and T. E. Emerson, 52–68. University of Nebraska Press, Lincoln.

Loren, D.
1998   Putting on the Ritz: Colonial Dress and Identity at the Eighteenth-Century Spanish Presidio of Los Adaes. Paper presented at the Fifty-fifth Annual Southeastern Archaeological Conference, Greenville, S.C.

Lowie, R. H.
1927   *The Origin of the State*. Harcourt Brace, New York.
1966   *Culture and Ethnology*. Basic Books, New York.

Lyman, R. L., and M. J. O'Brien
1998   The Goals of Evolutionary Archaeology. *Current Anthropology* 39:615–652.

Lyman, R. L., M. J. O'Brien, and R. C. Dunnell
1997   *The Rise and Fall of Culture History*. Plenum Press, New York.

Lyon, E.
1981   Spain's Sixteenth-Century North American Settlement Attempts: A Neglected Aspect. *Florida Historical Quarterly* 59:275–291.

MacArthur, R. H., and E. O. Wilson
1963   An Equilibrium Theory of Insular Zoogeography. *Evolution* 17:373–387.

Maceachern, S.
1998   Scale, Style, and Cultural Variation: Technological Traditions in the Northern Mandara Mountains. In *The Archaeology of Social Boundaries*, edited by M. T. Stark, 107–131. Smithsonian Institution Press, Washington, D.C.

Maher, T. O.
1989   The Middle Woodland Ceramic Assemblage. In *The Holding Site: A Hopewell Community in the American Bottom*, by A. C. Fortier, T. O. Maher, J. A. Williams, M. C. Meinkoth, K. E. Parker, and L. S. Kelly, 125–318. *American Bottom Archaeology FAI-270 Site Reports*, volume 19. University of Illinois Press, Urbana.
1996   Time, Space, and Social Dynamics During the Hopewell Occupation of the American Bottom. Ph.D. dissertation, University of North Carolina, Chapel Hill.
2000   Ceramic Assemblage. In *The Dash Reeves Site (11–Mo-80): A Middle Woodland Village and Lithic Production Center in the American Bottom*, by A. C. Fortier. Ms. on file, Illinois Transportation Archaeological Program, University of Illinois, Urbana.

Mainfort, R. C., Jr.
1985   Wealth, Space, and Status in a Historic Indian Cemetery. *American Antiquity* 50:555–579.
1996   Late Period Chronology in the Central Mississippi Valley: A Western Tennessee Perspective. *Southeastern Archaeology* 15(2):172–180.

Mainfort, R. C., Jr., and R. Carroll
1996   The Nodena Phase: Research Potential of Museum Collections. Paper presented at the Sixty-first Annual Meeting of the Society for American Archaeology, New Orleans.

Mainfort, R. C., Jr., and L. P. Sullivan
1998   Explaining Earthen Enclosures. In *Ancient Earthen Enclosures of the Eastern Woodlands*, edited by R. C. Mainfort, Jr., and L. P. Sullivan, 1–16. University Press of Florida, Gainesville.

Mann, R. B., and D. D. Loren
n.d.   Keeping Up Appearances: Dress, Architecture, Furniture, and Status at French Azilum. Manuscript in possession of the authors.

Marcus, G. E., and M. M. J. Fischer
1986   *Anthropology as Cultural Critique: An Experimental Moment in the Human Sciences.* University of Chicago Press, Chicago.

Marquardt, W. H.
1978   Advances in Archaeological Seriation. In *Advances in Archaeological Method and Theory*, vol. 1, edited by M. B. Schiffer, 257–314. Academic Press, New York.

Marquardt, W. H., and C. L. Crumley
1987   Theoretical Issues in the Analysis of Spatial Patterning. In *Regional Dynamics: Burgundian Landscapes in Historical Perspectives*, edited by C. L. Crumley and W. H. Marquardt, 1–18. Academic Press, New York.

Marrinan, R. A.
1993   Archaeological Investigations at Mission Patale, 1984–1992. In *The Spanish Missions of La Florida*, edited by B. G. McEwan, 244–294. University Press of Florida, Gainesville.

Martin, C.
1978   *Keepers of the Game: Indian-Animal Relationships and the Fur Trade.* University of California Press, Berkeley.

Martin, J. W.
1991   *Sacred Revolt: The Muskogee's Struggle for a New World.* Beacon Press, Boston.

Martin, P. S., and J. Rinaldo
1951   The Southwestern Co-Tradition. *Southwestern Journal of Anthropology* 7:215–229.

Maschner, H.D.G., editor
1996   *Darwinian Archaeologies.* Plenum Press, New York.

Mason, C. I.
1963   Eighteenth-Century Culture Change among the Lower Creeks. *Florida Anthropologist* 16:65–80.

McAlister, L. N.
1984   *Spain and Portugal in the New World, 1492–1700.* University of Minnesota Press, Minneapolis.

McCall, J. C.
1999   Structure, Agency, and the Locus of the Social. In *Material Symbols: Culture and Economy in Prehistory*, edited by J. Robb, 16–20. Occasional Paper 26. Southern Illinois University, Carbondale.
McElrath, D. L.
1993   Mule Road: A Newly Defined Late Archaic Phase in the American Bottom. In *Highways to the Past: Essays on Illinois Archaeology in Honor of Charles J. Bareis*, edited by T. E. Emerson, A. C. Fortier, and D. L. McElrath, 148–157. *Illinois Archaeology* 5 (1, 2).
1995   Defining Archaic Cultures in the American Bottom. Paper presented at the Sixtieth Annual Meeting of the Society for American Archaeology, Minneapolis.
McElrath, D. L., and A. C. Fortier
1983   The Missouri Pacific #2 Site. *American Bottom Archaeology FAI-270 Site Reports*, vol. 3. University of Illinois Press, Urbana.
2000   The Early Late Woodland Occupation of the American Bottom. In *Late Woodland Societies: Tradition and Transformation across the Midcontinent*, edited by T. E. Emerson, D. L. McElrath, and A. C. Fortier, 97–121. University of Nebraska Press, Lincoln.
McElrath, D. L., T. E. Emerson, and A. C. Fortier
2000   *Social Evolution or Social Response: A Fresh Look at the Good Grey Cultures after Four Decades of Midwest Research*, edited by T. E. Emerson, D. L. McElrath, and A. C. Fortier, 3–36. University of Nebraska Press, Lincoln.
McElrath, D. L., T. E. Emerson, A. C. Fortier, and J. L. Phillips
1984   Late Archaic Period. In *American Bottom Archaeology: A Summary of the FAI-270 Project Contribution to the Culture History of the Mississippi River Valley*, edited by C. J. Bareis and J. W. Porter, 34–58. University of Illinois Press, Urbana.
McEwan, B. G.
1991   The Archaeology of Women in the Spanish New World. *Historical Archaeology* 25:33–41.
1992a   *Archaeology of the Apalachee Village at San Luis de Talimali*. Florida Archaeological Reports 28. Florida Bureau of Archaeological Research, Tallahassee.
1992b   The Role of Ceramics in Spain and Spanish America during the Sixteenth Century. *Historical Archaeology* 26:92–108.
1993   Hispanic Life on the Seventeenth-Century Florida Frontier. In *The Spanish Missions of La Florida*, edited by B. G. McEwan, 295–321. University Press of Florida, Gainesville.
McGuckin, E.
1997   Tibetan Carpets. *Journal of Material Culture* 2:291–310.

McGuire, R. H.

1983   Breaking Down Cultural Complexity: Inequality and Heterogeneity. *Advances in Archaeological Method and Theory* 6:91–142.

1988   Dialogues with the Dead: Ideology and the Cemetery. In *The Recovery of Meaning*, edited by M. P. Leone and P. B. Potter, 435–480. Smithsonian Institution Press, Washington, D.C.

1992   *A Marxist Archaeology*. Academic Press, San Diego.

1994   The Sanctity of the Grave: White Concepts and American Indian Burials. In *Conflict in the Archaeology of Living Traditions*, edited by R. Layton, 167–184. Routledge, London.

McGuire, R. H., and D. J. Saitta

1996   Although They Have Captains, They Obey Them Badly: The Dialectics of Prehispanic Western Pueblo Social Organization. *American Antiquity* 61:197–216.

McGuire, R. H., and R. Paynter, editors

1991   *The Archaeology of Inequality*. Blackwell, London.

McKee, L.

1991   Summary Report of the 1990 Hermitage Field Quarter Excavation. *Tennessee Anthropological Association Newsletter* 16(1):1–17.

1993   Summary Report on the 1991 Hermitage Field Quarter Excavation. *Tennessee Anthropological Association Newsletter* 18(1):1–16.

1997   Summary Report on the 1994 Excavation at Alfred's Cabin. Manuscript on file, The Ladies' Hermitage Association, Hermitage, Tenn.

McKee, L., V. P. Hood, and S. Macpherson

1992   Reinterpreting the Construction History of the Service Area of the Hermitage Mansion. In *Text-Aided Archaeology*, edited by B. J. Little, 161–176. CRC Press, Boca Raton.

McKee, L., B. W. Thomas, and J. Bartlett

1994   Summary Report on the Hermitage Mansion Yard Area. Ms. on file, Ladies' Hermitage Association, Hermitage, Tenn.

McKenzie, D.

1964   The Moundville Phase and Its Position in Southeastern Prehistory. Ph.D. dissertation, Harvard University, Cambridge.

1966   A Summary of the Moundville Phase. *Journal of Alabama Archaeology* 12:1–58.

McKirvergan, D. A.

1991   Migration and Settlement among the Yamassee in South Carolina. M.A. thesis, University of South Carolina, Columbia.

McMurray, J. A.

1973   The Definition of the Ceramic Complex at San Juan del Puerto. Ph.D. dissertation, University of Florida, Gainesville.

Mead, M.

1951   Anthropologist and Historian: Their Common Problems. *American Quarterly* 3:3–13.

Mehrer, M. W.

1995   *Cahokia's Countryside: Household Archaeology, Settlement Patterns, and Social Power.* Northern Illinois University Press, De Kalb.

Mehrer, M. W., and J. M. Collins

1995   Household Archaeology at Cahokia and in its Hinterlands. In *Mississippian Communities and Households*, edited by J. D. Rogers and B. D. Smith, 32–57. University of Alabama Press, Tuscaloosa.

Milanich, J. T., A. S. Cordell, V. J. Knight, Jr., T. A. Kohler, and B. J. Sigler-Lavelle

1997   *Archaeology of North Florida, A.D. 200–900: The McKeithen Weeden Island Culture.* University Press of Florida, Gainesville.

Miller, C. F.

1949   The Lake Spring Site, Columbia County, Georgia. *American Antiquity* 15:254–258.

Miller, D., M. Rowlands, and C. Tilley, editors

1989   *Domination and Resistance.* Routledge, London.

Miller, J. E., Jr.

1982   Construction of Site Features: Tests of Mounds C, D, E, B, and the Embankment. In *Emerging Patterns of Plum Bayou Culture*, edited by M. A. Rolingson, 30–43. Arkansas Archeological Survey Research Series 18. Fayetteville.

Milner, G. R.

1984   The Robinson's Lake Site. *American Bottom Archaeology FAI-270 Site Reports*, vol. 10. University of Illinois Press, Urbana.

1998   *The Cahokia Chiefdom: The Archaeology of a Mississippian Society.* Smithsonian Institution Press, Washington, D.C.

Milner, G. R., T. E. Emerson, M. W. Mehrer, J. A. Williams, and D. Esarey

1984   Mississippian and Oneota Period. In *American Bottom Archaeology*, edited by C. J. Bareis and J. W. Porter, 158–186. University of Illinois Press, Urbana.

Mitchem, J. M.

1993   Beads and Pendants from San Luis de Talimali: Inferences from Varying Contexts. In *The Spanish Missions of La Florida*, edited by B. G. McEwan, 399–417. University Press of Florida, Gainesville.

Mooney, J.

1896   *The Ghost-Dance Religion and the Sioux Outbreak of 1890.* Fourteenth Annual Report of the Bureau of Ethnology to the Secretary of the Smithsonian Institution, 1892–93. Part 2. Washington, D.C.

Moore, C. B.

1907   Moundville Revisited. *Journal of the Academy of Natural Sciences of Philadelphia* 13:337–405.

1908   Certain Mounds of Arkansas and Mississippi. *Journal of the Academy of Natural Sciences of Philadelphia* 13:479–605.

Moore, D. G.

1990   An Overview of Historic Aboriginal Public Architecture in Western

North Carolina. Paper presented at the Forty-seventh Annual Meeting of the Southeastern Archaeological Conference, Mobile.

Moore, J. H.

1994a Ethnoarchaeology of the Lamar Peoples. In *Perspectives on the Southeast: Linguistics, Archaeology, and Ethnohistory*, edited by P. B. Kwachka, 126–141. University of Georgia Press, Athens.

1994b Putting Anthropology Back Together Again: The Ethnogenetic Critique of Cladistic Theory. *American Anthropologist* 96:925–948.

Morfí, F. J. A.

1935 *History of Texas, 1673–1779*. Translated and annotated by Carlos Eduardo Casteñeda. Quivera Society, Albuquerque.

Morgan, P. D.

1983 The Ownership of Property by Slaves in the Mid-Nineteenth-Century Low Country. *Journal of Southern History* 49:399–420.

1982 Work and Culture: The Task System and the World of Lowcountry Blacks, 1700–1880. *William and Mary Quarterly* 563–599.

Morrell, L. R., and B. C. Jones

1970 San Juan de Aspalaga: A Preliminary Architectural Study. *Bureau of Historic Sites and Properties Bulletin* 1:25–43.

Morris, M. J.

1993 The Bringing of Wonder: Creek and Euroamerican Trade in the Seventeenth Century. Ph.D. dissertation, Auburn University, Auburn, Ala.

Morse, D. F.

1989 The Nodena Phase. In *Nodena: An Account of Ninety Years of Archaeological Investigation in Southeast Mississippi County, Arkansas*, edited by D. F. Morse, 97–114. Arkansas Archeological Survey Research Series 30. Fayetteville.

1990 The Nodena Phase. In *Towns and Temples along the Mississippi*, edited by D. H. Dye and C. A. Cox, 69–97. University of Alabama Press, Tuscaloosa.

Morse, D. F., and P. A. Morse

1983 *Archaeology of the Central Mississippi Valley*. Academic Press, New York.

1990 The Spanish Exploration of Arkansas. In *Columbian Consequences*, vol. 2, *Archaeological and Historical Perspectives on the Spanish Borderlands East*, edited by D. H. Thomas, 197–210. Smithsonian Institution Press, Washington, D.C.

1996 Northeast Arkansas. In *Prehistory of the Central Mississippi Valley*, edited by C. H. McNutt, 119–136. University of Alabama Press, Tuscaloosa.

Morse, P. A.

1981 *Parkin: The 1978–1979 Archeological Investigations of a Cross County, Arkansas, Site*. Arkansas Archaeological Survey Research Series 13. Fayetteville.

1990   The Parkin Site and the Parkin Phase. In *Towns and Temples along the Mississippi*, edited by D. H. Dye and C. A. Cox, 118–134. University of Alabama Press, Tuscaloosa.

Mrozowski, S. A.

1988   Historical Archaeology as Anthropology. *Historical Archaeology* 22:18–24.

Muller, H. J.

1943   *Science and Criticism: The Humanistic Tradition in Contemporary Thought.* Yale University Press, New Haven.

Muller, J.

1987   Lower Ohio Valley Emergent Horticulture and Mississippian. In *The Emergence of Horticultural Economies in the Eastern Woodlands*, edited by W. F. Keegan, 243–273. Occasional Paper 7. Center for Archaeological Investigations, Southern Illinois University at Carbondale.

1997   *Mississippian Political Economy.* Plenum Press, New York.

Nassaney, M. S.

1987   On the Causes and Consequences of Subsistence Intensification in the Mississippi Alluvial Valley. In *The Emergence of Horticultural Economies in the Eastern Woodlands*, edited by W. F. Keegan, 129–151. Occasional Paper 7. Center for Archaeological Investigations, Southern Illinois University at Carbondale.

1991   Spatial-Temporal Dimensions of Social Integration during the Coles Creek Period in Central Arkansas. In *Stability, Transformation, and Variation: The Late Woodland Southeast*, edited by M. S. Nassaney and C. R. Cobb, 177–220. Plenum Press, New York.

1992a   Communal Societies and the Emergence of Elites in the Prehistoric American Southeast. In *Lords of the Southeast: Social Inequality and the Native Elites of Southeastern North America*, edited by A. W. Barker and T. R. Pauketat, 111–143. Archeological Papers of the American Anthropological Association 3, Washington, D.C.

1992b   Experiments in Social Ranking in Prehistoric Central Arkansas. Ph.D. dissertation, University of Massachusetts, Amherst.

1994   The Historical and Archaeological Context of Plum Bayou Culture in Central Arkansas. *Southeastern Archaeology* 13:36–55.

1996a   Aboriginal Earthworks in Central Arkansas. In *Mounds, Embankments, and Ceremonialism in the Midsouth*, edited by R. C. Mainfort, Jr., and R. A. Walling, 22–35. Arkansas Archeological Survey Research Series 46. Fayetteville.

1996b   The Role of Chipped Stone in the Political Economy of Social Ranking. In *Stone Tools: Theoretical Insights into Human Prehistory*, edited by G. H. Odell, 181–224. Plenum Press, New York.

1999   An Update on the Plum Bayou Survey Project and Recent Arkansas-Related Developments in Southwest Michigan. *Arkansas Archeological Society Field Notes* 288:9–11.

2000   The Late Woodland Southeast. In *Late Woodland Societies: Tradition and Transformation across the Midcontinent*, edited by T. Emerson, D. McElrath, and A. Fortier. University of Nebraska Press, Lincoln.

Nassaney, M. S., and M. Abel

2000   Urban Spaces, Labor Organization, and Social Control: Lessons from New England's Nineteenth-Century Cutlery Industry. In *Lines That Divide: Historical Archaeologies of Race, Gender, and Class*, edited by J. Delle, S. Mrozowski, and R. Paynter. University of Tennessee Press, Knoxville.

Nassaney, M. S., and C. R. Cobb

1991a   Patterns and Processes of Late Woodland Development in the Greater Southeastern United States. In *Stability, Transformation, and Variation: The Late Woodland Southeast*, edited by M. S. Nassaney and C. R. Cobb, 285–322. Plenum Press, New York.

Nassaney, M. S., and C. R. Cobb, editors

1991b   *Stability, Transformation, and Variation: The Late Woodland Southeast.* Plenum Press, New York.

Nassaney, M. S., and N. H. Lopinot

1986   The Significance of a Short-Term Late Archaic Occupation on the American Bottom. In *Foraging, Collecting, and Harvesting: Archaic Period Subsistence and Settlement in the Eastern Woodlands*, edited by S. W. Neusius, 195–219. Occasional Paper 6. Center for Archaeological Investigations, Southern Illinois University at Carbondale.

Nassaney, M. S., and K. Pyle

1999   The Adoption of the Bow and Arrow in Eastern North America: A View from Central Arkansas. *American Antiquity* 64:243–263.

Nassaney, M. S., and K. E. Sassaman

1995   Understanding Native American Interactions. Introduction to *Native American Interactions: Multiscalar Analyses and Interpretations in the Eastern Woodlands*, edited by M. S. Nassaney and K. E. Sassaman, xix–xxxviii. University of Tennessee Press, Knoxville.

Ndagala, D. K.

1988   Free or Doomed? Images of the Hadzabe Hunters and Gatherers of Tanzania. In *Hunters and Gatherers*, vol. 1, *History, Evolution, and Social Change*, edited by T. Ingold, D. Riches, and J. Woodburn, 65–72. Berg, London.

Nelson, M. C.

2000   Abandonment: Conceptualization, Representation, and Social Change. In *Social Theory in Archaeology*, edited by M. B. Schiffer, 52–62. University of Utah Press, Salt Lake City.

Nelson, S. M.

1997   *Gender in Archaeology: Analyzing Power and Prestige.* Alta Mira Press, Walnut Creek, Calif.

1998   Reflections on Gender Studies in African and Asian Archaeology. In *Gender in African Prehistory*, edited by S. Kent, 285–294. Alta Mira Press, Walnut Creek, Calif.

1999   Rethinking Gender and Power. In *Manifesting Power: Gender and the Interpretation of Power in Archaeology*, edited by T. L. Sweely, 184–189. Routledge, London.

Neusius, S., editor

1986   *Foraging, Collecting, and Harvesting: Archaic Period Subsistence and Settlement in the Eastern Woodlands*. Occasional Paper 6. Center for Archaeological Investigations, Southern Illinois University at Carbondale.

Norberg-Schulz, C.

1971   *Existence, Space, and Architecture*. Praeger, New York.

1980   *Genius Loci: Towards a Phenomenology of Architecture*. Rizzoli, New York.

Nöth, W.

1990   *Handbook of Semiotics*. Indiana University Press, Bloomington.

Nowell-Smith, P. H.

1977   The Constructionist Theory of History. *History and Theory* 16(4):1–28.

Nunley, M. C.

1986   The Mexican Kickapoo Indians: Avoidance of Acculturation through a Migratory Adaptation. Ph.D. dissertation, Southern Methodist University, Dallas.

1991   Contemporary Hunting and Gathering: The Foraging Ethos and the Mexican Kickapoo. In *Between Bands and States*, edited by S. A. Gregg, 341–358. Occasional Paper No. 9. Center for Archaeological Investigations, Southern Illinois University, Carbondale.

O'Brien, M. J.

1994   *Cat Monsters and Head Pots: The Archaeology of Missouri's Pemiscot Bayou*. University of Missouri Press, Columbia.

O'Brien, M. J., and T. D. Holland

1990   Variation, Selection, and the Archaeological Record. *Archaeological Method and Theory* 2:31–79.

O'Brien, M. J., R. L. Lyman, and R. D. Leonard

1998   Basic Incompatibilities Between Evolutionary and Behavioral Archaeology. *American Antiquity* 63:485–498.

O'Connell, M., and J. L. Jones

1991   Analysis of European-derived Ceramics at Mission San Pedro y San Pablo de Patale. Ms. on file, Department of Anthropology, Florida State University, Tallahassee.

O'Crouley, P. A.

1972   *A Description of the Kingdom of New Spain, 1774*. Translated and edited by S. Galvin. John Howell Press, New York.

Ohnuki-Tierney, E.
1990   The Historicization of Anthropology. Introduction to *Culture Through Time: Anthropological Approaches*, edited by E. Ohnuki-Tierney, 1–25. Stanford University Press, Stanford.

Okeley, J.
1983   *The Traveller-Gypsies*. Cambridge University Press, Cambridge.

Oliver, B. C.
1985   Tradition and Typology: Basic Elements of the Carolina Projectile Point Sequence. In *Structure and Function in Southeastern Archaeology*, edited by R. S. Dickens and H. T. Ward, 195–211. University of Alabama Press, Tuscaloosa.

Olwell, R.
1996   Loose, Idle, and Disorderly: Slave Women in the Eighteenth-Century Charleston Marketplace. In *More Than Chattel*, edited by D. B. Gaspar and D. C. Hine, 97–110. Indiana University Press, Bloomington.

Opler, M. E.
1952   The Creek "Town" and the Problem of Creek Indian Political Reorganization. In *Human Problems in Technological Change: A Casebook*, edited by E. H. Spicer, 165–180. New York,

Orser, C. E., Jr.
1992   Commodities Article. *Historical Archaeology* 26:95–104.
1996   *A Historical Archaeology of the Modern World*. Plenum Press, New York.
1998   The Archaeology of the African Diaspora. *Annual Review of Anthropology* 27:63–82.

Ortner, S. B.
1984   Theory in Anthropology Since the Sixties. *Comparative Studies in Society and History* 26:126–166.

O'Shea, J. M.
1984   *Mortuary Variability: An Archaeological Investigation*. Academic Press, New York.

Otto, J. S.
1984   *Cannon's Point Plantation, 1794–1860: Living Conditions and Status Patterns in the Old South*. Academic Press, Orlando.

Pagden, A.
1982   *The Fall of Natural Man: The American Indian and the Origins of Comparative Ethnology*. Cambridge University Press, Cambridge.

Parker, James M.
1840–41 James M. Parker Daybook, 1840–41, MSS 2067. Microfilm Edition, Western Reserve Historical Society, Cleveland.

Patterson, T. C.
1986   Ideology, Class Formation, and Resistance in the Inca State. *Critique of Anthropology* 6:75–85.

1987   Tribes, Chiefdoms, and Kingdoms in the Inca Empire. In *Power Relations and State Formation*, edited by T. C. Patterson and C. W. Gailey, 117–127. American Anthropological Association, Washington, D.C.

Pauketat, T. R.

1992   The Reign and Ruin of the Lords of Cahokia: A Dialectic of Dominance. In *Lords of the Southeast: Social Inequality and the Native Elites of Southeastern North America*, edited by A. W. Barker and T. R. Pauketat, 31–51. Archeological Papers of the American Anthropological Association 3, Washington, D.C.

1993   *Temples for Cahokia Lords: Preston Holder's 1955–1956 Excavations of Kunnemann Mound*. Museum of Anthropology Memoir 26. University of Michigan, Ann Arbor.

1994   *The Ascent of Chiefs: Cahokia and Mississippian Politics in Native North America*. University of Alabama Press, Tuscaloosa.

1996   The Foundations of Inequality within a Simulated Shan Community. *Journal of Anthropological Archaeology* 15:219–236.

1997a   Cahokian Political Economy. In *Cahokia: Domination and Ideology in the Mississippian World*, edited by T. R. Pauketat and T. E. Emerson, 30–51. University of Nebraska Press, Lincoln.

1997b   Specialization, Political Symbols, and the Crafty Elite of Cahokia. *Southeastern Archaeology* 16:1–15.

1998a   *The Archaeology of Downtown Cahokia: The Tract 15A and Dunham Tract Excavations*. Studies in Archaeology 1. Illinois Transportation Archaeological Research Program, University of Illinois, Urbana.

1998b   Refiguring the Archaeology of Greater Cahokia. *Journal of Archaeological Research* 6:45–89.

2000a   Politicization and Community in the Pre-Columbian Mississippi Valley. In *The Archaeology of Communities: A New World Perspective*, edited by M.-A. Canuto and J. Yaeger, 16–43. Routledge, London.

2000b   The Tragedy of the Commoners. In *Agency in Archaeology*, edited by M.-A. Dobres and J. Robb, 113–129. Routledge, London.

2001   Practice and History in Archaeology: An Emerging Paradigm. *Anthropological Theory* 1:73–98.

2002   Materiality and the Immaterial in Archaeology. In *Archaeological Theory 2002*, edited by C. S. VanPool and T. L. VanPool. University of Utah Press, Salt Lake City. In press.

Pauketat, T. R., and T. E. Emerson

1991   The Ideology of Authority and the Power of the Pot. *American Anthropologist* 93:919–941.

1997a   Domination and Ideology in the Mississippian World. Introduction to *Cahokia: Domination and Ideology in the Mississippian World*, edited by T. R. Pauketat and T. E. Emerson, 1–29. University of Nebraska Press, Lincoln.

1999 The Representation of Hegemony as Community at Cahokia. In *Material Symbols: Culture and Economy in Prehistory*, edited by J. Robb, 302–317. Occasional Paper 26. Southern Illinois University, Carbondale.

Pauketat, T. R., and T. E. Emerson, editors

1997b *Cahokia: Domination and Ideology in the Mississippian World*. University of Nebraska Press, Lincoln.

Pauketat, T. R., and N. H. Lopinot

1997 Cahokian Population Dynamics. In *Cahokia: Domination and Ideology in the Mississippian World*, edited by T. R. Pauketat and T. E. Emerson, 103–123. University of Nebraska Press, Lincoln.

Pauketat, T. R., M. Rees, and S. Pauketat

1996 Early Cahokia Project 1994 Excavations at Mound 49, Cahokia (11-S-34-2). Report submitted to the Illinois Historic Preservation Agency.

Payne, C.

1981 A Preliminary Investigation of Fort Walton Settlement Patterns in the Tallahassee Red Hills. *Southeastern Archaeological Conference Bulletin* 24:29–31.

1994 Mississippian Capitals: An Archaeological Investigation of Precolumbian Political Structure. Ph.D. dissertation, University of Florida, Gainesville.

Payne, C., and J. F. Scarry

1998 Town Structure at the Edge of the Mississippian World. In *Mississippian Towns and Sacred Places*, edited by R. B. Lewis and C. Stout, 22–48. University of Alabama Press, Tuscaloosa.

Paynter, R., and R. H. McGuire

1991 The Archaeology of Inequality: Material Culture, Domination, and Resistance. In *The Archaeology of Inequality*, edited by R. H. McGuire and R. Paynter, 1–27. Blackwell, Oxford.

Peacock, J. L.

1986 *The Anthropological Lens: Harsh Light, Soft Focus*. Cambridge University Press, Cambridge.

Pearson, M. P.

2000 *The Archaeology of Death and Burial*. Texas A and M Press, College Station.

Peebles, C. S.

1987 The Rise and Fall of the Mississippian in Western Alabama: The Moundville and Summerville Phases, A.D. 1000 to 1600. *Mississippi Archaeology* 22(1):1–31.

1991 Annalistes, Hermeneutics, and Positivists: Squaring Circles or Dissolving Problems. In *The Annales School and Archaeology*, edited by J. Bintliff, 108–124. New York University Press, New York.

Peebles, C. S., and S. M. Kus

1977 Some Archaeological Correlates of Ranked Societies. *American Antiquity* 42:421–448.

Penningroth, D.
1997   Slavery, Freedom, and Social Claims to Property among African Americans in Liberty County, Georgia, 1850–1880. *Journal of American History* 84:405–435.
Perdue, T.
1998   *Cherokee Women: Gender and Culture Change, 1700–1835.* University of Nebraska Press, Lincoln.
Peregrine, P. N.
1992   *Mississippian Evolution: A World-Systems Perspective.* Monographs in World Archaeology 9. Prehistory Press, Madison, Wis.
Pfaffenberger, B.
1992   Social Anthropology of Technology. *Annual Review of Anthropology* 21:491–516.
Phillips, J. L., and J. A. Brown, editors
1983   *Archaic Hunters and Gatherers in the American Midwest.* Academic Press, New York.
Phillips, P.
1970   *Archaeological Survey in the Lower Yazoo Basin, Mississippi, 1949–1955.* Peabody Museum of American Archaeology and Ethnology Papers 60. Harvard University, Cambridge.
Phillips, P., and J. A. Brown
1978   *Pre-Columbian Shell Engravings from the Craig Mound at Spiro, Oklahoma.* Part 1. Peabody Museum of American Archaeology and Ethnology, Harvard University, Cambridge.
Phillips, P., J. A. Ford, and J. B. Griffin
1951   *Archaeological Survey in the Lower Mississippi Alluvial Valley, 1940–47.* Peabody Museum of American Archaeology and Ethnology Papers 25. Harvard University, Cambridge.
Plog, F.
1973   Diachronic Anthropology. In *Research and Theory in Current Archaeology*, edited by C. L. Redman, 181–198. Wiley, New York.
1974   *The Study of Prehistoric Change.* Academic Press, New York.
Pohl, M.E.D., and J.M.D. Pohl
1994   Cycles of Conflict: Political Factionalism in the Maya Lowlands. In *Factional Competition and Political Development in the New World*, edited by E. M. Brumfiel and J. W. Fox, 138–157. Cambridge University Press, Cambridge.
Polanyi, K.
1957   The Economy as Instituted Process. In *Trade and Market in the Early Empires*, edited by K. Polanyi, C. Arensberg, and H. W. Pearson, 243–270. Free Press, New York.
Polhemus, R. R.
1990   Dallas Phase Architecture and Sociopolitical Structure. In *Lamar Archae-*

ology: Mississippian Chiefdoms of the Deep South, edited by J. M. Williams and G. D. Shapiro, 125–138. University of Alabama Press, Tuscaloosa.

Polhemus, R. R., editor

1987   *The Toqua Site: A Late Mississippian Dallas Phase Town.* Report of Investigations 39. Department of Anthropology, University of Tennessee, Knoxville.

Porter, J. W.

1964   *Thin Section Descriptions of Some Shell-Tempered Prehistoric Ceramics from the American Bottoms.* Lithic Laboratory, Research Report 7. Southern Illinois University, Carbondale.

Praetzellis, A., M. Praetzellis, and M. Brown III

1987   Artifacts as Symbols of Identity: An Example from Sacramento's Gold Rush Era Chinese Community. In *Living in Cities: Current Research in Urban Archaeology*, edited by E. Staski, 38–47. Arizona State University, Tuscon.

Preucel, R. W.

1991   The Philosophy of Archaeology. In *Processual and Postprocessual Archaeologies: Multiple Ways of Knowing the Past*, edited by R. W. Preucel, 17–29. Occasional Paper 10. Center for Archaeological Investigations, Southern Illinois University, Carbondale.

1995   The Postprocessual Condition. *Journal of Archaeological Research* 3:147–175.

Prezzano, S. C.

1997   Warfare, Women, and Households: The Development of Iroquois Culture. In *Women in Prehistory: North America and Mesoamerica*, edited by R. A. Joyce and C. Claassen, 88–99. University of Pennsylvania Press, Philadelphia.

Price, C. R., and J. E. Price

1980   An Inventory and Assessment of the Leo Anderson Collection of Archaeological and Historical Specimens. Center for Archaeological Research, Southwest Missouri State University, Springfield.

Purrington, B. L.

1983   Ancient Mountaineers: An Overview of the Prehistoric Archaeology of North Carolina's Western Mountain Region. In *The Prehistory of North Carolina: An Archaeological Symposium*, edited by M. A. Mathis and J. J. Crow, 83–166. North Carolina Division of Archives and History, Raleigh.

Raboteau, A. J.

1980   *Slave Religion: The Invisible Institution in the Antebellum South.* Oxford University Press, Oxford.

Ramenofsky, A. F.

1990   Loss of Innocence: Explanations of Differential Persistence in the Sixteenth-Century Southeast. In *Columbian Consequences*, vol. 2, *Archaeological and Historical Perspectives on the Spanish Borderlands East*, edited by D. H. Thomas, 31–48. Smithsonian Institution Press, Washington, D.C.

1998   Evolutionary Theory and the Native American Record of Artifact Replacement. In *Studies in Culture Contact: Interaction, Culture Change, and Archaeology*, edited by J. C. Cusick, 77–101. Occasional Paper 25. Center for Archaeological Investigations, Southern Illinois University, Carbondale.

Rands, R. L.
1956 Southern Cult Motifs on Walls-Pecan Point Pottery. *American Antiquity* 22:183–186.

Rapoport, A.
1969   *House Form and Culture*. Prentice-Hall, Englewood Cliffs, N.J.

Rathje, W. L.
1974   The Garbage Project: A New Way of Looking at the Problems of Archaeology. *Archaeology* 27:236–241.

Rawick, G. P., editor
1972   *Unwritten History of Slavery*. Social Science Institute, Fisk University, Nashville, 1945. Reprinted in *The American Slave: A Composite Autobiography*, vol. 18. Greenwood, Westport, Conn.

Redman, C. L.
1978   Multivariate Artifact Analysis: A Basis for Multidimensional Interpretations. In *Social Archaeology: Beyond Subsistence and Dating*, edited by C. L. Redman, M. J. Berman, E. V. Curtin, W. T. Langhorne, Jr., N. M. Versaggi, and J. C. Wanser, 159–192. Academic Press, New York.

Redmond, E. M.
1983   *A Fuego y Sangre: Early Zapotec Imperialism in the Cuicatlán Cañada, Oaxaca*. Museum of Anthropology Memoir 16. University of Michigan, Ann Arbor.

Redpath, J.
1968 *The Roving Editor; or, Talks with Slaves in the Southern States*. A. B. Burdick, New York, 1859. Reprint, Negro Universities Press, New York.

Rees, M. A.
1997   Coercion, Tribute, and Chiefly Authority: The Regional Development of Mississippian Political Culture. *Southeastern Archaeology* 16:113–133.

1998   From Moundville to Moon Lake: The Mississippian-Protohistoric Transition in West Central Alabama. Paper presented at the Fifty-fifth Annual Meeting of the Southeastern Archaeological Conference, Greenville, S.C.

1999   Mississippian Political Culture and the Decline of Moundville. Paper presented at the Sixty-fourth Annual Meeting of the Society for American Archaeology, Chicago.

Reichel-Dolmatoff, G.

1979   Desana Shamans Rock Crystals and the Hexagonal Universe. *Journal of Latin American Lore* 5:117–128.

1981   Things of Beauty Replete with Meaning—Metals and Crystals in Columbian Indian Cosmology. In *Sweat of the Sun, Tears of the Moon*, edited by H. Seligman, 17–33. Natural History Museum Alliance of Los Angeles County, Los Angeles.

Reidy, J. P.

1993   Obligation and Right: Patterns of Labor, Subsistence, and Exchange in the Cotton Belt of Georgia, 1790–1860. In *Cultivation and Culture: Labor and the Shaping of Slave Life in the Americas*, edited by I. Berlin and P. D. Morgan, 138–154. University of Virginia Press, Charlottesville.

Reitz, E. J.

1985   Spanish and Aboriginal Subsistence on the Atlantic Coastal Plain. *Southeastern Archaeology* 4(1):41–50.

1992   The Spanish Colonial Experience and Domestic Animals. *Historical Archaeology* 26:84–91.

1993   Evidence for Animal Use at the Missions of Spanish Florida. In *The Spanish Missions of La Florida*, edited by B. G. McEwan, 376–398. University Press of Florida, Gainesville.

Rice, P. M.

1987   *Pottery Analysis: A Sourcebook*. University of Chicago Press, Chicago.

Richards, C.

1996   Monuments as Landscape: Creating the Center of the World in Late Neolithic Orkney. *World Archaeology* 28:190–208.

Ridington, R.

1988   Knowledge, Power, and the Individual in Subarctic Hunting Societies. *American Anthropologist* 90:98–110.

Riggs, B. H.

1989   Interhousehold Variability among Nineteenth-Century Cherokee Artifact Assemblages. In *Households and Communities*, edited by S. Maceachern, D. Archer, and R. Garvin, 328–338. Archaeological Association of Calgary Proceedings 21. University of Calgary, Calgary.

Riley, T. J., G. R. Waltz, C. J. Bareis, A. C. Fortier, and K. E. Parker

1994   Accelerator Mass Spectrometry (AMS) Dates Confirm Early Zea Mays in the Mississippi River Valley. *American Antiquity* 59:490–497.

Robb, J. E.

1998   The Archaeology of Symbols. *Annual Review of Anthropology* 27:329–346.

Rodning, C. B.

1996   Gender and Social Institutions in Native Communities of the Appalachian Summit. Paper presented at the Fifty-third Annual Meeting of the Southeastern Archaeological Conference, Birmingham.

1999   Archaeological Perspectives on Gender and Women in Traditional Chero-
         kee Society. *Journal of Cherokee Studies* 20:3–27.
2001   Mortuary Ritual and Gender Ideology in Protohistoric Southwestern
         North Carolina. In *Archaeological Studies of Gender in the Southeastern
         United States*, edited by J. M. Eastman and C. B. Rodning, 77–100. Uni-
         versity Press of Florida, Gainesville.
Rogers, J. D.
1990   *Objects of Change: The Archaeology and History of Arikara Contact
         with Europeans.* Smithsonian Institution Press, Washington, D.C.
1991   Patterns of Change on the Western Margins of the Southeast, A.D. 600–
         900. In *Stability, Transformation, and Variation: The Late Woodland
         Southeast*, edited by M. S. Nassaney and C. R. Cobb, 221–248. Plenum
         Press, New York.
1996   Markers of Social Integration: The Development of Centralized Author-
         ity in the Spiro Region. In *Political Structure and Change in the Prehis-
         toric Southeastern United States*, edited by J. Scarry, 53–68. University
         Press of Florida, Gainesville.
Rolingson, M. A.
1982a   The Concept of Plum Bayou Culture. In *Emerging Patterns of Plum
         Bayou Culture*, edited by M. A. Rolingson, 87–93. Arkansas Archeologi-
         cal Survey Research Series 18. Fayetteville.
1990   The Toltec Mounds Site: A Ceremonial Center in the Arkansas River
         Lowland. In *The Mississippian Emergence*, edited by B. D. Smith, 27–49.
         Smithsonian Institution Press, Washington, D.C.
1998   *Toltec Mounds and Plum Bayou Culture: Mound D Excavations.* Arkan-
         sas Archeological Survey Research Series 54. Fayetteville.
Rolingson, M. A., editor
1982b   *Emerging Patterns of Plum Bayou Culture.* Arkansas Archeological Sur-
         vey Research Series 18. Fayetteville.
Rolland, V. L., and K. H. Ashley
2000   Beneath the Bell: A Study of Mission Period Colonoware from Three
         Spanish Missions in Northeast Florida. *Florida Anthropologist* 53:36–
         61.
Roseberry, W.
1988   Political Economy. *Annual Review of Anthropology* 17:161–185.
1989   *Anthropologies and Histories: Essays in Culture, History, and Political
         Economy.* Rutgers University Press, New Brunswick, N.J.
Rudolph, J. L.
1984   Earthlodges and Platform Mounds: Changing Public Architecture in the
         Southeastern United States. *Southeastern Archaeology* 3:33–45.
Ruhl, D. L., and K. Hoffman, editors
1997   Diversity and Social Identity in Colonial Spanish America: Native Ameri-
         can, African, and Hispanic Communities during the Middle Period. *His-
         torical Archaeology* 31:1.

Russell, A. E.
1997   Material Culture and African-American Spirituality at the Hermitage. *Historical Archaeology* 31:63–80.

Russo, M. A.
1992   Chronologies and Cultures of the St. Marys Region of Northeast Florida and Southeast Georgia. *Florida Anthropologist* 45:107–126.

Sabol, J. R.
1978   Trade and the Development of Local Status and Rank in Dallas Society. *Tennessee Anthropologist* 3:14–30.

Sackett, J. R.
1990   Style and Ethnicity in Archaeology: The Case for Isochrestism. In *The Uses of Style in Archaeology*, edited by M. Conkey and C. Hastorf, 32–43. Cambridge University Press, Cambridge.

Sahlins, M. S.
1981   *Historical Metaphors and Mythical Realities: Structure in the Early History of the Sandwich Islands Kingdom*. Association for Social Anthropology in Oceania, Special Publications 1. University of Michigan Press, Ann Arbor.

1985   *Islands of History*. University of Chicago Press, Chicago.

1994   Goodbye to Tristes Tropes: Ethnography in the Context of Modern World History. In *Assessing Cultural Anthropology*, edited by R. Borofsky, 377–393. McGraw-Hill, New York.

Saitta, D. J.
1994   Agency, Class, and Archaeological Interpretation. *Journal of Anthropological Archaeology* 13:201–227.

1997   Power, Labor, and the Dynamics of Change in Chacoan Political Economy. *American Antiquity* 62:7–26.

Sassaman, K. E.
1993   *Early Pottery in the Southeast: Tradition and Innovation in Cooking Technology*. University of Alabama Press, Tuscaloosa.

1997   Refining Soapstone Vessel Chronology in the Southeast. *Early Georgia* 25(1):1–20.

1998a   Crafting Cultural Identity in Hunter-Gatherer Economies. In *Craft and Social Identity*, edited by C. Costin and R. Wright, 93–107. Archeological Papers of the American Anthropological Association 8, Washington, D.C.

1998b   Distribution, Timing, and Technology of Early Pottery in the Southeastern United States. *Revista de Arqueologia Americana* 14:101–133.

2000   Agents of Change in Hunter-Gatherer Technology. In *Agency in Archaeology*, edited by M-A. Dobres and J. Robb, 148–168. Routledge, London.

n.d.   Articulating Hidden Histories of the Mid-Holocene Southeast. In *Archaeology of the Appalachian Highlands*, edited by L. Sullivan and S. Prezzano. University of Tennessee Press, Knoxville (in press).

Sassaman, K. E., K. Wilson, and F. Snow
1995   Putting the Ogeechee in Its Place. *Early Georgia* 23:20–40.

Sattler, R. A.
1995   Women's Status Among the Muskogee and Cherokee. In *Women and Power in Native America*, edited by L. F. Klein and L. A. Ackerman, 214–229. University of Oklahoma Press, Norman.

Saunders, R.
1992a Continuity and Change in Guale Indian Pottery, A.D. 1350–1702. Ph.D. dissertation, University of Florida, Gainesville.
1992b Guale Indian Pottery: A Georgia Legacy in Northeast Florida. *Florida Anthropologist* 45:139–147.
1993   Architecture of the Missions Santa María and Santa Catalina de Amelia. In *The Spanish Missions of La Florida*, edited by B. G. McEwan, 35–61. University Press of Florida, Gainesville.
1998   Forced Relocation, Power Relations, and Culture Contact in the Missions of La Florida. In *Studies in Culture Contact: Interaction, Culture Change, and Archaeology*, edited by J. G. Cusick, 402–429. Center for Archaeological Investigations, Southern Illinois University, Carbondale.
2000a *Stability and Change in Guale Indian Pottery, a.d. 1300–1702.* University of Alabama Press, Tuscaloosa.
2000b Pottery and Ethnicity: Yamassee Ceramics in Florida during the Mission Period. Paper presented at the Fifty-seventh Annual Meeting of the Southeastern Archaeological Conference, Macon, Ga.

Scarry, C. M.
1993a Agricultural Risk and the Development of the Moundville Chiefdom. In *Foraging and Farming in the Eastern Woodlands*, edited by C. M. Scarry, pp. 157–181. University Press of Florida, Gainesville.
1993b Plant Production and Procurement in Apalachee Province. In *The Spanish Missions of La Florida*, edited by B. G. McEwan, 357–375. University Press of Florida, Gainesville.
1993c Variability in Mississippian Crop Production Strategies. In *Foraging and Farming in the Eastern Woodlands*, edited by C. M. Scarry, 78–90. University Press of Florida, Gainesville.
1995   *Excavations on the Northwest Riverbank at Moundville: Investigations of a Moundville I Residential Area.* Report of Investigations 72. University of Alabama Museums, Office of Archaeological Services.

Scarry, C. M., editor
1993d *Foraging and Farming in the Eastern Woodlands.* University Press of Florida, Gainesville.

Scarry, C. M., and V. P. Steponaitis
1997   Between Farmstead and Center: The Natural and Social Landscape of Moundville. In *People, Plants, and Landscapes*, edited by K. J. Gremillion, 107–122. University of Alabama Press, Tuscaloosa.

Scarry, J. F.
1990   The Rise, Transformation, and Fall of Apalachee: A Case Study of Political Change in a Chiefly Society. In *Lamar Archaeology: Mississippian*

Chiefdoms in the Deep South, edited by J. M. Williams and G. D. Shapiro, 175–186. University of Alabama Press, Tuscaloosa.

1992   Political Offices and Political Structure: Ethnohistoric and Archaeological Perspectives on the Native Lords of Apalachee. In *Lords of the Southeast: Social Inequality and the Native Elites of Southeastern North America*, edited by A. Barker and T. R. Pauketat, 163–183. Archeological Papers of the American Anthropological Association 3, Washington, D.C.

1994   The Apalachee Chiefdom: A Mississippian Society on the Fringe of the Mississippian World. In *The Forgotten Centuries: Indians and Europeans in the American South, 1521–1704*, edited by C. Hudson and C. C. Tesser, 156–178. University of Georgia Press, Athens.

1995   Apalachee Homesteads: The Basal Social and Economic Units of a Mississippian Chiefdom. In *Mississippian Communities and Households*, edited by J. D. Rogers and B. D. Smith, 201–223. University of Alabama Press, Tuscaloosa.

1996a   Looking for and at Mississippian Political Change. In *Political Structure and Change in the Prehistoric Southeastern United States*, edited by J. F. Scarry, 3–11. University Press of Florida, Gainesville.

1996b   Stability and Change in the Apalachee Chiefdom. In *Political Structure and Change in the Prehistoric Southeastern United States*, edited by J. F. Scarry, 192–227. University Press of Florida, Gainesville.

1999   Elite Identities in Apalachee Province: The Construction of Identity and Cultural Change in a Mississippian Society. In *Material Symbols: Culture and Economy in Prehistory*, edited by J. Robb, 342–361. Occasional Paper 26. Center for Archaeological Investigations, Southern Illinois University, Carbondale.

Scarry, J. F., and C. M. Scarry

1995   Food Production and Food Storage in the Mississippian Lower Southeast. Paper presented at the Fifty-second Annual Southeastern Archaeological Conference, Knoxville.

Scarry, J. F., and M. D. Maxham

n.d.   Elite Actors in the Protohistoric: Elite Identities and Interaction with Europeans in the Apalachee and Powhatan Chiefdoms. In *Archaeology of the Protohistoric Period*, edited by C. Wesson and M. Rees.

Scarry, J. F., and B. G. McEwan

1995   Domestic Architecture in Apalachee Province: Apalachee and Spanish Residential Styles in the Late Prehistoric and Early Historic Period Southeast. *American Antiquity* 60:482–495.

Scarry, J. F., and M. F. Smith, Jr.

1988   Apalachee Settlement and Demographic Change. *LAMAR Briefs* 11:14–15.

Schiffer, M. B.

1976   *Behavioral Archaeology*. Academic Press, New York.

1996   Some Relationships Between Behavioral and Evolutionary Archaeologies. *American Antiquity* 61:643–662

Schmidt, P. R., and T. C. Patterson

1995   From Constructing to Making Alternative Histories. Introduction to *Making Alternative Histories*, edited by P. R. Schmidt and T. C. Patterson, 1–24. School of American Research Press, Santa Fe.

Schneider, J., and R. Rapp, editors

1995   *Articulating Hidden Histories: Exploring the Influence of Eric R. Wolf.* University of California Press, Berkeley.

Schrire, C.

1984   Wild Surmises on Savage Thoughts. In *Past and Present in Hunter-Gatherer Studies*, edited by C. Schrire, 1–25. Academic Press, Orlando.

Schroedl, G. F.

1989   The Overhill Cherokee Household and Village Patterns in the Eighteenth Century. In *Households and Communities*, edited by S. MacEachern, D. Archer, and R. Garvin, 350–360. Archaeological Association of Calgary Proceedings 21. University of Calgary, Calgary.

1998   Mississippian Towns in the Eastern Tennessee Valley. In *Mississippian Towns and Sacred Spaces: Searching for an Architectural Grammar*, edited by R. B. Lewis and C. B. Stout, 64–92. University of Alabama Press, Tuscaloosa.

Schroedl, G. F., editor

1986   *Overhill Cherokee Archaeology at Chota-Tanasee*. Report of Investigations 38. Department of Anthropology, University of Tennessee, Knoxville.

Schuyler, R. L., editor

1978   *Historical Archaeology: A Guide to Substantive and Theoretical Contributions*. Baywood, Farmingdale, New York.

Scott, G., and R. R. Polhemus

1987   Mortuary Patterning. In *The Toqua Site: A Late Mississippian Dallas Phase Town*, edited by R. R. Polhemus, 378–431. Report of Investigations 41. Department of Anthropology, University of Tennessee, Knoxville.

Scott, J. C.

1985   *Weapons of the Weak: Everyday Forms of Peasant Resistance*. Yale University Press, New Haven.

1990   *Domination and the Arts of Resistance: Hidden Transcripts*. Yale University Press, New Haven.

Sears, W. H.

1955   Creek and Cherokee Cultures in the Eighteenth Century. *American Antiquity* 21:143–149.

Seeman, M. F.
1995   When Words Are Not Enough: Hopewell Interregionalism and the Use of Material Symbols at the GE Mound. In *Native American Interactions: Multiscalar Analyses and Interpretations in the Eastern Woodlands*, edited by M. S. Nassaney and K. E. Sassaman, 122–143. University of Tennessee Press, Knoxville.

Seeman, M. F., and W. S. Dancey
2000   The Late Woodland Period in Southern Ohio: Basic Issues and Prospects. In *Late Woodland Societies: Tradition and Transformation in the Midcontinent*, edited by T. E. Emerson, D. McElrath, and A. C. Fortier. University of Nebraska Press, Lincoln.

Service, E. R.
1962   *Primitive Social Organization: An Evolutionary Perspective*. Random House, New York.
1975   *Origins of the State and Civilization: The Process of Cultural Evolution*. Norton, New York.

Shanks, M., and I. Hodder
1995   Processual, Postprocessual, and Interpretive Archaeologies. In *Interpreting Archaeology: Finding Meaning in the Past*, edited by I. Hodder, M. Shanks, A. Alexandri, V. Buchli, J. Carman, J. Last, and G. Lucas, 3–29. Routledge, London.

Shanks, M., and C. Tilley
1987   *Re-Constructing Archaeology*. Cambridge University Press, Cambridge.

Shannon, T. J.
1996   Dressing for Success on the Mohawk Frontier: Hendrick, William Johnson, and the Indian Fashion. *William and Mary Quarterly* 53:13–42.

Shapiro, G.
1987   *Archaeology at San Luis: Broad-scale Testing, 1984–85*. Florida Archaeology 3. Florida Bureau of Archaeological Research, Tallahassee.

Shapiro, G., and B. G. McEwan
1992   *Archaeology at San Luis: The Apalachee Council House*. Florida Archaeology 6, part 1. Florida Bureau of Archaeological Research, Tallahassee.

Shennan, S. J.
1989   Archaeological Approaches to Cultural Identities. Introduction to *Archaeological Approaches to Cultural Identity*, edited by S. Shennan, 1–32. Routledge, London.
1991   Tradition, Rationality, and Cultural Transmission. In *Processual and Postprocessual Archaeologies: Multiple Ways of Knowing the Past*, edited by R. Preucel, 197–210. Occasional Papers 10. Center for Archaeological Investigations, Southern Illinois University at Carbondale.
1993   After Social Evolution: A New Archaeological Agenda? In *Archaeological Theory: Who Sets the Agenda?* edited by N. Yoffee and A. Sherratt, 53–59. Cambridge University Press, Cambridge.

Sherratt, A.
1990   The Genesis of Megaliths: Monumentality, Ethnicity, and Social Complexity in Neolithic Northwest Europe. *World Archaeology* 22:147–167.

Shils, E. A.
1981   *Tradition.* University of Chicago Press, Chicago.

Singleton, T. A.
1998   Cultural Interaction and African American Identity in Plantation Archaeology. In *Studies in Culture Contact: Interaction, Culture Change, and Archaeology,* edited by J. Cusick, 172–188. Center for Archaeological Investigations, Southern Illinois University.

Singleton, T. A., editor
1999   *'I Too Am America': Archaeological Studies of African American Life.* University Press of Virginia, Charlottesville.

Smedley, A.
1993   *Race in North America: Origin and Evolution of a Worldview.* Westview, Boulder, Colo.

Smith, B. D.
1984   Mississippian Expansion: Tracing the Historical Development of an Explanatory Model. *Southeastern Archaeology* 3:13–32.

1986   The Archaeology of the Southeastern United States: From Dalton to de Soto, 10,500–500 B.P. In *Advances in World Archaeology,* vol. 5, edited by F. Wendorf and A. E. Close, 1–92. Academic Press, Orlando.

1989   Origins of Agriculture in Eastern North America. *Science* 246:1566–1571.

1990   Introduction to *The Mississippian Emergence,* edited by B. D. Smith, 1–8. Smithsonian Institution Press, Washington, D.C.

1992   *Rivers of Change: Essays on Early Agriculture in Eastern North America.* Smithsonian Institution Press, Washington, D.C.

Smith, B. W.
1991   The Late Archaic–Poverty Point Trade Network. In *The Poverty Point Culture: Local Manifestations, Subsistence Practices, and Trade Networks,* edited by K. M. Byrd, 173–180. Geoscience and Man 29.

Smith, C.
1996   Analysis of Plant Remains from Mound S at the Toltec Mounds Site. *Arkansas Archeologist* 35:51–76.

Smith, H. G.
1951   A Spanish Mission Site in Jefferson County, Florida. In *Here They Once Stood: The Tragic End of the Apalachee Missions,* by M. F. Boyd, H. G. Smith, and J. W. Griffin, 104–136. University of Florida Press, Gainesville.

Smith, M. F., Jr., and J. F. Scarry
1988   Apalachee Settlement Distribution: The View from the Florida Master Site File. *Florida Anthropologist* 41:351–364.

322 | Bibliography

Smith, M. T.

Smith, M. T.
1987   *Archaeology of Aboriginal Culture Change in the Interior Southeast: Depopulation during the Early Historic Period.* University of Florida Press, Gainesville.
1992   *Historic Period Indian Archaeology of Northern Georgia.* Laboratory of Archaeology Report 30. University of Georgia, Athens.
Smith, M. T., and D. J. Hally
1992   Chiefly Behavior: Evidence from Sixteenth-Century Spanish Accounts. In *Lords of the Southeast: Social Inequality and the Native Elites of Southeastern North America*, edited by A. W. Barker and T. R. Pauketat, 99–109. Archeological Papers of the American Anthropological Association 3, Washington, D.C.
Smith, M. T., and J. M. Williams
1990   Piedmont Oconee River. In *Lamar Archaeology: Mississippian Chiefdoms in the Deep South*, edited by J. M. Williams and G. D. Shapiro, 60–63. University of Alabama Press, Tuscaloosa.
1994   Mississippian Mound Refuse Disposal Patterns and Implications for Archaeological Research. *Southeastern Archaeology* 13:27–35.
Smith, S. D., editor
1976   *An Archaeological and Historical Assessment of the First Hermitage.* Research Series 2. Division of Archaeology, Tennessee Department of Conservation, Nashville.
Smith, S. D., F. W. Brigance, E. Breitburg, S. D. Cox, and M. Martin
1977   Results of the 1976 Season of the Hermitage Archaeology Project. Report prepared for the Ladies' Hermitage Association and the Tennessee American Revolution Bicentennial Commission, Nashville.
Sobel, M.
1988   *Tabelin On: The Slave Journey to an Afro-Baptist Faith.* Princeton University Press, Princeton.
Solís, F. G. J.
1931   Diary of a visit of inspection of the Texas missions made by Fray Gaspar José de Solís in the year 1767–1768. *Southwestern Historical Quarterly* 35:28–76.
Spain, D.
1992   *Gendered Spaces.* University of North Carolina Press, Chapel Hill.
Spector, J. D.
1993   *What This Awl Means: Feminist Archaeology at a Wahpeton Dakota Village.* Minnesota Historical Society Press, Saint Paul.
Spencer, C. S.
1997   Evolutionary Approaches in Archaeology. *Journal of Archaeological Research* 5:209–264.
Spencer, N.
1995   Multidimensional Group Definition in the Landscape of Rural Greece. In

Time, Tradition, and Society in Greek Archaeology: Bridging the "Great Divide," edited by Nigel Spencer, 28–42. Routledge, London.

Spicer, E. H.

1961   Types of Contact and Processes of Change. In *Perspectives in American Indian Culture Change,* edited by E. H. Spicer, 517–544. University of Chicago Press, Chicago.

1962   *Cycles of Conquest: The Impact of Spain, Mexico, and the United States on the Indians of the Southwest, 1533–1960.* University of Arizona Press, Tucson.

Spielmann, K. A.

1995   Glimpses of Gender in the Prehistoric Southwest. *Journal of Anthropological Research* 51:91–102.

1998   Ritual Craft-Specialists in Middle Range Societies. In *Craft and Social Identity,* edited by C. L. Costin and R. P. Wright, 153–159. Anthropological Papers of the American Anthropological Association 8, Washington, D.C.

Stahl, A. B.

1999   Pipes, Beads, Bottles, and Cloth: Embodying Colonial Change in Banda, Ghana. Paper presented at the Society for American Archaeology Annual Meeting, Chicago.

2001   *Making History in Banda: Anthropological Visions of Africa's Past.* Cambridge University Press, Cambridge (in press).

Stampp, K. M.

1956   *The Peculiar Institution: Slavery in the Ante-Bellum South.* Vintage Books, New York.

Stanyard, W. F.

1997   *The Big Haynes Reservoir Archaeological Project: A Perspective on the Native American History of North-Central Georgia between 8,000b.c. and a.d. 1838.* TRC Garrow and Associates, Inc., Atlanta.

Stark, M. T.

1998   Technical Choices and Social Boundaries in Material Culture Patterning: An Introduction. In *The Archaeology of Social Boundaries,* edited by M. T. Stark, 1–11. Smithsonian Institution Press, Washington.

1999   Social Dimensions of Technical Choice in Kalinga Ceramic Traditions. In *Material Meanings: Critical Approaches to the Interpretation of Material Culture,* edited by E. S. Chilton, 24–43. University of Utah Press, Salt Lake City.

Stark, M. T., M. D. Elson, and J. J. Clark

1998   Social Boundaries and Technical Choices in Tonto Basin Prehistory. In *The Archaeology of Social Boundaries,* edited by M. T. Stark, 208–231. Smithsonian Institution Press, Washington, D.C.

Stein, G.

1998   Diasporas, Colonies, and World Systems: Rethinking the Archaeology of

Inter-Regional Interaction. Distinguished Lecture, Archaeology Division, Ninety-seventh Annual Meeting of the American Anthropological Association, Philadelphia.

Steponaitis, V. P.

1978   Location Theory and Complex Chiefdoms: A Mississippian Example. In *Mississippian Settlement Patterns*, edited by B. D. Smith, 417–453. Academic Press, New York.

1983   *Ceramics, Chronology, and Community Patterns: An Archaeological Study at Moundville.* Academic Press, New York.

1986   Prehistoric Archaeology in the Southeastern United States, 1970–1985. *Annual Review of Anthropology* 15:363–404.

1991   Contrasting Patterns of Mississippian Development. In *Chiefdoms: Power, Economy, and Ideology*, edited by T. Earle, 193–228. Cambridge University Press, Cambridge.

1998   Population Trends at Moundville. In *Archaeology of the Moundville Chiefdom*, edited by V. J. Knight, Jr., and V. P. Steponaitis, 26–43. Smithsonian Institution Press, Washington, D.C.

Sterling, J.

1969 *Letters from the Slave States, 1857.* Reprint, Kraus Reprint Company, New York.

Stern, P.

1998   Marginals and Acculturation in Frontier Society. In *New Views of Borderlands History*, edited by R. H. Jackson, 157–188. University of New Mexico Press, Albuquerque.

Steward, J. H.

1955   *Theory of Culture Change: The Methodology of Multilinear Evolution.* University of Illinois Press, Urbana.

Stewart, C., and R. Shaw

1994   *Syncretism/Anti-Syncretism: The Politics of Religious Synthesis.* Routledge, London.

Stewart, M.

1997   *The Time of the Gypsies.* Westview, Boulder.

Stewart-Abernathy, J.

1982   Ceramic Studies at the Toltec Mounds Site: Basis for a Tentative Cultural Sequence. In *Emerging Patterns of Plum Bayou Culture*, edited by M. A. Rolingson, 44–53. Arkansas Archeological Survey Research Series 18. Fayetteville.

Stoianovich, T.

1976   *French Historical Method: The Annales Paradigm.* Cornell University Press, Ithaca.

Stoler, A. L.

1991   Carnal Knowledge, Imperial Power: Gender, Race, and Morality in Colonial Asia. In *Gender at the Crossroads of Knowledge*, edited by M. di Leonardo, 51–101. University of California Press, Berkeley.

1997   Sexual Affronts and Racial Frontiers: European Identities and the Colonial Politics of Exclusion in Colonial Southeast Asia. In *Tensions of Empire: Colonial Cultures in a Bourgeois World*, edited by F. Cooper and A. L. Stoler, 514–551. University of California Press, Berkeley.

Stoler, A. L., and F. Cooper
1997   Between Metropole and Colony: Rethinking a Research Agenda. In *Tensions of Empire: Colonial Cultures in a Bourgeois World*, edited by F. Cooper and A. L. Stoler, 1–58. University of California Press, Berkeley.

Storey, R.
1991   Bioanthropological Studies of the Lake Jackson Elite. Paper presented at the Forty-eighth Annual Southeastern Archaeological Conference, Jackson.

Struever, S.
1964   The Hopewell Interaction Sphere in Riverine–Western Great Lakes Culture History. In *Hopewellian Studies*, edited by J. Caldwell and R. L. Hall, 85–106. Scientific Papers 12. Illinois State Museum, Springfield.
1965   Middle Woodland Culture History in the Great Lakes Riverine Area. *American Antiquity* 31:211–223.
1968   A Re-Examination of Hopewell in Eastern North America. Ph.D. dissertation, University of Chicago.

Stuckey, S.
1987   *Slave Culture: Nationalist Theory and the Foundations of Black America.* Oxford University Press, New York.

Sturtevant, W. C.
1966   Anthropology, History, and Ethnohistory. *Ethnohistory* 13:1–51.

Sued Badillo, J.
1996   The Theme of the Indigenous in the National Projects of the Hispanic Caribbean. In *Making Alternative Histories: The Practice of Archaeology in Non-Western Settings*, edited by P. R. Schmidt and T. C. Patterson, 25–46. University of Washington Press, Seattle.

Sullivan, L. P.
1987   The Mouse Creek Phase Household. *Southeastern Archaeology* 6:16–29.
1989   Household, Community, and Society: An Analysis of Mouse Creek Settlements. In *Households and Communities*, edited by S. Maceachern, D. Archer, and R. Garvin, 317–327. Archaeological Association of Calgary Proceedings 21. University of Calgary, Calgary.
1995   Mississippian Community and Household Organization in Eastern Tennessee. In *Mississippian Communities and Households*, edited by J. D. Rogers and B. D. Smith, 99–123. University of Alabama Press, Tuscaloosa.
2001   Those Men in the Mounds: Gender, Politics, and Mortuary Practices in Late Prehistoric Eastern Tennessee. In *Archaeological Studies of Gender in the Southeastern United States*, edited by J. M. Eastman and C. B. Rodning, 101–126. University Press of Florida, Gainesville.

Swanton, J. R.
1911   *Indian Tribes of the Lower Mississippi Valley and Adjacent Coast of Mexico*. Bulletin 43. Bureau of American Ethnology, Smithsonian Institution, Washington, D.C.
1922   *Early History of the Creek Indians and Their Neighbors*. Bureau of American Ethnology, Washington, D.C.
1928   *Social Organization and Social Usages of the Indians of the Creek Confederacy*. Forty-second Annual Report of the Bureau of American Ethnology, 31–726. Smithsonian Institution, Washington, D.C.
1946   *The Indians of the Southeastern United States*. Bulletin 137. Bureau of American Ethnology, Smithsonian Institution, Washington D.C.
Swartz, M. J.
1958   History and Science in Anthropology. *Philosophy of Science* 25:59–70.
Swartz, M. J., editor
1968   *Local-Level Politics: Social and Cultural Perspectives*. Aldine, Chicago.
Swartz, M. J., V. W. Turner, and A. Tuden
1966a   Introduction to *Political Anthropology*, edited by M. J. Swartz, V. W. Turner, and A. Tuden, 1–41. Aldine, Chicago.
Swartz, M. J., V. W. Turner, and A. Tuden, editors
1966b   *Political Anthropology*. Aldine, Chicago.
Sztompka, P.
1991   *Society in Action: The Theory of Social Becoming*. University of Chicago Press, Chicago.
Tainter, J. A.
1975   Social Inference and Mortuary Practices: An Experiment in Numerical Classification. *World Archaeology* 7:2–15.
1978   Mortuary Practices and the Study of Prehistoric Social Systems. *Advances in Archaeological Method and Theory* 1:105–141.
Taylor, W. W.
1948   *A Study of Archaeology*. American Anthropological Association Memoir 69, Washington, D.C.
Thomas, B. W.
1995   Community among Enslaved African Americans on the Hermitage Plantation, 1820s–1850s. Ph.D. dissertation, State University of New York at Binghamton, Binghamton.
1998   Power and Community: The Archaeology of Slavery at the Hermitage Plantation. *American Antiquity* 63:531–551.
Thomas, B. W., and L. Thomas
n.d.   Gender and the Presentation of Self: An Example from the Hermitage. In *Engendering African-American Archaeology*, edited by A. L. Young.
Thomas, B. W., L. McKee, and J. Bartlett
1995   Summary Report on the 1995 Hermitage Field Quarter Excavation. Ms. on file, Ladies' Hermitage Association, Hermitage, Tenn.

Thomas, D. H.
1993   *Historic Indian Period Archaeology of the Georgia Coastal Zone.* Georgia Archaeological Research Design Paper 8, Laboratory of Archaeology Series, Report 31. University of Georgia, Athens.

Thomas, J.
1990   Monuments from the Inside: The Case of the Irish Megalithic Tombs. *World Archaeology* 22:168–178.

1996   *Time, Culture, and Identity: An Interpretive Archaeology.* Routledge, New York.

2000   Reconfiguring the Social, Reconfiguring the Material. In *Social Theory in Archaeology*, edited by M. B. Schiffer, 143–155. University of Utah Press, Salt Lake City.

Thomas, L. A.
2000   Images of Women in Native American Iconography. In *Interpretations of Native North American Life: Material Contributions to Ethnohistory*, edited by M. S. Nassaney and E. S. Johnson, 321–357. University Press of Florida, Gainesville

Thomas, N.
1989   *Out of Time: History and Evolution in Anthropological Discourse.* Cambridge University Press, Cambridge.

Thompson, R. H.
1956   An Archaeological Approach to the Study of Cultural Stability. In *Seminars in Archaeology: 1955*, edited by R. Wauchope, 31–58. Society for American Archaeology Memoir 11, Salt Lake City.

Tilley, C.
1989   Interpreting Material Culture. In *The Meanings of Things: Material Culture and Symbolic Expression*, edited by I. Hodder, 185–194. Unwin-Hyman, Boston.

1994   *A Phenomenology of Landscape: Places, Paths, and Monuments.* Berg, Oxford.

1996   The Powers of Rocks: Topography and Monument Construction on Bodmin Moor. *World Archaeology* 28:161–176.

Todorov, T.
1984   *The Conquest of America: The Question of the Other.* Harper and Row, New York.

Toren, C.
1999   *Mind Materiality and History: Explorations in Fijian Ethnography.* Routledge, London.

Trigger, B. G.
1976   *The Children of Aetensic: A History of the Huron Peoples to 1660.* McGill-Queen's University Press, Montreal.

1978   Cultural Unity and Diversity. In *Handbook of North American Indians*, vol. 15, *Northeast*, edited by B. G. Trigger, 798–804. Smithsonian Institution Press, Washington, D.C.

1980   Archaeology and the Image of the American Indian. *American Antiquity* 45:662–676.

1982   Ethnohistory: Problems and Prospects. *Ethnohistory* 29:1–19.

1984   Alternative Archaeologies: Nationalist, Colonialist, and Imperialist. *Man* 19:355–370.

1985   *Natives and Newcomers.* McGill-Queen's University Press, Montreal.

1986   Ethnohistory: The Unfinished Edifice. *Ethnohistory* 33:253–267.

1989a   *A History of Archaeological Thought.* Cambridge University Press, Cambridge.

1989b   History and Contemporary American Archaeology: A Critical Analysis. In *Archaeological Thought in America*, edited by C. C. Lamberg-Karlovsky, 19–34. Cambridge University Press, Cambridge.

1990a   Maintaining Economic Equality in Opposition to Complexity: An Iroquoian Case Study. In *The Evolution of Political Systems: Sociopolitics in Small-Scale Sedentary Societies*, edited by S. Upham, 119–149. Cambridge University Press, Cambridge.

1990b   Monumental Architecture: A Thermodynamic Explanation of Symbolic Behaviour. *World Archaeology* 22:119–131.

1991   Distinguished Lecture in Archaeology: Constraint and Freedom—A New Synthesis for Archaeological Explanation. *American Anthropologist* 93:551–569.

Trocolli, R.

1999   Women Leaders in Native North American Societies: Invisible Women of Power. In *Manifesting Power: Gender and the Interpretation of Power in Archaeology*, edited by T. L. Sweely, 49–61. Routledge, London.

Trouillot, M.

1995   *Silencing the Past: Power and the Production of History.* Beacon Press, Boston.

Turnbaugh, W. A.

1993   Assessing the Significance of European Goods in Seventeenth-Century Narragansett Society. In *Ethnohistory and Archaeology: Approaches to Postcontact Change in the Americas*, edited by J. D. Rogers and S. M. Wilson, 133–160. Plenum Press, New York.

Turnbull, C.

1961   *The Forest People.* Simon and Schuster, New York.

Turner, V.

1967   *The Forest of Symbols.* Cornell University Press, Ithaca.

Ulin, R. C.

1996   *Vintages and Traditions: An Ethnohistory of Southwest French Wine Cooperatives.* Smithsonian Institution Press, Washington, D.C.

Upton, D.

1996   Ethnicity, Authenticity, and Invented Traditions. *Historical Archaeology* 30:1–7.

Van den Berghe, P. L.
1981   *The Ethnic Phenomenon*. Elsevier, New York.
VanDerwarker, A. M.
1999   Feasting and Status at the Toqua Site. *Southeastern Archaeology* 18:24–34.
VanPool, C. S., and T. L. VanPool
1999   The Scientific Nature of Postprocessualism. *American Antiquity* 64:33–53.
Vernon, R.
1988   Seventeenth-Century Apalachee Colono-ware as a Reflection of Demography, Economics, and Acculturation. *Historical Archaeology* 22:76–82.
Vernon, R., and A. Cordell
1991   A Distributional and Technological Study of Apalachee Colono-ware from San Luis de Talimali. *Florida Anthropologist* 44:316–330.
1993   A Distributional and Technological Study of Apalachee Colono-ware from San Luis de Talimali. In *The Spanish Missions of La Florida*, edited by B. G. McEwan, pp. 418–442. University Press of Florida, Gainesville.
Vernon, R., and B. G. McEwan
1990   *Investigations in the Church Complex and Spanish Village at San Luis.* Florida Archaeological Reports 18. Florida Bureau of Archaeological Research, Tallahassee.
Vincent, J.
1990   *Anthropology and Politics: Visions, Traditions, and Trends.* University of Arizona Press, Tucson.
Vogel, J. O.
1975   Trends in Cahokia Ceramics: Preliminary Study of the Collections from Tracts 15A and 15B. In *Perspectives in Cahokia Archaeology*, 32–125. Illinois Archaeological Survey Bulletin 10. Urbana.
Voget, F. W.
1973   History of Cultural Anthropology. In *Handbook of Social and Cultural Anthropology*, edited by J. J. Honigmann, 1–88. Rand McNally, Chicago.
Walthall, J. A.
1980   *Prehistoric Indians of the Southeast: Archaeology of Alabama and the Middle South*. University of Alabama Press, Tuscaloosa.
Ward, H. T., and R.P.S. Davis, Jr.
1999   *Time Before History: The Archaeology of North Carolina.* University of North Carolina Press, Chapel Hill.
Waring, A. J.
1968   The Southern Cult and Muskogean Ceremonial. In *The Waring Papers: The Collected Works of Antonio J. Waring*, edited by S. Williams, 30–69. Peabody Museum of American Archaeology and Ethnology Papers 58. Harvard University, Cambridge.

Waring, A. J., and P. Holder
1945   A Prehistoric Ceremonial Complex in the Southeastern United States. *American Anthropologist* 47:1–34.
Waselkov, G. A.
1989   Seventeenth-Century Trade in the Colonial Southeast. *Southeastern Archaeology* 8:117–133.
1993   Historic Creek Indian Responses to European Trade and the Rise of Political Factions. In *Ethnohistory and Archaeology: Approaches to Postcontact Change in the Americas*, edited by J. D. Rogers and S. M. Wilson. Plenum Press, New York.
Watson, P. J.
1985   The Impact of Early Horticulture in the Uplands Drainages of the Midwest and Midsouth. In *Prehistoric Food Production in North America*, edited by R. I. Ford, 205–243, Anthropological Paper 75. Museum of Anthropology, University of Michigan, Ann Arbor.
1988   Prehistoric Gardening and Agriculture in the Midwest and Midsouth. In *Interpretations of Culture Change in the Eastern Woodlands during the Late Woodland Period*, edited by R. W. Yerkes, 39–67. Occasional Papers in Anthropology 3. Ohio State University, Columbus.
1991   A Parochial Primer: The New Dissonance as Seen from the Midcontinental United States. In *Processual and Postprocessual Archaeologies: Multiple Ways of Knowing the Past*, edited by R. Preucel, 197–210. Occasional Papers 10. Center for Archaeological Investigations, Southern Illinois University, Carbondale.
Watson, P. J., S. A. LeBlanc, and C. L. Redman
1971   *Explanation in Archaeology: An Explicitly Scientific Approach*. Columbia University Press, New York.
Weik, T.
1997   The Archaeology of Maroon Societies in the Americas: Resistance, Cultural Continuity, and Transformation in the African Diaspora. *Historical Archaeology* 31:81–92.
Weissner, P.
1983   Style and Social Information in Kalahari San Projectile Points. *American Antiquity* 48:253–276.
1985   Style or Isochrestic Variation? A Reply to Sackett. *American Antiquity* 50:160–166.
Welch, P. D.
1991   *Moundville's Economy*. University of Alabama Press, Tuscaloosa.
1996   Control over Goods and the Political Stability of the Moundville Chiefdom. In *Political Structure and Change in the Prehistoric Southeastern United States*, edited by J. F. Scarry, 69–91. University Press of Florida, Gainesville.
1998   Outlying Sites Within the Moundville Chiefdom. In *Archaeology of the Moundville Chiefdom*, edited by V. J. Knight, Jr., and V. P. Steponaitis, 133–166. Smithsonian Institution Press, Washington, D.C.

Welch, P. D., and C. M. Scarry
1995   Status-related Variation in Foodways in the Moundville Chiefdom. *American Antiquity* 60:397–419.

Wenhold, L. L.
1936   *A 17th Century Letter of Gabriel Diaz Vara Calderón, Bishop of Cuba, Describing the Indians and Indian Missions of Florida.* Smithsonian Miscellaneous Collections 95(16). Government Printing Office, Washington, D.C.

Wesson, C. B.
1997   Households and Hegemony: An Analysis of Historic Creek Culture Change. Ph.D. dissertation, University of Illinois at Urbana-Champaign.
1998   Mississippian Sacred Landscapes: The View from Alabama. In *Mississippian Towns and Sacred Spaces: Searching for an Architectural Grammar,* edited by R. B. Lewis and C. B. Stout, 93–122. University of Alabama Press, Tuscaloosa.
1999   Chiefly Power and Food Storage in Southeastern North America. *World Archaeology* 31:145–164.

Wetherell, N.
1982   Cross-Cultural Studies of Minimal Groups: Implications for the Social Theory of Intergroup Relations. In *Social Identity and Intergroup Relations,* edited by H. Tajfel, 207–240. Cambridge University Press, Cambridge.

Whelan, M. K.
1995   Beyond Hearth and Home on the Range: Feminist Approaches to Plains Archaeology. In *Beyond Subsistence: Plains Archaeology and the Postprocessual Critique,* edited by P. Duke and M. C. Wilson, 46–65. University of Alabama Press, Tuscaloosa.

White, J. R.
1975   Historic Contact Sites as Laboratories for the Study of Culture Change. *The Conference on Historic Site Archaeology Papers* 9:153–163.

White, L.
1959   *The Evolution of Culture: The Development of Civilization to the Fall of Rome.* McGraw-Hill, New York.

White, N. M.
1999   Reflections and Speculations on Putting Women into Southeastern Archaeology. In *Grit-Tempered: Early Women Archaeologists in the Southeastern United States,* edited by N. M. White, L. P. Sullivan, and R. A. Marrinan, 315–336. University Press of Florida, Gainesville.

Whitehead, N.
1992   Tribes Make States and States Make Tribes: Warfare and the Creation of Colonial Trade and States in Northeastern South America. In *War in the Tribal Zone: Expanding States and Indigenous Warfare,* edited by R. B. Ferguson and N. L. Whitehead, 127–150. School of American Research Press, Santa Fe.

Widmer, R. J.
1988   *The Evolution of the Calusa.* University of Alabama Press, Tuscaloosa.
Wiessner, P.
1990   Is There a Unity to Style? In *The Uses of Style in Archaeology,* edited by M. Conkey and C. Hastorf, 105–112. Cambridge University Press, Cambridge.
Wilk, R. R., and W. L. Rathje
1982   Household Archaeology. *American Behavioral Scientist* 25(6):617–639.
Wilk, R. R., and L. R. Wilk
1982   Household Archaeology. *American Behavioral Scientist* 25:617–639.
Willey, G. R.
1945   Horizon Styles and Pottery Traditions in Peruvian Archaeology. *American Antiquity* 11:49–56.
1966   *An Introduction to American Archaeology,* vol. 1, *North and South America.* Prentice-Hall, New York.
1993   *A History of American Archaeology.* 3d edition. Freeman, New York.
Willey, G. R., and P. Phillips
1958   *Method and Theory in American Archaeology.* University of Chicago Press, Chicago.
Willey, G. R., and J. A. Sabloff
1980   *A History of American Archaeology.* 2d edition. Freeman, San Franciso.
Williams, J. A.
1989   Lithic Assemblage. In *The Holding Site: A Hopewell Community in the American Bottom,* by A. C. Fortier, T. O. Maher, J. A. Williams, M. C. Meinkoth, K. E. Parker, and L. S. Kelly, 319–428. *American Bottom Archaeology FAI Site Reports,* vol. 19. University of Illinois Press, Urbana.
1993   Meridian Hills: An Upland Holding Phase Middle Woodland Habitation Site. In *Highways to the Past: Essays on Illinois Archaeology in Honor of Charles J. Bareis,* edited by T. E. Emerson, A. C. Fortier, and D. L. McElrath. *Illinois Archaeology* 5:193–200.
Williams, M.
1990   Middle Ocmulgee River. In *Lamar Archaeology: Mississippian Chiefdoms in the Deep South,* edited by M. Williams and G. D. Shapiro, 63–64. University of Alabama Press, Tuscaloosa.
Williams, M., and G. Shapiro
1990b   Paired Towns. In *Lamar Archaeology: Mississippian Chiefdoms in the Deep South,* edited by M. Williams and G. D. Shapiro, 163–174. University of Alabama Press, Tuscaloosa.
1996   Mississippian Political Dynamics in the Oconee Valley, Georgia. In *Political Structure and Change in the Late Prehistoric Southeastern United States,* edited by J. F. Scarry, 128–149. University Press of Florida, Gainesville.

Williams, M., and G. D. Shapiro, editors
1990a   *Lamar Archaeology: Mississippian Chiefdoms in the Deep South*. University of Alabama Press, Tuscaloosa.

Williams, R.
1961   *The Long Revolution*. Columbia University Press, New York.
1977   *Marxism and Literature*. Oxford University Press, Oxford.

Williams, S., and J. P. Brain
1983   *Excavations at the Lake George Site, Yazoo County, Mississippi, 1958–1960*. Peabody Museum of American Archaeology and Ethnology Papers 74. Harvard University, Cambridge.

Willoughby, C. C.
1932   History and Symbolism of the Muskogeans. In *Etowah Papers*, edited by W. K. Moorehead, 7–67. Yale University Press, New Haven.

Wilmsen, E.
1989   *Land Filled with Flies: A Political Economy of the Kalahari*. University of Chicago Press, Chicago.
1995   Who Were the Bushmen? Historical Process in the Creation of an Ethnic Construct. In *Articulating Hidden Histories: Exploring the Influence of Eric R. Wolf*, edited by J. Schneider and R. Rapp, 308–321. University of California Press, Berkeley.

Wilson, H. H.
1986   Burials from the Warren Wilson Site: Some Biological and Behavioral Considerations. In *The Conference on Cherokee Prehistory*, compiled by D. G. Moore, 42–72. Warren Wilson College, Swannanoa, N.C.

Wilson, S. M., and J. D. Rogers
1993   Historical Dynamics in the Contact Era. In *Ethnohistory and Archaeology: Approaches to Postcontact Change in the Americas*, edited by J. D. Rogers and S. M. Wilson, 3–15. Plenum Press, New York.

Winterhalder, B., and E. Alden Smith
1981   *Hunter-Gatherer Foraging Strategies: Ethnographic and Archaeological Analyses*. University of Chicago Press, Chicago.

Wolf, E. R.
1974   *Anthropology*. Prentice-Hall, Englewood Cliffs, N.J., 1964. Reprint, Norton, New York.
1982   *Europe and the People Without History*. University of California Press, Berkeley.
1984   Culture: Panacea or Problem? *American Antiquity* 49:393–400.
1990   Facing Power—Old Insights, New Questions. *American Anthropologist* 92:586–596.
1999   *Envisioning Power*. University of California Press, Berkeley.

Wood, B.
1995   *Women's Work, Men's Work: The Informal Slave Economies of Lowcountry Georgia*. University of Georgia Press, Athens.

Woodburn, J.
1982   Egalitarian Societies. *Man* 17:431–451.
1988   African Hunter-Gatherer Social Organization: Is It Best Understood as a Product of Encapsulation? In *Hunters and Gatherers*, vol. 1, *History, Evolution, and Social Change*, edited by T. Ingold, D. Riches, and J. Woodburn, 31–64. Berg, London.

Worth, J. E.
1995   *The Struggle for the Georgia Coast: An Eighteenth-Century Spanish Retrospective on Guale and Mocama.* Anthropological Papers of the American Museum of Natural History 75. University of Georgia Press, Athens.

Wright, H. T.
1977   Recent Research on the Origin of the State. *Annual Review of Anthropology* 6:379–397.
1984   Prestate Political Formations. In *On the Evolution of Complex Societies, Essays in Honor of Harry Hoijer, 1982*, edited by T. Earle, 41–77. Undena Publications, Malibu, Calif.

Wright, J. L., Jr.
1986   *Creeks and Seminoles: The Destruction and Regeneration of the Muscogulge People.* University of Nebraska Press, Lincoln.

Wylie, A.
1995   Alternative Histories: Epistemic Disunity and Political Integrity. In *Making Alternative Histories*, edited by P. R. Schmidt and T. C. Patterson, 255–272. School of American Research Press, Santa Fe.

Wynn, J. T.
1990   *Mississippi Period Archaeology of the Georgia Blue Ridge Mountains.* Laboratory of Archaeology Report 27, University of Georgia, Athens.

Yarnell, R. A., and M. J. Black
1985   Temporal Trends Indicated by a Survey of Archaic and Woodland Plant Foods Remains from Southeastern North America. *Southeastern Archaeology* 4:93–106.

Yellen, J. E.
1989   The Present and the Future of Hunter-Gatherer Studies. In *Archaeological Thought in America*, edited by C. C. Lamberg-Karlovsky, pp. 103–116. Cambridge University Press, Cambridge.

Yerkes, R. W.
1987   *Prehistoric Life on the Mississippi Floodplain: Stone Tool Use, Settlement Organization, and Subsistence Practices at the Labras Lake Site, Illinois.* University of Chicago Press, Chicago.
1991   Specialization in Shell Artifact Production at Cahokia. In *New Perspectives on Cahokia: Views from the Periphery*, edited by J. B. Stoltman, 49–64. Monographs in World Archaeology No. 2. Prehistory Press, Madison, Wis.

Yoffee, N.
1993   Too Many Chiefs? (or, Safe texts for the 90s). In *Archaeological Theory: Who Sets the Agenda?* edited by N. Yoffee and A. Sherratt, 60–78. Cambridge University Press, Cambridge.

Yoffee, N., and A. Sherratt
1993   The Sources of Archaeological Theory. Introduction to *Archaeological Theory: Who Sets the Agenda?* edited by N. Yoffee and A. Sherratt, 1–9. Cambridge University Press, Cambridge.

Young, A. L.
1997   Risk Management Strategies among African-American Slaves at Locust Grove Plantation. *International Journal of Historical Archaeology* 1(1): 5–37.

Zagarell, A.
1986   Structural Discontinuity—A Critical Factor in the Emergence of Primary and Secondary States. *Dialectical Anthropology* 10:155–177.

Zubrow, E. B. W.
1971   Carrying Capacity and Dynamic Equilibrium in the Prehistoric Southwest. *American Antiquity* 36:127–138.

Contributors

Susan M. Alt is a graduate student in anthropology conducting doctoral research at the University of Illinois, Champaign-Urbana. She has directed excavations over the last four years at Cahokia and nearby upland villages. Her recent papers include "Spindle Whorls and Fiber Production at Early Cahokian Settlements," published in *Southeastern Archaeology*, and "Gendered Politics and the Southeastern Ceremonial Complex," presented at the Society for American Archaeology meetings in 2000. Her research interests focus on social organization, gender, community, and identity.

Thomas E. Emerson is director, Illinois Transportation Archaeological Research Program, and an adjunct professor of anthropology, University of Illinois, Champaign-Urbana. He is the author of *Cahokia and the Archaeology of Power* (1997) and coeditor of *Late Woodland Societies: Tradition and Transformation across the Midcontinent* (2000) and of *Cahokia: Domination and Ideology in the Mississippian World* (1997). He has also edited other volumes, contributed book chapters, and written numerous articles. For ten years he was chief archaeologist for the Illinois Historic Preservation Agency. Current research endeavors include archaeometric isotope studies of diet and sourcing of material sources as well as the historical interplay of practice and power in the construction of inequality and social and political complexity.

Andrew C. Fortier is special projects coordinator at the Illinois Transportation Archaeological Research Program, University of Illinois, Champaign-Urbana. He received a Ph.D. in anthropology from the University of Wisconsin, Madison, in 1981. He has coedited *Late Woodland Societies: Tradition and Transformation across the Midcontinent* (2000) and is the author of "Pre-Mississippian Economies in the American Bottom of Southwestern Illinois, 3000 B.C.–A.D. 1050," published in *Research in*

Economic Anthropology. He is the author of twelve volumes in FAI-270 Site Reports Series, University of Illinois Press.

Kent Lightfoot is professor of anthropology at the University of California, Berkeley. He received his Ph.D. from Arizona State University in 1981, undertaking research on the sociopolitical organization of prehistoric Pueblo societies. Over the last twenty years he has been involved in archaeological fieldwork in southern New England, Alaska, Hawaii, and California. His current fieldwork focuses on the archaeology of prehistoric and colonial California. His publications include two monographs on the archaeology and ethnohistory of Fort Ross, California, a series supported by the University of California Archaeological Research Facility.

Diana DiPaolo Loren is curatorial assistant in southeastern archaeology at the Peabody Museum of Archaeology and Ethnology at Harvard University. She received her doctorate from SUNY-Binghamton in 1999. Her recent research has focused on processes of creolization and the social negotiations of race and identity in Spanish and French colonial contexts. Her work has appeared in several journals, including *Historical Archaeology* and the *Journal of Social Archaeology.* She is currently conducting research on colonial sites in northwestern and southeastern Louisiana.

Dale McElrath received his M.A. in 1973 from the University of Wisconsin-Madison and has recently returned there to complete his Ph.D. Over the last twenty-five years he has worked in Illinois and is currently the statewide survey coordinator for the Illinois Transportation Archaeological Research Program, University of Illinois, Champaign-Urbana. He has written extensively on Late Archaic and Late Woodland period archaeology. Special interests include lithics, storage, emergence of complexity, political economy, and philosophy of archaeology.

Michael S. Nassaney is associate professor of anthropology at Western Michigan University, Kalamazoo. His research interests include social archaeology, political economy, and ethnohistory. He coedited *Interpretations of Native North American Life: Material Contributions to Ethnohistory* (2000). He is currently directing the Fort St. Joseph Archaeological Project, a long-term multidisciplinary investigation of interactions and cultural traditions on the colonial frontier in southwest Michigan.

Timothy R. Pauketat is associate professor of anthropology at the University of Illinois, Champaign-Urbana. He received his doctorate from the University of Michigan in 1991 and is an author or editor of seven books and monographs and numerous other articles focusing on Mississippian political economy and cultural history. His interests in historical processes, social movements, inequality, and North American archaeology are exemplified by chapters in *Agency in Archaeology* (2000) and *The Archaeology of Communities* (2000). Since 1993 he has directed field research at and around Cahokia in southwestern Illinois.

Mark A. Rees is research archaeologist with the Center for Archaeological Research at Southwest Missouri State University, Springfield. He received his Ph.D. in anthropology from the University of Oklahoma in 2001 and holds a master's degree in historical archaeology from the University of Massachusetts at Boston. He has directed or assisted in fieldwork throughout the eastern United States, ranging from colonial and historic Native American sites in New England, the mid-Atlantic, and Missouri, to Mississippian mound sites in Alabama and Illinois. His research examines regional political development and decline in the Mississippian Southeast and was funded by a National Science Foundation dissertation improvement grant. He is the author of numerous reports and a contributor to several edited publications, including *Southeastern Archaeology*. His research interests include political culture, ethnogenesis, and historical anthropology.

Christopher B. Rodning is a Ph.D. candidate in anthropology at the University of North Carolina, Chapel Hill. His dissertation is an archaeological study of native public architecture and the cultural landscape of southwestern North Carolina during the seventeenth and early eighteenth centuries. He is coeditor of *Archaeological Studies of Gender in the Southeastern United States* (2001).

Kenneth E. Sassaman is assistant professor of anthropology at the University of Florida, Gainesville. He received his Ph.D. in anthropology from the University of Massachusetts–Amherst in 1991. His research centers on social and technological change among ancient small-scale societies of the American Southeast. He recently began long-term research in the St. Johns Basin of Florida after twelve years investigating Stallings culture of the Savannah River Valley.

Rebecca Saunders is associate curator of anthropology at the Museum of Natural Science, Louisiana State University, Baton Rouge. She received her Ph.D. from the University of Florida in 1992. Her major research interest areas are southeastern U.S. prehistoric and early historic Native American archaeology. She is the author of *Stability and Change in Guale Indian Pottery*, A.D. *1300–1702* (2000) and of numerous papers. Most recently, she has focused on Archaic period coastal adaptations and the rise of cultural complexity, Mission period Native American/European interaction and acculturation, and pottery technology, style, and ethnicity.

John F. Scarry is research associate professor of anthropology at the University of North Carolina, Chapel Hill. He received his Ph.D. from Case Western Reserve University in 1984. He is the author of numerous works on the political organization and cultural history of the Mississippian societies of the Lower Southeast. He is particularly interested in the creation of social and ethnic identities and the relationships between identities and the construction of social institutions such as political inequality and hierarchy. This recent work is exemplified by his paper in *Material Symbols* (1999). He has been studying the archaeology of the Apalachee since 1980. He has recently initiated a research project with Margaret Scarry that is focused on changes in the articulation of households with larger social formations associated with the emergence of the Moundville chiefdom.

Lynne P. Sullivan is curator of archaeology at the Frank H. McClung Museum at the University of Tennessee, Knoxville. Her research interests in eastern North America archaeology focus on social inequality, gender roles, mortuary practices, community and household organization, and the history of archaeology. She received her doctorate from the University of Wisconsin-Milwaukee in 1986 and is an author or editor of six books, including *Archaeology of the Appalachian Highlands* (2001) and *Grit-Tempered: Early Women Archaeologists in the Southeastern United States* (1999), and numerous articles. She has directed fieldwork in Tennessee, New York, and Illinois.

Brian W. Thomas is archaeology program director for the Atlanta office of TRC Garrow Associates. He received an M.A. in anthropology from Wake Forest University and a Ph.D. in anthropology from the SUNY–Binghamton with a specialization in historical archaeology. Recent publications include "Power and Community: The Archaeology of Slavery at the Hermitage Plantation" published in *American Antiquity.*

Cameron B. Wesson is assistant professor of anthropology at the University of Illinois at Chicago. He holds degrees in anthropology and architecture from Auburn University and received his Ph.D. in anthropology from the University of Illinois at Champaign-Urbana. His research interests include household archaeology, architecture and culture, and political economy. His current research addresses the sociopolitical dynamics of Mississippian polities in central Alabama.

Index